virgin film
BOND FILMS

virgin film

BOND FILMS

**Jim Smith and
Stephen Lavington**

First published in Great Britain in 2002
by Virgin Books Ltd
Thames Wharf Studios
Rainville Road
London
W6 9HA

A catalogue record for this book is available from the British Library.

ISBN 0 7535 0709 9

Typeset by TW Typesetting, Plymouth, Devon
Printed and bound in Great Britain by Mackays of Chatham PLC

Dedicated to

Alex Comer – a friend indeed

JES

My family – for tolerating my obsessions
Laura – for keeping me sane

SEL

Contents

Acknowledgements

The authors gratefully acknowledge the assistance and co-operation of:
Kirstie Addis (our editor at Virgin Books), Scott Andrews (valuable discussion),
Kevin Burns (dispenser of wisdom), Mark Clapham (comments, sarcasm, coffee),
James Clive Matthews ('My face! My beautiful face!'), Laura Cook (you can have
him back now), Jason Douglas (alternative opinions), Nick Edwards (special field
agent), Michael Mason (a great critic and a great teacher), Lawrence Miles
(discussions), Jonny (de Burgh) Miller ('Try to take over the world!'), Johnny
Minkley (bok?), Eddie Robson (who knows the score), Rowan Searle (our man in
Sydney), Louisa Smith (cheers, kid), Rob Stradling (enthusiasm and advice), Alan
Stevens (useful comments), John Sutherland (an influence always), Matt Symonds
('You're a cigarette!') Harris Watson (wit and insight) and Ben Williams (the wily
Welshman). Apple Macintosh, Carlsberg, Coca-Cola, Ericsson, Fortnum & Mason,
Haribo, Nokia, The New Culture Revolution, Sony Computer Entertainment
Europe, Stella Artois, Unwins and the staff of the BFI Library, the British Library,
The Spread Eagle in Camden, The Platinum Bar in Highgate and GOSH! Comics.

Special thanks to the late Ian Fleming without whom there'd be nothing to
write about.

Extra special thanks to our mums and dads – for everything . . .

Introduction

A white circle moves from left to right on a black screen and then expands into a gun barrel; a suited figure emerges and walks purposefully from right to left – always in the gun's sights. Lightning fast, he turns, draws a gun and fires. The screen drips red with blood to the sound of clashing chords.

It has been estimated that more than half the population of Earth have seen at least one James Bond film. Bond was a creation of British novelist and ex-Naval Intelligence Officer, Ian Fleming, brought to the cinema screen by producers Albert R 'Cubby' Broccoli and Harry Saltzman in 1962. The series in which he appears is the longest-running, most commercially successful and perhaps most recognisable film series in the history of the medium. Bond has outlived his literary and cinematic creators and emerged into the new century perhaps more popular than ever. But you knew that. Everyone knows that. And that's the point.

Bond has been around a long time, surviving, shifting and adapting through numerous changes: in lead actor, in filmmaking and in the world in which his films are released. The aim of this book is to assess each Bond picture both on its own and as part of the series; as a product on its own merits and (as is often the case) as an adaptation of a 1950s novel, while investigating its attitude to, and role in, the world around it. The book provides a commentary on each picture's plot, characters and production. The idea is not to nail down a Bond 'formula', but to establish the progression of a unique cinematic phenomenon across nearly two dozen films and the last four decades of the twentieth century.

Each film is broken up into several 'categories' so that it can be tackled from several different angles, without getting bogged down in minutiae.

We have also inserted several capsules into the text, which deal with general Bondian themes, such as smoking or accusations of sexism, and cover the whole series. The categories look something like this:

The Title of the Film (Year)
Producers
Writers
The Director of Photography
Those responsible for the music
The Editor(s)
The Director

PRINCIPAL CAST

PRE-CREDITS AND TITLES: The nearly omnipresent 'bit before the music' often vital to setting the tone of a Bond picture, and provider of many of the series' most memorable scenes. Under this we also include the inspirational pop art title design of Maurice Binder and his imitators/successors.

SUMMARY: What happens in the film. We're unlikely to dwell on plot holes either here or in other sections – unless they particularly offend us. The Bond films are driven by spectacle, style and sex appeal, and there's not really a single one of them that *entirely* hangs together in a story sense. Well, except maybe *On Her Majesty's Secret Service*.

UNIVERSAL EXPORTS: The cover name for the service which Bond works for. Under this blanket heading we examine the service's key employees, such as:

BOND, JAMES BOND: The cinematic James Bond is not one character played by six actors or six characters played by one actor each. Neither is he 22 separate characterisations portrayed by six actors. He's all of the above and then something else again. The Bond of *Dr. No* is precious little like the Bond of *Diamonds Are Forever* despite them both being played by Sean Connery. The same goes for the very different Moore Bonds of *Live and Let Die* and *For Your Eyes Only*. Under this heading we look at the characteristics displayed by 007 in each particular film, including lifestyle habits, skills, inconsistencies and things particularly likeable or dislikeable.

M: Bond's boss, from admirable admiral to gutsy female civil servant.

MONEYPENNY: M's secretary.

Q: A key member of Bond's world, Q is the man who provides the gadgets. These are dealt with in a separate section, but the man himself has enough prominence in the films to justify mention on his own merits.

OHMSS: A more generic category to cover all other aspects of the service, such as where its base is located what its resources seem to be.

ALLIES: Those on Bond's side but not based in London – the collection of foreign secret service agents, thieves, smugglers, civilians and members of other intelligence agencies who are frequently found in alliance with Bond.

THE OPPOSITION: The bad guys and their henchmen and -women. From cackling world-domination-obsessed lunatics to petty dope smugglers and everyone in between.

PRINCIPAL CASTING: The casting of the principals. Also notable roles and cameos from interesting or unlikely actors.

DIRECTOR AND CREW: Directors of Bond films have often been overlooked, regarded by critics as hack-men behind cameras. Unfair? Undoubtedly, and we intend to examine how, for example, *You Only Live Twice* fits into the distinguished career of Lewis Gilbert, or how John Glen's status as a 'resident director' during the whole of the 1980s affected the series.

FASHION VICTIMS: The clothes – sometimes they're great, sometimes they're ghastly. Bond's style is key to the character, especially when his definition of style clashes with everyone else's.

SET PIECES: Things blowing up, people jumping off buildings, spectacular stunts and scenes. A key component of the Bond films.

POSITIVELY SHOCKING: The particularly brutal despatching of characters. A chance to comment on the levels of violence in a series initially depicted as the ultimate in screen sadism and now regarded as all-round family entertainment.

MEMORABLE QUOTES: Witty lines, pithy bon mots, amusing insults.

GADGETS: Another important part of Bond's world. The toys he uses to beat the enemy, or the ingenious components of their villainous schemes.

CULTURE VULTURE: Cultural references, relevant and irrelevant, deliberate and accidental, references to other films or to literature. They're all part of how the Bond pictures fit into the world.

IN THE REAL WORLD: Although no one could, sanely, label a Bond film socially realistic, everything is inevitably a product of its time. How topical influences make themselves felt.

SOURCE TO SCREEN: Most Bond films are, to some degree, adaptations of the work of Ian Fleming. Here we chart the progression from the page to celluloid. A wide-ranging section covering script development, the incorporation of elements from Fleming's writing and, as the series' wears on, the cannibalisation of past Bond films.

MUSICAL NOTES: The tunes. Everything from the background score to the series only number one hit single, and the composers responsible.

BOX OFFICE: The financial rewards.

AWARDS: Bond films have won few awards. Those that some bodies were good enough to give out are acknowledged here.

CRITICS: Critical reaction to Bond has changed over time, from Nina Hibbin's declaration in the *Daily Worker* of 12 October 1963 that 'James Bond is not "fun" – he's just sick!' to the indulgent 'welcome back old friend'-style reviews of recent years. All are vital to the public perception of 007.

CUT SCENES: A category for discussing both sequences cut from screenplays and/or shot but never included in the finished picture and commenting on the various styles of film editing employed across the series.

TRIVIA: A lot of facts about various Bond productions are interesting, but don't sit happily in other areas. This is where they can be found.

PRODUCT PLACEMENT: The cinematic manifestation of one of Fleming's personal obsessions – the brand name.

MARTINIS, GIRLS AND GUNS: Notching up all of Bond's onscreen seductions, kills and Martinis. An attempt to resolve three disputes based around Bond's career. The section covers just those from the specific film in question, putting all three in context; the box at the very end of each film gives running totals of all three, up to and including the film under discussion. *Never Say Never Again* has its own total but is not included in the overall counter due to its 'unofficial' status. *Casino Royale* does not have a counter because of its incredibly complex and convoluted nature.

THE ONE WITH . . .: Explain to your auntie (who has seen all the Bond films on various bank holidays but can't tell the difference between them) which one is which in one easy sentence.

THE LAST WORD: A final qualitative judgement on the picture in question. We don't expect you to always agree with us. In fact we'd be disappointed if you did.

The Man with the Golden Typewriter (and his attempts to bring his hero to the screen)

Ian Fleming, James Bond's literary creator – and the only person to be credited on every single James Bond film – was born in 1908.

The path of his most famous creation to the big screen was not a quick or easy one. Some reports state that as early as 1953 the legendary producer, Sir Alexander Korda, contacted Fleming about the possibility of a Bond picture, or pictures, and because of this Fleming designed his next Bond novel, *Moonraker*, in such a way as it would be eminently suitable to be filmed. Nothing ultimately came of Korda's suggestion. Whether it was Korda's initial approach that convinced Fleming that the transition of Bond from the printed page to the screen was both desirable and possible is difficult to ascertain. What is certainly true is that he devoted much of the last decade of his life to attempting to arrange such a transition.

In May 1954, Gregory Ratoff bought the screen rights to Fleming's first Bond novel, *Casino Royale*, for a period of just six months. Fleming was paid, by all accounts, £1,000 for the privilege. Ratoff took this option to US TV network CBS, who produced and broadcast a live, black-and-white one-hour version of the novel on Thursday 21 October 1954. The teleplay, although generally faithful to the structure and story of the novel, cast actor Barry Nelson as American agent 'Card Sense' Jimmy Bond, and recreated Bond's CIA contact Felix Leiter as a British agent named Clarence. In the central villainous role of Le Chiffre was Peter Lorre, back then a fading film star whose most famous roles included *Casablanca* (Michael Curtiz, 1942) and Hitchcock's original version of the *The Man Who Knew Too Much* (1934). The resultant programme is very much a product of the television production techniques of its time, with bad editing and a slackness of pace caused by the actors literally having to move from set to set 'live' during takes, as if they were on a theatrical stage. It's entertaining only as a curio, with Nelson a particularly witless and stiff Bond.

A year later, perhaps happy with the success of this production, perhaps convinced that more could and should be done with the story, Ratoff purchased *Casino Royale* in perpetuity for a further $6,000. Nothing would come of this arrangement for many years and, even then, it would be something neither Fleming nor Ratoff had envisaged (see **Casino Royale**).

In 1956, having written *From Russia with Love*, a novel which seemingly ended with James Bond's demise, Fleming began work on

James Gunn – Secret Agent (aka *Commander Jamaica*), a television script for mogul Henry Morgenthau III, a New Yorker who had designs on a media empire. Morgenthau intended to found a regional Jamaican television industry to provide home-grown programmes for the Caribbean islands.

James Gunn was Fleming's attempt to create a Jamaican action series with the eponymous Gunn a thinly Americanised Bond. A girl named Pearl was to be one of the regular characters, and Fleming suggested that local calypso music be used to open and close each episode. Despite Fleming's best efforts, Morgenthau's plans for such an industry collapsed within a year and *Commander Jamaica* was not made. Never one to waste promising material, Fleming cannibalised the story into a new Bond novel published in 1958, one that would see his hero survive the conclusion of *From Russia with Love* to be despatched to Jamaica on Gunn's mission. Pearl became Honeychile Ryder and the novel *Doctor No* was born.

At some point in the mid-50s, Fleming wrote a screenplay based on *Moonraker*, apparently at the behest of the Rank organisation, but this would not result in a finished film. There is some evidence of the suggestion of another television series, this time from US TV network CBS, for which Fleming dusted off the Gunn script (dutifully altered to feature Bond in name as well as spirit). This also collapsed without any concrete results, although many of the Bond short stories Fleming wrote around this time, (later made available in posthumous collections) are thought to have originated as ideas for television episodes (see **For Your Eyes Only**).

Of more lasting consequence, although perhaps not in a positive way, was Fleming's involvement with young Irish filmmaker, Kevin McClory. A mutual friend, Ivar Bryce, had introduced McClory to Fleming. The novelist and the filmmaker, along with Bryce, screenwriter Jack Whittingham and Fleming's friend Ernest Cuneo, collaborated on a number of ideas, one of which they hoped would make a suitable basis for an original James Bond picture, rather than an adaptation of one of Fleming's pre-existing novels. The project floundered when it proved impossible to finance what would undoubtedly have been a more ambitious and spectacular project than Ratoff's static, and already forgotten, *Casino Royale* TV play.

Judging the affair to be over, Fleming incorporated many of the ideas discussed with McClory into a new James Bond novel, *Thunderball*, published in 1961. McClory and Whittingham would sue over this appropriation, and the result of the case would have protracted and complex effects on the smooth running of the eventual Bond film series (see **Thunderball** and **Never Say Never Again**).

This series would be set up by producers Harry Saltzman and Albert R 'Cubby' Broccoli (referred to as such because during childhood his siblings felt he resembled a cartoon bear; the nickname remained with him for life). Saltzman and Broccoli weren't close friends – they had been introduced by mutual acquaintance, screenwriter Wolf Mankowitz – and their partnership had come about solely because they both wished to work on Bond pictures. Saltzman owned the rights to the novels, having bought them from Fleming earlier that year, and Broccoli, as a protégé of Howard Hughes and former employee of Charles K Feldman's Famous Artists company, had the industry contacts to get the series off the ground.

They went into partnership in 1960 with the specific intent of producing films based on Fleming's novels. They had formed two companies: Danjaq (named after their respective spouses Dana and Jaqueline) to hold the various copyrights attached to Bond, and Eon to manage production of the films.

Talks were held with Columbia Pictures, but broke down over finance. Broccoli turned to Arthur Krim and David Picker at United Artists, and on 20 June 1961 the two men flew to New York to make a presentation before the board of United Artists. Less than an hour later they'd shaken hands with Picker on a deal, an arrangement Broccoli trusted implicitly. The more practical Saltzman refused to celebrate until contracts were signed and sealed, but to all intents and purposes the deal was done. James Bond's celluloid career was a reality. Now all they had to do was go out and make the films . . .

Dr. No (1962)

Produced by Harry Saltzman and Albert R Broccoli
Screenplay by Richard Maibaum, Johanna Harwood,
Berkley Mather
Director of Photography: Ted Moore, BSC
Production designed by Ken Adam
Music by Monty Norman
'James Bond Theme' played by John Barry & Orchestra
Edited by Peter Hunt
Directed by Terence Young

PRINCIPAL CAST: Sean Connery (*James Bond*), Ursula Andress (*Honey Ryder*), Joseph Wiseman (*Doctor No*), Jack Lord (*Felix Leiter*), Bernard Lee (*M*), Anthony Dawson (*Professor Dent*), Zena Marshall (*Miss Taro*), John Kitzmiller (*Quarrel*), Eunice Gayson (*Sylvia*), Lois Maxwell (*Miss Moneypenny*), Peter Burton (*Major Boothroyd*), Yvonne Shima (*Sister Lily*), Michel Mok (*Sister Rose*), Marguerite Le Wars (*Photographer*), William Foster-Davis (*Superintendent*), Dolores Keator (*Mary*), Reginald Carter (*Jones*), Louis Blaazer (*Pleydell-Smith*), Colonel Burton (*General Potter*), Lester Prendergast (*Puss Feller*), Timothy Moxon (*Strangways*).

NOTE: The film is called *Dr. No*, abbreviated and with a prominent full stop. The character is called 'Doctor No', as is the novel. The reason for the change is a mystery.

PRE-CREDITS AND TITLES: No pre-credits action. The first-ever gun-barrel sequence is hugely impressive though. Maurice Binder creates an iconic motif by photographing the inside of a gun barrel with a pin-hole camera. It's stuntman Bob Simmons, not Connery, who walks the walk and the *James Bond Theme* doesn't begin until after 007 has fired his shot, unlike on every subsequent sequence. Instead, the moving circle is accompanied by a discordant piece of pseudo musique concrète. The titles run over circles and rounded squares in primary and pastel colours and against a black background. The Bond theme fades, to be replaced by a metallic calypso rhythm and the images change to dancing female bodies; these are in turn replaced by the silhouettes of three men walking from left to right across the screen accompanied by the strains of *Three Blind Mice*. Groovy, alarming and ever evolving, it still looks both wonderful and strange forty years on.

SUMMARY: Sent to Jamaica to investigate the disappearance of fellow government agent, Strangways, James Bond discovers that the man has been murdered. Strangways was investigating the 'toppling' of American space rockets. Working with the CIA, Bond traces responsibility for both Strangways's murder and this 'toppling' to a man named Doctor No. Travelling to No's private island, Bond is imprisoned, but escapes, kills No and destroys his base.

UNIVERSAL EXPORTS:

BOND, JAMES BOND: James Bond is agent 007, employed by the British Government. According to Bond's cantankerous superior, M, a 'double-0' number indicates that an agent carries a licence to kill in the line of duty. Bond has used a Beretta 25-calibre pistol for a decade, and claims never to sleep on the firm's time. He has keen detective skills, and is devoted to the mission in hand, but can always find time for a beautiful lady. He is a member of, or at least a frequent visitor to, Le Cercle at Les Ambassadeurs, a London gambling club where he plays chemin de fer with great skill. He has golf clubs in his apartment indicating a familiarity with the game (see **Goldfinger**). He drinks vodka Martinis if circumstances allow (see **MARTINIS, GIRLS AND GUNS**) or straight vodka if they don't, and smokes filterless cigarettes.

Bond appears as an amalgam of sexually voracious playboy and efficient secret agent. Suave, confident and sophisticated yet ruthless and brutal when required, he can switch from charming lover to callous professional effortlessly – as seen in his encounter with Miss Taro.

M: A man in late middle age who smokes a pipe and briefs Bond about his forthcoming mission. While he clearly has faith in 007's competence, he does not entirely trust him to obey the letter as well as the spirit of his orders. He insists that Bond leave behind his trusted Beretta, seemingly well aware that Bond intends to dump the new Walther that has been forced on him at the first chance he gets. M's office contains paintings of sea battles and a bust of former Secretary to the Admiralty and celebrated diarist Samuel Pepys, perhaps indicating a naval background (see **On Her Majesty's Secret Service**). He also displays a bust of Winston Churchill and a portrait of Lord Palmerston, two of Britain's more bellicose prime ministers. Entry to his office is controlled by a traffic-light system – the visitor must wait for a red light to turn to white before entering.

MONEYPENNY: A woman of roughly Bond's age, she is M's secretary and, considering the personality of her boss, a surprisingly upbeat and flirtatious employee. She enjoys a friendly relationship with Bond, the exact basis and nature of which is not revealed, though she clearly would like their association to be more than professional. M is aware of this relationship and admonishes both of them for wasting the agency's valuable time.

MAJOR BOOTHROYD: Never referred to as 'Q' onscreen or in the credits (see **Goldfinger**), Major Boothroyd (Peter Burton) is described by M as the 'Armourer'. He's a serious-minded, fastidious man who regards Bond's choice of firearm with a degree of contempt. He equips Bond with a Walther PPK (see **GADGETS**).

OHMSS: The service for which all the above personnel work is either MI6 or MI7. In the communications room someone asks a colleague to call MI6, but later on M refers to himself as head of MI7. The code for MI6/MI7's base in Jamaica is W6N. London Control is G7W.

ALLIES:

QUARREL: A Cayman islander, fisherman and freelance boatman. Bond is told that Quarrel was commissioned by Strangways to sail him to local islands. Initially an abrasive and suspicious figure, he warms to Bond as soon as it is revealed that Bond is working for the British and not 'the opposition'. He is brave and trustworthy, and in plot terms supplies Bond with vital skills (such as local knowledge and sailing expertise). He meets a grisly end at the hands of Doctor No's 'Dragon'.

FELIX LEITER: M briefs Bond on this man – the CIA's local agent. At first he appears to the audience as a rather sinister figure, but when assured of Bond's identity becomes friendlier. What help he provides is negligible (probably due to his absence from the source novel). When he finally turns up with a detachment of marines, all he can offer is a tow to the mainland, help Bond eschews in favour of more time with . . .

HONEY RYDER: The daughter of a marine biologist whom she believes was murdered by Doctor No, a fact that does not seem to prevent her from searching for shells on the Doctor's island. She has a rather sad history: after her father's demise she was sexually assaulted by her former landlord. She took revenge by putting a female black widow spider ('they're the worst', she says) in her attacker's bed. It then 'took him a whole week to die'. She is strong willed and independent, with knowledge of Crab Key that is useful to Bond in completing his mission. Doctor No has her staked out by a sluice gate for no adequately explained reason, although he does suggest that he hopes she finds 'the guards amusing', implying an exceptionally unpleasant fate.

SYLVIA TRENCH: Shapely fellow-card player at Bond's club. It is she who is on the receiving end of Bond's famous screen introduction. Shortly afterwards he hands her one of his cards and she turns up at his London flat later.

THE OPPOSITION:

DOCTOR NO: The unwanted son of a German missionary and a Chinese woman of high birth, No previously worked for the Tongs (the Chinese mafia) from whom he embezzled $10 million that fund his life of crime. Doctor No is a member of SPECTRE, the Special Executive for Counter intelligence, Terror, Revenge, Extortion. For some unexplained reason this society's aims are assisted by interference with American experimental space rockets. No has metal prosthetic hands, having lost his own as a result of experiments with radioactivity. After it becomes clear that Bond would rather avenge the murders of Strangways and Quarrel than join SPECTRE, Doctor No dismisses him as 'a stupid policeman'. This is an insult he comes to regret as Bond throws him into a vat of boiling radioactive water, and then for an encore destroys his base.

Despite the frequent incompetence of his employees and his incomprehensible plan, Doctor No is a menacing and impressive villain. It's 38 minutes into the film before we even hear his voice, and an hour and twenty before we actually see him. Before this he's built up by the obvious fear all of the Doctor's employees have of him, especially the pathetic Dent.

PROFESSOR DENT: A bridge partner of the unfortunate Strangways, he's ostensibly a metallurgist who runs a test laboratory. He works for, and is terrified of, Doctor No, and sets up the assassination of Strangways. He panics when Bond questions him about Crab Key, arousing the agent's suspicions further. After failing to kill Bond with a poisonous spider, he has a go at shooting him while he sleeps. Rather unwisely he empties the entire chamber of his revolver into a strategically positioned bolster pillow. Bond, who has been hiding behind the door, taunts him about this waste of bullets before shooting him twice.

MISS TARO: Doctor No's spy in Government House, who blows her cover by ineptly listening at the door during Bond's meeting with the Principal Colonial Secretary. She allows Bond to seduce her, inviting him to her home in the mountains, and makes sure the three blind mice are waiting for him. Seemingly unaware that Bond has suspected her motives all along, she then attempts to distract him for long enough for an assassin to arrive. Bond is quite happy to go along for the ride, and then arranges for her arrest, waiting in her apartment for the assassin.

'THE THREE BLIND MICE': Three local hitmen in the employ of Doctor No. Masquerading as blind men, they are responsible for the death of both Strangways and his secretary. They attempt to kill Bond at least twice. Their first attempt (shooting him) fails when they are interrupted by an inconvenient passing car. Their subsequent try, running him off the road in their hearse, somewhat backfires when they drive off the cliff, smashing themselves into pieces on the jagged rocks below. Good work, lads.

THE PHOTOGRAPHER: Though not provided with a name, this photographer acts as the first stage of No's Jamaican intelligence service, collecting photographs of possible enemies. The then reigning Miss Jamaica, Marguerite LeWars, gives a physical and delightfully snarling performance. The moment where she licks the light bulb is awesome.

PRINCIPAL CASTING: Although largely distanced from the production process, Bond's creator Ian Fleming inevitably had some casting suggestions, including David Niven for the role of Bond (see **Casino Royale**). However, producers Albert R Brocoli and Harry Saltzman wanted to create a more mid-Atlantic character with greater mass-market appeal. To this end Cary Grant (who had been best man at Cubby's wedding in 1958) was suggested, but Broccoli was aware that Grant would only be interested in playing the role once. Broccoli was planning a series from the beginning and knew that this would be disastrous with any potential successor having to compete with the memory of a great movie star in the role. Peter Hunt, who was scheduled to edit *Dr. No*, was working on a comic picture, *On the Fiddle*

(Cyril Frankel, 1961), which featured little-known Scottish actor, Sean Connery. The film's producer, Ben Fisch, was a friend of Harry Saltzman's, and he suggested Connery for the lead. Broccoli remembered Connery from an introduction made by mutual friend Lana Turner some time before and he arranged a screening of Connery's film, *Darby O'Gill and the Little People* (Robert Stevenson, 1959) for him and his wife. Dana Broccoli was hugely impressed by Connery and lobbied her husband to cast him in the series' main role. Though initially sceptical, United Artists let the producers choose their man, and Connery signed a contract to play James Bond in *Dr. No*. This contract also contained the option for Eon to retain Connery's services for up to four further Bond film appearances. In the finished picture Connery does not disappoint – he's suave but with a tense coiled quality to his movements. He is able to bridge the gap between the charming casino dweller and intensely physical man of action.

Ian Fleming wanted either his cousin, actor Christopher Lee, or his friend and neighbour Noël Coward for the role of the eponymous villain. Lee has publicly stated that he was never contacted about the role and, although Fleming wrote to Coward on UA's behalf asking him if he would be interested in the part, the then 63-year-old writer/actor/director/songwriter declined. Attention turned to accomplished New York stage actor Joseph Wiseman, who delivers an intelligent and coldly menacing performance, establishing No as one of the series' best villains.

The casting of Bond's love interest, Honey Ryder, was tricky, and was not resolved until shortly before filming. Swiss actress Ursula Andress was suggested without audition, on the basis of a photograph of her which had been taken by her husband (actor John Derrick) in Greece. Unsure whether or not to take the role, she was swayed by the advice of a friend, actor Kirk Douglas, who liked the script Young had sent her. Following Douglas's advice made her an icon. Her Venus-like emergence from the waves is the most memorable entrance in the series, save that of Bond himself.

Anthony Dawson, portraying the wretched Professor Dent, had had a long career in films, including an appearance in Hitchcock's *Dial M for Murder* (1954), and had worked with director Terence Young more than once. He would return, uncredited, in both of Young's subsequent Bond pictures (*From Russia with Love* and *Thunderball*). He also assisted the director with casting on *From Russia with Love* by performing the – arduous – task of playing James Bond opposite many a screen-testing lovely. Dawson imbues Dent with a nervous, sweaty, suppressed hysteria and his scene in the meeting room, where he converses with Doctor No's offscreen voice, is a highlight of the film.

Casting for the film also required the creation of a small company of actors who, like Connery, would be expected to be in for the long haul should Broccoli and Saltzman's plans for a series come to fruition.

Cast as M was Bernard Lee, a respected film actor who had contributed splendid performances to such important pictures as *The Third Man* (Carol Reed, 1949) and *The Blue Lamp* (Basil Dearden, 1950). Lee was the very incarnation of Fleming's crusty admiral. He would continue to play M in every subsequent Bond film until shortly before his death from cancer in 1981.

Lois Maxwell came to the role that would be hers for 23 years due to personal tragedy. Her husband was gravely ill, and Maxwell was subsequently returning to acting after a long break in order to provide for her family. One of the many directors she called with a view to acquiring work was Terence Young, who offered her the roles of either Bond's London fling, Sylvia Trench, or M's secretary. Maxwell chose the more demure role, feeling Sylvia Trench's immodest pyjama sequence to be inappropriate for her.

Appearing for only a single time as CIA man, Felix Leiter, is the swaggering Jack Lord, later a star in his own right through television series *Hawaii 5-0*. Lord's performance is excellent, an effective American version of James Bond, and it's a shame he didn't reprise the role for any of the character's later appearances.

DIRECTOR AND CREW: Terence Young was an established director, with a selection of low-key British films such as *They Were Not Divided* (1950) and *No Time to Die* (1958) on his résumé. He had worked with Albert Broccoli before (on *The Red Beret* [1953]) and although other directors (including future Bond 'four-timer' Guy Hamilton) were considered, Young got the job. As a result he came to shape the character of Connery's Bond, with 007's taste in food and suits, and his fondness for throwaway humour. His direction is accomplished and unobtrusive, maintaining the distinctiveness of the setting without collapsing completely into bland travelogue photography.

The crew largely consisted of previous associates of Broccoli, Saltzman or Young, and most of them would return to work on future Bond productions. Editor Peter Hunt would provide final cut of all Bond films up to *You Only Live Twice*, and direct *On Her Majesty's Secret Service*. In *Dr. No* he creates an editing style suitable to a film which called for quick-fire action over narrative substance. The fight scenes benefit from this, Hunt overriding traditional editing wisdom which held that cutting during action or movement would disorientate an audience. In fact it makes for a visceral experience.

Ken Adam, hired as production designer, had worked with Broccoli on *The Trials of Oscar Wilde* (Ken Hughes, 1960) – a film which (bizarrely) featured an actor named Ian Fleming who was no relation of the author. Adam is one of cinema's most distinctive production designers; in this film his style is most visible in Doctor No's refined underwater study and the cold, clinical control centre. Adam also designed all the rather more mundane, but important, interiors, notably creating a style for M's office that would endure until 1995's *GoldenEye*.

MUSICAL NOTES: Monty Norman, a theatrical composer, was persuaded to do the film by the promise of a trip for him *and* his wife to Jamaica. His calypso-based score is hugely infectious, especially the hit single 'Jump Up!', and is expertly performed by Byron Lee and The Dragonaires, both then and now Jamaica's number one musical act. His 'James Bond Theme' is practically omnipresent too, far more ubiquitous in the score than it would later become.

SET PIECES: For most of its running time *Dr. No* is a detective story. The only remarkable example of 'Bondian' action comes at the climax, where extras fling themselves off the pier of Doctor No's exploding bauxite mine, a stunt reputedly achieved by offering actors extra money to throw themselves into the sea.

POSITIVELY SHOCKING: Bond's first screen kill is conducted with a degree of unpleasantness. Professor Dent is shot in cold blood when Bond knows that his opponent's gun is empty. In fact his scene had to be cut down from the original at the behest of the censor. Terence Young's preferred version had the unfortunate Professor being shot a further four times. As it was the director had to argue that Bond's apparently cold-blooded behaviour was justified after the mental trauma of seeing 'himself' – the bolster pillow set-up in Miss Taro's bed – being shot. Indeed it could be said that Bond is simply extending the same courtesy – six bullets – to Dent that Dent tried to extend to him.

The most horrific death in the picture is the burning alive of Quarrel. This is particularly poignant given the affection the character has engendered in the audience. At the time Bond is deeply affected by the end that his friend meets. It is rather sad that this seems to slip his mind upon meeting Felix Leiter after the Doctor's death: though Quarrel had been friends with the CIA agent, Leiter doesn't enquire as to the fisherman's absence and it doesn't occur to Bond to tell him.

CUT SCENES: Controversy surrounds Doctor No's intended fate for Honey Ryder. The review in the *Daily Express* (5 October 1962) referred at length to a scene in which she was 'shackled to the ground . . . as poisonous crabs crawl over her limbs' in a fashion similar to the end of the book. Official materials claim that such a scene was planned but proved unworkable and so was never shot. The substitute scene shows Honey being threatened by a slowly filling pool of water. If the crab scene was filmed (and photographs of it do exist) it was swiftly cut, and all currently extant versions of the film utilise the more mundane, but probably less laughable, water scene.

MEMORABLE QUOTES:
Bond to Doctor No: 'Tell me, does toppling American rockets really compensate for having no hands?'

Honey: 'Are you looking for shells?'
Bond: 'No, just looking.'

Bond (depositing a corpse outside Government House): 'Sergeant, make sure he doesn't get away.'

FASHION VICTIMS: Director Terence Young has been regarded as the model for James Bond by many of the cast and crew on account of his sartorial elegance and fondness for fine living. Cubby Broccoli's autobiography gave credit to Young for ensuring that Sean looked 'like Bond, Terence . . . took Sean to his tailor and his shirtmaker, and persuaded him to go out in the evenings wearing the clothes, so that he'd feel . . . at ease in them.'
  In the film Sean Connery's suits are made by Anthony Sinclair and his shirts by Turnbull & Asser. As in Fleming's books, Bond prefers slip-on shoes. The feel of the film as a whole is one of tailored elegance. Everyone is fitted perfectly. Even the gauche American feels the need to respond to Bond's Savile Row barb with the assertion that his suits are supplied by a man 'in Washington'. Doctor No rises to the challenge by providing an entire wardrobe for his 'guests', though in Bond and Honey's case apologies are made for the measurements only arriving a day before.

PRODUCT PLACEMENT: There are conspicuous appearances by Smirnoff Red vodka and Red Stripe lager which are made all the more suspicious by how carefully everything else in the picture is non-branded.

GADGETS: In this initial outing Bond has little to rely on other than his wits. However, at the beginning, his trusted Beretta is replaced by a Walther PPK, a widely respected 7.62mm pistol. Bond seems excessively attached to his .25 cal Beretta, despite Boothroyd's assertions that it belongs 'in a lady's handbag'. The literary Bond had been relying on this gun for several novels. Bond also uses a (comically huge) Geiger counter, sent to him in the field.

The only other noteworthy gadget consists of the fire-breathing, diesel-propelled 'Dragon' employed by Doctor No. An adapted swamp buggy, running on planks set up by the production team, this fearsome vehicle proves more than a match for Bond. It remains the only obstacle that Bond has failed to beat directly.

SOURCE TO SCREEN: *Doctor No* was actually the sixth James Bond novel written by Ian Fleming and was published in 1958. The Harry Saltzman/Albert Broccoli partnership had access to all of Fleming's writings, with one exception (see **Casino Royale**). Once the partnership began production on their initial Bond film, writer Richard Maibaum was told to write a script based on *Thunderball*, a novel itself based on an abandoned 1950s screen treatment, co-authored with Kevin McClory and Jack Whittingham (See **Introduction** for details). It quickly became clear that Fleming's former partners were legally questioning his propriety over *Thunderball* (see **Thunderball**) and so attention sensibly switched to *Doctor No* (the only other Bond novel based on material initially prepared for the screen – see **Introduction**) to avoid involving the filmmakers in any unnecessary legal entanglements.

A screenplay eventually emerged to which four writers contributed, three of whom are credited. The fourth, Wolf Mankowitz, asked to have his name removed. This writing and rewriting was a far from smooth process. In one of the first treatments, Mankowitz and Maibaum decided that a fiendish Chino-German doctor with metal claws wasn't an acceptable villain and that the eponymous doctor should in fact be the real villain's pet ape. Cubby Broccoli found it hard to forget or forgive this creative, if flawed, suggestion. As Richard Maibaum often recalled, 'Even . . . fifteen films later, if we got into an argument – we argued all the time – he hit me with "DOCTOR NO IS A MONKEY!" '

Although it is unclear who contributed what to the final draft, the result is effective and faithful to the sense of the novel. There are key differences: Felix Leiter doesn't appear in Fleming's *Doctor No* but both Quarrel and Strangways are known to Bond from his earlier visit to Jamaica in the book *Live and Let Die*. Professor Dent was invented for the screen and Miss Taro's role was expanded. A more easily filmed tarantula replaces the book's five-inch tropical centipede. The car chase that appears on screen is developed from an episode in the book where lookalikes – hired by Quarrel to drive around and draw off hostile interest – are killed in a car crash. The most important change is in the nature of the villain. Doctor No is the highly territorial owner of a guano mine with a sideline in Soviet-funded missile 'toppling', not a member of SPECTRE, an organisation which had yet to appear in the novels when Fleming wrote *Doctor No*. On paper, Strangways is investigating the suspicious death of a pair of bird wardens on Crab Key and it is not until the end that No's involvement in the sabotage of the US space programme is revealed. This plot idea is brought right forward to become part of M's briefing in the film. This was a canny move by the filmmakers, the invocation of American interests making the film easier to sell to the all-important US market.

Bond's assignment for the mission also has a different basis in the novel. While it is tricky to see why a valuable 00 agent would be assigned to this apparently simple detective case, in the book Bond is recovering from a Soviet nerve poisoning (see **From Russia with Love**) and M assigns him the case because of its apparently simple nature. The main objective is to ease him back into duties after his suffering. In this context, a torturous obstacle course that Doctor No puts Bond through serves as confirmation that Bond is not only as capable as before, but has a physical endurance beyond most men.

This 'trial by pain' is missing from the film. Its nearest equivalent occurs during Bond's escape from his cell – onscreen there is no indication he is being observed or his reactions monitored. This also allows the quiet dropping of the climax of the book – a fight between Bond and a giant squid. This sequence could not have been made to work on the film's budget, and remains the most interesting Fleming set piece not to appear in any Bond picture.

Having said all this, *Dr. No* is one of the most faithful adaptations in the series. Many of the films bear no resemblance to Fleming's novels save the titles and a few character names. What changes there are allow this film to stand alone, unshackled by continuity to previous (as yet unfilmed) novels, and to act as a good introduction to a previously unknown cinematic hero.

It is generally accepted that few of the 'trademarks' of the Bond series are present in *Dr. No*. However, this picture features numerous aspects which would be seen to be recurring motifs of the Bond series. These include an initial London briefing in M's office; a flirtation with Moneypenny; an exotic location; numerous minor henchmen; a friendly ally who shows Bond the ropes and meets a bloody end; and a selection of girls – some good, some bad, one of the former of which canoodles with our hero as the end credits roll. Most importantly, *Dr. No* establishes a pattern for the climactic chain of events. The culturally refined villain will wine and dine Bond, taking the opportunity to pontificate at length about his fiendish plans and superior intellect, before imprisoning Bond or consigning him to a gruesome, if impractical, fate. This conversation establishes sufficient personal antipathy between the characters to act as a backdrop to a final confrontation where Bond finishes his adversary off. This is the case in the cinematic *Dr. No*, where there is a fierce hand-to-hand battle. The novel has an even less dignified fate awaiting the villain, as he is buried alive under several hundred tonnes of bird dung – and that almost as an afterthought.

IN THE REAL WORLD: The film's topicality and subsequent box-office rentals benefited, in the UK at least, from its release coinciding with developments in the Cuban Missile Crisis. The plot itself was focused on missiles located a few hundred miles north of Cuba – the space rockets both the British and Americans are so concerned about are launched from Cape Canaveral, Florida. The American space program had experienced many problems in its early days and Ian Fleming employed this in his books to suggest deliberate sabotage. In the novel this was the action of a Soviet-funded agent. In the film it is the work of SPECTRE. This creates a minor plot problem: it is easy to see how, in the era of the space race, disrupting American space probes would be in Soviet interests, but for SPECTRE, a self-confessed criminal organisation, to do such a thing seems motiveless. Certainly if such a motive does exist it is never explained to either Bond or the audience.

There is something very late 40s, early 50s about the atmosphere of *Dr. No*, with its colonial houses, British ex-pats playing bridge and general air of British superiority. The appearance of a 'Queen's Club' in Kingston, 'Government House' and the Colonial Secretary must have appeared rather dated, even at the time of filming. In fact, Jamaica was already well on the way to full independence, achieving it in the year of the film's release.

One final, topical joke can be seen as Bond walks in to Doctor No's office. The painting that the camera lingers on is a copy of a Goya portrait of Wellington that had been stolen from the National Gallery in August 1961. The painting was to have been purchased by Charles Wrightman, an American oil baron and art collector, for $392,000. He planned to take it to America, but a public outcry followed this revelation and the Government felt obliged to find an equal sum of money in order to buy the painting from its seller and keep it in the country. In the third week of its residency at the National Gallery the picture was stolen. The thief demanded a ransom of $392,000. During production of *Dr. No*, screenwriter Johanna Harwood suggested that a reproduction of the Goya be made up and placed in Doctor No's lair, suggesting that the then still missing painting had been snatched by Bond's fiendish opponent. In 1965 the real thief (an unemployed bus driver named Kempton Bunton) revealed the picture's location to the *Daily Mirror*. The painting was picked up by police, and few weeks later Bunton gave himself up. He claimed he would have used the ransom money to buy TV licences for the poor. He served three months for the crime.

CULTURE VULTURE: The most important thing to appreciate about Bond – in the context of film culture – was that it had no immediate precedent. Films such as *The 39 Steps* (1935) had spy rings, and *Saboteur* (1942) involved German spies. Long-running British heroes (such as Sherlock Holmes) often *fought* spies, and stiff-jawed American or British heroes were frequently shown working undercover against the Nazis, but there are no prior examples of *heroic* cinematic spies operating in peacetime. In this sense, the filmic incarnation of Bond was to start a genre. With elements of the amateur heroics of Richard Hannay and Bulldog Drummond, but officially working for the Government against a real foe – Communism – James Bond was created by Ian Fleming as a man who lived both in the real world of the rich – fast cars, gambling, beautiful women, name-brand drink and exotic food – and in the unreal twilight world of a secret war. The films took these elements and added more to give a fully rounded cinematic creation; action in rising increments as the series went on and, most distinctly, humour. The political dimension was underplayed, outlandish super-villains were the true opponents, their schemes taking place against the backdrop of global tension. A new type of film was born, the spirit of a 1920s/30s cliffhanger serial packed into a 105-minute film with its own rules and higher production values. Bond was the first manifestation of the action adventure hero, whose influence is substantial still. That is why *Dr. No* was such a success on release: above all else it is like little else, and the shock of the new translated into box-office dynamite and, eventually, widespread homage and pastiche.

CRITICS: Most reviewers went for a light-hearted approach, and viewed Bond as escapism. They generally rejected accusations of bad taste, and noted the inherent self-deprecating humour. David Robinson, writing in the *Financial Times* of 5 October 1962 judged the sadism 'played down or played for laughs', arguing that the picture had 'the carefree fantasy of a thirties sub-Hitchcock thriller'. The *New Statesman*'s John Goldman (9 October) acknowledged that 'occasions for sadistic day-dreaming are kept down by a certain astringency of dialogue and cutting' in a generally positive review which commented that 'no one could take these antics seriously', and predicted a succession of sequels, 'a chain . . . of Bonded goods'. Penelope Gillat in the *Observer* of 7 October commented on the film's 'self parody', and compared it favourably with the source novels. Best of all, the reviewer felt that viewing James Bond's excesses was no more likely to damage a viewer's sensibilities than 'Sherlock Holmes' beastliness to Dr Watson encourages . . . the taking of cocaine.'

Director Terence Young received a rather back-handed compliment from Derek Hill in *Scene* for displaying 'the kind of rock-hard competence more usually associated with Hollywood' and Sean Connery won praise for his performance. *Variety*'s Rich wrote on 17 October that Connery was a 'stalwart, confident actor who . . . may have landed himself a career as Bond'. *Time* magazine's issue of 31 May 1963 liked the way Connery moved, his 'tensile grace . . . excitingly suggests the violence that is bottled in Bond' but dismissed the rest of the picture out of hand. Some critics' suggestions of excess in the film were rejected by Iain Cameron in the *Spectator* of 9 October. He found the film restrained in its depiction of 007's activities, singling out for complaint the 'insidious economy on girls' while labelling the film 'inept' and 'grotesque'.

Principal among the film's ideological opponents was Nina Hibbin of the *Daily Worker*, who used her column of 6 October to attack the film as 'vicious hokum skilfully designed to appeal to the filmgoer's basest instinct'. It also had 'sinister racialist implications' due to the ethnicity of some (not all) of the villains. Principal among her objections was the way the 'brutalised film' asked its audience to 'laugh along with it at blood and torture and slow death'. Thus the tongue-in-cheek elements that made the picture acceptable to some critics were the very source of Ms Hibbin's deepest rage. Nearly three years after the film's release it was reported that an article in the Vatican's newspaper, *Observatore Romano*, had condemned the film as 'deplorable'.

Despite these ideologically separate but curiously similar condemnations, the general view was broadly tolerant of the film's excess, and recognised its nature as pop entertainment. There was even some enthusiasm for the inevitable development of a series, or as the *Sunday Times'* Dilys Powell put it, 'now for the next, please'.

BOX OFFICE: Released in early October 1962, *Dr. No*'s budget was more than covered by its UK box-office returns – and so United Artists' delay in releasing the film in the potentially crucial US market ultimately had little effect on the series. (The film wasn't released in the US until 8 May the following year, and **From Russia with Love** had begun shooting in April.) *Dr. No* has taken $60 million at the box office in present-day values. This is sixty times the cost of its manufacture, and this figure doesn't take into account video, TV, and DVD sales and merchandising revenue.

AWARDS: Sean Connery was placed in the Golden Laurel Awards for 'top action performance' in 1964. He came third. The Laurels were a non-prestigious award given out by the *Motion Picture Exhibitor* magazine; there was no ceremony – the results were merely printed in the magazine. This poor showing, combined with the picture's huge box-office gross, goes a long way towards fulfilling the prophecy in *Variety* at the time of the movie's UK release that 'James Bond . . . will win no Oscars, but a heck of a lot of enthusiastic followers'.

MARTINIS, GIRLS AND GUNS: Three confirmed seductions: Sylvia, Miss Taro and Honey. He could have had the receptionist at the hotel if he'd wanted to, judging by the way she constantly sizes him up. Two Martinis are drunk, neither ordered onscreen by Bond but both mixed to his specifications. He tallies up five kills: Professor Dent, the guard in the swamps, the guard whose uniform he steals, the scientist he flings into the reactor and Doctor No himself.

THE LAST WORD: 'Bond, James Bond.' An effective screen introduction for 007, *Dr. No* is a satisfyingly glossy pseudo-detective story. It *has* dated in places, though less than many far more expensive films of its era, and while it lacks some of the elements that have become widely anticipated in Bond films, it retains an entertainment value that isn't easy to dismiss. To overlook it on the basis of its lower budget and modest aims is to overlook gorgeous location filming, a great ensemble cast, a few truly iconic screen moments and the achievement of a skilled crew in establishing the series as a popular brand.

GIRLS	3
MARTINIS	2
DEATHS	5

Bond vs Nina Hibbin: 'World socialism will be achieved peaceably.'

One of Bond's most vociferous early critics was Nina Hibbin, the film reviewer of the left-wing newspaper, the *Daily Worker* (later the *Morning Star*). Though eventually reconciled to the films – even indicating something approaching approval for *You Only Live Twice* – she initially railed against what she saw as monstrous sources of sex and violence in rather melodramatic terms. Of *From Russia with Love* she memorably said that it was 'about as amusing as watching someone slip on a banana skin. To be more precise a blind-man slipping on a banana skin personally placed there by his own mother.'

She did not limit herself to criticising just James Bond. In 1959 she spoke in shocked tones of *Dracula* (Terence Fisher, 1958), starring Christopher Lee. 'I went to see Dracula . . . prepared to enjoy a nervous giggle. I was even ready to poke gentle fun. I came away revolted and outraged.'

Somewhat incongruously, she went on to write a history of the *Carry On* films, *What a Carry On . . . The Official Story of the Carry On Film Series* with her daughter Sally Hibbin. Keeping to the family business, Sally Hibbin would go on to write more books on film. Ironically these included *The Official James Bond Movie Book*, *The Official James Bond Movie Poster Book* and *The Making Of Licence To Kill*.

From Russia with Love (1963)

Produced Harry Saltzman and Albert R Broccoli
Screenplay by Richard Maibaum
Adapted by Johanna Harwood
Director of Photography: Ted Moore, BSC
Art Director: Syd Cain
Orchestral music composed and conducted by John Barry
Title song written by Lionel Bart

'From Russia with Love' sung by Matt Monro
Edited by Peter Hunt
Directed by Terence Young

PRINCIPAL CAST: Sean Connery (*James Bond*), Daniela Bianchi (*Tatiana*), Pedro Armendáriz (*Kerim Bey*), Lotte Lenya (*Rosa Klebb*), Robert Shaw (*Grant*), Bernard Lee (*M*), Eunice Gayson (*Sylvia Trench*), Walter Gotell (*Morzeny*), Francis de Wolff (*Vavra*), George Pastell (*Train Conductor*), Nadja Regin (*Kerim's Girl*), Lois Maxwell (*Miss Moneypenny*), Aliza Gur (*Vida*), Martine Beswick (*Zora*), Vladek Sheybal (*Kronsteen*), Leila (*Gypsy Dancer*), Hasan Ceylan (*Foreign Agent*), Fred Haggerty (*Krilencu*), Neville Jason (*Kerim's Chaufeur*), Peter Bayliss (*Benz*), Nushet Ataer (*Mehmet*), Peter Brayham (*Rhoda*), Desmond Llewelyn (*Boothroyd*), Jan Williams (*Masseuse*), Peter Madden (*McAdams*).

PRE-CREDITS AND TITLES: 'James Bond' is hunted through a moonlit garden by a muscular blond man (later identified as Donald Grant) who garrottes him. The dead man is then revealed to be an actor in a mask. It's all been a training exercise. The title sequence and credits are projected onto the body of a dancing woman in a simple, but effective sequence put together in imitation of Maurice Binder's style by his former assistant Richard Brownjohn.

SUMMARY: SPECTRE (see **Dr. No**) formulate a plan to trick the British Secret Service into sending James Bond to steal a Lektor decoder from the Russian Consulate in Istanbul. Once Bond has done this, SPECTRE will kill him, take the decoder from his body and sell the stolen goods back to the Russians. The motivation to do this is threefold: financial gain; to increase tensions between East and West; and to gain revenge on Bond for his killing of SPECTRE operative Doctor No in Jamaica. By way of subsidiary benefit, and as a smokescreen, SPECTRE intend to smear the reputation of Bond and of the British Secret Service. Explicit film of Bond and Russian cipher girl Tatiana Romanova (Tania) will be placed on the agent's body along with a suicide note. It will look as though Tania intended to extract a promise of marriage from Bond, that 007 discovered this, killed the girl and then himself.

UNIVERSAL EXPORTS:

BOND, JAMES BOND: We see Bond 're-acquainting' himself with Sylvia Trench for the first time since their abortive golf match six months

previously. In the course of this encounter we discover that he has a scar
on his lower left back and can quote from Shakespeare's *Henry V* (Act
III Scene i 'once more into the breach'). He tips well, and is au fait with
Turkish coffee (which he takes medium sweet) and cuisine (he orders
'green figs, yoghurt and coffee, very black' for breakfast). He shows a
remarkable adaptability to local moonshine, taking rather a fancy to
raki, not the most palatable of drinks. He is partial to grilled sole, and is
understandably shocked by the idea of a man who would drink red wine
with fish.

Outside of culinary matters we see an extreme example of his reaction
when deceived. Miss Taro's treachery (see **Dr. No**) is treated with good
humour, however, Bond is deeply affected by the murder of Kerim Bey
and is particularly brutal to Tania, whom he suspects knows more than
she has said, in the aftermath of this event. This is uncomfortable to
watch, largely because the audience have become attached to the idea of
Bond and Tania as a couple. To see Bond's professional side intrude so
suddenly is extremely discomfiting.

This is Bond's first real outing as a secret agent, as opposed to the
glorified policeman of *Dr. No*. He is involved in a field operation against
the Russians, one which necessitates the employment of his 00 licence to
a greater degree. Here we see him as a Cold Warrior, conspiring against
a foe in one of many covert battles assumed to be occurring at this time.
We have a rare glimpse of Bond as a shadow-dwelling, secret-stealing,
professional spy of a more conventional kind.

M: We learn very little about Bond's superior – though even what we do
find out may be too much. When Tania asks how she compares with
Western girls, Bond begins to relate a story about himself and M in
Tokyo. M is visibly embarrassed and swiftly turns the incriminating tape
off, only resuming play after fast-forwarding a safe distance.

M is smart enough to detect the trap behind the proffered Lektor, but
pragmatic enough to know that this is the service's best chance to
procure a piece of equipment that they have wanted for a long time, and
so he chooses to send Bond.

MONEYPENNY: She flirts and pouts, but seems resigned that any
relationship with Bond is a lost cause. She is cleared for analysis of top
secret sources and has no compunction in eavesdropping on information
she is not officially permitted to hear – a trait that M is aware of and
seems to accept.

MAJOR BOOTHROYD: Still credited as such, but this time referred to as 'Equipment Officer'. Boothroyd is allowed even less emotion than we see in *Dr. No* where he at least gets to rubbish Bond's choice of side arm. Here he serves only to brief 007 on the features of his new briefcase. Former theatre actor and prisoner of war, Desmond Llewelyn took the role of Q for the first of seventeen appearances.

CAPTAIN NASH: An ill-fated secret service agent based in Zagreb. Nash is a 00 agent as can be seen from his possession of the standard issue 'trick briefcase' (see **GADGETS**). He plays only a small part in the film, his arrival at Zagreb station is swiftly followed by his departure from this mortal coil, facilitated by Grant.

OHMSS: Regional Secret Service stations are known by the initial letter of their host country. Station 'Y' is based in Zagreb, Yugoslavia and Station 'T' is based in Istanbul, Turkey. There is a uniform pass-code for the whole service; SPECTRE are able to torture this code out of an agent in Tokyo and subsequently use it to fool both Bond and the local Yugoslav MI6 agent. The service employs foreign nationals, both as station officers and, in the shape of the gypsies, as proxy agents who carry out the dirty work that the secret service would prefer not to be directly associated with. The Russians follow a similar practice, employing Bulgars. Kerim Bey displays less than genuine sorrow for the consequences of this: 'I am afraid it has created a blood feud between them' he blithely states.

With only a few details the tone of the Cold War in Istanbul is well established. The uneasy balance of power is shattered with a few surgical moves by SPECTRE and an escalating war erupts. *From Russia with Love* gives a detailed view of a service which, in latter times, becomes little more than the supplier of Bond's equipment and the manufacturer of his excuses to various appalled foreign governments.

ALLIES:

KERIM BEY: Former circus strongman and head of Station 'T', Kerim Bey has allocated all-important positions within his organisation to his sons – his motto is 'Blood is the best security in this business.' He also employs a troop of gypsies, with whom he has become friendly. Though he is initially sceptical about Bond's mission they become friends and he is willing to back Bond whatever he does. He clearly has a great time and seems to revel in the fact that Bond's arrival marks the end of a long (and boring) truce with the Russians. He is a wonderful character, and one of

27

Bond's most memorable allies. It is unfortunate that the death he meets on the Orient Express comes in the form of a messy knife fight with a Russian agent.

Kerim is a particularly good example of the 'sacrificial lamb' – an ally of Bond who becomes well established before being killed later in the film, providing Bond with added impetus to complete his mission and bringing a touch of pathos to the proceedings – a recurring feature of the series. This can come as a real blow if the deceased has been accepted by the audience. His/her death can feel like a genuine loss to the story. If handled badly, it becomes little more than an obstacle to the narrative. Quarrel in *Dr. No* is a good example of the former whereas Chuck Lee in *A View to a Kill* belongs firmly in the latter category.

TATIANA ROMANOVA (TANIA): A trained ballerina who grew an inch over regulation height, necessitating her leaving the ballet. She carries the rank of corporal and works in the Russian embassy in Istanbul, having previously been employed by the English Decoding Crew in Moscow, where she gained knowledge of Rosa Klebb (see **KLEBB**). She is initially recruited by Klebb and ordered to pretend to be in love with Bond as part of a Soviet operation to feed information to the West. It is implicit that she is expected to have sex with Bond in the course of this mission. She believes she is 'doing all this for Mother Russia' and is unaware of the true nature of what she is involved with. She defects to the West at the end of the film. Her KGB file is sufficiently detailed as to number her previous lovers (three). Bond is obviously impressed by the picture of her M gives him.

Tania is the first character in Bond films to exhibit what will become a common trait in female leads: in critical terms, the 'ideological repositioning' of a female character through 'knowledge' of Bond, a simple variation on the idea of a character being redeemed by love. What this boils down to is 'having sex with Bond makes an evil or misguided woman good'. This is so well established by *Thunderball* (1965), that the series itself begins to mock the excesses of this approach. Tania is initially ordered to pretend to be in love with 007; she genuinely becomes so enraptured with him that she completely changes her allegiance. This realignment is finally confirmed in the penultimate scene, where she supports Bond over her military superior, Klebb.

THE OPPOSITION:

SPECTRE: The criminal organisation has connections with international espionage, its fund-raising methods are a cut above bank robbery. James

Bond has already become a named enemy of the 'Special Executive' to be dealt with by its revenge division.

KLEBB: Colonel Rosa Klebb, former head of SMERSH (see **Casino Royale** and **The Living Daylights**) and now SPECTRE Number Three. She prefers experience to training and seems only passably impressed with Grant. She uses a combination of guile and the wielding of her old SMERSH authority to bludgeon Tania into taking the mission. There is also more than a hint that she would like to take relations with Tania beyond the professional. The one person by whom she is intimidated is Ernst Blofeld.

While not as colourful as Doctor No, Klebb is a fine Bond villain. She is gruesome and thoroughly evil, making for a nice counterpoint with the beautiful and misguided Tania. Though she forms the focus for the opposition in the film, she does little more than enact Kronsteen's plan and report progress to Blofeld. She is, to all intents and purposes, a middle-grade civil servant of evil. It is not until the final moments that we have the requisite big confrontation with Bond, and despite his flicker of recognition there is little of the personal animosity the scene should have – ultimately it is more about Klebb and Tania than Bond and Klebb.

GRANT Donald Grant (never referred to by the commonly used name 'Red Grant' on screen) is a thirty-something blond psychopath. A 'homicidal paranoic' who escaped from Dartmoor in 1960 and was recruited by SPECTRE in 1962, he is now a highly regarded assassin and takes great pleasure in his job. He has undergone a programme of intensive indoctrination and training including the simulated hunting and killing of 007, a fight that takes him a minute and 52 seconds. He is established as a man to be feared as he stalks Bond through the streets of Istanbul. He stirs up the Russians against the British and tacitly assists Bond (at one point even killing a would-be assassin) as far as such assistance aids SPECTRE. He follows Bond and Tania as they make their escape, imitating an English MI6 agent (whom he has previously killed) to get Bond's trust. He carries out his tasks with such smooth professionalism that there are serious doubts about 007's chances of survival.

However, he takes a sadistic pleasure in the prospect of killing Bond and this is his downfall – he draws out the execution long enough for Bond to turn the tables. Grant is strangled with his own garrotte watch.

Grant is the first (and greatest) in a long line of menacing, taciturn henchmen, employed by Bond's opponents as hatchet men, usually charged with 007's assassination and always failing in this task. He is also the first of quite a few to try this on a train.

KRONSTEEN: Grand chess master and SPECTRE Number Five, it is Kronsteen who formulates SPECTRE's basic plan (see **SUMMARY**) although the choices of Grant and Tania as the players in the game appears to be Klebb's. Kronsteen believes the British mentality is such that they always treat an obvious trap as a challenge. Just as well really. When his plan fails (and it's Klebb's fault, not his), Blofeld has him killed. His chess-playing skills and trademark sneer are no protection against a dagger in the leg.

ERNST BLOFELD: Credited as such, but only referred to as 'Number One' onscreen, Blofeld's feline-loving hands belong to Antony Dawson, and his sibilant voice to actor Eric Pohlman. He's cunning and proud, has a twisted sense of honour (he's almost offended by the idea that SPECTRE won't deliver the promised Lektor back to the Russians) but doesn't seem to realise that it's Klebb, not Kronsteen, who has caused his plan to fail. He disposes of a potentially valuable resource as a result, which isn't actually very smart.

Despite this he is a menacing figure, due in part to his ambiguity. We see nothing of his personal features, only his cold ruthlessness in official business. He strikes fear into the hearts of even his closest lieutenants.

KRILENCU: A vicious killer employed by the Russians. He leads the Bulgar assault on the gypsy camp, an attack unrelated to SPECTRE's plot but a Soviet action resulting from the rising tension in Istanbul. Krilencu is shot by Kerim Bey while trying to escape from his hideout based behind a movie poster billboard (see **PRODUCT PLACEMENT**).

FASHION VICTIMS: 'Not mad about his tailor, are you?' quips Bond to Kerim as they tie up the KGB man on the train. This is harsh, but fair. His suit is several sizes too big and made of unpleasant, itchy-looking material. Bond's grey suit, on the other hand, is impressive, as is his hat. Tania's pink blouse and her white and blue striped belted dress are lovely, but she's rather more impressed than we are by the lace dresses Bond picks out for her. The majority do seem to be designed solely for wearing at night. Most other characters wear fairly anonymous garb. The two exceptions worthy of mention are the flamboyant blouses sported by the gypsy chief, and the fine tailoring enjoyed by Kerim Bey – a man who can make an oversized linen suit and cheap cigarette holder combo look good. On the other side of the Iron Curtain, Donald Grant, like all thugs, looks uncomfortable in a suit. Surely this should have alerted Bond to the fact he's a scoundrel?

SET PIECES: The furiously edited fight on the train, courtesy of Peter Hunt, is a sequence much imitated even by later Bond films. The balletic brutality of the Bulgars' attack on the gypsy camp is brilliant for the way it portrays Bond as walking through the melee, only occasionally being embroiled in the action. The suspenseful *North by Northwest*-influenced fight with a helicopter is impressive too. Also noteworthy is 007's little trick with the flare gun, the SPECTRE motor-craft and several thousand gallons of petrol. Nice. One of the most memorable set pieces, the opening chess match, has nothing to do with Bond. It takes place on a brilliant set courtesy of production designer Syd Cain, and is a spectacular – perhaps too spectacular – introduction for the weasely Kronsteen.

POSITIVELY SHOCKING: *From Russia with Love* is more violent than *Dr. No*. It opens with a garrotting, proceeds to show a brutal girl-on-girl cat fight degenerate into a confused gypsy/Bulgar melee, a man being stabbed with a poisoned blade, the aftermath of a bloody knife fight and the visceral train battle. This is finished off with the last boat scene, where the camera lingers on the burning forms of the SPECTRE boat crews.

Given the darker nature of the film's plot and the character of Bond's adversaries, this is largely appropriate. The violence serves as a way to mark the warming up of the Cold War in Istanbul and also as a way to distinguish Bond's acts of self-defence from the sadistic pleasure Grant takes in killing.

Ian Fleming was reportedly disappointed that the gypsy girls' fight didn't, as the one in his book did, feature one girl biting another's breast. Director Terence Young was understandably disingenuous when asking the author how he expected such a scene to be a) filmed and b) pushed past the censors.

MEMORABLE QUOTES:

Bey (to a gagged and bound man): 'I've led a particularly fascinating life, would you like to hear about it?'

Bey (of returning to the arms of his beautiful, but demanding, mistress): 'Back to the salt mines.'

Tanya: 'I think my mouth is too big'.
Bond: 'No, it's the right size . . . for me that is.'

GADGETS: Q-branch supply their first gadget to Bond here – a dapper but lethal leather briefcase, which has recently been made standard issue for all 00 personnel. It comes equipped with storage space for ammunition, throwing knives and fifty gold sovereigns for emergency bribery. A tear-gas grenade disguised as a tin of talcum powder provides security. The case also contains a sniper rifle, used to off Krilencu and down the SPECTRE helicopter.

Though low key, it is a nice addition to the film, and the knowledge of this ace up Bond's sleeve adds tension to the confrontation on the train where it, and its sister case pinched by Grant from the dead Captain Nash, prove vital.

Not mentioned by the Equipment Officer, though presumably supplied by Q-branch, is the cine-camera/tape recorder with which Bond records Tania's description of the Lektor to confirm its authenticity. Bond is also one of the first people in the world to have a beeper and mobile telephone with which he can be contacted by headquarters.

Once again, the opposition are well armed. Grant has his garrotte watch and Rosa Klebb is kitted out with a poison-tipped dagger in her left shoe.

CULTURE VULTURE: Terence Young claimed that the famous pre-credit teaser is based on the 1961 Alain Resnais film *Last Year at Marienbad (L'Année Dernière à Marienbad)*.

The Orient Express has played a leading role in many classic films, the most memorable being Agatha Christie's oft-filmed *Murder on the Orient Express*, the 1974 version of which starred Sean Connery.

When Bond comments of SPECTRE that 'One of their aircraft is missing' (something he has ensured by shooting down their helicopter), there is a clear reference to the 1942 Michael Powell and Emeric Pressburger war film, *One of Our Aircraft is Missing*.

In an architectural vein, it should be noted that the crew shot many scenes on location at some of Istanbul's most beautiful landmarks. The Blue Mosque can be seen in several location shots, Kerim Bey's headquarters are located in the labyrinthine Great Bazaar, Bond and Tania's boat ride takes them past the spectacular Topkapi Palace and Grant disposes of a Russian/Bulgarian agent in the San Sophia Mosque (the soundtrack in the background is that of an actual tour taking place). There are also some fine shots of Venice, a city that Bond would return to in *Moonraker*.

IN THE REAL WORLD: In changing the central villains from the Communists to a criminal organisation which owed its allegiance to no country or creed, Broccoli and Saltzman essentially decided that the

Bond films should be apolitical. Throughout the Cold War Bond would fight criminal masterminds with private aims that were above international politics. However these objectives would often involve the manipulation of the two sides, relying on their mutual mistrust.

What is especially interesting about *From Russia with Love* is its invocation of Britain as the power against which Russia is pitted. When America is mentioned it is as an opponent of sorts, another Western power eager to get its hands on a Lektor, and M takes relish in the idea of Britain securing one first. In some ways this shows the greatest departure from reality in the film. In the post-Cuban Missile Crisis world, Russia and America were the key players. Just as *Dr. No* harkened back to a time of colonialism that had all but disappeared, so *From Russia with Love* envisioned a scenario where a major crime syndicate would choose Britain as the ideal foil for the Russians. Tellingly, Bond would not be involved in another purely Anglocentric mission until *For Your Eyes Only* in 1981. The apolitical tone of the films would last until a similar time (see 1983's **Octopussy**).

For the 60s and 70s the Cold War would form only the backdrop to a series of distinctly more outlandish battles, or as Richard Maibaum termed them, 'capers'.

SOURCE TO SCREEN: *Dr. No* performed well at the box office. It had done moderate business in America, but the bulk of its earnings came from the European and British markets. It had earned its spurs and a second instalment of the series was guaranteed. Although it immediately preceded *Doctor No* in the books' own chronological order, *From Russia with Love* was chosen as the next Bond film. In addition to being a tightly plotted, conventional spy story (and so relatively easy to adapt) there were other points in its favour. Its European setting (Turkey, the Balkans and Paris in the book) made it more viable for the profitable European film markets; additionally it had featured in a list of the ten favourite books of the current US president, John F Kennedy, compiled by *Time* magazine.

Richard Maibaum is credited with the screenplay for this film, though Johanna Harwood – one of the three credited for writing *Dr. No* – is given mention for 'adapting' the book. As it stands, *From Russia with Love* is, like its predecessor, a generally faithful screen version of Fleming's novel; what changes there are result from the change of Bond's enemies. In the book the overly elaborate plot is devised by SMERSH (see **The Living Daylights**).

Rather than being a side benefit of the scheme, as in the film, here the humiliation of Bond, and through him the British Secret Service, is the key goal. Rosa Klebb is still loyal to the Russians and assigns Grant (here known as Donovan 'Red' Grant) and Tania to this mission at the behest of another equally grotesque Russian spymaster. Replacing malign Russian influence with SPECTRE added a nice twist to the plot – Bond suspects the Russians all through the book. Onscreen however, he is completely hoodwinked until Grant's train-carriage explanation.

The other major change was designed solely to add a cinematic flourish to the end of the film (and an excuse to insert the already requisite explosive finale). The fight on the Orient Express is a brief encounter in the novel – Nash/Grant menaces Bond with a gun concealed in a book while explaining the fiendish SMERSH plot to the confused agent. Bond then feigns death by using his cigarette case to block the bullet meant for his heart before disposing of Grant with the book-gun. The scene swiftly changes to Paris where Bond confronts Klebb. In the film we have a helicopter chase lacking in imagination but tensely staged and shot, and the climactic boat chase across the Gulf of Venice. This is well done and far from gratuitous given the liberties taken by other adaptations. With the mooring of Blofeld's yacht near Venice, and the time needed by Bond to traverse the stretch of water, this confrontation seems almost plausible.

Additionally this allows for a more realistic conclusion in the film. The book had seen Grant blab top secret information about the location of one of Russia's spymasters – he is quite happy to tell Bond the exact details surrounding the planned rendezvous with Klebb in Paris after his mission's conclusion. It is noteworthy that the screen version avoids this cheap opportunity to advance the plot, especially as the filmmakers are quite happy to take this route in later outings. Instead it is Klebb who tracks Bond and Tania down to their hotel room. She makes straight for the Lektor and is on the point of shooting Bond before Tania intervenes.

This differs from the novel, which ends with Bond being poisoned by Klebb's venomous stiletto, crashing to the floor near to death (his Beretta jams and it is this that M is referring to, with a slightly paradoxical effect, at the start of the cinematic *Dr. No*). The film avoids any such maudlin ending. Instead, Bond and Tania triumphantly cruise Venice's Grand Canal. Indeed, the sense of triumph is so great that, for the first time, Eon felt duty-bound to announce the next Bond film before it was even made. After teasing us with the prospect of this being 'The End', the credits reveal that it is 'Not quite the end' and that 'James Bond will return in the next Ian Fleming thriller, *Goldfinger*.' It is ironic that a novel which, in its original form, seems to end with Bond's death, should pave the way to the character's cinematic immortality.

DIRECTOR AND CREW: After the success of *Dr. No*, Terence Young was hired to direct the sequel. With a rapport with Connery and an established visual style of his own, as well as a personal stake in the series, Young readily agreed. While some crew members, such as Peter Hunt, also returned there were several changes behind the camera. Production designer Ken Adam, whose work had contributed greatly to *Dr. No*'s success, had gone off to design Stanley Kubrick's *Dr. Strangelove or, How I Learned to Stop Worrying and Love the Bomb*, and was consequently unavailable. Syd Cain, a former assistant of Adam's, was hired instead. Another former assistant promoted due to a crew member's lack of availability was Richard Brownjohn who was responsible for *From Russia with Love*'s striking title sequence. Brownjohn had worked under Maurice Binder on *Dr. No*, but was here called upon to replace him when a dispute of royalties led to Binder refusing to work on the new picture.

PRINCIPAL CASTING: Lotte Lenya had been married to German composer/dramatist Kurt Weill, confidant of the great German Communist writer Bertolt Brecht. She had first appeared onscreen in the film adaptation of Brecht's *Threepenny Opera* (G. W. Pabst, 1931). Principally known for 'victim' roles, and playing long-suffering figures, Klebb was a major departure for her. Critics at the time found her performance unconvincing, so wedded were they to her previous screen persona; this seems strange from the vantage point of the early 21st century, where Lenya is principally known for her brutal presence in *From Russia with Love*. Interestingly she is 'name checked' in her husband's most famous composition, 'Mack the Knife'.

Daniela Bianchi was a former Miss Rome, who gave up acting soon after this film. She bought a real sense of naivety to the part of Tania, perfectly conveying the wide-eyed innocence demanded of the character.

Pedro Armandáriz was a Mexican actor who frequently worked with director John Ford. Soon after filming began it became apparent that Armandáriz was gravely ill and his continued involvement was only assured after a personal call by Ford to the filmmakers. Here Armandáriz turns in the finest performance of his career. Sadly, his illness turned out to be terminal cancer, and he only just managed to finish filming his part before being hospitalised. He later took his own life rather than waste away under the effects of painful chemotherapy.

Robert Shaw was a novelist and actor whose first screen appearance had been in the classic *The Dam Busters* (Michael Anderson, 1954). Following *From Russia with Love* he continued with both his writing and film acting, most memorably in *A Man For All Seasons* (Fred Zinnemann, 1966) for which his outstanding performance as King Henry VIII garnered him an Academy Award nomination. One of his final screen appearances was as Quint in Steven Spielberg's classic *Jaws* (1975), to which he also contributed some of the dialogue.

MUSICAL NOTES: It was initially John Barry's intention to use local music on the *From Russia with Love* soundtrack, much as Monty Norman had on *Dr. No*, and he accompanied the crew to Istanbul to research Turkish music. Unfortunately he didn't much like what he heard in the town's bar and clubs, and so composed a more traditional-sounding score in the vein of movie composers like Alexander Korngold instead. Whereas Monty Norman's bravura calypso music had suited the previous film's Jamaican locale, Barry's score seems more suited to Bond the man, following him around the world rather than greeting him where he arrives. This movie also sees the debut of a recognisable 'Bond Song' with Lionel Bart's 'From Russia with Love' ably performed by former north London bus conductor, Matt Monro, once at the beginning and once at the end of the film.

BOX OFFICE: Breaking box-office takings and house admissions levels at the time, *From Russia with Love* took $79 million, an increase of almost a third on *Dr. No*'s takings.

AWARDS: *From Russia with Love* picked up a BAFTA for Best British Cinematography (Colour) for returning Director of Photography, Ted Moore. It received a Golden Globe nomination for Best Song in a Motion Picture but failed to win the award.

CRITICS: Critical reaction to *From Russia with Love* was largely indulgent, if occasionally a touch patronising. *Variety*'s Rich (16 October) called it a 'preposterous skilful slab of hardhitting, sexy hokum', praised Young for directing 'at a zingy pace' and concluded that it was all 'topnotch escapism'. The performances of Pedro Armandáriz and Robert Shaw were singled out for particular praise, as was that of Sean Connery – although it was already being noted that he may come to regret being so strongly associated with one character and yearn to avoid 'being identified entirely with James Bond'. 'Don't Miss It!' exhorted Bosley Crowther of *The New York Times* (21 April 1964) of this 'delightfully wild film' which was both 'deliciously fantastic and delightfully well played' and had its 'tongue blithely wedged in cheek'. The *Sunday Times* critic Dilys Powell was more simplistic in its praises: 'a film to be simply and uproariously enjoyed' she exclaimed in her review of 18 October.

Other critics were keen to emphasise the difference between Saltzman and Broccoli's Bond and Fleming's original. The *Financial Times*' David Robinson, writing on 11 October 1963, felt Fleming himself took his super-spy rather seriously, but that director Terence Young and screenwriter Richard Maibaum were 'not so fooled . . . they recognise the inherent self-parody', and that made the picture all the more entertaining. For him, however, there was little relish in the realisation that the 'James Bond will Return' ending, 'threaten[ed] a third film in the series'. For the *Saturday Review*, Hallis Alpert found the prospect of further screen James Bond adventures inviting: 'you . . . need another, and United Artists has one in the works this very minute' he wrote on 18 April 1964.

The *Sunday Express*, the daily sister of which had run James Bond comic strips in the 50s and early 60s, ran an article by Thomas Wiseman on 13 October. This called Bond 'the arch exponent of pop fascism . . . the patriot-libertine, always ready to seduce a pretty spy for his country' and described the film as 'an expensive penny dreadful' (comparing it to the gruesome, substandard popular fiction of the nineteenth century) while conceding it was 'enjoyably absurd'. It also asked perhaps the most sensible question from any reviewer during the film's initial release: why does Bond's escape route from Turkey (a non-Communist country) take him through Communist Bulgaria, when he's carrying stolen Communist equipment?

As before, the most stringent criticism came from Nina Hibbin in the *Daily Worker* (12 October) whose main question was 'What sort of people are we becoming if we can accept such perversion as a giggle?' She condemned Connery's Bond as 'dividing his time . . . between assassination and fornication' and posed the question 'Do you find this amusing?' Yes, Nina. Thanks for asking.

CUT SCENES: Peter Hunt performed above and beyond the duty of a film editor. Because the script was constantly rewritten during the shoot, the plot of the finished film did not hang together well, with several contradictory scenes. Working with Terence Young, Peter Hunt improvised with the available footage. The opening scenes were reordered to indicate a different flow to the story and some footage was used twice, once in reverse to create coverage that hadn't been shot.

Because the face of the actor playing Blofeld was never seen, it was a simple matter to record new dialogue and dub it over the scenes. It was also necessary to rewrite some of Klebb's dialogue and this necessitated re-shooting. However, it was prohibitively expensive to rebuild struck sets. Hunt came up with a masterstroke: he blew up footage of Klebb sitting talking to Blofeld, and used it as a back projection plate. Director Young then got actress Lotte Lenya to sit in front of her own screen image, effectively masking herself. She could therefore deliver new plot expositional dialogue without breaking the continuity of the scene.

PRODUCT PLACEMENT: In a move of marketing genius, Broccoli and Saltzman make a slight change to the murder of Krilencu as depicted in the book. Yes, he crawls out of a billboard, yes this billboard advertises a movie, but rather than Marilyn Monroe in *Niagara* (Henry Hathaway, 1953), the Bulgarian hitman crawls out of the mouth of Anita Ekberg, advertising a film called *Call Me Bwana* (Gordon Douglas, 1963) produced by . . . Albert R Broccoli and Harry Saltzman.

MARTINIS, GIRLS AND GUNS: Like Grant, Bond is an efficient killing machine, notching up seventeen kills (if you include the nine boatmen) plus one KO, and another KO/possible knifing. He scores with Sylvia, Tanya and the two gypsy girls. No Martinis though, the wimp.

THE ONE WITH . . .: that woman who kicks people to death with a dagger in her shoe.

THE LAST WORD: 'The Cold War in Istanbul will not remain cold for very much longer.' Things which are great about *From Russia with Love*: Kerim Bey; the helicopter sequence; Blofeld; the fight on the train; the scenes in the San Sofia mosque; Klebb; the chess match; Grant's habit of putting his gloves on before a kill; the Cold-War atmosphere; Bond walking untouched through the chaos of the battle at the gypsy encampment . . . you need more?

GIRLS	7
MARTINIS	2
DEATHS	22

Goldfinger (1964)

Produced by Albert R Broccoli and Harry Saltzman
Script by Richard Maibaum, Paul Dehn
Director of Photography: Ted Moore, BSC
Production designed by Ken Adam
Music composed and conducted by John Barry
Title song lyrics: Leslie Bricusse, Anthony Newley
Title song sung by Shirley Bassey
Edited by Peter Hunt
Directed by Guy Hamilton

PRINCIPAL CAST: Sean Connery (*James Bond*), Honor Blackman (*Pussy Galore*), Gert Frobe (*Auric Goldfinger*), Shirley Eaton (*Jill Masterson*), Tania Mallet (*Tilly Masterson*), Harold Sakata (*Oddjob*), Bernard Lee (*M*), Martin Benson (*Solo*), Cec Linder (*Felix Leiter*), Austin Willis (*Simmons*), Lois Maxwell (*Moneypenny*), Bill Nagy (*Midnight*), Michael Mellinger (*Kisch*), Peter Cranwell (*Johnny*), Nadja Regin (*Bonita*), Richard Vernon (*Smithers*), Burt Kwouk (*Mr Ling*), Desmond Llewelyn (*Q*), Mai Ling (*Mai-Lei*), Varley Thomas (*Swiss Gatekeeper*), Margaret Nolan (*Dink*), John McLaren (*Brigadier*), Robert Macleod (*Atomic Scientist*), Victor Brooks (*Blacking*), Alf Joint (*Capungo*), Gerry Duggan (*Hawker*), Denis Cowles (*Brunskill*), Hal Galili (*Strap*), Lenny Rabin (*Henchman*), Raymond Young (*Sierra*).

PRE-CREDITS AND TITLES: This film marks the beginning of the pre-credit sequence as a mini-adventure with a merely tangential link to the story about to unfold in the film. Bond infiltrates an unspecified installation somewhere in Central/South America (with the aid of a fake seagull) and destroys it. He meets up with an unnamed local ally at a nearby bar and indicates that the purpose of his action was to prevent the smuggling of heroin to finance revolutions. The link with the main plot is that he is to take a flight to Miami. First he has an appointment to keep with one of the bar's dancers who betrays him to a local thug, an action that Bond describes, after electrocuting said ruffian, as 'positively shocking'.

The title sequence is a development of the style of *From Russia with Love*. Here, instead of the credits being projected onto the body of a woman, a series of clips from Bond films are projected onto the actress Margaret Nolan, while the actual credits run in the black spaces beside her. Gorgeous, iconic, seminal.

SUMMARY: Goldfinger's plan is a brilliant basis for a movie, and has been justifiably praised down the years. Goldfinger is going to break into Fort Knox and explode a cobalt/iodine atomic bomb, rendering the US gold reserves radioactive, and therefore inaccessible, for 58 years. In doing so he will increase the value of his own gold stash tenfold, and cause the economic chaos in the West desired by his paymasters, the Red Chinese.

At the film's opening, Bond is in the luxury Fountainebleau hotel, Miami, with orders to keep an unobtrusive eye on Auric Goldfinger. Bond interprets this loosely, taking the opportunity ostentatiously to ruin a card-sharking scam that Goldfinger is running then seducing Goldfinger's assistant/escort Jill. Enraged by this, Goldfinger has his henchmen Oddjob beat up Bond, and has Jill murdered for her treachery.

Returning to London, (where M notes that Bond hasn't distinguished himself lately), 007 is told that the secret service suspects Goldfinger of smuggling gold.

Bond is ordered to shadow Goldfinger, and plays golf against the industrialist in a guarded game where both men cheat and each pretends not to recognise the other. This makes far more sense in the book where Goldfinger has no reason to believe Bond is anything other than his new golf partner.

Bond trails Goldfinger to Switzerland, where he is captured. Bond tells Goldfinger that he knows about Operation Grand Slam, and that if Goldfinger kills him 008 will be assigned to take over the case. Because Goldfinger cannot take the risk of Bond being replaced by an agent who is at liberty – and who knows everything Bond does – he chooses to take Bond with him to his Kentucky base rather than kill him. He believes that if he keeps Bond conspicuously alive, then the British and the Americans will continue to believe that Bond is undercover and on top of the situation. Later, after Bond has accidentally uncovered more details of Goldfinger's plan, he is keen to let the mogul know how much of the specific detail of the plot he is familiar with. This further guarantees his safety by suggesting an even greater scale to the knowledge that 008 might have access to.

Bond then spends most of the rest of the film in a cell apart from the sequence where he tries and fails to warn the CIA about Operation Grand Slam. Goldfinger's henchwoman, Pussy Galore, changes sides and contacts the CIA on Bond's behalf, leading to an intervention by the US military at Fort Knox. The only further role Bond takes is to neutralise Oddjob. Having done that he is forced to wait for the US bomb-disposal team to deactivate the atomic device to which he is chained.

In an exciting coda Goldfinger escapes and infiltrates the plane Bond is taking to meet President Johnson, making one last attempt to kill him. Bond gets the advantage and Goldfinger gets blown out of the side of the plane. Bond parachutes to safety for a final tryst with Pussy.

UNIVERSAL EXPORTS:

BOND, JAMES BOND: Bond seemingly decides that the best way to achieve his mission is to spend the entire film being as rude as possible to everyone he meets including his enemy, his superior and a woman he's trying to seduce. No wonder Goldfinger wants his death to be a particularly painful one. Some more aspects of his personal life are revealed. He doesn't like The Beatles but enjoys bourbon and branch water and mint juleps. He is a competent golfer and his ball of choice is a Penfold hearts.

There's far less to 007 than meets the eye here; Connery is magnificent, swaggering, smirking and deals out stylish violence. The indestructible superman Bond of *Thunderball* has its seeds in *Goldfinger*. Having said this, the character is peripheral at best, and plays no real part in the plot's resolution. He is, however, so cool that this largely goes unnoticed by audiences.

M: M's increasing despair at 007 and his methods continues apace. He doesn't trust Bond to take a gold bar (bait to interest Goldfinger) one night early, and is eye-rollingly displeased with Bond's showing off over the quality of the brandy at dinner. His office appears to have changed shape slightly, and all his pictures have changed again.

MONEYPENNY: Another rather twittering outing for Moneypenny. Even M seems to tire of her gabbling on about her knowledge of gold being limited to that found in a wedding ring, telling her to 'cut short the customary by-play'.

Q: Now credited and referred to as such, Q seems unimpressed by Bond, and has no qualms about taking up over an hour of his time in order to explain how to work the specially adapted Aston Martin correctly.

OHMSS: M threatens Bond with replacement by 008 if he begins to treat this case as a personal vendetta. Bond's mission seems more a case for Customs and Excise, the secret service apparently taking it on at the request of Colonel Smithers's department.

ALLIES:

FELIX LEITER: A first return appearance for Felix, here played as a bumbling middle-aged type in a pork-pie hat. Bond mentions their previous meeting in Jamaica, but there's no resemblance between Jack Lord's stateside Bond and this finger-lickin' fool. This film's portrayal of the CIA is not exactly flattering: their operation consists of two conspicuous men in a car, hanging around with binoculars. They seem unable to act on their own initiative and need to call in the armed forces to get anything.

JILL MASTERSON: A bikini-clad lovely, initially working for Goldfinger – she watches him playing cards through binoculars and informs him of his opponent's hand. She tells Bond that Goldfinger pays her to be seen with him but 'nothing else', specifying that she is an escort rather than a prostitute. She succumbs to Bond's charms willingly and playfully and seems rather self-assured and direct. It is Jill whom Goldfinger has painted gold, a process which kills her through skin suffocation and provides one of the most memorable images in movie history.

TILLY MASTERSON: Sister to Jill, the charming (if snooty) Tilly follows Goldfinger to Switzerland, planning to shoot him in revenge for her sister's murder. After a brief acquaintance with Bond and a shared car chase, she's killed by Oddjob's steel hat. Along with the Havelocks (see **For Your Eyes Only**) the Mastersons must rank as the joint unluckiest family in the Bond canon.

COLONEL SMITHERS: A civil servant in charge of the security of Britain's gold, Smithers briefs M and Bond on his worries about Goldfinger. This briefing takes place over a sumptuous black-tie dinner. Smithers loans Bond a gold bar obtained from a Nazi hoard at Lake Topling to help investigation of Goldfinger's operation.

THE OPPOSITION:

GOLDFINGER: A very rich man, with a licence to smelt gold, he's also the owner of (among other things) a golf club in England and a stud farm in Kentucky, USA. He habitually cheats at golf and cards, and is too mean to pay off the mobsters who have provided him with the materials to facilitate his plan (see **SUMMARY**), choosing to gas them instead.

Before they die he treats them to a long-winded explanation of the nature of his enterprise just to show them all how clever he is. It appears the sole aim of his plan is to increase the value of his gold.

Goldfinger's objectionable traits are compounded by his greed. Despite his wealth and his thriving legitimate jewellery business he's also into gold smuggling, which he accomplishes using his Rolls-Royce to ferry two tonnes of 18 carat gold per trip. With his six annual trips, Britain is losing 12 tonnes of gold a year thanks to Auric. His Chinese associate suggests that it might be time to suspend such operations and concentrate fully on 'Grand Slam'. Goldfinger poo-poos this idea, perhaps foolishly, given that it is these trips that have aroused the suspicion of the British Government.

He demonstrates lack of judgement in suggesting that Pussy Galore entertain James Bond alone (Bond knows the full details of his plan; Pussy doesn't) and is a rampant egoist. He has enough sense to know his enterprise might fail, however, and has an escape plan worked out, concealing a US army uniform under his heavy greatcoat in the Fort Knox scenes and wielding a natty gold-plated revolver. Even so, he can't resist having one last pop at Bond and gets sucked out of a plane for his troubles.

Frobe's Goldfinger is one of the great screen villains of all time, as witty and cocky as Bond with a scheme to match. The little touches, such as the way he briefly switches sides during the battle of Fort Knox, all add to his onscreen impact.

ODDJOB: Mute Korean henchman and caddy, Oddjob is armed with a brutal karate chop and a deadly metal-brimmed hat. He uses this to intimidate Bond by decapitating a statue at the golf club and to kill the fleeing Tilly Masterson. It is also the indirect cause of his undoing: while retrieving it from a Fort Knox vault he is electrocuted by Bond.

A fine villain, even tougher than Grant and with less of a vocabulary (reduced to two strangled yells), Oddjob is one of the two most famous Bond henchmen (along with Jaws, see **The Spy Who Loved Me**) due to his menacing presence, eccentric dress and infamous hat. It is testament to the character's longevity and Harold Sakata's performance that his appearances onscreen are accompanied by suitable apprehension on the part of the audience.

PUSSY GALORE: The glamorous, blonde head of Pussy Galore's Flying Circus, an all-female flying troupe. She can shoot and fly well and claims to be 'immune' to Bond's charms, although we later discover this is far from the case.

Goldfinger has promised her a share of the bounty from the heist (she seems to believe that he is going to steal the bullion, rather than irradiate it) and she doesn't know that the gas her planes will be spraying over Fort Knox is lethal.

In Fleming's book Pussy is a dark-haired lesbian who is 'straightened out' when Bond forces himself on her. However, it is not really clear if the film's Pussy is meant to be gay at all. The sexual tension between Connery and Blackman steams off the screen from the moment they first look at one another (indeed Ms Blackman has repeatedly described Connery as 'the sexiest man I've ever met') and her 'immunity' seems more a matter of playing hard to get than an indication of another sexual preference.

It has been suggested that Pussy simply becomes 'good' after her sexual encounter with Bond, and this *could* be what happens. It seems more likely that once told of the true nature of Goldfinger's plan, perhaps miffed that she's unlikely to be paid (there would be no gold to share out) and probably shocked by the mass slaughter planned, she informs on her boss to the CIA. However, she still rescues Goldfinger from Fort Knox with her helicopter, and is flying with him to Cuba when he makes his final attempt to kill Bond. Although Goldfinger says that he will 'deal with' Pussy later, it appears that he has accepted her role in his defeat and that she has accepted that he lied to her – and that they can still somehow work together after this.

Bond's seemingly miraculous realigning of Miss Galore's loyalties is his most significant contribution to the plot of *Goldfinger*. Does a film which reduces Bond to Britain's most inspiring sexual athlete do the character justice? Even if he is so potent that he can alter someone's moral sense with a single, literal roll in the hay.

MR LING: The Red Chinese agent and nuclear fission expert, Mr Ling is closely supervising Goldfinger's operation on behalf of the Chinese government who are supplying the nuclear bomb required for irradiating Fort Knox in the hope of securing 'economic chaos in the West' (see **THE REAL WORLD**). He is among the first to be killed in the battle for Fort Knox, shot by Goldfinger, who is quick to see which way the wind is blowing and changes into his American Army guise.

DIRECTOR AND CREW: Denied a percentage of the profits for what would have been his third consecutive James Bond film adventure, Terence Young jumped ship during pre-production preferring instead to direct *Moll Flanders*. Guy Hamilton, who had been originally approached to shoot *Dr. No* and who had refused, was asked – and jumped at this second chance to be a part of the Bond series. Hamilton had started out in films as a clapper-boy, and had risen to the position of director via the assistant director's chair, a capacity in which he worked on *The Third Man* (Carol Reed, 1949) and *The African Queen* (John Huston, 1951). Hamilton's primary aim for this Bond picture was that it was to be fun, and he was very keen to propel the series to new realms of tongue-in-cheek ludicrousness. He would direct a further three Bond pictures over the next ten years.

PRINCIPAL CASTING: German actor Gert Frobe was hired by producer Broccoli, who had seen the actor's German language Swiss film *Es Geschah am hellichten Tag* (Ladislao Vadja, 1958). Assured by Frobe's agent that the actor could speak English, Hamilton was appalled to discover that Frobe could do no such thing. As a result most of his lines in the film are dubbed by voice-over artiste Michael Collins, who arguably deserves at least as much credit as Frobe for bringing the character to such vivid life. His most famous role aside from the eponymous *Goldfinger* is in another Saltzman/Broccoli Fleming adaptation, *Chitty Chitty Bang Bang* (Ken Hughes, 1968).

Honor Blackman had had a successful film career in the 40s and 50s, including an appearance in Roy Ward Baker's *A Night To Remember* (1958), a sumptuous black-and-white Kenneth More picture which remains, to this day, the best film representation of the sinking of the Titanic. By the early 60s she was of course best known for her role as karate-kicking, sex-bomb female investigator Cathy Gale in ATV's espionage and adventure series *The Avengers*. She left the series to make *Goldfinger*, causing the producers of that series several headaches as a result. As Pussy Galore, Blackman is simply wonderful. She matches Bond's machismo with her sardonic putdowns, and struts and preens with as much confidence as Connery, if not more. The only point at which she looks slightly ill at ease is when forced to play the damsel in distress to Bond's rescuing hero at the end.

Hawaiian wrestler Harold Sakata was cast in the role of mute Korean Oddjob. He delivers a splendidly menacing performance that, were such a thing to exist, would surely feature in a textbook of Bond villainy.

FASHION VICTIMS: Bond's hideous short-legged blue towelling dressing gown is best forgotten. His tuxedo-concealing wetsuit, however, is exceptionally cool. The grey suit he wears around Goldfinger's farm is stylish and flattering and on the golf course his neat trilby and Slazenger top far outclass Goldfinger's outrageous plus fours. Pussy always looks amazing, but special mention to her shiny lamé waistcoat and cleavage-enhancing purple blouse.

SET PIECES: The pre-credit sequence is awesome – a five-minute summary of everything great about the Bond film. The fight in Fort Knox is hugely satisfying, especially considering Peter Hunt's usual editorial approach of lightning cuts and confusing action. These are swapped for a slowly paced match of wits. The two stalk around each other deliberately before Bond eventually overcomes his foe using brains rather than brawn. This vies with the train fight of *From Russia with Love* for the title of best one-on-one battle in the series.

POSITIVELY SHOCKING: Bond casually kills a Mexican bandit with an electric heater thrown in the bath. Tilly's sad fate is compounded by the knowledge of the gruesome effect Oddjob's hat has.

MEMORABLE QUOTES:
Pussy: 'My name is Pussy Galore.'
Bond: 'I must be dreaming.'

Bond: 'An ejector seat? You're joking.'
Q: 'I never joke about my work, 007.'

Leiter: 'I told them liquor for three.'
Bond: 'Who are the other two?'
Leiter: 'Oh, there are no other two.'

And, inevitably,
Bond: 'Do you expect me to talk?'
Goldfinger: 'No Mr Bond I expect you to die!'

GADGETS: We are finally invited into Q-branch, the workshop of the Secret Service. The noisy home of numerous eccentric gadgets, such as a gas-spewing parking meter and a bullet-proof vest (the technician testing it seems unperturbed by the fact it has not been perfected). Bond is given access to the famed Aston Martin DB5. Machine guns, smokescreens, oil-slick dispensers, tyre-slasher hubcaps, bullet-proof screens and windows, revolving number plates and the infamous ejector seat. The last of these is built up beautifully in the film. Bond toys knowingly with the gear stick while his unwelcome passenger looks in ignorance and the audience salivate in anticipation. Though initially planning to keep this last feature a secret, the filmmakers made a wise choice in explaining its functions beforehand. For Bond to escape through such an apparently contrived device would have induced incredulity. That the audience is aware of, and thus eagerly awaits its use produces a sense of satisfaction when finally employed.

However, this undoubtedly beautiful car is of negligible value in the field. Its tyre-slashers force Tilly off the road, but none of its devices allow Bond to escape Goldfinger's compound and it ends up as a heap of junk. Though many critics chose this point to start accusing Bond of being taken over by machines and gadgets, here they fail to save him from the villain's clutches.

Goldfinger has access to an industrial laser. This device had only recently been invented and, at that point, had no practical applications. The Bond team produced the effect of metal being cut by having a member of the production team operate a blowtorch underneath or behind the sheet being cut. This is probably the reason for Connery's visible tension in the torture scene. Goldfinger gets extra marks for re-using this handy tool to cut into Fort Knox.

CULTURE VULTURE: The entry of Bond into a smoky, exotic bar, wearing a white tuxedo is more than a little reminiscent of Humphrey Bogart's Rick Blaine in *Casablanca* (Michael Curtiz, 1942).

IN THE REAL WORLD: In a puzzling move, given the producers' non-political stance, Goldfinger is linked with Communist China, a country which is presented as a driving force behind Operation Grandslam. Chairman Mao's China was a wild card in international affairs. A communist country, but with enough differences with its neighbour Russia to prevent a solid alliance, it existed as a third super-power in world affairs, technologically behind its co-powers but with a huge army, massive population and subject to the West's traditional mistrust of the East.

Clashes had occurred between United Nations forces and the Chinese during the Korean war (1950–53) and they had become the oriental variant of the traditional Cold War communist bugbear – a feature of many films of the period (for instance in John Frankenheimer's 1962 thriller *The Manchurian Candidate*). Crucially, 1964 had seen the detonation of the first Chinese atomic bomb. China had become the perfect backer for Goldfinger's fictional villainy: a newly nuclear power, largely feared and mistrusted by the people in the West and with a government not even recognised by the United States (China's seat on the

UN Security Council was occupied by Taiwan – a province under the control of Chinese nationalists, opposed to the communist revolution). They also backed Blofeld's scheme in *You Only Live Twice* and, even after Richard Nixon opened peace overtures with China in the early 1970s, appeared as backers to several of Bond's latte-day opponents (see **The Man with the Golden Gun** and **Tomorrow Never Dies**).

Goldfinger's laser represented a new technological development. So new in fact that the producers issued a press release, explaining the scientific fact behind this apparently fictional death ray. Invented by Californian physicist Ted Maiman in 1960 the 'Light Amplification by Stimulated Emission of Radiation' has since become a common tool, as predicted in the film.

By and large one of the great selling points of the film is its timelessness. For example, there was great fear of crop dusters being used to spread toxins from the air in the aftermath of the attacks on America on 11 September 2001. In fact, so easily adaptable were the bases of the plot that the producers tried to replicate it in 1985's *A View to a Kill*.

SOURCE TO SCREEN: Ian Fleming's seventh James Bond novel was a natural choice to be filmed third, due to the plot's obvious appeal to an American audience. *Goldfinger* provided an American setting for a series that had hitherto been confined to the Caribbean and Europe, and the climax – a full-on military assault on Fort Knox, site of the USA's gold reserves – had great cinematic potential. It also had a strong villain in the eponymous Goldfinger, something that other books set in the USA, such as *Diamonds are Forever*, conspicuously lacked.

Richard Maibaum wrote a first draft script, and then Paul Dehn, the film critic and Oscar-winning screenwriter, was brought in to do rewrites.

In the book, Bond first meets Goldfinger by chance in Miami, while returning from a mission in Mexico (an episode adapted for the pre-credit sequence). Later M briefs him on the Government's worries about the wealthy metallurgist who is also a SMERSH paymaster, entrusted with financing Soviet operations in Europe. The screenplay deleted this clumsy coincidence. On the page, Bond dines with Goldfinger after their golf match and is there appraised of Oddjob's unique skills (this sequence was included in early scripts but rests uneasily even in the original novel). Bond then follows Goldfinger to Switzerland, and witnesses a drop-off of smuggled gold which is destined for retrieval by Soviet agents. Bond secures the gold himself, and takes it to the regional British Secret Service station. As in the film he encounters

Tilly Masterson en route to Goldfinger's compound. Here the two stories begin to differ greatly. Both Bond and Tilly are taken alive and, and while Bond *is* tortured, Goldfinger decides not to kill him, as he will be able to play a role in Goldfinger's upcoming Operation Grand Slam. In the book this is a 'straightforward' bullion robbery involving American mobsters, with Goldfinger planning to escape on a Soviet cruiser. A no-fallout atomic device ('bought' from an American airbase!) will be used to blow open the security doors. This idea was reworked by Maibaum and Dehn into the irradiating plotline when they worked out just how unfeasible it was to physically carry away that amount of gold. When Bond explains the impracticality of Goldfinger's ostensible plan it is Maibaum's own thoughts he is expounding. In order to fit in with these alterations the novel's clean bomb becomes a 'particularly dirty' one.

In the book the bomb is never detonated as Bond manages to get a message out by taping it to the underside of a plane toilet and the Americans – led by Felix Leiter – intervene. Goldfinger never reaches the inside of Fort Knox.

These expansions of the plot are, in general, welcome, as are the changes made to the character of Pussy Galore. In the book she is, explicitly, a lesbian but this identification serves little purpose other than to allow Fleming to salivate over her 'conversion' by the virile Bond. Though the toning down of Pussy in the film might seem cowardly, it is necessary, on a par with cutting Fleming's casual racism and some of his more grotesque sexist assertions. The cinematic Pussy is resistant to Bond's charm and is head of a female flying circus but this is where any implications begin and end. The film lingers on ideological conversion from bad to good rather than any sexual repositioning.

MUSICAL NOTES: With a release for the film predetermined, John Barry apparently had to score some sequences straight from the cutting room. This is far from evident from the finished picture, the score for which has colossal panache. The music that accompanies the very start of the film, and the sweeping shots over Miami beach, is eminently hummable. The title song is suitably strident and superbly orchestrated, but Shirley Bassey's much-celebrated delivery of it could equally be judged as raucous and grating.

BOX OFFICE: *Goldfinger* took $125 million worldwide, over twice the amount *Dr. No* had taken and a substantial increase on *From Russia with Love*, reflecting the Bond series' increased popularity in the American market.

AWARDS: *Goldfinger* became the first Bond film to win an Academy Award when Norman Wanstall was given the Oscar for Best Sound Effects. Wanstall and his wife attended the Awards ceremony at producer Broccoli's expense.

Wanstall would go on to work on two further Bond Eon films, *Thunderball* and *You Only Live Twice*, as well as Francois Truffaut's adaptation of Ray Bradbury's *Fahrenheit 451* (1966), before retiring from the movie business to become Britain's only Oscar-winning plumber. He has returned to the movie industry only once, at Sean Connery's personal request, to work on the renegade Bond feature *Never Say Never Again* in 1983.

CRITICS: Derek Prouse in the *Sunday Times* (20 September 1964) had not thought highly of the previous films but praised *Goldfinger* as 'superbly engineered. It is fast, it is most entertainingly preposterous and it is exciting.' The *Time* review of 18 December described it as 'a thriller exuberantly travestied.' *Punch* (30 September) felt the tone of the film to be 'little short of burlesque. The audience is there to laugh and does so on the slightest excuse.' Along with this came the first claims of overreliance on gadgets. The same *Punch* review bemoaned the fact that 'the gadgets have finally taken over'. Iain Crawford in the *Sunday Express* (20 September) described James Bond as a man of the time, saying how he 'goes in heavily for automation' perhaps tying in with Prime Minister Harold Wilson's contemporaneous comment about the 'white heat of technology'. Critics also commented on the high production values, Derek Prouse paying 'tribute to the set designers and special effects department' while Philip Oakes in the *Sunday Telegraph* (20 September) spoke of the film being 'dazzling in its technical ingenuity'. Oakes also felt that while 'the occasional *Goldfinger* can be fun, there are obvious limits. A surfeit of the breed would be like sharing a house with a herd of mammoths.' This enigmatic analogy aside, the point about audiences being saturated by Bond films was a fair one. Henceforth, the films would be made and released at two-year intervals rather than annually.

CUT SCENES: No scenes were cut per se, but a proposed gadget for the DB5 – a dispenser that dropped spikes onto the road ahead of pursuing cars – was removed after fears that this practice would be copied. The same worries oddly were not expressed about the oil-slick dispenser or tyre-slasher devices.

TRIVIA: For the first time Sean Connery's name is above the title of the film, rather than immediately following it. Albert R Broccoli and

Harry Saltzman's credits are reversed, so that Broccoli comes first. Saltzman had been the first credited on the previous two pictures. From the next film onwards it's seemingly a lottery as to who gets credited first. Oddly, given that *On Her Majesty's Secret Service* was very much Saltzman's film, Broccoli receives first credit, and the reverse is true of the Broccoli-led *Diamonds Are Forever*.

The character of Sylvia Trench was dropped after Terence Young's departure from the series. Though Young later returned Trench did not.

PRODUCT PLACEMENT: The use of the DB5 ranks as one of the most effective pieces of product placement ever, single-handedly making Aston Martin a viable company after years of financial insecurity.

The use of Kentucky Fried Chicken in the background as Felix Leiter muses on Bond's fate was accidental. Guy Hamilton was filming scenes supposedly set in Kentucky while on location in Miami for the opening sequence. He saw it as an opportunity to establish Leiter as being in Kentucky, not realising that the fast food outlet was a national franchise.

There was also an example of product placement that never was. Hamilton arrived on set to shoot the sequence in Goldfinger's private Jetstar aircraft (another product referenced, though it is doubtful that the film influenced sales of this particularly luxurious item) to find that producer Harry Saltzman had dressed the set with a multitude of Gillette products, having signed a deal with the company. Though the director removed the items from the set, in future he would ask for a checklist of companies with whom deals had been done. He would then check off those that could be included in the film.

MARTINIS, GIRLS AND GUNS: Bond scores once with the delicious, unfortunate Jill and at least twice with Pussy Galore. On Goldfinger's plane he orders a single Martini, shaken not stirred and notches up a few more kills, although not as excessive a body count as in his last outing. There's the Mexican in the pre-credits, the four people in the car, and one with the ejector seat gives six. Plus, a shooting in a firefight, one cell guard (a particularly nasty blow to the chin), of course Oddjob (burn baby burn!) and Goldfinger himself; a nicely homicidal ten.

THE ONE WITH . . .: Honor Blackman, Shirley Bassey's delivery of 'GOLD-FIN-GAH!' and Oddjob.

THE LAST WORD: 'My apologies Goldfinger, it's brilliant!' Perhaps the most highly and consistently praised Bond picture of them all,

Goldfinger is far slower and more low-key than you remember it being and gives its leading man little or nothing to do. Despite this it is fluid, witty, sexy, excitingly shot and brilliantly performed – physical proof that you can make an undeniably great film with an episodic script, characters that don't so much develop as stroll around pouting and a resolution in which the ostensible lead character plays no real part.

GIRLS	9
MARTINIS	3
DEATHS	32

Thunderball (1965)

Executive Producers: Harry Saltzman and Albert R Broccoli
Produced by Kevin McClory
Screenplay by Richard Maibaum and John Hopkins
Based on an Original Screenplay by Jack Whittingham
Based on the Original Story by Kevin McClory,
Jack Whittingham and Ian Fleming
Director of Photography: Ted Moore, BSC
Production designed by Ken Adam
Music composed and conducted by John Barry
Title song words by Leslie Bricusse
Supervising Editor: Peter Hunt
Directed by Terence Young

PRINCIPAL CAST: Sean Connery (*James Bond*), Claudine Auger (*Domino*), Adolfo Celi (*Largo*), Luciana Paluzzi (*Fiona*), Rik Van Nutter (*Felix Leiter*), Guy Doleman (*Count Lippe*), Molly Peters (*Patricia*), Martine Beswick (*Paula Caplan*), Bernard Lee (*M*), Desmond Llewelyn (*Q*), Lois Maxwell (*Moneypenny*), Roland Culver (*Foreign Secretary*), Earl Cameron (*Pinder*), Paul Stassino (*Palazzi*), Rose Alba (*Madame Boitier*), Philip Locke (*Vargas*), George Pravda (*Kutze*), Michael Brennan (*Janni*), Leonard Sachs (*Group Captain*), Edward Underdown (*Air Vice Marshal*), Reginald Beckwith (*Kenniston*), Harold Sanderson (*Hydrofoil Captain*).

PRE-CREDITS AND TITLES: Bond is in France at the funeral of one Jacques Boitier (see **TRIVIA**) – a man who murdered two of Bond's Secret Service colleagues and whom he had been sent to France to kill.

Finding on his arrival that Boitier was ostensibly already dead, Bond decides to attend the funeral. While there he deduces that Boitier is alive, and is disguised as one of the female mourners. Bond kills him, and escapes the scene with assistance from a jet pack, his Aston Martin and a swish brunette who seems rather keen on him.

The titles are eye-popping. Two women swim around in a vast widescreen morass of bright colours, firing harpoons and splashing around. To shoot this sequence designer Maurice Binder reportedly hired two dancers who had swum in tanks in 'clubs' and persuaded them to swim around naked for him. He tinted and assembled the footage at a later date, resulting in the awesome sequence which opens this picture.

SUMMARY: SPECTRE steals two thermonuclear devices from the RAF and then blackmail 'the NATO powers', demanding £100 million/ $280 million from the British and US governments in return for not destroying a major city in either country. The British Government sends the 00 agents out to various places across the world to try and locate these bombs, firstly because they hate the idea of paying SPECTRE their 'blood money' but also because they rightly don't trust SPECTRE not to explode the weapons anyway. (Indeed, at the end of the film, after we see the Government's preparing to pay up, SPECTRE move to detonate the bombs regardless.) Bond, acting on a hunch, is sent to the Bahamas, where he encounters SPECTRE Number Two Emilio Largo, discovers the bombs and after a bloody fracas prevents them from being detonated.

UNIVERSAL EXPORTS:

BOND, JAMES BOND: At the film's opening Bond is staying at Shrublands, a health farm, where he is recuperating from his recent exertions. His suspicions are aroused by an encounter with the mysterious Count Lippe, who appears to be wearing a SPECTRE ring and has a tattoo which may indicate membership of a Tong. Bond decides to investigate.

This consists of breaking into the rooms of Lippe and his wheelchair-bound associate, 'Mr Angelo', rifling through their things and then stealing their grapes. Though he uncovers nothing, this nosiness makes him a target for the paranoid Lippe. Angelo is later said to have died, and his body is taken away (see **ANGELO**). Bond is playful and wilful all the way through the Shrublands sequences, although to his credit he is far more focused and restrained when actually on his mission.

After leaving Shrublands, 007 is briefed on the matter of the missing Vulcan bomber, and he recognises one of the people in the photographs given to him and the other 00 agents as the 'Angelo' he encountered at Shrublands. This man is in fact Major Derval of NATO, a passenger on the missing bomber. This incongruity is enough for M to send Bond to Nassau in search of Derval's sister, Domino (also pictured in the folder), who may have clues to the case. This is rather contrived but it all flies by wonderfully on screen.

Bond once again decides that being as rude as possible to his host is the best way to proceed with his mission (see **Goldfinger**). He states that Largo's gun is more suitable for a woman, flirts with his mistress, and shows him up by being a much better shot than he is. He doesn't quite slap Largo round the face and call him a 'cycloptic buffoon' but he might as well have done.

Compounding his rudeness is his initial ineptness as a secret agent. On first meeting Largo he makes as many unsubtle references to 'spectres' as possible. Short of tattooing '007 of the Secret Service' on his forehead it's difficult to see how Bond's mission could have got off to a more obtrusive start. Despite this, he is effective later, tracking down the missing bombs through persistence and keen deductive skills.

This rudeness also marks one of the film's failings. As first indicated in *Goldfinger*, Bond was no longer really apprehensive of any event. This Bond is so utterly sure of himself that he treats almost every obstacle with what amounts to yawning indifference. Bond still shows his penchant for luxury, toying with Largo over the chemin de fer tables and then ordering Dom Perignon 55 (see **Dr. No**) and caviar for a light supper with Domino.

M: M has sufficient faith in Bond's instincts to change his assignment on the vaguest of hunches – correctly as it turns out. He also shows the high regard he has for Bond, something normally concealed by his curmudgeonly ways. He will take no criticism of 007, even from government ministers.

MONEYPENNY: A far more sparkling than usual Moneypenny refers to M as 'the old man', and seems to relish the idea of being spanked by Bond. The office banter between Bond, Moneypenny and M reaches its zenith here – laugh-out-loud funny and skilfully played by all.

Q: Desmond Llewelyn has one brilliant scene, as he goes out in the field for the first time, handing Bond his equipment in Nassau. 'Oh no,' murmurs 007 as the irascible major enters, seemingly ungrateful for the equipment that will later save his life.

PAULA CAPLAN: Played by Hammer starlet Martine Beswick, who had also featured in *From Russia with Love*, Paula is a field assistant assigned to Bond by the Secret Service. She develops some sort of attachment to Bond, albeit unrequited and, in a rather chilling scene, commits suicide by taking a cyanide capsule when captured by SPECTRE.

OHMSS: There are, it seems, nine 00 agents including Bond. Moneypenny says that all the 00 agents in Europe have been recalled and when Bond enters the meeting room there are nine chairs, including the empty chair reserved for him. Overall rather circumstantial evidence, but it seems likely – the idea of a '0010' sounds silly.

ALLIES:

DOMINO: The beautiful ward/mistress of Emilio Largo and the sister of murdered NATO pilot Francois Derval. Domino is a headstrong, fiery young woman who takes to Bond quickly, seeing him as an opportunity for a harmless fling. Once the details of Largo's scheme and past crimes are revealed she swiftly agrees to join forces with Bond but is captured in the act of searching for the atom bombs and is threatened by Largo in a particularly unpleasant torture scene, made worse because much is implied. We never know exactly what Largo does or intends to do, only that it involves the use of heat (cigars) and cold (ice cubes) applied 'scientifically and slowly. Very slowly.' One enduring mystery from the film is how the sister of murdered airman Derval ended up on Largo's ship. If it's a coincidence, the suspension of disbelief required is enormous. A possible explanation is that she caught Largo's fancy while he was scouting for the man whom SPECTRE would create a double of for the mission. This implausibility comes about because of the addition of the Angelo subplot. In the novel, the NATO pilot (there called Petachi) is himself involved in SPECTRE's scheme. In an echo of the end of *From Russia with Love*, it is she who kills Largo rather than Bond.

FELIX LEITER: This Felix looks more like Jack Lord's smooth spy than Cec Linder's ageing buffoon, clad as he is in Bermuda fashions and shades. Rik Van Nutter's relaxed and charming performance works well, but there's more than a hint of the stoner/surfer beach bum about him at times. He doesn't quite tell Bond to 'simmer down and like take a chill-pill, man' but he looks as though he's about to.

PINDER: Filling the same role as *Dr. No*'s Quarrel, Pinder provides local assistance to Bond. He provides key assistance to Bond in blacking out Palmyra, allowing 007 to infiltrate Largo's property.

PATRICIA FEARING: A nurse working at Shrublands who, despite Bond's bullish flirting, doesn't seem to be giving in to his charms. After Count Lippe uses the back-stretching machine at the clinic as part of a bungled attempt to kill 007, it is Pat who rescues him. Bond's offhand comment that 'someone will pay' for his 'accident' (meaning Lippe) is interpreted by Patricia as Bond threatening to have her removed from her job. Bond is quick to jump on this misapprehension, suggesting that he could be persuaded not to complain . . . for a price. Initially reluctant, she has sex with him in the steam room; and when we next see them she clearly can't get enough of him. Nonetheless it is difficult to excuse his earlier behaviour.

When Bond leaves she gives him an invitation to get together with her, 'any time, any place'. Bond's reply, 'another time, another place', is a reference to the film of that title Sean Connery had made with Lana Turner in 1958.

THE OPPOSTION:

SPECTRE: We discover more about SPECTRE in this film than ever before. Their base is now hidden inside an attractive mews house in Paris, operating under the cover of the 'International Brotherhood for the Assistance of Stateless Persons'. SPECTRE Number One is still Blofeld (played again by Antony Dawson/Eric Pohlman). We discover that Jacques Boitier was Number Six and see several other SPECTRE agents, all of whom report to Blofeld. Number Five is British, Number Seven is Chinese, Number Ten is French and Numbers Nine and Eleven American. We discover that they are involved in everything from drug smuggling to the Great Train Robbery, SPECTRE agents either initiating the crimes or acting as consultants and taking a cut of the loot.

BLOFELD: A malevolent background presence, who disposes of treacherous and incompetent minions via death traps and his 'execution division' but insists that SPECTRE has 'absolute integrity'. It is his voice which appears on the tape sent to the British and (presumably) American governments.

EMILIO LARGO: A cruel, handsome pirate of a man, Largo is SPECTRE Number Two and the field commander of the operation. He is working out of a luxurious beachside villa, Palmyra, and a modified hydrofoil craft, the *Disco Volante*. He is using the latter to ferry the stolen atomic warheads.

Largo seems happy to live the playboy lifestyle as the atom-bomb smuggling progresses, going to casinos and happily showing Bond around his villa. Though outwardly genial there is a vicious streak near the surface, emerging most prominently when he is preparing to torture Domino. He indulges in innuendo-laden verbal battles with Bond. Simultaneously the brains and brawn of the enemy outfit, Largo is one of Bond's most imposing adversaries and the film culminates in a vicious physical hand-to-hand battle, ending only when Domino kills Largo.

FIONA VOLPE: Cast from the same mould as Pussy Galore, but this time actually immune to Bond's charm, Volpe is part of SPECTRE's execution division (it is she who disposes of the incompetent Count Lippe) and acts as a troubleshooter for Largo in Nassau. She captures the unfortunate agent Caplan and then seduces Bond before attempting to kill him. He escapes into a passing carnival, and in the confusion it is Fiona who is killed.

Most interestingly, Fiona represents the early realisation on the filmmakers of the tendency for the Bond character to 'convert' female opponents to his side by having sex with them, as demonstrated in both *Goldfinger* and, to an extent, *From Russia with Love*. Here Bond expressly states that sleeping with Fiona gave him 'no pleasure', and that he did it 'for King and country'. In other words, to initiate such a change in her loyalties. Fiona counters Bond's comments by pointing out that she is aware of this character trait/plot device and the way Bond expects his conquests repent and return 'to the side of right and virtue'. Bond's rather feeble comeback is, 'You can't win them all.' Although this is a smart, post-modernistic handling of the issue head on, it sadly resulted in a new Bond stereotype, – the beautiful female villain who sleeps with Bond, but is not 'ideologically realigned', so to speak, and subsequently 'has' to be killed off.

COUNT LIPPE: Apparently a member of the Red Dragon Tong, a criminal organisation from Macau (though this is never confirmed), Count Lippe is a SPECTRE agent based at Shrublands health farm assisting in the handling of the unpredictable Angelo. His Tong membership discovered by Bond, he engages in a childish battle of wills trying to tear Bond apart on a stretching machine before Bond attempts to poach him to death in a Sitz bath. However, it is Lippe's failure to control Angelo that leads to his death – Blofeld decides that the choice of a duplicate for Derval was flawed and orders Lippe's execution.

VARGAS: 'Vargas does not drink, does not smoke, does not make love. What do you do Vargas?' Hang around the place looking shifty before being harpooned by Bond, it seems.

ANGELO: A man of indeterminate origin who is in the pay of SPECTRE. He has undergone a two-year course of speech therapy and plastic surgery to make him resemble Major Francois Derval of NATO. He has done this so he can steal the RAF Vulcan bomber on SPECTRE's behalf, a service for which he will be rewarded with $100,000. At the last moment he ups his fee to $250,000 for which avarice he is forcibly drowned by Largo's men. After he's committed the robbery of course.

FASHION VICTIMS: 'On you everything looks good', Felix tells Bond, and he might be right, given the way Connery manages to look good in red cheesecloth. Domino's black-and-white bikini is almost as awesome as the girl wearing it and the fiendish Miss Volpe looks lovely as well.

For once, Bond's adversary is an equal in the sartorial stakes. Largo almost outclasses him in the casino (despite the burden of a white tux) and wins hands down in the final underwater battle – sleek black wetsuits against the violent orange of the aqua-paratroops is hardly a contest, especially when Bond's embarrassingly tiny swimming trunks are considered.

SET PIECES: There are two real stand-out sequences in *Thunderball*. The chase through the carnival (itself set up for the benefit of the production – certain dancers have made costumes which prominently display the 007 logo) is suspenseful and well paced, though nothing compared to the later sublime pursuit scenes of *On Her Majesty's Secret Service*. However, the climactic underwater battle is simply amazing. Brilliantly shot and disgracefully violent, the great clash between US forces and SPECTRE frogmen deserves its screentime. One of the finest Bond battles, made all the more so by the hectic boat chase with which it ends. Both Bond's opening scene fight with Boitier and his hectic clash with Largo in the cabin of the *Disco Volante* were filmed with an undercranked camera, resulting in the sequences appearing to run slightly too fast in the finished film. This adds a furious energy.

POSITIVELY SHOCKING: The suicide of Bond's assistant Paula is really rather unpleasant. Some have taken issue with the sheer ferocity of the underwater battle, which features Bond firing a harpoon into someone's eye. Similarly, the cold-bloodedness of Bond quipping as Fiona dies in his arms has provoked strong reactions.

MEMORABLE QUOTES:
Bond (at Shrublands health farm): 'See you later . . . irrigator.'

Domino: 'My, what sharp little eyes you've got.'
Bond: 'Wait 'til you get to my teeth.'

Invited to shoot clay pigeon at Palmyra and confronted by Largo with shotgun:
Bond: 'That gun . . . it looks more fitting for a woman.'

And when actually shooting:
Bond: 'It seems terribly difficult . . . [effortlessly blows clay pigeon away] . . . no, it isn't is it?'

GADGETS: Bond is well provided for by Q-branch here. Within minutes of the start he has taken to the skies in a jet pack – an actual working prototype developed by the Bell aeronautic corporation. He also utilises his Aston Martin – this time fitted with high-pressure water hose. This is effective at keeping SPECTRE thugs at bay but, as many spoilsports have pointed out, requires so much water that the sports car would have to be effectively a stationary tank of fluid.

He also has a Geiger counter concealed within a watch (and another concealed within a camera that he gives to Domino), a radioactive tracer in pill form, a miniature flare gun (used in conjunction to guide in a rescue team allowing Bond to be involved in the underwater battle), a propeller-powered SCUBA pack armed with harpoons and doubling as a hefty explosive charge and, very hi-tech for the time, an underwater camera with infra-red film. Additionally he has a pocket-sized re-breather giving five minutes' worth of air, which is used to great effect in Largo's shark tank and the climactic battle. So impressive was this apparatus that representatives from the military got in touch with special effects man John Stears asking for details on the device's construction. When told that the effective operating time for the unit was simply for as long as the actors could hold their breath the army slunk away quietly.

SPECTRE are a well-financed and well-armed organisation. Their execution branch has rocket-firing motorbikes, Blofeld has his conference chairs booby-trapped with high-voltage electricity for disposal of traitors and their underwater division has access to submarine sleds armed with harpoons. Largo has the *Disco Volante* at his disposal. In its original incarnation a lavishly equipped yacht, it's capable of splitting into two parts – a heavily armed 'cocoon' section designed to hold off hostile forces and a super-fast hydrofoil section for its getaway.

CULTURE VULTURE: The success of *Goldfinger* led to many attempts to cash in on the Bond name which began to emerge around the time of *Thunderball* (see **PARODY AND PASTICHE**).

The most interesting series to be developed because of the cinematic success of Bond was the Harry Palmer trilogy, produced by Bond's own Harry Saltzman. *The Ipcress File* (Sidney Furie, 1965), *Funeral in Berlin* (Guy Hamilton, 1966) and *Billion Dollar Brain* (Ken Russell, 1967) were based on early 60s novels by Len Deighton and presented a blue-collar spy in the form of Michael Caine's Harry Palmer, a man who appreciates the finer things in life, but on a smaller scale to 007 – he prefers home-ground coffee, and has a liking for tinned champignon. A spy who saves the world while simultaneously being a more human figure, one who grumbles about his bosses, gets in late to work and reads the *Racing Post*, Palmer existed in a more morally dubious, less certain world than Bond, one comparable to that inhabited by the spies in John Le Carré's work – represented by the film of *The Spy Who Came in from the Cold* (Martin Ritt, 1965). These films had close links with the Bond series. John Barry composed the laidback, jazzy theme-tune to *The Ipcress File*, Bond regulars Peter Hunt and Norman Wanstall edited and provided sound effects respectively and Ken Adam designed the sets. Guy Hamilton went on to direct *Funeral in Berlin* after *Goldfinger* and Ken Adam returned as production designer while *Billion Dollar Brain* saw production design by *From Russia with Love*'s Syd Cain and titles designed by Maurice Binder. The greatest link comes in the shape of Harry Saltzman as producer of all three.

It seems as though, by the mid-60s, the dynamic Saltzman was developing itchy feet, despite the success of the Bond films, and was looking to new projects, including the Palmer pictures which were tantamount to a rival franchise. Saltzman would become involved in Orson Welles's financially troubled *Chimes at Midnight* (1966) and produce the lavish *The Battle of Britain* (Guy Hamilton, 1969) before becoming a major investor in Technicolor. Meanwhile, Broccoli was content to stick with the successful, established, profitable Bond pictures.

It is little surprise that tension would grow between two men with such different attitudes to their careers.

IN THE REAL WORLD: Like *Goldfinger*, *Thunderball* is a film with very few specific links to its time. In fact, it was remade as recently as 1983 (see **Never Say Never Again**) and the basic idea of criminals using nuclear bombs to hold the world hostage remains compelling.

DIRECTOR AND CREW: *Goldfinger*'s Guy Hamilton was asked to return for *Thunderball*, and did some preparatory work, but later left the project, saying he wanted some time off following the exertions of directing *Goldfinger*. Instead Terence Young returned to the series, attracted by the chance to shoot a film on such a scale. He would later express regret at having returned to Bond, comparing *Thunderball* unfavourably with his own earlier efforts. This was to be his last film and his departure was a great loss to the series. His films ultimately look the most old-fashioned of the series, but it is he who shaped the image of Bond and introduced the element of travelogue that was to become such a vital part of the character's adventures. Though Guy Hamilton is credited with the 'best' of the early Bonds it is Young who had the more consistent record, producing two low-key works of light espionage action and one brilliantly epic adventure.

After a two-film absence, title designer Maurice Binder also returned, having come to terms with Saltzman and Broccoli. He would now contribute to every Bond film until his death in 1991. The ravishing titles for *Thunderball* are among his best work. Apart from this, and the addition of McClory as producer (Saltzman and Broccoli became 'executive producers' for the duration), the creative team is a remarkably stable continuation of those responsible for the previous three Bond films. Screenwriter Richard Maibaum, production designer Ken Adam, editor Peter Hunt, cinematographer Ted Moore, soundman Norman Wanstall, special effects man John Stears and musician John Barry all returned from the previous picture.

PRINCIPAL CASTING: A filmmaker as well as an actor (his films as writer/director include 1950s Portuguese language film *Caicara*) Adolfo Celi was – like Gert Frobe – an actor who had distinguished himself in European cinema, but who was not terribly well known in Britain or America. Immediately prior to *Thunderball* he had been seen as Giovanni de Medici in Carol Reed's *The Agony and The Ecstasy* (1965). For some (although far from all) of *Thunderball*, his voice was dubbed by actor Robert Rietty on account of Celi's thick accent occasionally causing problems.

After *Thunderball* he would continue to work mainly in European language films. Worthy of note is his appearance alongside a variety of other Bond actors (Lois Maxwell, Bernard Lee, Daniela Bianchi and Anthony Dawson) in *OK Connery* aka *Operation Kid Brother* aka *Operation Double 007* aka *Secret Agent 00* (Alberto De Martino, 1967), an execrable Bond spoof starring Sean Connery's younger brother Neil. In early 1981 he would star as Pope Alexander VI in the BBC's lavish, much-criticised *The Borgias*. He died in 1986.

Actor Rik Van Nutter who plays Bond CIA contact Felix Leiter was married to Anita Ekberg, who had featured in Saltzman and Broccoli's *Call Me Bwana* (Gordon Douglas, 1963). He was offered the part without audition while having dinner with Cubby and Dana Broccoli.

SOURCE TO SCREEN: *Thunderball* remains the most controversial Bond film in terms of tracing authorship. In 1958 Ian Fleming's friend, Ivar Bryce, had financed a film produced and directed by a young Irishman named Kevin McClory (*The Boy and the Bridge*). McClory began talks with Fleming about bringing James Bond to the cinema screen, using an entirely original script rather than adapting one of the pre-existing novels. The three men, together with attorney Ernie Cuneo and screenwriter Jack Whittingham, began putting together a story with Bond searching the globe for stolen atomic bombs. Script development trundled along with deadlines for final versions set and missed, and Fleming, tired of waiting, converted the half-finished screenplay into his eighth James Bond novel, published in 1961.

This sparked off a court case as McClory and Whittingham sued Fleming, claiming breach of copyright for the adaptation of a co-authored screen treatment. This legal battle altered Broccoli and Saltzman's plans to adapt *Thunderball* into Eon's first James Bond film (see **Dr. No**). The case was finally resolved in 1963. It was agreed that all future editions of the novel should carry the attribution, 'This story is based on a screen treatment by Kevin McClory, Jack Whittingham and Ian Fleming', and in addition McClory received all film rights to the story.

Initially McClory planned to produce his own Bond picture, independent of Saltzman and Broccoli. However, the three producers struck a deal to work together to film *Thunderball*. On the finished picture McClory is credited as producer, and Saltzman and Broccoli are listed as executive producers. As part of the film deal with Eon, McClory kept the film rights to the story, albeit with an exclusion clause preventing him from making any further pictures based on this material for another ten years. After this McClory would periodically claim to be producing new Bond films with *Thunderball* as the basis (see **Never Say Never Again**).

In the event, the book followed the standard route of Bond production. Richard Maibaum and playwright John Hopkins produced a script; Terence Young and many veteran Bond crew members returned to work behind the camera and returning actors took up familiar roles.

The end result is very close to the book. A lot of the novel is descriptive padding with little narrative function, the SPECTRE operation being outlined in (often fascinating) detail. The film strips this down and adds a few more confrontations such as the femme-fatale figure of Fiona Volpe and Bond's infiltration of Palmyra, along with the 'sacrificial lamb' of Paula Caplan. Often it overcomplicates matters, notably with the identity of the hijacker. The novel gives a simple motive of the bribery of an Italian Air Force pilot (Giuseppe Petacchi), which the film replaces with a convoluted story of plastic surgery and murderous double identity.

In the book, the health farm sequence serves no plot function. Bond happens across Count Lippe, they fight, Bond leaves to take part in Operation Thunderball and is sent to the Bahamas on the orders of M. In the film Angelo serves to link the Shrublands sequence with the main narrative.

Interestingly the greatest change is in the climax. The film's aqua-paratroop attack is a wonderful sequence, but Fleming describes a more suspenseful battle. Bond and Felix are assigned a nuclear submarine which, though effective, is unable to pursue the *Disco Volante* into shallow water. A small group of frogmen, led by Bond and Leiter, volunteer to swim after the SPECTRE team and attack with makeshift spears. This remained unfilmed even after 1983's remake, *Never Say Never Again*.

MUSICAL NOTES: The theme song for the film was originally to be Barry/Bricusse's 'Mr Kiss Kiss Bang Bang', performed by either Dionne Warwick or Shirley Bassey (recordings of both artistes singing the song exist). Towards the end of production, the producers became worried about the film's song not featuring its title among the lyrics, and so commissioned Barry/Briscusse for another tune to be entitled 'Thunderball'. This was recorded late in the day by Welsh singing star Tom Jones, who legendarily fainted after hitting the top note at the very end of the song. With cheerfully nonsensical, vaguely homoerotic lyrics, 'Thunderball' is a great Bond theme. One consequence of the late change is that much of Barry's score is based around the melody to 'Mr Kiss Kiss Bang Bang' rather than 'Thunderball'. A similar problem arose over thirty years later (see **Tomorrow Never Dies**).

BOX OFFICE: *Thunderball*'s worldwide gross was a little over $141 million, a substantial increase on even *Goldfinger*. In the US, admissions (that is to say, the number of people admitted to see the film) was an astounding 74.8 million, a figure not bettered in that market by any Bond film since.

AWARDS: The second Academy Award given to the Bond series was presented to John Stears, for Best Effects, Special Visual Effects work carried out on this film. Stears was unaware that he was even nominated for such an award until the statuette was handed to him during a routine day's work. The picture was also nominated for a BAFTA, for Ken Adam's masterful Production Design/Art Direction.

CRITICS: Critical reception for *Thunderball* was mixed. Some reviewers welcomed this addition to a film series they were enjoying, and others questioned how long Bond's screen adventures could keep going. '*Thunderball* packs a wallop in its tongue in cheek treatment of an agent at work' commented *Variety*'s Whit (22 December 1965), going on to praise the production values as 'posh all the way'. The resulting film was thus a 'tight exciting melodrama in which novelty of action figures importantly'. In summary it was 'action at fever pitch' and in total 'superb'.

The *Daily Mail*'s Cecil Watson (writing on 19 December) had also enjoyed the picture: 'Terence Young directs with his usual tongue in cheek flair and 007 maintains his usual throwaway tone of speech' he commented, concluding that *Thunderball* was 'A rare bout of aquatic all-in wrestling, dagger duels and harpoon shooting'. Writing in the *Observer* on 2 January 1966, Kenneth Tynan called the film 'a prodigious toy shop come travel agency', and while he compared the role played by the picture's hero favourably to his non-involvement in *Goldfinger*, he was quick to conclude that 'Bond's world has been conquered by the dreaded cohorts of gadgetry'.

Bond's dismissal of The Beatles in *Goldfinger* also came back to haunt him, with Tynan comparing *Thunderball* unfavourably with the band's own excursion into Bahamas-based cinematic excess, *Help*! (Richard Lester, 1965).

The Times review of 19 December, however, found more to like in the picture, claiming it to be 'not so good as *From Russia with Love*, not so bad as *Goldfinger* and about level pegging with *Dr. No*'. Ken Adam's sets were singled out for praise as 'even larger and more lavish than before', although even this positive, albeit unnamed, reviewer detected in *Thunderball*'s repetition of earlier Bond films 'alarming signs that the series is going to seed'.

Perhaps surprisingly, Bond's old foe Nina Hibbin of the *Daily Worker* (writing on 1 January 1966) initially seemed to be giving some ground by claiming that '*Thunderball* . . . isn't quite as vicious as the others' and that the filmmakers were now 'playing for laughs' (hadn't they always been?). Hibbin, too, felt the Bond formula was already tired. 'It doesn't work well enough to make me angry any more. It just bores me to tears' she concluded.

TRIVIA: On the cast list the SPECTRE man Bond kills in the pre-credit sequence is called Jacques Boitier even though onscreen it's pronounced Beauvard. Equally, Paul Stassino is credited as 'Palazzi' when he actually plays two roles: Francois Derval and Angelo when disguised as Derval. It is possible that Palazzi is meant to be Angelo's surname (although he's called 'Mr Angelo' in one conversation) but even so it is strange that the credits omit mention of his dual role.

MARTINIS, GIRLS AND GUNS: Bond definitely scores with Fiona, Pat and a sub-aqua Domino. He almost certainly has his way with the French girl at the start as well (it's doubtful that when she asks him if there's anything she can do for him and he lasciviously replies 'maybe later' that he has a cup of tea in mind), but there's no confirmation of this so it doesn't count. Although he orders no Martinis in this picture, Bond's death toll is an astounding 22 – partially excused by the fact that he's directly involved in an honest-to-God battle for the first time in the series. There's Jacques Boitier in the pre-credits; two men shot in the raid on Palmra; the SPECTRE flunkey he knifes and then feeds to a shark; the wetsuited guard underneath the *Disco Volante*; another knifing in the atom-bomb storage cave plus the endless casualties of the (brilliant) underwater fight sequence between Bond and the marines and the SPECTRE goons, which includes him shooting someone through the eye with a harpoon.

THE ONE WITH . . .: The grand underwater battle.

THE LAST WORD: 'Our Mr Bond must have a very high opinion of himself.' Perhaps even more so than any other Bond picture, *Thunderball* has a storyline plagued with problems and which only hangs together thanks to ludicrous coincidences. It seems as if, encouraged by the grosses of *Goldfinger*, the producers upped the ante, making *Thunderball* bigger in every sense, paying attention only to incident and spectacle, not story, logic or character. It's a beautifully shot piece, with Terence Young gaining real benefits from some stunning locations and the series' first use of proper widescreen photography. Connery was still running at his Bondian prime and John Barry's score is an absolute knock-out. *Thunderball* is far more epic than any Bond film before it, and despite its manifest flaws is magnificent and absorbing entertainment.

GIRLS	12
MARTINIS	3
DEATHS	54

Parody and pastiche: 'We're renaming all our agents James Bond 007.'

The press coined a term to describe the popular appeal of the Bond films in the mid-60s – Bondmania. So began the obsession of people and the media with Bond; the girls, the stunts, the locations and, overwhelmingly, the actor who played him. Other studios and producers weren't blind to this market for 'the most extraordinary gentleman spy in all fiction' nor to the possibility of rival characters and series exploiting it.

The most interesting series to be developed, mainly due to its many links with the Bond franchise, was the Harry Palmer trilogy, (see Thunderball).

James Coburn played Derek Flint, suave CIA super-spy in *Our Man Flint* (Daniel Mann, 1965) and *In Like Flint* (Gordon Douglas, 1967). These two enjoyable pastiches of the Bond style featured a criminal organisation called ZOWIE (Zonal Organisation World Intelligence Espionage), a multi-purpose cigarette lighter and Flint's ability to converse with dolphins.

Hard-drinking, hard-singing Rat Pack legend Dean Martin appeared as agent Matt Helm in *The Silencers* (Phil Karlson, 1966), co-produced by Irving Allen, Cubby Broccoli's old business partner. Three equally disappointing sequels followed this disappointing film: *Murderers' Row* (Henry Levin, 1966), *The Ambushers* (Henry Levin, 1967) and *The Wrecking Crew* (Phil Karlson, 1969).

Dirk Bogarde, Terence Stamp and Monica Vitti starred in comic-strip adaptation *Modesty Blaise* (Joseph Losey, 1966). A psychedelic piece of self-indulgence, this is dull, badly lit and gratuitously of its time. Indeed, all these imitators were even more rooted in the age than Bond, a fact that can be clearly seen in contemporary Bond spoof Casino Royale.

Austin Powers: International Man of Mystery (Jay Roach, 1997) and its sequels, *Austin Powers: The Spy Who Shagged Me* (Jay Roach, 1999) and *Austin Powers in Goldmember* (Jay Roach, 2002), successfully played on this to produce a parody that targeted not just Bond, but the whole attitude of the 60s spy film and of 'swinging London' in general, making it much funnier than far weaker attempts such as Leslie Nielsen's *Spy Hard* (Rick Friedberg, 1996).

The 90s saw attempts to produce an American Bond. The ill-judged *True Lies* (James Cameron, 1994) rejected the 'blue collar' hero image of its star, Arnold Schwarzenegger, to present him as a professional 'white collar' CIA agent. The modelling of this character on Bond was made explicit by use of the famous wetsuit/tuxedo entrance from Goldfinger. The only notable difference to the British agent is the incorporation of Agent Harry Tasker's married home life. Similarly, Tom Cruise used the forum of the *Mission Impossible* movies to present his own version of the cinematic Bondian figure. Indeed, this young franchise, based on the popular 60s/not so popular 80s TV series, already has its Living Daylights in the tense and enjoyable *Mission Impossible* (Brian De Palma, 1996) and its Man With the Golden Gun in the episodic, overblown and confused *MI:2* (John Woo, 2000).

Casino Royale (1967)

Charles K Feldman presents
A Famous Artists Production
Screenplay by Wolf Mankowitz, John Law, Michael Sayers*
Director of Photography: Jack Hildyard, BSC
Additional photography: John Wilcox, BSC, Nicolas Roeg, BSC
Production Designer: Michael Stringer
Music composed and conducted by Burt Bacharach
Lyrics by Hal David
'The Look of Love' sung by Dusty Springfield
Main title theme played by Herb Alpert and the Tijuana Brass
Suggested by the novel *Casino Royale* by Ian Fleming
Film Editor: Bill Lenny
Directed by John Huston, Kenneth Hughes, Val Guest, Robert Parrish, Joseph McGrath. Additional Sequences Val Guest

*plus Woody Allen, Orson Welles, Peter Sellers, Terry Southern and Val Guest uncredited

PRINCIPAL CAST: Peter Sellers (*Evelyn Tremble – James Bond 007*), Ursula Andress (*Vesper Lynd – 007*), David Niven (*Sir James Bond*), Orson Welles (*Le Chiffre*), Joanna Pettet (*Mata Bond*), Daliah Lavi (*The Detainer – 007*), Woody Allen (*Jimmy Bond – Dr Noah*), Deborah Kerr (*Agent Mimi – alias Lady Fiona*), William Holden (*Ransome*), Charles Boyer (*Le Grand*), John Huston (*McTarry – M*), Kurt Kasznar (*Smernov*), George Raft (*Himself*), John-Paul Belmondo (*French Legionnaire*), Terence Cooper (*Cooper – James Bond 007*), Barbara Bouchet (*Moneypenny*), Angela Scoular (*Buttercup*), Gabriella Licudi (*Eliza*), Tracey Crisp (*Heather*), Elaine Taylor (*Peg*), Jacky Bisset (*Miss Goodthighs*), Alexandra Bastedo (*Meg*), Anna Quayle (*Frau Hoffner*), Derek Nimmo (*Hadley*), Ronnie Corbett (*Polo*), Colin Gordon (*Casino Director*), Bernard Cribbins (*Taxi Driver*), Tracy Reed (*Fang Leader*), John Bluthal (*Casino Doorman and MI5 Man*), Geoffery Bayldon (*Q*), John Wells (*Q's Assistant*), Duncan Mcrae (*Inspector Mathis*), Graham Stark (*Cashier*), Chic Murray (*Chic*), Jonathan Routh (*John*), Richard Wattis (*British Army Officer*), Burt Kwouk (*Chinese Army Officer*), Vladek Sheybal (*Le Chiffre's representative*), Percy Herbert (*1st Piper*), Penny Riley (*Control Girl*), Jeanne Roland (*Captain of the Guards*).

SIGNIFICANT UNCREDITED CAST: John Le Mesurier (*Chauffeur*), Peter O' Toole (*Imaginary Piper*), Valentine Dyall (*Voice of Dr Noah*).

PRE-CREDITS AND TITLES: Peter Sellers sticks his head round a French public toilet with 'Les Beatles' graffitied on it, and smirkingly offers to show a colleague his 'credentials'. There then follows the most beautiful title sequence imaginable. Tiny squares of film run in huge animated letters on a black background backed by an irresistible, comically up-tempo piece of music. Genius.

SUMMARY: As simply as possible: Sir James Bond 007 is asked to come out of retirement by M and representatives of the Russian, American and French secret services; the four countries have pooled their resources because they are all losing agents to a mysterious fifth power. Bond refuses their offer, so M blows up his house. Unfortunately M is killed in the explosion and Bond (for no discernible reason) travels to his old boss's ancestral home and delivers his remains to his widow. Unfortunately she has been replaced by SMERSH agent Madam Mimi and a group of giggling girls, who have orders either to kill Bond or to besmirch his reputation by corrupting him. They fail in their mission; Madam Mimi falls in love with Sir James and saves him from being

killed by a robot pheasant, which is attracted to a homing device
in a button on his cloak. Madam Mimi tells Sir James that she and her
girls were employed by Berlin-based organisation, International
Mother's Help.

Then Sir James travels to London to assume M's position as the head
of the Secret Service, where (for no discernable reason) he enlists
sometime double agent Vesper Lynd to acquire the services of
world-class baccarat player, Evelyn Tremble, who is to go to the Casino
Royale in France and play baccarat against Le Chiffre, a SMERSH agent
who owes the organisation a great deal of money.

Sir James then orders that all British agents be renamed James Bond
007 in order to confuse the enemy and that one agent Cooper be trained
to resist the charms of any woman who attempts to seduce him.

Sir James then recruits the services of his daughter, Mata Bond, who is
sent to Berlin to infiltrate the Mata Hari dancing school founded by her
mother. Sir James believes (for no discernable reason) that the school is a
cover for SMERSH (which it is). Once there Mata retrieves some
incriminating photographs, which Le Chiffre was going to auction to
pay off his gambling debts, and returns home to London.

Evelyn Tremble plays cards against Le Chiffre, wins and is then
captured by Le Chiffre's men. Le Chiffre tortures Tremble with a
psychedelic dream sequence in which the dream Vesper turns out to be a
double agent and kills the dream Tremble. Le Chiffre is then killed by
SMERSH for his 'failure' and the real Vesper and Tremble disappear (for
no discernable reason).

Then, SMERSH send a flying saucer to London to kidnap Mata Bond
in order to lure her father to SMERSH headquarters, which appears to
be in/under and/or next to the Casino Royale. Bond follows his daughter
to resuce her, where it is revealed that Dr Noah, the head of SMERSH, is
in fact his nephew, Little Jimmy Bond. Jimmy is planning to (a) release a
bacteriological weapon which will make all women beautiful and kill all
men over four foot six, (b) to replace all the world's leaders with
duplicates (this is where the missing agents have gone, they're the
physical basis for the duplicates – for no discernable reason) and (c) get
someone to swallow a pill which is actually a miniature thermonuclear
device.

Sir James and his party, which includes Moneypenny and Agent
Cooper (who appears out of nowhere between scenes – for no
discernable reason) try to escape the Casino, which comes under attack
from marines, the US cavalry, Indians, the French Foreign legion, two
sealions and God knows what else (again, for no discernable reason).

Little Jimmy Bond, who has swallowed his own nuclear pill, explodes, killing everyone. All the characters go to heaven except Jimmy, who goes to hell.

UNIVERSAL EXPORTS:

BOND, SIR JAMES BOND: The one, the only, the original. Apparently. 'The greatest spy in history', according to M. Bond is an elderly man who was a spy during the earliest days of the twentieth century. He won a Victoria Cross at Mafeking, and retired after leading his lover (and the mother of his daughter), Mata Hari, to death in front of a firing squad. He is said to play Debussy on his piano every day, enjoy standing on his head and eat a lot of Royal Jelly. While in the Orient he learned how to take his intestines 'down' and wash them by hand. He is killed when the Casino explodes.

EVELYN TREMBLE – 007: Expert on baccarat employed by Sir James to bankrupt Le Chiffre. He is trained in spycraft by Vesper Lynd and beats Le Chiffre only to be taken captive and psychologically tortured. After an incomprehensible marching bagpiper sequence it appears as though Tremble is killed by Vesper Lynd. Of course we can't be sure of this.

M: This M, who's real name is McTarry, is a Scottish aristocrat who has been head of the British Secret Service for many, many years. He is known to Sir James Bond, although it isn't clear whether he was head of section in Bond's time.

MONEYPENNY: Or rather Miss Moneypenny's daughter, also called Miss Moneypenny (so she's illegitimate) who's taken her mum's old job in the service, played with wit and grace by the astonishingly beautiful Barbara Bouchet. Bond snogs her when he sees her, assuming her to be her mother, indicating that this Bond's relationship with his Moneypenny went far beyond flirtation.

Q: Played by future *Catweazle* star Geoffery Bayldon as an absent-minded Boffin, Q features briefly despite not appearing in the novel on which the film is (ostensibly) based.

THE DETAINER – 007: Another of Sir James's 007s, The Detainer is a beautiful brunette whose slipping of the nuclear pill into Jimmy Bond's drink causes the film's explosive 'climax'.

OHMSS: The service is based in London, somewhere near the Foreign Office by the looks of things.

THE OPPOSITION:

SMERSH: SMERSH were the villains of Fleming's earliest Bond novels, including this one. In those it was – as in reality – a branch of the Russian Secret Service whose name was a contraction of the Russian for 'Death to Spies' – *Smiert Spionem* (see **The Living Daylights**). Here SMERSH is portrayed as an international criminal organisation more like SPECTRE than anything else. Presumably SPECTRE was avoided in order to prevent Kevin McClory becoming involved in the murky legal quagmire surrounding this project. (see **Thunderball, Never Say Never Again.**)

DR NOAH: The head of SMERSH. Initially a disembodied voice giving orders, Dr Noah is actually James Bond's nephew, Little Jimmy Bond, who has always been unable to speak in the presence of his uncle due to the high regard in which he holds him. Jimmy has more than a few plans for world domination and a massive inferiority complex.

VESPER LYND: *Dr. No*'s Ursula Andress using her real voice to play a (perhaps) double agent named after a character from the novel. Vesper, like Tremble, disappears after the end of the dream sequence in which Tremble is (possibly) killed.

LE CHIFFRE: The torture-loving villain of Fleming's novel is played by writer/actor/director Orson Welles. Welles's performance is very funny, especially his tendency to do magic tricks at inopportune moments; but he disappears quickly and in an arbitrary manner.

MUSICAL NOTES: Burt Bacharach is a genius. (Arguably only Paul McCartney has written more instantly recognisable and well-loved pop songs.) His brass-heavy score is an utter delight, totally 60s in a *Blow Up* style, and thus perfectly of the era while being nothing like the score to any Eon Bond film.

SET PIECES: The whole film is nothing but set pieces, or to be more accurate, sketches. Some of them are great (anything with Joanna Pettet, the SMERSH headquarters at the end), others are dull (the stuff set in Scotland) and some are bland (most of the Peter Sellers/Ursula Andress scenes). There aren't many 'action' sequences though, but we do have a fondness for the chase as Sir James makes his way from Scotland to London in his Bentley. The flying saucer landing in Trafalgar Square is quite special too.

CUT SCENES: A contemporary interview with Sellers (in the *Sun*, 8 March 1966) indicates a scene in which he is attacked by a midget who climbs out of a toilet bowl to get him. This is nowhere to be seen in the picture as released. This is odd: judging by the way non-sequitur sequences of Sellers are edited in as dreams/hallucinations, Feldman was obviously keen to use every available scrap of footage featuring his ostensible star.

MEMORABLE QUOTES:
Sir James: 'Have you noticed me stuttering since I came in?'
Moneypenny: 'No.'
Sir James: 'Good. I don't have time for that any more.'

Sir James (describing the kind of spy who operated in his era): 'vocationally devoted, sublimely disinterested. Hardly a description of that sexual acrobat who leaves a trail of dead beautiful women like so many blown roses behind him – that bounder to whom you gave my name and number.'

FASHION VICTIMS: An undeniable strength of the film. The men wear tailored suits, the women wear flawless 60s fashions, and even the tunic adopted by Woody Allen's Dr Noah looks good. The only dodgy spot is Vesper's inexplicable desire to see Tremble dressed as Napoleon, Hitler and Toulouse Lautrec.

GADGETS: A pen which fires acid into the eye of the writer and is 'perfect for poison pen letters'. The head of the CIA has a carnation that squirts cyanide, the head of the French Secret Service has deadly poisons in each of his fly buttons, the Russian KGB representative has an 'arsenal' concealed in his shoes. Vesper Lynd once had a miniature submarine shaped like a shark. Le Chiffre has special sunglasses allowing him to read the value of playing cards laid face down. Dr Noah has a UFO-type flying device with matching mini speedboat type thing, perfect replicas of all the world leaders and is skilled in biological warfare.

SOURCE TO SCREEN: Having acquired the screen rights to the one Ian Fleming James Bond novel not optioned by Eon, producer

Charles K Feldman initially planned to make a straight adaptation of the book. He approached Sean Connery to play Bond, only to be told by the star that he would require $1 million before he would even consider it. Presumably Saltzman and Broccoli were unaware of this contact; one can hardly imagine them approving. By 10 September 1965 the *Daily Express* was reporting that Feldman's *Casino Royale* would be 'played strictly for laughs', and announcing that Peter Sellers would feature alongside Shirley MacLaine and actor Terence Cooper as Bond. The script was, at this stage, credited to Wolf Mankowitz (who had contributed to Eon's *Dr. No* and *Goldfinger*) and Michael Sayers, and was to be 'faithful to the line of the original Fleming novel'. Mention of Shirley Maclaine proved to be premature, but the casting of Sellers was real enough.

Sellers had become involved through Feldman, whom he had worked with on the hugely successful *What's New Pussycat?* (Clive Donner, 1965). It may or may not have been Sellers's involvement which pushed the production into becoming a comedy (reports vary) but it certainly hastened the process. Sellers had many demands of the production before he would agree to come aboard, including the appointment of his friend, Scottish TV director Joe McGrath, to shoot the picture. McGrath had been in charge of the Peter Cook/Dudley Moore TV series *Not Only . . . But Also* on which Sellers had once guested. To this demand, and to a huge salary for Sellers, Feldman agreed.

Filming began at Shepperton Studios, London in January 1966, with the script being rewritten on set to accommodate the performers. Some of this rewriting was done by Sellers himself, some by his friend John Law (a cohort of Sellers's fellow Goon, Michael Bentine) and yet more by Terry Southern, who'd been brought onto the picture by producer Feldman.

Executives at Columbia reacted to early rushes positively, but somewhere along the line things began to go wrong. Sellers and McGrath quarrelled badly, a situation compounded by Sellers's reported mental instability and his fear of appearing opposite Orson Welles. This fear led to him refusing to act opposite him, and so their sequences were shot on alternate days with stand-ins for each actor to react to. Other demands of Sellers's during the shoot included the destruction, unused, of a set he had had a nightmare about and the insistence that actor John Bluthal (who was to have played numerous minor roles in the film) be fired, apparently because he was 'conspiring' against him. Most parties involved also agree that Sellers was continually late. In order to accommodate Sellers, McGrath was fired, only to be rehired days later.

He then walked off the picture. He was replaced by a new director, Robert Parrish, who took over and attempted to complete Sellers's sequences with a minimum of fuss.

At some point parallel shooting, both at Elstree Studios and on location in Ireland, began of other sequences for the movie. These featured David Niven as Sir James Bond, and were written and directed by John Huston. Huston had directed nearly a dozen great movies, such as *The Treasure of the Sierra Madre* (1948) *Key Largo* (1948) *The Maltese Falcon* (1941) and *The African Queen* (1951) and openly took the assignment on the condition that Feldman paid him enough money to clear his gambling debts. Reports differ as to whether there was always an intention to make the film in segments or whether the decision came as a result of Sellers's behaviour. Certainly a contemporary press report (in the *Sun*, 8 March) contains an interview with Sellers where he is fully aware of Niven's involvement.

Feldman then decided to hire two further directors, Val Guest and Ken Hughes, to shoot two new sections which would be edited together with Parrish, McGrath and Huston's sequences to produce a final picture. Guest was to shoot material featuring (and partially written by) Woody Allen. Hughes's section would be set in Berlin and feature Bond's daughter, Mata. Guest had been a regular director at Hammer studios in the 50s, and had won a British Academy Award for *The Day the Earth Caught Fire* (1961). Hughes had worked with Cubby Broccoli on *The Trials of Oscar Wilde* (1960) and would later collaborate with him on Eon's adaptation of Fleming's *Chitty Chitty Bang Bang* (1968). His chosen cinematographer for his section would himself later become an accomplished and much-respected feature director, Nic Roeg, whose later work would include *Performance* (1970) *Don't Look Now* (1973) and *The Man Who Fell to Earth* (1976).

There were now further problems at Elstree. Sellers had walked away from the production as soon as his contract allowed him to despite the fact that his scenes were unfinished. Production, never orderly, had finally descended into utter chaos.

By late summer 1966, principal photography was still in full swing, and yet another director – the septuagenarian ex-stuntman Robert Tamludge – was shooting an extended finale/fight sequence set in the eponymous casino. Val Guest, now based at MGM Borehamwood Studios, was desperately trying to complete linking material (some featuring Niven, who had become free when Huston's segment had wrapped on time) which circumstances (including the departure of screenwriter Wolf Mankowitz) had forced him to both write *and* direct.

Production finally stopped (it is hard to say it was 'completed') in November after nearly eight months of shooting. Guest, Feldman and co-producer Joseph Bresler then began the torturous process of editing the footage together into something resembling a motion picture. It would be April 1967 before they were ready to show the results of their efforts to the world.

It is barely worth considering the influence of Fleming's original novel. In this, Bond is trying to bankrupt SMERSH paymaster Le Chiffre by beating him at baccarat (Le Chiffre is desperately trying to recoup Soviet funds lost in the collapse of his empire of brothels). Bond meets up with British agent Vesper Lynd, and manages to beat Le Chiffre, but Lynd is kidnapped, so Bond chases after Le Chiffre and is himself captured. Le Chiffre tortures Bond by beating his genitals with a carpet beater and is about to kill him when a SMERSH agent arrives and 'liquidates' Le Chiffre for misuse of Soviet money. Bond survives (the SMERSH agent has no instructions regarding his treatment) and is ready to settle down with Vesper, only to discover that she is a double agent and had been helping Le Chiffre. She commits suicide and he returns to England. Yes, there is a (possible) double agent called Vesper Lynd, yes there is a baccarat game and yes, Welles's Le Chiffre does torture 007, though not in such a gruesome way. (A carpet beater, like that used by Fleming's Le Chiffre, is visible in the scenes where Tremble is tortured. However, it's stuck to the back of the chair he's tied to.)

CULTURE VULTURE: George Raft – Hollywood star noted for playing gangster roles – appears in a cameo performing his famous 'coin-flipping' trick. Jean-Paul Belmondo, the hero of French new wave cinema, briefly appears as a member of the Foreign Legion. The cast may be the most bizarrely eclectic in screen history.

CRITICS: While the critics weren't absolutely unanimous in condemning outright Feldman's epic folly, few had anything positive to say about it. Perhaps the nicest single thing said about it was: 'I can honestly say with my hand on my stomach that *Casino Royale* is the worst film I ever enjoyed', (the *Mirror*'s Donald Zec, 14 April). Rather a generous assessment, given Zec's long-term association with the Broccoli family. (He had known Cubby since the 50s and would later collaborate with him on his autobiography, *When the Snow Melts*.) Dilys Powell, writing in the *Sunday Times* (15 April), decided to use the film's own publicity against it: '*Casino Royale*, the adverts say, is too much for one James Bond. I find it too much for one critic.'

BOX OFFICE: Despite itself, *Casino Royale* made around $17 million for Columbia, more than covering the $12 million it cost to make.

AWARDS: 'The Look of Love' was nominated for an Academy Award for Best Original song, but failed to win. The statuette was instead picked up by 'If I Could Talk to the Animals' from *Dr. Dolittle*.

THE LAST WORD: 'We'll run amok. If you're too tired we can walk amok.' *Casino Royale* is almost irresponsibly stupid, and had malign affects on the careers and health of many of the cast and crew. It makes little sense on any level and some of the performances are absolutely atrocious, yet it is somehow impossible to hate. The Joe McGrath/Robert Parrish sequences indicate that the planned *Casino Royale* would have been an efficient, if dull, spy spoof in which Sellers would frequently drop into his interminable 'amusing' ethnic accents and Welles would try and earn enough easy money to get *Chimes at Midnight* finished. That this version was abandoned (see **SOURCE TO SCREEN** above) is no great loss. Many would cheerfully swap those scenes that *were* filmed for more of the strange poetry of the early Niven scenes (right up until M dies the entire film looks as though its going to be fantastic) and the beautiful pop madness of Val Guest's finale. The 'finished' film's cinematic schizophrenia ensures that it's brilliant one moment and dreadful the next. This is why you cannot really explain *Casino Royale*, you simply have to experience it. So what if this is a nonsensical collection of ludicrous set pieces with a lousy narrative and which is only held together by the art direction and the magnificence of the actor playing James Bond? So is *Thunderball*.

You Only Live Twice (1967)

Produced by Albert R Broccoli and Harry Saltzman
Screenplay by Roald Dahl
Additional Story Material: Harold Jack Bloom
Director of Photography: Freddie Young, BSC
Music composed, conducted and arranged by John Barry
Title song lyrics by Leslie Bricusse
Title song sung by Nancy Sinatra
Production designed by Ken Adam
Second Unit Director and Supervising Editor: Peter Hunt
Directed by Lewis Gilbert

PRINCIPAL CAST: Sean Connery (*James Bond*), Akiko Wakabayashi (*Aki*), Mie Hama (*Kissy*), Tetsuro Tamba (*Tiger Tanaka*), Teru Shimada (*Mr Osato*), Karin Dor (*Helga Brandt*), Donald Pleasence (*Blofeld*), Bernard Lee (*M*), Lois Maxwell (*Miss Moneypenny*), Desmond Llewelyn (*Q*) Charles Gray (*Henderson*), Tsai Chin (*Chinese Girl – Hong Kong*), Peter Fanene (*Maivia Car Driver*), Burt Kwouk (*SPECTRE Number Three*), Michael Chow (*SPECTRE Number Four*). Ronald Rich (*Blofeld's Bodyguard*), Jeanne Roland (*Bond's Masseuse*), David Toguri (*Assassin – Bedroom*), John Stone (*Submarine Captain*), Norman Jones, Paul Carlson (*Astronauts – 1st American Spacecraft*), Laurence Herder, Richard Graydon (*Astronauts – Russian Spacecraft*), Bill Mitchell, George Roubicek (*Astronauts – 2nd American Spacecraft*).

PRE-CREDITS AND TITLES: An American two-man space capsule is hijacked by a space vehicle of unknown origin that swallows it with metal jaws before disappearing off radar scopes. At a top-secret conference of major powers (America, Russia and Britain), the Soviets are accused by the Americans of stealing the craft in order to dominate space. The British are convinced that the vehicle in fact landed in the vicinity of Japan and pass on the matter to their 'man in Hong Kong', James Bond. Bond is, unsurprisingly, in bed with a Chinese girl who betrays him, allowing a group of gunmen to riddle him with bullets. As the Maurice Binder titles roll, and the beautiful Nancy Sinatra song plays, the audience is supposed to wonder 'is this it for Bond?'

SUMMARY: Well, of course it isn't. Bond's 'murder' is an attempt to get his adversaries off his back, and allow him more freedom with his next investigation. Bond is charged with finding the missing spacecraft before the next American launch three weeks hence (if that craft goes missing, the Americans promise that war will result). He is sent to Japan to rendezvous with agent Henderson, who is swiftly killed off by an employee of the Osato corporation. Bond then meets with 'Tiger' Tanaka, head of the Japanese Secret Service who believes a private enterprise is involved – possibly SPECTRE. Tiger arranges for the analysis of documents taken from Osato, which reveal that the company is supplying liquid oxygen (rocket fuel) to an unknown party and that tourists are being killed for taking photos of a particular stretch of coastline, and a particular vessel, the *Ning Po*. After a meeting with Osato and two more encounters with his murderous employees, Bond carries out aerial reconnaissance of some extinct volcanoes on the coastline where the *Ning Po* was spotted. He is attacked but discovers nothing. Meanwhile a Russian spacecraft is captured. Bond is disguised as Japanese and trained in the art of ninjitsu. It is during this training that Aki is murdered by a SPECTRE hitman. Bond teams up with another of Tanaka's female agents and heads to a fishing village near to the volcano where he was attacked. He discovers Blofeld's base hidden in a hollow volcano and the madman's plan to cause World War Three. With the aid of ninja commandos the base is infiltrated and the plan foiled.

UNIVERSAL EXPORTS:

BOND, JAMES BOND: Seen in full naval uniform and mentioned (for the first time) as carrying the naval rank of commander, Bond is accorded the honour of a full (albeit phoney) military burial at sea. He sets about his mission relentlessly, tracking down suspects and pursuing leads. He expresses distaste at Siamese vodka though is happy to drink sake (at the correct temperature of 98.4 degrees Fahrenheit). He has made an effort to cut down on his smoking habit, his chosen brand now being loaded with rocket bullets. He also claims to have taken a first in Oriental Languages from Cambridge, a degree not referred to in any other film or book.

It is also judged that Bond's combat skills are insufficient. He is given a crash course in ninjitsu. It is decided that for Bond to gain access to Blofeld's base he must disguise himself as Japanese. This leads to a bizarre sequence where the 'transformation' is carried out by a group of bikini-wearing beauties. It is not a success. The combination of ineffective eye implants, fake tan lotion and black wig applied to a six-foot Scotsman do not create an oriental fisherman. Tanaka is absurdly pleased with the result, proclaiming that all Bond needs is a wife to complete the effect. The man himself seems somewhat more aware of how foolish he looks. His expression upon reaching his destination conveys embarrassment and shame.

M: Temporarily based in a submarine, M has made himself thoroughly comfortable in an office that bears a distinct resemblance to his room in Whitehall. M gives Bond an initial briefing, and leaves no doubt as to the importance of the mission – that failure could very well lead to war. He too is seen in naval uniform and his rank insignia indicates he is an admiral. For the majority of the film, 007 reports to the head of the Japanese Secret Service – see **TIGER TANAKA**.

MONEYPENNY: Despite the cunning plan of getting Bond to repeat the Secret Service code phrase, 'I love you', Moneypenny still fails to get anywhere with 007. She plays little part in the film except for the end: when M's submarine surfaces under Bond's escape dinghy Moneypenny is only too keen to interrupt his tryst with Kissy.

Q: For the second time Q heads out to 'the field' to equip 007, and for the first time Bond requests Q's involvement rather than having it foisted upon him. Though separated from his workshop he brings a veritable army of assistants to help with the assembly of 'Little Nelly'. He takes offence at the ridicule heaped on this small aircraft by Tanaka, but Q's faith is vindicated by the autogyro's performance. Given their acerbic relationship to date, Bond's utter confidence in Q in the face of Tiger's mocking is pleasing. Unlike Bond, M and even Moneypenny, Q doesn't appear in uniform, wearing non-distinct khaki fatigues. Given that his rank is Major (see **From Russia with Love**) he can't be Navy personnel; presumably HMSS draws from all branches of the armed forces.

OHMSS: They have good relations with the Japanese Secret Service. While not given their due credit by the Americans, their intelligence-gathering apparatus, at least in the Far East, is greatly superior to that of the United States.

ALLIES:

'TIGER' TANAKA: A man of the world who enjoys drink and women, Tanaka (his friends call him Tiger) is physically fit and takes part in missions on the frontline. He is comparable with the great Kerim Bey, but occupies M's rank in the Japanese Secret Service. This incongruity aside, Tiger proves a valuable friend, providing Bond with the help he needs in tracking down Blofeld's lair, and the ninja muscle required to take it out. He quickly warms to Bond, sparing no expense in helping with the man's mission. He even, a rare thing among Bond's allies, survives the events of the film.

AKI: Bond's first contact with the Japanese Secret Service in Tokyo, Aki leads him through sumo hall, city street and subway before dumping him in Tanaka's lap. An effective agent, Aki is also rather charming. When she is assigned to help Bond in his investigation, the two become very close. This leads to tragedy, Aki receiving the poison intended to kill Bond as he sleeps. Few crtitics recognise the number of times Bond has to see a loved one or trusted friend brutally murdered, and Aki's death is one of the more poignant of those suffered by a 'sacrificial lamb'.

KISSY SUZUKI: Called Kissy on the credits, and never named onscreen, she is thus more commonly known as 'that girl that Bond marries so that he can unconvincingly pretend to be Japanese'. She's is another of Tanaka's female agents, selected as an assistant for Bond. Though Tanaka suggests she possesses a 'face like a pig', this is far from the truth. She is also part of Bond's cover on the volcano island. For some reason this necessitates a full-blown ceremony (unlike in *From Russia with Love*, it is not enough to knock up fake passports and pretend to be married). It is a strange state of affairs and one suspects an attempt to boost the presence of the largely anonymous Suzuki. The name Kissy Suzuki is taken from the original Fleming.

HENDERSON: The debonair and charming Henderson has been the Secret Service's man in Japan for 28 years but 'is only just beginning to find [his] way around'. He fought at the battle of Singapore in 1942 and lost a leg for his troubles. A seasoned ex-pat who 'refuses to go entirely Japanese', Henderson is sceptical of his host country's involvement in the space-jackings but is ready to help Bond. Sadly he never really gets the chance to do this as he is knifed in the back shortly after their meeting.

Though he initially is said to employ Aki, her involvement with Tanaka either implies the very close relationship of the British and Japanese agencies or that she has been a Japanese mole, reporting to Tanaka the whole time.

THE OPPOSITION:

ERNST STAVRO BLOFELD: The (previously unnamed onscreen) SPECTRE Number One introduces himself as he and Bond come face to face for the first time. Despite the failure of his previous three schemes, Blofeld has picked up funding from the Red Chinese for the setting up of his space-jacking rocket base, fitted out both a piranha pool and monorail.

This Blofeld is a disappointment with his nondescript grey Mao tunic and ugly scar. He creeps around in an unpleasant way, but does not seem up to the job of world-threatening megalomaniac. In any confrontation with Bond there is little doubt as to who would win, which is probably why Blofeld is all too ready to scurry away.

Though sporting a suitably insane plan, Blofeld does not seem worthy of being the boss of Doctor No, Colonel Klebb or Emilio Largo. To compound matters he has the cheek to tell Osato that 'This organisation does not tolerate failure'. Why not? They've had enough experience of it.

HELGA BRANDT: Flame-haired secretary to Mr Osato, Miss Brandt is an assassin along the lines of Fiona Volpe. She interrogates Bond after his capture at Kobe Docks but seems to be swayed by his somewhat flimsy cover of trying to smuggle a new formula for monosodium glutamate out of the country. However, like Volpe, she is not 'converted' by Bond and tries to kill him by the bizarrely convoluted method of pretending to escape with him only to sabotage the escape plane and parachute to safety. Bond escapes death, unlike Helga who is pitched into Blofeld's piranha pool. There is not much to say in Blofeld's favour but, at least since *From Russia with Love*, he has learned to punish the correct people for making mistakes.

OSATO: A Japanese industrialist assisting in the fuelling and supply of Bird-1, Osato is a key member of Blofeld's organisation. He is a respected man of business who believes in a no-smoking environment but is happy to wolf down champagne at any time of day.

His motives are even less clear than Blofeld's; it is difficult to imagine this man's lifestyle being more comfortable in a nuclear wasteland. Osato is a plot device to link Bond with Blofeld. When he is finally dispatched for 'failure' the audience is overcome with indifference.

HANS: Blofeld's silent Aryan bodyguard, and heir to the spirit of Donald Grant, exists to compensate for his boss's feeble appearance. Though his actions are limited to a brief scrap with Bond over the self-destruct key, the scene is a tense one and Connery looks outclassed once again, winning despite the odds.

THE RED CHINESE: Not mentioned by name, but it is pretty clear who Blofeld means when referring to a 'new power'. Despite their unsuccessful arrangement with Goldfinger, the forces of Red China are still looking for super-criminal help in their battles against the West and against Russia. Rather unwisely they plump for a man whose organisation has screwed up its last three big operations.

PRINCIPAL CASTING: Mie Hama and Akiko Wakabayashi were initially picked to play Aki (known as Suki in early scripts) and Kissy respectively. A major problem the filmmakers had was finding Japanese girls able to speak English. Lessons were given on set and, while

Wakabayashi picked up the language quickly, Hama was less successful. It was decided that Hama would have to return to Japan and the part be recast. However, this decision was swiftly reversed after Lewis Gilbert found out from Tetsuro Tamba (the Japanese martial artist cast as Tanaka) that Hama intended to commit suicide to make up for this 'dishonour'. A compromise was reached and Wakabayashi took the more dialogue-intensive role of Aki with Hama playing Kissy. As it is, they both turn in fine performances, though it has to be said that Wakabayashi gains more sympathy from the audience.

Blofeld was originally to be played by Czech actor Jan Werich. Reports differ as to the reason behind his last-minute replacement by Donald Pleasence. Though several sources cite illness on Werich's part, Lewis Gilbert recalls being personally unhappy with Werich's performance and asking the producers for permission to hire a replacement. Donald Pleasence is merely adequate as Blofeld. Though creepy and obviously 'evil', the performance comes close to parody and fails to match the stentorian, authoritative Blofeld of *Thunderball* and *From Russia with Love*.

The most shocking piece of casting news came from Sean Connery. At the end of both his contract with Saltzman and Broccoli and his tether with constant press intrusion, Connery announced that this would be his final Bond film. That he was growing tired of 'being' Bond really comes through in his performance. By no means ineffective, the James Bond of *You Only Live Twice* lacks the sparkle of previous films. As recently as *Thunderball*, Connery can be seen to be having fun with the character. By this stage he is just playing it by numbers.

DIRECTOR AND CREW: For what was again intended to be the biggest Bond film yet, Broccoli and Saltzman hired Lewis Gilbert to direct. The appointment of Gilbert, whose previous successes included the magnificent *Alfie* (1966) and wartime epic *Sink the Bismarck!* (1960), was to have far-reaching consequences for the series. It is no exaggeration to say that Gilbert's take on Bond, as developed across both this and his two later pictures, *The Spy who Loved Me* (1977) and *Moonraker* (1979), is the most iconic. Gilbert accompanied Broccoli and Saltzman to Japan on their first location hunt, and had input into the general direction of the scripting as well as the choice of location.

Ken Adam provided one of the finest sets in his career. Blofeld's volcano cost £350,000 (or $1 million at 1967 values), and was, for a time, the biggest film-set in Europe. Special effects maestro John Stears has suggested that Adam got away with this because the (British) crew thought that the (German) Adam was working in feet. He was in fact working in metres. The result is amazing. The crater entry point was wide enough to allow a full-size helicopter to land and take off while the spacecraft, Bird-1, was capable of performing the first stage of a rocket take-off. To cap it all, the whole set was spectacularly destroyed to represent the effect of Blofeld's self-destruct device. In an unforgivable omission, Ken Adam was not even nominated for an Oscar.

Aerial photographer John Jordan filmed the helicopter dogfight scenes. A skilled cameraman who was to return to shoot the skiing sequences of *On Her Majesty's Secret Service*, Jordan was badly injured during filming when turbulence caused two helicopters to collide. The skid of one of the helicopters was severed, along with Jordan's leg. Though the leg was re-attached by surgeons, the injury later became gangrenous and Jordan requested his leg be amputated.

Heading up the British team of stuntmen was former army officer Richard Graydon, who would return for *On Her Majesty's Secret Service* and would be recalled by Lewis Gilbert for work on *The Spy Who Loved Me* and *Moonraker*. (He also carried out uncredited stunt work on *For Your Eyes Only*, *Octopussy* and *A View to a Kill*.) On set, Graydon and his ex-British Army stunt team worked closely with Japanese martial artists. However, when called upon to perform the abseiling stunt at the end of the film the Japanese expressed a distaste for heights and so the entire stunt was carried out by Graydon's team.

MUSICAL NOTES: The theme song was heavily sampled by Robbie Williams for his number one hit 'Millennium' in 1999. The score itself is magnificent with heavy oriental influences and outstanding use of the '007' tune, during the helicopter dogfight to accentuate the action. This music had previously been used during the underwater battle of *Thunderball*. Monty Norman's 'James Bond Theme' itself, however, is hardly used at all.

SET PIECES: The car dropped from the helicopter is great fun, despite its total lack of narrative sense (who's filming the act and broadcasting it to Aki's car anyway?). The pitched battle in the volcano base acts as a great climax – so good that Gilbert repeated it ten years later in *The Spy Who Loved Me*. However, the best moment in the film (and possibly the series) is the fight on Kobe docks. The slow revelation of hostility to Bond, the sudden outbreak of violence and the glorious running battle across the rooftops as the camera slowly pans out from a close-up to a wide shot that takes in several buildings is all shot from the air and done in one long take.

POSITIVELY SHOCKING: Aki's death is harrowing and Bond's instinctive reaction to shoot first in retaliation may seem cold-blooded but is indicative of his professionalism – he grieves afterwards. Blofeld has the monopoly on nastiness here also being equipped with a piranha tank for disposal of awkward assistants.

CUT SCENES: Peter Hunt removed half an hour of footage after the producers decided that Lewis Gilbert's cut was too long.

MEMORABLE QUOTES:
Bond: 'Why do Chinese girls taste different from all other girls?'
Ling: 'You think we better?'
Bond: 'No, just different, like Peking Duck is different from Russian caviar but I love them both.'
Ling: 'Darling, I give you very best duck.'

Tanaka: 'You know what they're fascinated by? It's the hair on your chest. All Japanese men have beautiful bare skin.'
Bond: 'Japanese proverb say, "Bird never make nest in bare tree".'

FASHION VICTIMS: Notoriously, *You Only Live Twice* sees the emergence of the grey suit with the Mao collar favoured by super-villains throughout time and brilliantly parodied in the Austin Powers films. Bond keeps up his usual standards with the nicely cut light suit sported in Tokyo. However, his Beatle fright-wig-cum-Japanese haircut distracts attention from his stylish kimono. The volcano battle may have seen Tanaka's ninjas emerge victorious but there are no winners in the fashion stakes. The brightly coloured SPECTRE boiler suits versus the nasty nylon of the ninja outfits produce a no-score draw.

PRODUCT PLACEMENT: When Tanaka drops enemy spies to certain doom, he relays the event on a Sony TV screen. Apart from this the only advert is for the beautiful Japanese landscape. Anyone who sees this film is invariably going to want an autogyro of their very own.

GADGETS: Another toy-happy outing. Even in death 007 is well equipped, his shroud containing SCUBA gear to allow him to survive until picked up by Royal Navy divers. Q-branch has also outfitted secret agents with a safe-cracking device (efficient but without the ability to deactivate alarms – a major oversight). They also operate a delivery service, supplying a collapsible autogyro 'Little Nelly', perfect for reconnaissance of suspect volcanic lakes and armed with air-to-air missiles, unguided rockets, rear-firing flame throwers, aerial mines and machine guns. Q also supplies a cine-camera in Bond's flying helmet, to record the aerial combat for posterity. Ken Adam suggested the use of the craft after hearing about it and its inventor, Wing Commander Ken Wallace, on the radio. Wallace would clock up some 42 hours of flying time to record the brief aerial battle.

Tanaka's ninja unit uses a hefty range of gadgets: rocket guns with explosive bullets, metal throwing stars and a cigarette with built-in anti-personnel missile. The Japanese have a perfect device for getting rid of pesky enemy agents – a helicopter with an electro-magnet scoops them up and drops them in the sea.

Blofeld's volcano lair is heavily fortified and equipped with a self-destruct device. He also supplies Helga Brandt with a lipstick-bomb, which she uses to disable the plane she and Bond are travelling in. Most importantly he has access to the Bird-1 which he uses to capture the Russian and American vessels. Perhaps the luckless super-villain deserves greater recognition for perfecting a reusable spacecraft – something even NASA weren't to develop for another thirteen years.

SOURCE TO SCREEN: The novel *You Only Live Twice* provided an opportunity to use Japan as the setting for a Bond film. With regular screenwriter Richard Maibaum unavailable, Broccoli and Saltzman turned to short-story writer and children's author Roald Dahl. Though never having written a screenplay before, Dahl, who had known Fleming, produced a piece of science fiction, so highly original it bore almost no resemblance to the book of the same name. Dahl was given free rein in his writing except for three things: he had to retain the location, was not permitted to alter the established character of Bond and had to follow a mysterious 'girl rule'. This, as Dahl explained in the June 1967 edition of *Playboy*, was to 'put in three girls no more, no less'. The use of girls was carefully demarcated. 'Girl number one is pro-Bond. She stays around . . . the first reel of the picture. Then she is bumped off by the enemy, preferably in Bond's arms.' Girl number two 'is anti-Bond. She works for the enemy . . . She must capture Bond and Bond must save himself by bowling her over with sheer sexual magnetism. This girl should also be bumped off.' Finally, Dahl referred to girl number three, who was once again on Bond's side and who 'must [not] be killed. Nor must she permit Bond to take any lecherous liberties with her until the end of the story. We keep that for the fade out.' These 'rules' are only really seen in this film and (arguably) *Thunderball*. Many other Bond pictures have either fewer or more girls than the 'requisite three', and it is very rare to see Bond wait until the fade out. The 'rule' is ineffective here – it leaves audiences in mourning for Aki with too little time to accept 'girl number three', Kissy.

The book sees Bond, still grieving for his wife Tracy, killed by Blofeld (see **On Her Majesty's Secret Service** – once again the films fail to follow the chronology of the books). On the advice of the Service's neurosurgeon, M sends Bond on an 'impossible' mission. This takes the form of a diplomatic assignment to try and gain access to secrets from the Japanese Secret Service (the subtext is that Bond must convince the Japanese that Britain is still a world power). However, M's opposite number in Japan, a modern-day samurai named Tanaka, gives Bond a task to perform in exchange for this information. Bond must infiltrate the castle of a 'Dr Shatterhand', a foreigner who has collected a large garden of poison plants and animals, and assassinate him. The doctor has been encouraging those Japanese who wish to commit suicide to do so in his custom garden of death. Carrying out this mission will affirm that Britain still has some fight and is worthy of receiving the grade-A intelligence. This first half of the book is couched in the style of an urbane travelogue as, through Bond's eyes, we experience Japanese life and culture – a life and culture which is alien to much of the West even now and would have been more so in the 1960s. The second half is a more straightforward, well-constructed battle of good versus evil. Bond discovers that, coincidentally, Shatterhand is Blofeld. He starts off in the 'good' village of a group of simple oyster fishermen, working undercover and helped by a girl called Kissy Suzuki. He then travels to the 'bad' castle to fight and defeat the 'dragon' (Blofeld). However, he is left with amnesia and, though cared for by Kissy, is seen, as the book ends, setting out for somewhere called 'Russia' which he feels has something to do with his former life.

Only a very few elements from the novel are employed in Dahl's script. In Fleming's novel, Henderson is secret agent Dikko Henderson, a hard-drinking Australian. A swinging trap door seen in Blofeld's castle in the novel is employed by the Japanese Secret Service to lead Bond into his meeting with Tanaka, who has a secret HQ based in the incomplete Japanese subway system in both versions. In the novel 007, partially disguised to look Japanese, is given ninja tools, though no real training, and is based in a fishing village before infiltrating Blofeld's base. However that is where the similarities end. The film follows the established path of action and spectacle, exaggerating the sci-fi elements already present and that would become standard in Bond films over the next decade (especially those directed by Lewis Gilbert). Sadly, one of Fleming's most interesting books was lost in the process.

In a sense this film sees the emergence of what may be recognised as the Bond 'formula'. Although the preceding films had contained recurring elements and motifs, they were generally faithful adaptations of the novels. *You Only Live Twice*, written as it is directly for the screen, brings together elements from all of its filmic predecessors, becoming in a sense Roald Dahl's *idea* of what 'a Bond *film*' is. Dahl's script created the iconic screen Bond, a version of the cinematic 007 adventure that would be held up as an ideal. It would later be both imitated and referenced, consciously and unconsciously, in the making of later Bond films (see particularly **The Spy Who Loved Me, Moonraker, GoldenEye, The World Is Not Enough**).

IN THE REAL WORLD: The space-race was a real source of national pride and international tension in the late 60s. The Americans had overcome early problems with their rockets and were catching up with the Soviets. The first successful launch of the one-man 'Mercury' capsule took place in 1962 (one year after Russian cosmonaut Yuri Gagarin became the first man in space). This programme was followed by the introduction of the two-man 'Gemini' capsule in 1965. This was the craft used by the Americans in the film. President Kennedy had promised a man on the moon before the end of the decade and his successors would ensure this in 1969. The Russians had always been one step ahead of the Americans until this point, creating real fear of a 'communist conquest of space', making the use of orbital technology a political issue rather than the commercial concern it is today.

CULTURE VULTURE: The title comes from a haiku written by Ian Fleming for the book. A seventeen-syllable poetic form made famous by the seventeenth-century Japanese poet Bashu, the haiku relies on the magnification of minor events to suggest a deeper meaning to life. Fleming's work doesn't quite reach these intellectual heights (and is overlong by one syllable) but is a nice piece of work all the same. 'You only live twice/Once when you're born/And once when you look death in the face.'

CRITICS: *Time* magazine's critic (30 June 1967) judged that 'Bond himself seems to be weakening' while Patrick Gibbs in the *Daily Telegraph* (16 June) commented on how Connery was 'showing his age

[and] the signs of exhaustion after gallant service in four films'. Gibbs went on to pinpoint the second reason for critical discontent, 'this [exhaustion] seems to be tacitly acknowledged by giving the star role in effect to Ken Adam . . . By this really remarkable studio set . . . poor Bond is quite dwarfed.' Dilys Powell's review in the *Sunday Times* (18 June) echoed this judgement: 'In the design of the production Ken Adam has outdone himself . . . technically, *You Only Live Twice* is overpowering. So overpowering in fact that it threatens to extinguish the players.' After a long list of the gadgets and machines used in the film, Powell's conclusion was simple: 'The machines have taken over at last.'

Surprisingly, one voice of dissent belonged to old adversary, Nina Hibbins. Across two reviews in the *Morning Star* (13 June) she defended the film as one of those 'workable fantasies that stretch the imagination without actually snapping it' and as 'way ahead of all previous Bond films'. If the increased sci-fi bent of the film went in its favour with Hibbins, so did the moral and political message that she drew. 'There's no racialism, no Cold-War stuff (almost the opposite) only an occasional gloating over sudden death.'

BOX OFFICE: *You Only Live Twice* took around $112 million worldwide, down around $30 million on *Thunderball*, perhaps indicating that the negative critical reception had an impact on admissions.

AWARDS: Ken Adam's production design was nominated for a BAFTA award, for Best British Art Direction (Colour), but failed to win it.

TRIVIA: The 2000 GT convertible sports car driven by Aki in the film was not a model produced by Toyota at the time. It was specially adapted for the production by the simple process of having its roof sawn off.

MARTINIS, GIRLS AND GUNS: Dahl's strict adherence to 'the girl rule' gives us the standard three girls for this mission (tellingly, Bond says that 'five more minutes' and he would have found out 'about' the Chinese girl, Ling, in the pre-credit sequence). One Martini is served to Bond by Henderson (albeit stirred not shaken). Another excessively violent mission, eleven SPECTRE assassins are despatched at Osato's building, in the aerial battle above the volcano, at the ninja training school and at Kobe docks (where several others are knocked out – not obvious kills). Once in Blofeld's base Bond eliminates another eight adversaries (including the sinister Hans and an unfortunate technician, hit with a rocket cigarette). To cap it all Bond destroys Bird-1, killing its two-man crew in the process.

THE ONE WITH . . .: the volcano base and all the ninjas.

THE LAST WORD: 'It won't be the nicotine that kills you, Mr Bond.' *You Only Live Twice* is a loving tribute to the idea that nothing succeeds like excess. From Ken Adam's frankly astonishing production design to the simple conceit of filming most of the picture in Japan, *You Only Live Twice* screams that this is a production team at the very top of their game, and ready to take on the entire world. It's more Fleming pastiche than actual Fleming, with elements of the previous Eon Bond films liberally sprinkled through a mechanical (yet inspired) screenplay. There wouldn't be another Bond film like it for another ten years, and its immediate successor would have a radically different style. This is pop art, delivered with punch and panache. More froth than substance, but froth of the highest quality.

GIRLS	15
MARTINIS	4
DEATHS	75

On Her Majesty's Secret Service (1969)

Produced by Albert R Broccoli and Harry Saltzman
Screenplay by Richard Maibaum
Additional dialogue by Simon Raven
Director of Photography: Michael Reed, BSC
Production designed by Syd Cain, GFAD
Music composed, conducted and arranged by John Barry
Lyrics by Hal David
'We Have All the Time in the World' sung by Louis Armstrong
Editor and 2nd Unit Director: John Glen
Directed by Peter Hunt

PRINCIPAL CAST: George Lazenby (*James Bond*), Diana Rigg (*Tracy*), Telly Savalas (*Blofeld*), Gabriele Ferzetti (*Draco*), Ilse Steppat

(*Irma Bunt*), Lois Maxwell (*Moneypenny*), George Baker (*Sir Hilary Bray*), Bernard Lee (*M*), Bernard Horsfall (*Campbell*), Desmond Llewelyn (*Q*), Yuri Borienko (*Grunther*), Virginia North (*Olympe*), Geoffrey Cheshire (*Toussaint*), Irvin Allen (*Che Che*), Terence Mountain (*Raphael*), James Bree (*Gumbold*), John Gay (*Hammond*), Angela Scoular (*Ruby*), Catherina von Schell (*Nancy*), Julie Ege (*Scandinavian Girl*), Mona Chong (*Chinese Girl*), Sylvana Henriques (*Jamaican Girl*), Dani Sheridan (*American Girl*), Joanna Lumley (*English Girl*), Zara (*Indian Girl*), Anouska Hempel (*Australian Girl*), Ingrit Back (*German Girl*), Helena Ronee (*Israeli Girl*), Jenny Hanley (*Irish Girl*).

PRE-CREDITS AND TITLES: While hunting for Blofeld on the continent, 007 spots a woman who is trying to commit suicide by walking into the sea. He saves her from herself, only to be attacked by two armed thugs. Although he bests them, the woman runs off leaving him alone on the beach. The sequence is terrifically shot and lit, with almost painfully loud sound design adding a fury to what might otherwise look like excessively arty photography. The editing style is markedly different, taking the discontinuous, non-naturalistic edge of earlier films to new levels. Characters are not necessarily in the same positions from shot to shot, increasing the pace and scale of the scene in a subtle way. The titles to *On Her Majesty's Secret Service* run over a deep purple sequence, replete with images from previous Bond films and filled with images of monarchy. All this is accompanied by John Barry's terrific synth-laden instrumental.

SUMMARY: M relieves Bond of his responsibilities to the hunt for Blofeld and grants him two weeks' leave. While officially off the case, Bond receives information from Marc Ange Draco (whose daughter he rescued in the pre-credits sequence, and whom he is now courting) that Blofeld has links with a Swiss solicitor. Breaking into the solicitor's office, Bond discovers papers suggesting Blofeld is the Director of Piz Gloria, an allergy clinic in the Alps; and that he is attempting, via the Royal College of Arms in London, to establish his right to the hereditary title of the Count de Bleuchamp. Bond takes this information to M, who then allows him to travel to Piz Gloria masquerading as Sir Hilary Bray of the Royal College. Ostensibly 'Sir Hilary' is to assess the director's claim to the title, but in fact his mission is to ascertain whether or not the director is Blofeld, and what his plans for the institute are.

Once at Piz Gloria, it becomes apparent that the Count is indeed the SPECTRE Number One, and that he is planning to use the patients of his allergy clinic to distribute an 'omega virus' which can induce infertility in any species of flora or fauna. Once the virus is in place at several key points across the globe, Blofeld will blackmail the world via the United Nations. His terms? Not millions of dollars nor world domination, but simply a pardon for all his past crimes, legal recognition of his title as Count and the opportunity to retire into private life. Bond escapes from Piz Gloria after Blofeld uncovers his identity. The United Nations are willing to give in to Blofeld's demands and so Bond organises a private raid on Piz Gloria using men and machines provided by Draco. The raid succeeds, although Blofeld escapes – this is to have tragic consequences (see below).

UNIVERSAL EXPORTS:

BOND, JAMES BOND: 007 has spent two years trying to track down Ernst Stavro Blofeld (presumably since the events of *You Only Live Twice*) under the official name Operation Bedlam. Though unsuccessful he is totally unwilling to give in, going so far as to offer his resignation, which fortunately proves unnecessary.

Bond is very well informed about caviar, being able to identify which part of the Caspian Sea a particular sample originates from. He drinks Dom Perignon 57, still plays golf and still occasionally wears a hat. He tries to pass for Sir Hilary Bray, but despite his earnest swotting up on genealogy, his old habits cause him to be unmasked. His attempt to sleep with several of Blofeld's 'Angels' is as revealing as his uncertain knowledge of genealogy.

M: M's home, a large mansion-like house called Quarterdeck, is revealed as is his interest in lepidoptery (butterfly collecting). We also see a softer side to his abrasive relationship with Bond, when he thanks Moneypenny for presenting Bond's resignation. This doesn't change things when Bond requests assistance in raiding Piz Gloria – M is unable to accommodate him, but it is clear from his reaction that he is disgusted with the UN's decision to give in to Blofeld's demands.

MONEYPENNY: Plays a key role (for once). She is overjoyed to see Bond, proclaiming him the 'same old James . . . only more so!' (a reference to the change in actor). She is quite devastated when, after Bond's confrontation with M over the pursuit of Blofeld, she is asked to pen his letter of resignation. By changing this to a request for leave she saves face for both men and keeps Bond in the Service. There is a touching scene where both M and Bond privately reveal their gratitude to Moneypenny for solving this problem. She is later seen crying at Bond's wedding.

Q: After a brief appearance in the pre-credits, Q does not pop up again until Bond's wedding where his offers of future assistance are politely turned down by Bond's assurance that he 'has all the gadgets now'.

OHMSS: Their headquarters seem to be within sight of the Palace of Westminster – it can be seen the reflected in the company's nameplate. We see Bond's own office for the first (and so far only) time in the series. He has a portrait of the Queen on the wall, and keeps souvenirs of his previous missions in his desk (Honey's knife, Grant's watch and the re-breather from *Thunderball*) along with a hip flask of whisky.

ALLIES:

CONTESSA TERESA DI VICENZO: Marc-Ange Draco is aware that Bond saved the life of his daughter Teresa (see **PRE-CREDITS AND TITLES**), and later spent the night with her. Draco offers Bond £1 million to marry his daughter in the hope that this will break her rebellious spirit. Bond admits to Draco that although he is interested in Tracy he will have no part of such a deal; what he will do, however, is spend time with her in return for Draco using his underworld connections to find Blofeld

Bond is told that Tracy has been married once before, to a count whom Draco did not approve of and who died in a car accident alongside one of his mistresses (there is the faintest implication that Draco organised this). It is also clear that she has not simply a rebellious nature, but a tendency towards excess and a love of dangerous situations.

Tracy and Bond encounter one another again at Draco's birthday celebrations, where she instantly works out what her father has planned and insists that Draco give Bond the information he seeks with no caveats. After this Bond and Tracy begin spending time together (illustrated by a glorious montage accompanied by Louis Armstrong singing 'We Have All The Time In The World') and Tracy admits to her father that they are falling in love.

Bond is then despatched to Piz Gloria by M, and during his escape he unexpectedly encounters Tracy who has followed him to Switzerland. In a glorious subversion of the filmic status quo, *she* rescues *him* from

Blofeld's men, and as they rest while on the run he asks her to marry him.

Tracy is later captured by Blofeld and imprisoned in Piz Gloria, from where Bond and her father rescue her during their raid on the installation. Bond and Tracy marry in a lavish ceremony in the presence of both Draco's family and friends and many of Bond's Secret Service colleagues. Later that day Tracy is murdered by Irma Brunt, leaving a weeping Bond cradling her body in his arms.

MARC-ANGE DRACO: The head of the Union Corse, a criminal organisation based in French Corsica, roughly equivalent to the Sicilian Mafia. Draco's original request to Bond to marry his daughter for money is phrased in unequivocal terms which suggest a rather, er, traditional view of sexual politics. 'What she needs is a man to dominate her. To make love to her enough to make her love him,' he explains as if this is the most obvious thing in the world. Later (after knocking his daughter unconscious to prevent her from attempting to rescue Bond) he explains to one of his minions, 'spare the rod and spoil the child.'

We later find out that Draco was involved in a bullion robbery committed in 1964, in which his organisation lost three of its best men. He holds M responsible for this loss, but cheerfully jokes about it at James's and Tracy's wedding.

CAMPBELL: A Secret Service man, played with vigour by Bernard Horsfall, Campbell assists Bond during his break-in at the solicitor's office (odd, given that Bond is on leave at the time) and later shadows him to Piz Gloria, presumably on M's instructions. Campbell, who is posing as a tourist, is murdered by Piz Gloria security and his frozen body is shown to Bond by a gloating Blofeld.

SIR HILARY BRAY: The Sable Basilisk of the Royal College of Arms is persuaded by Bond to allow him to impersonate him in order to gain access to Blofeld's hideaway. Sir Hilary is only convinced by Bond's assurances that this is a matter of national importance. Sir Hilary likes brass rubbing, and intends to lose himself among the churches of Brittany for the duration of Bond's impersonation

THE OPPOSITION:

BLOFELD: Played with calm assurance, robust physicality and total urbanity by Telly Savalas, this Blofeld is by far the most effective of the character's onscreen manifestations. He is equally at home with a cigarette and a drink, cheerfully patronising Bond in a warm lounge, or rocketing down a mountainside on skies in pursuit of the fleeing secret agent. We do not learn much about the bald supervillain, it is not even certain whether he has re-formed SPECTRE (in the novel it is clear that he has). He does seem rather to have tired of the life of crime, and planned this as his 'last big score' – a way of retiring with a noble title and no chance of being arrested.

IRMA BUNT: Sour-faced 'old cow'. Loyal assistant to Blofeld, she runs the allergy clinic with an iron fist and is no doubt intimately acquainted with his plan. She does not seem impressed when Bond, in Sir Hilary mode, informs her that her name means 'the baggy parts of a sail'. It is she who pulls the trigger in the drive-by shooting which closes the film.

THE ANGELS: A dozen or so girls from all over the world, unwitting carriers of Blofeld's Virus Omega.

BEACH ASSAILANTS: It must be assumed that the ruffians attacking Bond on the beach are SPECTRE thugs, trying to prevent him from finding Blofeld. In the book they are Union-Corse men looking for Tracy, but that doesn't make sense in the context of the film's version of the sequence.

FASHION VICTIMS: It is easy to imagine that much of the negative criticism attracted by George Lazenby is a result of the truly hideous wardrobe he is forced to wear. Things start off nicely with a well-fitted evening shirt and a smart suit. However, he swiftly dons a disgusting brown zip cardigan/orange nylon turtleneck combo. The low point of the film comes with the full highland wear he adopts in the character of Sir Hilary Bray. Somehow, infuriatingly, Lazenby manages to pull this off. His confident stride melts any ill effect of the unfortunate cardigan and the nasty kilt (he even manages to find a use for the sporran, using it to conceal the device fashioned to bypass Blofeld's electric doors).

The many fashion faux pas of Bond almost make the rest of the cast nondescript, but only almost. It's nice to see Blofeld ditch the nasty grey pyjamas of *You Only Live Twice* and all his 'Angels' look lovely.

Special mention must be made of many great looks sported by the gorgeous Tracy, especially the cleavage-enhancing gown she wears in the casino early on, and her jaw-droppingly wonderful wedding dress.

SET PIECES: The final raid on Piz Gloria is impressive, and the magnificent pre-credit sequence is notable for its hectic editing and tongue-in-cheek referencing. Top honours have to go to the ski chase. As Bond launches himself down the slope, John Barry's pounding score sets in and Blofeld's men give chase. What is remarkable about this is the way the chase just won't end. Not for Bond the simple ditching of a couple of heavies with a pithy comment. Upon reaching the village he is still pursued by Bunt and Blofeld's security force. He knocks two out in a brutal fist fight then retires to a café where, about to break down, he is saved by Tracy. But the pursuit does not end here, it merely changes to a car chase. A break follows, as Bond proposes and pursuit is renewed on skis. It is only after the grisly demise of an enemy skier (see **POSITIVELY SHOCKING**) that the end comes in the shape of an avalanche, created not from stock footage but set up, by Peter Hunt, specifically for the film. That tension is maintained throughout this multi-stage chase, that a key plot element (Bond's proposal to Tracy) is fitted in to its framework and that its end (with Tracy captured by Blofeld) sets up the climax of the film is testimony to careful pacing.

POSITIVELY SHOCKING: The fight scenes created by Peter Hunt are worth a mention for the combination of fast, non-sequential editing and brutal sound effects. Additionally, the ski chase holds two gory delights: two SPECTRE agents fall to their death, a fall taking an indecently long time, and one SPECTRE skier suffers a grisly fate, falling into a snow blower and graphically demonstrating, as Bond puts it, that he 'had a lot of guts'.

Of the critics who claim Bond is a sadist, none appears to appreciate the tragedies he suffers himself. By this film he has seen close friends burned to death (*Dr. No*) or discovered their bodies after sordid knife-fights (*From Russia with Love*), had to see colleagues commit suicide under duress (*Thunderball*), had his lover poisoned before his eyes (*You Only Live Twice*) and, in this one, seen his new wife brutally slain on their wedding day. He is not a psychopath or heartless murderer but a professional who, in the line of duty, has received many personal blows, providing justification for his sometimes heavy-handed approach.

MEMORABLE QUOTES:
Blofeld: 'It will take more than a few props to turn 007 into Sir Hilary Bray, Baronet.'
Bond: 'And it'll take more than cutting off your earlobes to turn you into a count, Blofeld.'

Sir Hilary: 'Good motto, eh? "The World Is Not Enough".'

Tracy (on why she prefers to use a diminutive of her name): 'Therese was a saint. My friends call me Tracy.'

Blofeld (describing Campbell's frozen body): 'A dumb show for morbid tourists'.

Blofeld: 'We'll head him off at the precipice!'

GADGETS: There are rather fewer than before, a fact remarked on by critics and in keeping with the novel's own approach. Bond has a gigantic photocopier-cum-safe-cracker, and Q is trying to interest M in radioactive lint – this apparently would be of use in keeping tabs on all kinds of people, including the absent 007.

CULTURE VULTURE: *On Her Majesty's Secret Service* took the self-referential humour of the Bond films to a new level. Lazenby's line, 'This never happened to the other fella', was a way of acknowledging the signing over of the Bond mantle to a new actor, while simultaneously using the opportunity for a knowing joke. It's a genuine breaking of the fourth wall, which the film neither lingers on nor is embarrassed by.

When left alone on the beach, Bond picks up one of the Contessa's shoes, left behind in her rush to get away, and looks wistfully after his departing Cinderella.

IN THE REAL WORLD: Blofeld's mention of a 'particularly nasty outbreak of foot-and-mouth disease in England last spring' is particularly topical; the disease ravaged livestock across the country throughout 2001 (the reference in the film is to a similarly destructive outbreak of the disease in 1967).

Blofeld's choice of target for blackmail – the United Nations – is very much an institution of the time. It is difficult to imagine a terrorist choosing to target the largely irrelevant UN in today's more cynical world. The UN's decision to capitulate so quickly demonstrated how attitudes to this institution were changing. Its 24 years as a Cold War talking shop had not inspired confidence.

SOURCE TO SCREEN: The choice of this, the tenth Bond novel written by Fleming, was interesting given the continuity of the books, but ultimately logical. Eon had been planning to film it for some time, initially straight after *Goldfinger*, but events (such as the opportunity to collaborate with McClory on *Thunderball*) got in the way.

As touched upon in previous chapters, the novels have quite a strong sense of continuity, some of them dovetailing closely and with very few occasions when the opening pages of one book do not, in some small way, refer to its predecessor. This was especially the case for *Thunderball*, *On Her Majesty's Secret Service* and *You Only Live Twice*, a sequence of books that amounted to a trilogy based on the SPECTRE crime syndicate. Of course, the films ignored any continuity from the off, apart from a few half-hearted gestures such as the staff of the Secret Service. This is particularly so with the SPECTRE trilogy. Not only had the organisation already been the source of the opposition in all but one of the previous films, but the trilogy itself had been shot out of sequence. This causes a particular problem in *On Her Majesty's Secret Service* as Bond and Blofeld have explicitly never met before despite having come face-to-face in *You Only Live Twice*. However, these were ultimately minor considerations. The real benefit of choosing *On Her Majesty's Secret Service* was the potential for location-shooting in the Swiss alps and especially for the employment of spectacular ski-based set pieces, now regarded as commonplace in the Bond series.

This is not to say that the screenplay was dashed off haphazardly. The script is exceptionally strong, and many have credited this to its faithful rendering of Fleming's novel. Though the core of the plot is similar, there are subtle but important changes. As with *From Russia with Love*, they are also ultimately beneficial.

The book opens with Bond witnessing Tracy's suicide attempt on the beach. This same scene makes up the pre-credit sequence of the film but the book reveals that Bond has already met, and spent the night with the Contessa. The script reverses the order so that Bond and Tracy's first night together follows his saving her life. In Fleming's novel the beach scene takes place in the evening rather than the early hours of the morning. This encounter, in the book, results with Bond being taken to see Draco, whereas the screenplay moves this meeting to a little later, adding a short scene to explain how it comes about.

The film's plot deviates more seriously from the novel once Bond is given the desired information on Blofeld's location by Draco. Bond returns to London, cooks up the College of Arms plot with M and infiltrates Blofeld's operation. He encounters the ten 'Angels' as he does in the film, but escapes before Blofeld has realised his ruse. A brief, but very intense ski chase follows and Bond is rescued, as in the film, by Tracy, but this time they both manage to get away. The film's addition of a plot thread concerning Tracy's capture by Blofeld gives Diana Rigg and Telly Savalas some excellent scenes together – and gives Draco a strong motivation to provide manpower and machinery for Bond's assault on Piz Gloria (see below).

Bond does not discover the exact nature of Blofeld's plot in the book and this is explained in a most unsatisfactory way: a civil service official deduces what is going on and explains it to M and Bond at great length. Blofeld's target for agricultural chaos is limited to Britain, though his motives are never explained. It is hinted that Russia is involved, but this part as a whole is an ill-thought-out affair.

In the novel M, rather bizarrely, gives Bond the go-ahead to terminate Blofeld's operation as part of an independent action set up with the help of Draco. This assistance is Draco's wedding present to James. In the film the British Government intends to give in to Blofeld's demands, and M is therefore in no position to authorise military action against him. Bond's enlisting the Union-Corse in his attempt to rescue his would-be bride is the only option available to him, which is a far more satisfactory conclusion.

This is one of Fleming's more slapdash novels. As ever, the gambling and action scenes are good – the skiing one especially – but the attempts to deepen Bond's character are ill thought out and badly implemented. Bond's initial motive for resignation is flimsy (he is just bored, whereas in the film he is angry at being removed from Operation Bedlam). There is no sense of true build-up to Bond and Tracy's marriage, which deadens the impact of her death. The scenes with M are lifeless and contrived and, with the exception of the ski chase, there is no menace to the scenes with Blofeld. The villain's motivation (see **BLOFELD**) is entirely the creation of the filmmakers.

There are one or two nice touches. This book was published after the film series started (1963) and Fleming has a gentle dig at the cinematic Bond's gadgets, as well as having Bond mention that he comes from Scotland. The novel's Bond travels clean – without even a weapon – and is glad of the fact when his room is searched. However, it must be said that any good reputation the book has stems from its association with a superior screenplay.

DIRECTOR AND CREW: By 1969 Peter Hunt had been working on the Bond films for seven years. He had been offered the chance to direct *You Only Live Twice* but the offer had been withdrawn when Lewis Gilbert became available. Hunt remained on the picture as Editor/2nd Unit Director and was promised the director's chair for *On Her Majesty's Secret Service*. Hunt hired John Glen, a young editor whose experience lay largely in television, to take up his own old role. Glen would ultimately direct many of the film's action sequences, and would go on to direct five Bond films of his own.

This was to be Hunt's last Bond film. He would not work, in any capacity, on subsequent instalments. The position of director allowed Hunt a chance to hone his unusual editorial style. He also demonstrated a skill for stylish touches – the casino sign reflected in a swimming pool as light slowly fades, the beautiful pre-credit sequence – and for pacing a film over a longer period than the fight scenes he had previously displayed such ability with.

PRINCIPAL CASTING: Eon had found themselves in the difficult position of having to re-cast their leading man. Despite the posters for *You Only Live Twice* boasting that 'Sean Connery IS James Bond' there was never any question of ending the series simply because of his refusal to take part. Although the Bond films had dropped in frequency to bi-annually, there was still a 'production line' aspect to them, and the hunt for a new Bond became a race against time. Broccoli made overtures to Timothy Dalton, a young Welsh actor who had made a striking debut in *The Lion in Winter* (Anthony Harvey, 1968) but Dalton ruled himself out, claiming he was too young for the part.

George Lazenby eventually emerged as the front runner for the role. An Australian model with no acting experience, Lazenby was known as the 'Big Fry Man' in a series of chocolate commercials. There are many stories about Lazenby's casting. One is that Broccoli spotted him in his barber's and commented to the man cutting his hair that Lazenby would make a good James Bond. Another insists that Lazenby knew that Broccoli frequented the barbershop, and was himself there as part of an already ongoing campaign to become James Bond. Yet another story claims that he presented himself in Harry Saltzman's office one day, and told him to call off his search for the new 007. What is certain is that Lazenby quickly established himself as Saltzman's and director Hunt's favourite for the role. He performed two screen tests, and impressed both men with his wit and sheer physical agility. Some later reports suggest that Broccoli always had doubts, but these may simply be hindsight. With both little time left to them, and confidence that they had found their second James Bond, Saltzman and Hunt engaged Lazenby for what would be the first screen role of his career.

Diana Rigg, like Honor Blackman before her (see **Goldfinger**), chose to move from *The Avengers* TV series to the big screen via a Bond film.

Ironically, much of Rigg's subsequent career would be on the legitimate stage where she would carve out a justified reputation as one of the finest dramatic actresses of her generation.

Telly Savalas, suggested to Hunt by Broccoli for the role of Blofeld, had recently appeared in *The Dirty Dozen* (Robert Aldrich, 1967) but was best known for his Oscar-nominated role in *Birdman of Alcatraz* (John Frankenheimer, 1962). He would later find fame as television's *Kojak*. There was never any question of Donald Pleasence reprising his role due to the overly physical nature of Blofeld's involvement in the plot and action sequences of *On Her Majesty's Secret Service*.

Experienced German stage and film actress Ilse Steppat was yet another example of a star of European cinema tempted into an English-speaking role by the Bond series. *On Her Majesty's Secret Service* was to be her last film. She died on 22 December 1969.

MUSICAL NOTES: The strange thing about John Barry's score for *On Her Majesty's Secret Service* is that the 'James Bond Theme', when it occurs in it, seems both obtrusive and inappropriate compared with the melodies of either Barry's own opening instrumental or the magnificent 'We Have All the Time in the World'.

Time and again in this picture Barry delivers the goods, a sensitive orchestral score skilfully augmented by low-key synthesiser doodles. The music for the scene in the lawyer's office, the ski-chase theme, the accompaniment to the assault on Piz Gloria, are all perfectly judged.

BOX OFFICE: *On Her Majesty's Secret Service* was the most financially successful film on release in Britain in 1970. Worldwide however, its gross of $64.6 million, half that of *You Only Live Twice*, was enough to give Saltzman and Broccoli cause for concern.

AWARDS: Somewhat ironically, as it turned out, George Lazenby was nominated for a 'Most Promising Newcomer' Golden Globe in 1970.

CRITICS: There were two overwhelming areas of consensus on *On Her Majesty's Secret Service*: Lazenby was (at best) adequate as Bond but the film was enjoyable escapism in the spirit of the series. Most critics seemed unable to get through their first or last paragraph without mentioning the 'Big Fry' commercials. Donald Zec (who would ghost-write Cubby Broccoli's posthumous autobiography) summed up the opinion of many others in his *Daily Mirror* column (16 December

1969): 'In the . . . "ZAP!" and "WOWIE!" department the producers have left no neck un-broken, no stomach un-turned.' He was less impressed with the man playing Bond: 'I have doubts about Mr Lazenby . . . he jostles uncomfortably in the part like a size four foot in a size twelve gumboot.'

Some critics were more generous than others. The *Sunday Telegraph* review suggested that the inexperienced Lazenby was being overworked, while Dilys Powell in the *Sunday Times* (21 December) was quite positive about the new 007, albeit with some caveats: 'George Lazenby I find too amiable; one doesn't get the rasping indifference to danger.' Penelope Houston was not so much upset with the change of actor as with the general trend of the character: 'George Lazenby is a slow reactor, but in any case there is precious little left of the just human hero of the earlier films,' she wrote in the *Spectator* review of 27 December. Others were quite vicious. The *Sunday Mirror*'s review spoke of Lazenby as a 'great, big tall nothing' (Madeline Harmsworth, 21 December). Pauline Kael, in the *New Yorker* on 27 December, followed a similar line to Zec: 'George Lazenby [is] quite a dull fellow and the script isn't much either, but the movie is exciting anyway.'

Few disagreed with this evaluation. Writing in the *Guardian* of 16 December, Derek Malcolm called it 'a jolly frolic in the familiar money spinning fashion. Not a penny spared on production values [and] smart direction from Peter Hunt.' Surprisingly few critics took the sad ending seriously. Many speak of it in their reviews with a joking air. Only the pro-Lazenby Alexander Walker credits Bond with 'a reassuring sentimental streak. When his new wife is shot dead . . . the chap actually gets a bit moist-eyed' (16 December).

Dissent at the near-universal dislike of Lazenby was neatly expressed by John Gordon in the *Sunday Express* of 21 December, where he attacked the self-satisfied consensus on the actor: 'What's wrong with these critics that their view rarely agrees with most people's? Do they just write for each other?'

CUT SCENES: *On Her Majesty's Secret Service* remains, despite the general bloating in film running times during the 80s and 90s, the longest Bond film by some margin, running at 2 hours and 32 minutes. Two sequences are believed to have been lost from the finished version. One was an extended chase across the rooftops of London after Bond realises that his conversation with Sir Hilary is being monitored. Though photographs suggest this scene exists, Peter Hunt has explained in interviews that while it was storyboarded and some shooting undertaken, the sequence was never completed and he never had the option of including it in the finished film. The other is a brief sequence where Irma Bunt spies on Bond as he buys his wedding ring for Tracy. That the first sequence never came to be is a shame, but the loss of the second merely adds to the shock value (and it is shocking, even when you know what's coming) of the film's final minutes.

TRIVIA: At one point Bond walks past a dwarf who is rhythmically sweeping the floor with a large broom while whistling the theme to *Goldfinger*. It's like something out of a David Lynch film.

MARTINIS, GIRLS AND GUNS: Bond adds another three notches to his bedpost: the awesome Tracy, the amusing Ruby Bartlett and the nondescript second-girl-at-Piz-Gloria (the character doesn't actually have a name). This film further advances the idea that having sex is inevitably part of 007's mission. His seduction of Ruby in particular is carried out as part of his efforts to uncover what is actually going on at Piz Gloria. With regards to killing *On Her Majesty's Secret Service* is positively restrained compared with recent efforts. Bond only kills eight people in total – two on the beach in the pre-credits, two during the ski chase, and four during the final assault on Piz Gloria. He consumes one Martini. While undercover he drinks whisky and branch water, presumably because ordering a vodka Martini shaken not stirred would blow his cover even more quickly than his lack of knowledge about De Bleuchamp burials. Bond is more subdued on all counts in this picture, as befitting the more restrained tone of the film.

THE ONE WITH . . .: The other fella.

THE LAST WORD: 'We have all the time in the world.' It is difficult to know what to say about *On Her Majesty's Secret Service* that hasn't already been said. The passing years have been more than good to it, and it now stands revealed as perhaps the most beautifully shot, and certainly the best-scripted Bond picture ever committed to film. It's mature, reflective and rich in character, but all this is achieved without sacrificing pace or action. Lazenby's inexperience rarely shows, and when it counts (such as his conversation with Blofeld or any of his scenes with Tracy) he inarguably rises to the occasion. Peter Hunt not only directs both the action-adventure and romantic plots in resolutely different but absolutely appropriate ways, he also pays attention to thematic concerns (note the recurring imagery of monarchy throughout the film) in a way that few action-adventure directors have ever managed. There are many shots that display real imagination. Most powerful of these is perhaps when Tracy's capture is reflected in the glass as Bond stares out of the window of M's office. Equally impressive is the way the sun glares off the ice behind Blofeld, making it impossible for the inquisitive Campbell to distinguish Blofeld's features clearly. Gabriel Ferzetti is exceptionally brilliant, and the regulars, particularly Bernard Lee, are never better than here. *On Her Majesty's Secret Service* is an honest-to-God great movie.

GIRLS	18
MARTINIS	5
DEATHS	83

Continuity 1: 'This never happened to the other fella.'

Up until *You Only Live Twice* the James Bond films had been consistent, with recurring cast members and strong internal continuity. The first problem with this progressive continuity comes with *On Her Majesty's Secret Service*. This is not due to the re-casting of both Bond and Blofeld (anyone bothered by the re-casting of actors in a work of fiction should get out more) but the strange way that the two characters have never met before despite having been face to face in *You Only Live Twice*. This problem arises because *On Her Majesty's Secret Service* is a largely faithful adaptation of the novel in which the literary Bond and Blofeld meet for the first time, and the film *You Only Live Twice* dispensed with all but the vaguest props from Fleming's novel. Thus, in the film series, Bond and Blofeld meet for the first time. Twice. This essentially makes it impossible for the two pictures to exist in one internally consistent series.

This problem is compounded by *Diamonds Are Forever*, which steadfastly refuses to follow on from the end of *On Her Majesty's Secret Service* at all. Tracy is not mentioned once, and if (as some fans have suggested) the leave Bond has returned from is a period of convalescence following his 'killing' of Blofeld in revenge for the end of *On Her Majesty's Secret Service*, then M and Moneypenny are insultingly non-circumspect when referring to 007's recent activities. M criticises Bond for taking so much time off, and demands that he do some 'plain, solid work', while Moneypenny jokes at some length on the topic of marriage. Later, when Bond confronts Blofeld, there is again no mention of the circumstances of their last meeting. In fact, *Diamonds Are Forever* opens in Japan, as if the film is intended to follow on from the end of *You Only Live Twice*. The audience is expected to treat the previous film (as Eon clearly did at the time) as some sort of aberration, and this one as normal service being resumed. This attitude would continue with the next two Bond films, neither of which would refer to the events of *On Her Majesty's Secret Service* while maintaining broad continuity with the other films in the series.

Later, as the critical stock of *On Her Majesty's Secret Service* began to rise, this attitude would drastically change (see CONTINUITY 2).

Diamonds Are Forever (1971)

Produced by Harry Saltzman and Albert R Broccoli
Screenplay by Richard Maibaum and Tom Mankiewicz
Director of Photography: Ted Moore, BSC
Music composed, conducted and arranged by John Barry
Lyrics by Don Black
Title song sung by Shirley Bassey
Production designed by Ken Adam
Editors: John W Holmes, Bert Bates, ACE
Directed by Guy Hamilton

PRINCIPAL CAST: Sean Connery (*James Bond*), Jill St John (*Tiffany Case*), Charles Gray (*Blofeld*), Lana Wood (*Plenty O'Toole*), Jimmy Dean (*Willard Whyte*), Bruce Cabot (Saxby), Putter Smith (*Mr Kidd*) Bruce Glover (*Mr Wint*), Norman Burton (*Leiter*), Joseph Furst (*Dr Metz*), Bernard Lee (*M*), Desmond Llewelyn (*Q*), Leonard Barr (*Shady Tree*), Lois Maxwell (*Moneypenny*), Margaret Lacey (*Mrs Whistler*), Joe Robinson (*Peter Franks*), David de Keyser (*Doctor*), Laurence Naismith (*Sir Donald Munger*), David Bauer (*Mr Slumber*).

PRE-CREDITS AND TITLES: From Japan to Cairo, Bond, clad in a variety of unflattering items of clothing, brutalises various extras and demands to know Blofeld's location. He finds him in some kind of plastic surgery clinic, and throws him headfirst into a vat of boiling mud. Lacklustre editing, some bad dubbing and a distinct lack of pizzazz combine to make this the first pre-credits sequence in the series to disappoint. The titles are so-so too, although the theme song is great.

SUMMARY: Millions of pounds' worth of diamonds are being smuggled out of British mines in Africa, and Bond is sent to investigate the smuggling pipeline. Masquerading as smuggler Peter Franks, he meets up with the pipeline's Amsterdam connection, Tiffany Case. Together they smuggle diamonds to Los Angeles and then to Las Vegas.

Bond passes the diamonds to the next 'link', a comedian named Shady Tree, who, along with the other criminals involved in earlier parts of the operation, is murdered by fey assassins Wint and Kidd.

Bond reveals his true identity to Tiffany, who shows him the next hand-over point for the gems (Las Vegas airport) and they follow the man who makes the pickup to a remote desert installation, Whyte Techtronics, owned by reclusive billionaire Willard Whyte. Whyte has not been seen in three years, and during that time has ruled his business empire from the penthouse suite of a hotel in Las Vegas, communicating only by phone.

Bond investigates Whyte's penthouse where he discovers Blofeld. The villain has imprisoned the mogul in a safe house and has taken control of his business empire. The man killed by Bond in the plastic surgery clinic was a double of Blofeld seemingly created so that Bond *would* kill him.

Wint and Kidd again try and kill Bond but he again escapes and tricks Blofeld into revealing the location of the real Willard Whyte.

With Whyte rescued, Bond and the CIA investigate Whyte Techtronics and, specifically, a mysterious satellite built by laser expert Dr Metz. This satellite has just been launched and turns out to be an orbital energy weapon. Blofeld kidnaps Tiffany, and takes her to his oil-rig base off Baja, California. Bond tracks him down and tries to sabotage the satellite controls. He then calls in a helicopter strike. In the confusion Blofeld tries to escape in a submarine. Despite Bond's best efforts, Blofeld's final fate is uncertain.

In a coda, Bond and Tiffany Case are attacked by Wint and Kidd. This time the hitmen are decisively beaten and Bond and Tiffany sail into the night musing on the fate of all those orbiting diamonds.

UNIVERSAL EXPORTS:

BOND, JAMES BOND: Bond has just returned from an undisclosed period of leave. There is no mention of the tragic events of *On Her Majesty's Secret Service*. In form the mission Bond is given is very similar to that in *Goldfinger*, only this time the authorities have no idea who is behind the smuggling scheme.

Bond's knowledge of wines saves his life when he is threatened by a prospective assassin posing as a wine waiter. Suspicious of the man, Bond expresses surprise that no claret is available as the waiter pours from a bottle of Mouton Rothschild. The assassin apologises – but, of course, Mouton Rothschild *is* a claret.

M: M is on top irascible form. Irritated by Bond's lack of interest in his lecture on diamonds, M demands a little 'plain, solid work' from the agent. Though thwarted in calling Bond's bluff on knowing the year for a sherry (see **MEMORABLE QUOTES**) M is amused to hear that diamonds are something which Bond is not an expert in. M's appearance here is limited to making (delicious) acidic observations about Bond's abilities.

MONEYPENNY: Appears briefly at Dover to give Bond a false passport. They flirt and she suggests he could bring her a diamond ring, the sort used for proposing marriage perhaps? Surprisingly Bond doesn't respond by shouting, 'My wife was murdered at the end of the last film you heartless cow!' at her.

Q: No briefing scene, but Q gets more to do here than in any previous film. Once again he links up with 007 in the field, providing assistance and, in this instance, showing off his fruit-machine rigging skills to Tiffany. He also reveals a little of life outside the workshop. He has a family and irresponsibly built a voice-changing device for his children the Christmas before Bond's mission. He also, rather oddly, acts as the conveyer of the information about Peter Franks's escape – surely such a vital message would have been sent to Bond more urgently?

OHMSS: Once again, the service is working as a branch of customs and excise. Bond and M believe that diamond smuggling is unworthy of their attention, but Sir Donald Monger, an influential man in the diamond trade, has convinced the Prime Minister otherwise. They also enjoy very close relations with the CIA. Whether it is just Bond who enjoys this authority (he has been of vital help to America in the past) is unclear, but for a British agent to lead a mission to rescue an American citizen on American soil seems most irregular.

ALLIES:

FEIX LEITER: An elderly, portly man in a government-issue suit, it is impossible to imagine him and Bond as close friends. With neither the cool of Jack Lord nor the laidback style of Rik Van Nutter, he is of the Cec Linder (see **Goldfinger**) school of anonymous, orthodox American agents.

THE CIA: It would seem that three years of the constitutional unorthodoxy of the Nixon presidency have seriously affected the CIA.

Their agents quite happily operate within American borders. This is prohibited by US law: only the FBI can investigate on a national level.

WILLARD WHYTE: Whyte has been held captive by Blofeld for anything up to three years, while the wily supervillain used Whyte's resources to build a laser-armed satellite. Whyte is an amusing, authoritative man and, once freed from his penthouse, does everything he can to help in the defeat of Blofeld. Jimmy Dean's performance is terrific.

PLENTY O'TOOLE: Amusingly monikered casino floozy, Plenty provides brief distraction for Bond who rather shamelessly picks her up by handing her a big wedge of cash and then escorting her to his bedroom. One of the less respectable moves made by 007. Plenty is later killed, possibly because she has been mistaken for Tiffany Case (see **CUT SCENES**).

THE OPPOSITION:

ERNST STAVRO BLOFELD: It is implied by the opening sequences and the conversation in Blofeld's office that Blofeld looks and sounds as he does because he's had extensive plastic surgery and has some kind of modulator in his throat. This Blofeld is an entirely different animal to any of his previous screen incarnations and, while Gray is hugely amusing and entertaining in the part, you can't help wondering why they didn't just create a new character for the actor to play.

This Blofeld hates martial music, smokes through a cigarette holder and at one point cavorts around in a floral-patterned dress. He also obviously fancies Tiffany, making several lecherous comments about her. He has created two decoys, identical to him in appearance and voice. Bond despatches one before the credits have rolled and the other saves the original Blofeld from death at the hands of Bond's piton gun. This is a great scene, but the plot device is underemployed.

The exact nature of Blofeld's plan in this picture is confused. He's convinced Dr Metz that his laser satellite (which has the power to destroy nuclear weapons) will be used to force the governments of the world into total nuclear disarmament, but this is clearly not his intention. Towards the end of the film the real Willard Whyte says that Blofeld has contacted the president directly and that the US has until noon tomorrow to pay up (making this sound like a simple case of extortion) but later adds that Blofeld is holding an auction with world nuclear supremacy going to the highest bidder. (Presumably the nuclear weapons of all other countries would be destroyed). These two plans aren't really the same at all, and neither is confirmed by the man himself onscreen. The question is, if Blofeld really is in this for the money, why doesn't he just sit back and enjoy Whyte's fortune, to which he seems to have unlimited access?

TIFFANY CASE: Like Pussy Galore, Case is essentially an ally of the villain, 'repositioned' by Bond's charms. There is more to Case's change of heart though. While she is enamoured of James it isn't until the threat of prison is made that she fully co-operates with Bond and the CIA. Even after this there are several moments on the oil rig where she seems to be supporting Blofeld – although she comes through in the end, attempting to sabotage Blofeld's satellite.

Initially tough and headstrong, then a manipulative seductress with her own interests foremost, the wearing of a bikini in Blofeld's base seems to scramble Tiffany's character. She suddenly becomes a squeamish bimbo, comically inept with a machine gun and of no effective help during the battle on the cruise ship.

MR WINT AND MR KIDD: Homosexual hitmen in the employ of Blofeld, Wint and Kidd are assigned the task of eliminating all members of the diamond pipeline once all necessary shipments have been delivered. They eliminate a South African dentist, Mrs Whistler, Shady Tree and possibly Plenty O'Toole but have no luck in dealing with Bond despite three tries. An odd but effective addition to the roster of henchmen, they are not as obviously deadly as Oddjob or Jaws but have a more subtle menace of their own.

DR METZ: The world's leading expert on laser refraction and 'a committed idealist to peace', Dr Metz is employed directly by Blofeld, and clued in on every aspect of the operation. Blofeld convinces him to build the laser satellite as a solution to nuclear proliferation. It can and does destroy missiles, rocket silos and submarines. Metz seems to realise what sort of a man Blofeld is when Washington is targeted. Even then his reasons for dissent seem more rooted in his fear of an airstrike than objection to the destruction of Washington. His ultimate fate is uncertain – in all likelihood he is killed in the oil-rig explosion.

DIRECTOR AND CREW: Guy Hamilton, director of the much-admired *Goldfinger*, returned to the Bond series, as did director of photography Ted Moore and long-time production designer Ken Adam. Ted Moore's lush style seems strangely muted while Ken Adam's set designs, with the possible exception of Blofeld's office at The Whyte House, lack pizzazz.

PRINCIPAL CASTING: In early 1970 Eon forwarded the first instalment of George Lazenby's fee for *Diamonds Are Forever* to him. He returned it. It was clear that another actor would have to be found to play James Bond. Director Guy Hamilton favoured Burt Reynolds, but Cubby Broccoli could not be persuaded. It has been suggested that Broccoli was against casting an American, but this seems unlikely given who was considered next. After much deliberation and more than a few screen tests, Eon felt confident they had found their third Bond – American actor John Gavin, best known for his roles as Julius Caesar in Stanley Kubrick's *Spartacus* (1960) and Sam Loomis in *Psycho* (Alfred Hitchcock, 1960). The head of United Artists, David Picker, was unconvinced. It seems that it was not Gavin's casting, per se, that he was unhappy with, but the appearance of a new 007 in two successive films. Picker flew to Britain to discuss personally terms with the one man he felt could guarantee that *Diamonds Are Forever* would be a commercial success: Sean Connery. The man who had played Bond in five of the previous six films agreed – for a fee of $1,250,000, plus 12.5 per cent of the gross profits of the picture. This amount, a huge sum in 1970s film salary terms, was donated by Connery in full to The Scottish International Educational Trust, a charity Connery had recently set up with racing driver Jackie Stewart, to provide opportunities for disadvantaged Scottish youngsters. It was also agreed that United Artists would fund any two films Connery wished to make either as star or as director. The actor hoped to produce his own film version of Shakespeare's *Macbeth*, but was put off by the imminent release of Roman Polanski's version. Ultimately only one film, *The Offence* (Sidney Lumet, 1973) was made off the back of Connery's deal. It does, however, feature one of his most compelling screen performances.

American actress Jill St John (Tiffany Case) had appeared in Bond spoof *The Liquidator* (Jack Cardiff, 1965). St John initially tested for the smaller role of Plenty, but impressed Guy Hamilton sufficiently to be made the film's leading lady. Playing the part of an independent woman who, nevertheless, melts in Bonds arms at the end, St John delivers a solid performance despite the occasional inadequacies of the script.

Charles Gray had appeared briefly as Henderson in *You Only Live Twice*. His other film work included *The Devil Rides Out* (Terence Fisher, 1968) and *Cromwell* (Ken Hughes, 1970). Towards the end of his life he gained plaudits for his recurring role as Sherlock Holmes's brother Mycroft in Granada television's various Sherlock Holmes projects. He died in 1999.

Two key supporting parts were cast through serendipity. A keen jazz fan, Guy Hamilton saw Patrick 'Putter' Smith (Mr Kidd) playing bass fiddle and cast him on the basis of his 'hangdog' appearance. Smith was a renowned musician who had played with Thelonious Monk and later toured with Shirley Bassey. Though this was his first acting role he, along with later *Chinatown* (Roman Polanski, 1974) star, Bruce Glover, made memorable villains of Wint and Kidd.

Jimmy Dean (playing Willard Whyte) was also a musician – a country singer whose most famous hit was 'Big, Bad John'. The producers had seen him performing in a Vegas hotel and offered him the part on that basis.

MUSICAL NOTES: John Barry's score is one of his most accomplished for the series, almost as if he is trying to make up for the lacklustre action presented onscreen. The whole thing is tailor-made for Las Vegas – jazzy and funky with a slightly sleazy feel. The music used over the early Wynt/Kidd scenes is particularly memorable (yet frustratingly difficult to hum). Shirley Bassey's title song is vastly superior to her far more famous efforts on *Goldfinger* too.

SET PIECES: There is something rather subdued about the action in the film. There are plenty of bangs in the Las Vegas car chase, and explosions in the final oil-rig attack, but there is nothing wildly original here. Even the best fight in the film, the intense lift brawl, was very much inspired by the train carriage sequence in *From Russia with Love*. Sadly, the thing about this film that most people remember is the insipid desert chase with the moon buggy.

POSITIVELY SHOCKING: A nasty little film. The breast-pocket finger-trap, the immersion in boiling mud, the scorpion, Plenty's death, the immolation at the end and the cold-blooded piton gun execution. In the case of the first and last examples, the camera seems to linger on the violence in a rather gruesome way.

CUT SCENES: Several sequences were trimmed from the released version of *Diamonds Are Forever*, possibly because part of the reason that *On Her Majesty's Secret Service* hadn't made as much money as it could have done was due to its length. This made it difficult to schedule more than a few showings of it in any one cinema day. A number of short sequences explain how Plenty O' Toole ends up dead in Tiffany Case's pool. After Plenty and Bond are interrupted by Tiffany and her gangster pals, and Plenty has been thrown out of the window, she returns to Bond's room for her clothes. On hearing Bond and Tiffany in the bedroom, she takes Tiffany's wallet as a small act of revenge. It must be assumed (as Bond says in the finished film) that Plenty went to Tiffany's home to confront her and, unfortunately, her visit coincided with that of Wint and Kidd who mistook her for Miss Case. This doesn't solve the problem that having seen her on the plane (and indeed commented on her attractiveness) Wint and Kidd are well aware of what Tiffany looks like. Maybe they simply kill Plenty for kicks?

Also shot was a scene featuring a cameo by multi-talented Rat Packer Sammy Davies Jnr – a legend in cabaret circles who often performed in Vegas. Jnr was to be seen arguing about the terms of his contract to Willard Whyte. This hugely amusing sequence was also taken out of the finished film.

MEMORABLE QUOTES:
Bond (tasting his sherry): 'Fifty-one?'
M: 'There is no year for sherry, 007.'
Bond: 'I was referring to the original vintage on which the sherry is based, sir. Eighteen fifty-one.'

Bond (on being told that Tiffany is so named because she was born in the New York department store): 'You're lucky it wasn't Van Cleef & Arples'.

Bond (when asked if he prefers blondes or brunettes): 'As long as the collars and cuffs match.'

On arrival at Los Angeles airport:
Leiter: 'I know the diamonds are in the body but where?'
Bond: 'Alimentary, Dr Leiter.'

After Plenty has been thrown out of the window and into a swimming pool:
Bond: 'Exceptionally fine shot.'
Gangster: 'I didn't know there was a pool down there.'

FASHION VICTIM: A shambles. Tiffany walks away unharmed from this plane crash of fashion but shame on the rest of them. Bond's terrible wig and bizarre eyebrows (apparently blackened with shoe polish) are bad enough, but the horrendous beachwear in which he confronts Marie gives way to linen suit and a nasty salmon-pink tie. Leiter and his CIA goons look uncomfortable in ill-fitting dark suits and greasy sideburns. It's an ugly situation when Blofeld's Mao-collared tunics start looking rather fetching by comparison.

PRODUCT PLACEMENT: Although previous films had seen placements of products like Smirnoff vodka (*Dr. No*) or companies like Sony (*You Only Live Twice*), from here onwards this activity would become more common, with many companies paying for their brands and products to be used by or just seen on the same screen as James Bond. Director Guy Hamilton has often said that he was presented with a list of companies and asked to approve those whose appearance could be convincingly written into the screenplay (see **Goldfinger**).

In *Diamonds Are Forever* Bond flies Lufthansa and travels on a Seaspeed hovercraft (see **IN THE REAL WORLD**). Though he orders no vodka Martini cocktails, he enjoys a glass of Martini Rosso and knows his Mouton Rothschild. The biggest deal of the film was with Ford. In exchange for showing their new Mustang being driven by James Bond, Ford provided all the cars for the film's chases.

GADGETS: More gadgets than *On Her Majesty's Secret Service*, but in the same subdued style. Q supplies Bond with fake fingerprints, allowing him to impersonate Peter Franks, and a version of Blofeld's voice-changer, allowing him to impersonate Blofeld's employee, Bert Saxby. Bond is also equipped with a piton gun for climbing skyscrapers (improvised for use in killing the second decoy Blofeld) and a vicious mousetrap-type device for catching those who try to disarm him. He makes use of a bizarre hamster-ball craft to travel to Blofeld's oil rig after being dropped into the sea by parachute. Blofeld also has a voice-changer and a rather swish little 'bath-o-sub'. Oh yes, and an orbiting satellite equipped with a death ray.

SOURCE TO SCREEN: With the perceived failure of both *On Her Majesty's Secret Service* and Lazenby's Bond, not to mention the general downturn in critical notices and box-office receipts since *Thunderball*, Eon decided to try and recreate the success of perhaps the one Bond film that everyone agreed had an unimpeachable reputation – *Goldfinger*. Having secured the services of the star and director of the picture, Broccoli and Saltzman decided to go one further, and bring back the villain. Given that there was no remotely sensible way for Auric Goldfinger to have survived being ejected from his plane,

Richard Maibaum was instructed to prepare a script which featured Goldfinger's brother as the villain. It was anticipated that he too would be played by Gert Frobe. Maibaum's screenplay appears to have revolved, like the finished film, around diamond-smuggling, and reportedly featured Goldfinger building a laser-powered super weapon on some sort of oil tanker.

This 'Goldfinger II' version of *Diamonds* is faintly visible beneath the finished film. It is also true that many of the picture's concerns and incidental details are those of *Goldfinger*. The villain is a megalomaniac in it for the money; Felix Leiter is a middle-aged buffoon; there's some fun with lasers; the heroine is a little harder and less overtly 'good' than is normal and the settings are almost exclusively American.

The concentration on America extends beyond location. Bond himself becomes an American proxy and, though assertive of his affiliation (it is not the FBI or the CIA behind Whyte's rescue but 'British Intelligence'), is ultimately not involved with a threat to the UK. The case is explicitly put by Blofeld musing on Bond's arrival at the oil rig: 'Your pitiful little island hasn't even been threatened.' Neither is his mission conducted in the interest of the Western powers (*Thunderball*) or world peace (*You Only Live Twice*). Bond is fighting for America.

Diamonds Are Forever takes only a few elements from the book. The title, of course, and a few of the names (Shady Tree, Wint, Kidd and Tiffany Case) but the story was very different onscreen to that which unravelled on the page. Fleming described a smuggling operation set up by the Spangled Mob of Las Vegas. Bond traced them to a crooked race meeting in the town of Saratoga in New York state, then to Vegas, then to a ghost town and then, after a brutal beating and railroad chase, back to the operation's origin in Sierra Leone. Saving the use of Las Vegas, the cruise ship ending and the plot device of diamond-smuggling, little of Fleming's novel remains.

IN THE REAL WORLD: *Diamonds Are Forever* was a product of its time in more ways than any of its predecessors, the tone and style undeniably that of the early 70s. This deserves mention by itself; the world was changing and Bond had to change with it. The 60s style of Connery's early Bond films was becoming dated, and had been tainted by its use in the many spoof films. This film saw the series achieve a brasher, brighter style. There is something rooted in the lighting, the costumes, even the way the actors are made up that is unashamedly 1971. This readiness to adapt to changing attitudes and changing audiences, to shake off 60s chic and adapt to decades of changing aesthetics in fashion and filmmaking would be a vital part of the series' ability to sustain its appeal.

This willingness to mesh with the values of the day is also evident in various plot devices. In the late 60s/early 70s cosmetic surgery was becoming increasingly popular and affordable, and the public's awareness of it was increasing. Indeed, it had been suggested that this be used as an explanation for the change in Bond's appearance resulting from the casting of George Lazenby in *On Her Majesty's Secret Service*.

Also very contemporary is Bond's use of the hovercraft to cross the English Channel. The first working prototype of this vehicle was put together by Christopher Cockerell in 1956 but it was not until the very end of the 60s that such craft were entering regular cross-channel service. Bond had to be at the cutting edge of everything – including travel. Unfortunately novelty does not always equal longevity: hovercraft travel was uncomfortable in rough weather and its fate was sealed by the opening of the Channel Tunnel. The last commercial crossing was made in September 2000.

Willard Whyte was openly based on famous industrialist Howard Hughes. Born in 1906, Hughes inherited a fortune, which he used to found an aeronautics company, make motion pictures (he was to meet the young Cubby Broccoli in Hollywood) and, in the 60s, run Las Vegas casinos. In his last few years he became a recluse, hardly ever seen in public. He died in 1976. The idea of Blofeld's impersonation of Willard Whyte is said to have come from Cubby Broccoli. The producer dreamed of visiting his old friend and calling out to him, but the man in Hughes's seat turned out to be a total stranger.

In another way the film was very much ahead of its time. Though science fiction dreamed of satellite-mounted death rays, the idea of space-based lasers was not seriously mooted until US President Ronald Reagan's 'star wars' program of the 1980s. Even then the concept was way beyond the abilities of scientists and technicians (as was, somewhat more mundanely, the swipe-card entry systems in the lab). While Goldfinger's laser has become an everyday tool, the laser-satellite is just an idea in a movie. Which is probably just as well.

CULTURE VULTURE: Given that the Bond films are viewed as slapdash entertainment (and this one is more slapdash than most) it is interesting to note the theme of falseness running through the whole film: the fake Blofelds, counterfeit diamonds and money, the false identities adopted by Bond and Blofeld, the voice changing equipment, the simulated moon surface and the phoniness of Las Vegas as a whole. It's almost as though someone sat down and thought about it.

CRITICS: Reviewers were generally enthusiastic about *Diamonds Are Forever*. 'Very enjoyable indeed', beamed George Melly in the *Observer* on 21 January 1972, who conceded that, while it bore almost no resemblance to Ian Fleming's work, it really didn't matter. The story was 'a bit of escalating nonsense' and the players 'grotesque strip cartoon characters' but the film as a whole was a successful 'monument to low camp'. This was typical. Paul Temol, writing in the *Sunday Express*, called it 'glorious mind-boggling hokum' (21 January). Others went further still. 'Close to being the ideal Bond film', claimed the *Sunday Telegraph*, 'fast, exciting and ingenious' (2 January). The *Spectator*, though, was having none of it, claiming that Connery looked 'as if he has just been woken against his will from a deep sleep'. Perhaps more condemningly the critic took the film to task for being 'clearly a product of a decade gone by' (Terry Palmer, 8 January). This comment seems especially odd from the vantage point of the early 21st century where *Diamonds Are Forever* comes across as the most unashamedly 70s, determinedly un-60s looking Bond picture of all.

Finally, *Time* Magazine enjoyed the new Bond style: '*Diamonds Are Forever* is like a Loony Tune' it said approvingly, and exclaimed that Connery was 'the perfect, the only James Bond' (Jay Cocks, 10 January). For the sake of the next instalment in their series, Broccoli and Saltzman had to hope that this would not prove true.

BOX OFFICE: The worldwide gross for *Diamonds Are Forever* was $116 million, a major improvement on *On Her Majesty's Secret Service*, and a step up from *You Only Live Twice*. Significantly, US admissions were around $26.5 million, an increase of $10 million on *On Her Majesty's Secret Service*. David Picker's belief in Connery had proved well founded.

AWARDS: *Diamonds* was nominated for an Academy Award for best sound, but it lost out to *Fiddler on the Roof* (Norman Jewison, 1971). This can't have been much of a disappointment to Gordon K McCallum, who had supervised the sound editing on both.

MARTINIS, GIRLS AND GUNS: This is the only film in which 007 scores with just a single girl. Bond sends seven bad guys to meet their maker: two security guards in the pre-credits, three ersatz Blofelds (one mid-transformation) and Wint and Kidd. Not a solitary Martini cocktail in sight, although he does have a glass of Martini Rosso with Tiffany early on.

115

THE ONE WITH . . .: that moon-buggy chase.

THE LAST WORD: 'You've suddenly become tiresome, Mr Bond.'
Despite a few great scenes here and there – the fight in the lift, Bond
versus two Blofelds, the briefing with M – and much wit, *Diamonds are
Forever* just doesn't work. The first hour or so after the pre-titles are
pleasingly bizarre, with Bond doing a lot of detective work and plenty of
screen time for the fabulous Wint and Kidd, but after this it falls off
considerably. This is despite the best efforts of Sean Connery who,
although having aged considerably since *You Only Live Twice* and
hampered here by a ghastly wardrobe, is clearly enjoying himself
tremendously. Far from offensively bad, *Diamonds Are Forever* is
uninspired and slackly paced – and certainly the least enjoyable Bond
film in the series up to this point.

GIRLS	19
MARTINIS	5
DEATHS	90

Live and Let Die (1973)

Produced by Harry Saltzman and Albert R Broccoli
Screenplay by Tom Mankiewicz
Director of Photography: Ted Moore, BSC
Supervising Art Director: Syd Cain
Music by George Martin
Title song written by Paul and Linda McCartney
Title song performed by Paul McCartney & Wings
Editors: Ben Bates, Raymond Poulton, GBFE, John Shirley
Directed by Guy Hamilton

PRINCIPAL CAST: Roger Moore (*James Bond*), Yaphet Kotto
(*Kananga/Mr Big*), Jane Seymour (*Solitaire*), Clifton James (*Sheriff
Pepper*), Julius W Harris (*Tee Hee*), Geoffrey Holder (*Baron Samedi*),
David Hedison (*Leiter*), Gloria Hendry (*Rosie*), Bernard Lee (*M*), Lois
Maxwell (*Moneypenny*), Tommy Lane (*Adam*), Earl Jolly Brown
(*Whisper*), Roy Stewart (*Quarrel*), Lon Satton (*Strutter*), Arnold
Williams (*Cab Driver*), Ruth Kempf (*Mrs Bell*), Joie Chitwood (*Charlie*),
Madeline Smith (*Beautiful Girl*), Michael Ebbin (*Dambala*), Kubi Chaza
(*Sales Girl*), BJ Arnau (*Singer*).

PRE-CREDITS AND TITLES: Three bizarre but disparate killings occur simultaneously. In New Orleans a man is knifed while watching a funeral parade, in New York a delegate at the United Nations is killed on the debating floor of the conference room with some kind of sonic earpiece, and on the Caribbean island of San Monique a man is murdered as part of a voodoo ritual. These give way to a fantastic title sequence in which naked women vie for the audience's attention with human skulls writhing in flames against a black background. The credits appear in really evocative undulating type too. Wings' theme song, a driving rock/pseudo-reggae anthem courtesy of Paul McCartney, underpins the whole thing. Brilliant.

SUMMARY: Bond is sent to see if there is any link between the three killings (see **PRE-CREDITS AND TITLES**), and discovers the victims were all separately investigating different aspects of Mr Big's operations. Bond works out that a drugs syndicate, headed by the villainous Kananga, is planning to flood the United States with $2 million worth of free heroin, driving the Mafia's drug-dealers out of business, and creating millions more addicts in the process. The smack that he has stockpiled will then be sold at vastly inflated prices. Bond locates and destroys the heroin plantation and kills Kananga.

UNIVERSAL EXPORTS:

BOND, JAMES BOND: Bond is now drinking Bollinger, but seems unfussy about the year. He's taken to smoking long cigars, and is a lot more casually lascivious than recently (watch the way he eyes up the singer in the bar). He's more manipulative than before too, playing with Solitaire's religious beliefs in order to get her into bed – presumably because he believes that she'll be on his side afterwards – and then lying to her after they flee San Monique. Bond also varies his choice of gun for the first time, carrying a magnum .44 (Dirty Harry's 'most powerful hand gun in the world') for the final assault on San Monique. He owns a monogrammed dressing gown. Whereas George Lazenby had seemingly chosen to play Bond the same way as Sean Connery had, with perhaps more humility and humanity, Roger Moore's approach is to wrap Bond around his own established screen persona, as developed across *The Saint* and the then recently cancelled *The Persuaders*. A debonair old-style English charm is added to Bond's previously established super-cool confidence. The result is an amusing, detached performance.

M: For reasons known only to himself, M, the man in sole charge of the entire British Secret Service, calls on James Bond early in the morning to give him instructions rather than, as one might expect, contacting him to demand his presence.

MONEYPENNY: Moneypenny accompanies M on his sojourn to 007's home. Bond and Moneypenny's relationship here is not flirtation-based at all: she willingly helps him hide from M's prying eyes the buxom Italian agent he's spent the night with, and seemingly regards him with a gently mocking, distanced eye. She's amused by his antics, not hurt or impressed. Lois Maxwell is very effective in such a role.

Q: Q doesn't appear. The character is mentioned, and his gadgets and recommendations passed to Bond via M and Moneypenny. Q-branch carries the official title of 'Special Ordnance Section'.

ALLIES:

SOLITAIRE: Solitaire has the power to predict the future via tarot cards, and this is vital to Kananga's plans. She is a virtual prisoner because of this. Her mother fulfilled this role in Kananga's organisation before she did. Solitaire knows, as do Bond and Kananga, that should she lose her virginity she will also lose her magical powers. Bond seduces her by tricking her into believing that the cards themselves have predicted they become lovers – something which, as someone who believes in tarot, she cannot go against. After this she (inevitably) goes over to Bond's side and helps him against Kanaga's organisation.

FELIX LEITER: Felix has again been re-cast, this time as the gravel-voiced cop-like David Hedison. He again gets little to do, but has a genuine rapport with Bond (Moore and Hedison were old friends).

QUARREL JNR: Presumably the son of the Quarrel killed in *Dr. No* (though this earlier relationship is not mentioned in this film), he and Bond already know each other and it is implied they have worked together before. A solid, dependable ally, he provides key assistance in the final assault on San Monique. Unlike his father, Quarrel Jnr has no truck with magic and is not presented as the stereotypical superstitious native. 'My regards to Baron Samedi man,' he says, 'right between the eyes.'

THE OPPOSITION:

DR KANANGA/MR BIG: Kananga is the prime minister of San Monique, a Carribean island. He is running a heroin-smuggling operation, moving tonnes of the narcotic into the United States via a chain of restaurants (Fillet of Soul) which he owns. A respected international statesman, he moves between his two worlds by disguising himself as 'Mr Big', a clichéd black crime lord with a fearsome reputation, all the time surrounded by an entourage who are aware of his double life.

On San Monique, Kananga's power is backed up by a voodoo cult, which he uses as a method of controlling the population (effectively abusing their religion) and the precognitive power of Solitaire, a young girl who can read tarot cards with frightening accuracy. The character of Kananga is urbane and charming when he needs to be, yet still a ruthless opponent and one of the greatest (and largely unsung) of the Bond villains.

TEE HEE: Tee Hee is the 'hulking henchman with a gimmick', this time a metal claw replacing an arm lost to one of the crocodiles (named Albert) at the reptile farm. Limited to striding around and grinning menacingly (which is done well) he remains underemployed, being largely absent for most of the film. He appears briefly in the standard Guy Hamilton action coda where he is trounced by Bond in a battle aboard a train.

BARON SAMEDI: First glimpsed as a participant in a musical extravaganza at the hotel where Bond is staying on San Monique, Baron Samedi turns out to be one of Kananga's henchmen. It appears as though the Baron is finished off at the voodoo ceremony on San Monique, when thrown into a snake-filled coffin. However, supernatural origins referred to during the show at the hotel clearly have a basis in reality: at the close of the film Samedi is seen, laughing maniacally, on the front of Bond's train.

ROSIE CARVER: Rosie announces herself as Bond's CIA contact in San Monique, and she certainly knows of Felix Leiter, but her provenance is never confirmed. Given that she later turns out to be working for Kananga all along, it may be that she's simply a plant. She is supposed to lead Bond to his death but falls victim to the trap herself. Nicely played, with an appropriate mix of toughness and escalating fear, Carver perhaps fails to approach the heights of the best of Bond's femmes fatales such as Fiona Volpe. Like Volpe, her loyalties aren't altered as a result of sleeping with Bond; but as Carver is clearly not an entirely willing accomplice to Kananaga, maybe Bond shouldn't regard this as too much of a failure.

PRINCIPAL CASTING: Born 14 October 1927, Roger Moore had been one of the actors discussed when it came to casting James Bond for *Dr. No*, and his name had also come up during discussions for *On Her Majesty's Secret Service* and *Diamonds Are Forever*. Although not an established movie actor – his only significant film being *The Man Who Haunted Himself* (Basil Dearden, 1970) – his name was a considerable draw on both sides of the Atlantic thanks to his extraordinarily popular television work. He had played the eponymous hero of *Ivanhoe* (1958–59), Beau Maverick in *Maverick* (1960–61) and Simon Templar in *The Saint* (1962–69). Immediately prior to the role of 007 he had been playing Lord Brett Sinclair, alongside Tony Curtis's Danny Wilde in the hugely expensive *The Persuaders!* for Lew Grade's ITC company. The unexpected cancellation of this series before a second season could be filmed released Moore from his cast-iron five-year obligation to ITC, and allowed him to sign up for three pictures as 007.

The son of a Cameroonian crown prince, who claims a (plausible) blood link with the British Royal Family, Yaphet Kotto had his screen debut in *Nothing But A Man* (Michael Roemer, 1964) and appeared in top-notch criminal romance *The Thomas Crown Affair* (Norman Jewison, 1968) with Steve McQueen and Faye Dunaway. He is also an experienced stage actor, having appeared on Broadway many times, and an accomplished writer, having penned episodes of several US television series. When contacted by Eon he was working on *Across 110th Street* (Barry Shear, 1972), also a Harlem-based tale of drug dealing. He has since appeared in *Alien* (Ridley Scott, 1979), *The Running Man* (Paul Michael Glaser, 1987) and in the long-running TV crime drama, *Homicide*.

This was Jane Seymour's first major film role. The script had initially called for a black actress to play the part of Solitaire (Mankiewicz wanted to cast Diana Ross), but the producers insisted that a white actress play the part. A film with a white leading man and black leading lady would have been unacceptable in many parts of America. Unlike most other Bond girls, Seymour went on to forge a decent acting career, playing parts in many TV movies and miniseries including the successful *Dr Quinn: Medicine Woman*.

DIRECTOR AND CREW: Director Guy Hamilton was persuaded to stay by the argument that he had initially signed up to help smooth over the transition to the new 007, something that hadn't happened because of Sean Connery's brief return to Bondage. For the first time in the series, one scriptwriter would provide the screenplay – in this case returning scribe, Tom Mankiewicz.

Ted Moore rarely gets his due, and here he provides his usual very high standard of photography. The bayou chase is well handled but it is the scenes set on San Monique that really summon memories of his work on *Dr. No.* This was his sixth Bond film.

As 'supervising art director', Syd Cain was responsible for the high quality of set design. Managing to strike a balance between his own low-key style of *From Russia with Love* and the excess of Ken Adam, Cain does some excellent work on this picture.

MUSICAL NOTES: George Martin had initially been a producer of comedy records (including some with former 'Bond', Peter Sellers) before becoming the primary producer for The Beatles, as well as their principal arranger of orchestral parts and a close confidant of all four men. There had been talk of him providing the score to *Diamonds Are Forever*, but ultimately that honour fell to John Barry. For *Live and Let Die*, Martin supplied a score which mixed orchestral pieces with some great fat guitar licks. Some of his orchestration for this film is reminiscent of his work with The Beatles – the meeting between Solitaire and Bond in Harlem is accompanied by a musical flourish very similar to one found in his score for *Yellow Submarine* (George Dunning, 1968). At the very end of the pre-credits sequence there is a sharp orchestral sting which is an almost exact reprise of the Martin orchestrated end to The Beatles masterpiece, 'A Day In The Life'.

The style of the whole score is distinctive and recognisably Martin's, and thanks to his association with McCartney it utilises musical phrases from his title song. When it appears the score is powerful, appropriate, even exhilarating, but there are long periods when the absence of any backing music detracts from the action. This is particularly true of the bayou boat chase.

SET PIECES: Publicity for this film tends to trumpet the boat chase across the Louisiana bayou that ends the second third of the film. While intermittently entertaining, the chase is far too long, and the novelty of seeing a boat leap over/into a car or slide across a narrow piece of land swiftly wears thin.

Much more impressive is Bond's escape from the alligator farm. Location scouts for the production happened across the famous sign that features in the movie, 'Tresspassers will be eaten!' and found that it referred to a crocodile/alligator reserve run by Ross Kananga. A scene was quickly added to the story and Kananga himself volunteered to run across the alligator 'bridge'. There were four failed crossings (two nearly resulting in serious injury) before the take that appears in the film. In recognition of this insane individual, the film's villain was named after him.

POSITIVELY SHOCKING: There are a number of quite brutal deaths (the weird assassination at the United Nations, the two New Orleans stabbings) and a rather suspenseful, eerie tone created by the voodoo references.

MEMORABLE QUOTES:
Bond (to Tee Hee): 'Butter-hook.'

Bond: 'It's just a hat darling. Belonging to a small-headed man of limited means who lost a fight with a chicken.'

Rosie: 'There's a . . .'
Bond: 'A snake? Oh I forgot, I should have told you. You should never go in there without a mongoose.'

Black CIA man Strutter (questioning the wisdom of Bond's attempted infiltration of Mr Big's New York base): 'That clever disguise you were wearing . . . a white face in Harlem. Good thinking Bond.'

Bond: 'My name is B–'
Mr Big: 'Names is for tombstones, baby! Take this honky outside and waste him!'

FASHION VICTIMS: Bond looks great in the long coat and gloves he wears in New York and the all-black night assault gear seen at the end is even better. A Goldfinger moment comes when he strips off the jumpsuit worn during his hang-glider reconnaissance to reveal the neat tan single-breasted suit he wears to woo Solitaire. However, it is difficult to imagine him upstaging the supporting cast. The influence of flamboyant black American fashion is overwhelming; especially when Kananga and his gang take off sober suits to put on outrageous caricature 'disguises'. The pinnacle of this is the New Orleans funeral parade – a riot of huge afros, massive flares and feathered umbrellas. It looks brilliant.

PRODUCT PLACEMENT: Bond's long-running choice of a brand name watch with Q-branch modifications begins here with a hyper-magnetic Rolex, though he earlier sports a Pulsar LED watch. Bond flies Pan-Am while the CIA rely on surveillance equipment supplied by Panasonic. Bond is happy knocking back Bollinger while the Louisiana bayou chase features signs for the *New Orleans Times Picayune* newspaper.

GADGETS: Despite the official rejection of many of the tenets of *On Her Majesty's Secret Service*, the three films which followed it remained very light on gadgets. Bond's only piece of hi-tech kit here is a modified watch equipped with a 'hyper intensified magnetic field, powerful enough to deflect the path of a bullet'. A clear reference to the accusations that Bond had become dominated by technology comes when this watch-magnet fails to save Bond at the reptile farm – he has to rely on good old ingenuity (and nifty stunt-work). Slightly less admirably the watch is later revealed to have a built-in buzz saw as well. With no prior reference to this, it feels as though the filmmakers are cheating in some way. When it comes to Bond's gadgets there is much enjoyment to be found in waiting for him to use them. When he starts getting out of situations using devices that we have never seen before, the film is lessened.

Somewhat less extravagant is a hairbrush with radio transmitter and bug-detector and the compressed-air shark gun. Designed literally to 'blow up' the offending fish by firing a compressed air pellet, Bond uses the device to provide a particularly explosive end for Kananga.

SOURCE TO SCREEN: *Live and Let Die* was one of the earliest Bond novels, Fleming's second, and had been published back in 1954. Unsurprisingly, after nearly twenty years, the plot had become somewhat dated, as had the social attitudes expressed in the book. Indeed, the novel's setting – a Jamaica still part of the British Empire – no longer existed in 1972.

Fleming's plot recalled much earlier adventure tales, such as H Rider Haggard's *King Solomon's Mines*. It took for its subject gold-smuggling, specifically a seventeenth-century pirate's treasure hoard that was being siphoned from a small island off Jamaica by a group of American gangsters. Fleming's twist was to make the gang a voodoo cult and to have it led by a black criminal mastermind – Mr Big. As was often the case in the novels, Mr Big was carrying out this activity at the behest of SMERSH, using the money to pay Soviet agents.

Bond travels to New York where he confronts Mr Big and carries off his tarot high priestess (Solitaire), tracing the route of the gold to a fish and bait warehouse in St Petersburg, Florida (where his friend Felix Leiter is captured and tortured – see **Licence to Kill**) and from there to Jamaica. He destroys Big's yacht by limpet mine, the explosion taking place just as Bond and Solitaire are being keel-hauled across coral (see **For Your Eyes Only**).

While many elements from the book found their way into other films, little of it is used for *Live and Let Die*. Of key importance is the general idea of a smuggling story, but gold is changed for a more topical contraband – heroin. The producers also keep the idea of a predominately black gang, and of a wide network of informants across Harlem acting as its 'eyes'. Some of the book's key scenes are adapted for the screen. The tommy-gun attack on a train becomes Tee Hee's last attempt on Bond's life (though the train scene in *From Russia with Love* was undoubtedly also an influence) and the cave in which Morgan's treasure had been stored is re-invented as Kananga's smuggling base. For once, the villain's name is changed for the screen – Fleming's Mr Big is here just an alias for Kananga (see **SET PIECES** for the origin of the new name).

Additionally, some of Fleming's fascination with voodoo found its way onto the film, though in a somewhat contradictory manner. The religion is presented in the same light as it is in the novel – as a way of guaranteeing loyalty. However, unlike the novel's villain, Kananga may even believe in it all himself, although he is not averse to engineering false magic to keep up appearances.

IN THE REAL WORLD: The 1970s saw a substantial rise in recreational heroin use, and this provided a fertile topic for films, including *The French Connection* (William Friedkin, 1971), based on the true story of a major New York drug bust. For the first time, Bond films were taking their plots straight from the headlines.

The way in which this story was told also showed up contemporary geopolitics. The 'big' countries such as Britain and especially America have always been disproportionately concerned about the activities of much smaller countries within their immediate sphere of influence. Over the last forty years of the twentieth century, America became especially concerned about activities in the Caribbean and South America, largely due to fear of communist insurgency. Though this particular 'threat' is not implied in *Live and Let Die*, the idea of a Caribbean state hostile to North America, and especially of such a state using the United Nations General Assembly to express such hostility, is not a fantastical one. San Monique, an island nation with an international drug smuggler criminal at its head, looks forward to the equally fictional country of Isthmus in **Licence to Kill**.

CULTURE VULTURE: The overall style of the film borrows heavily from the prevalent film genre of the early 70s, Blaxploitation. Studio bosses deduced, rather cynically, from audience figures that a lot of box-office revenue came from black cinema-goers in urban areas. This led to a whole slew of low-budget releases made specifically for this audience including films such as *Shaft* (Gordon Parks, 1971), *Superfly* (Gordon Parks Jnr, 1972), *Blacula* (William Crain, 1972) and *Cleopatra Jones* (Jack Starrett, 1973). These introduced many new black stars into the public consciousness, many of whom, such as Richard Roundtree and Pam Grier, went on to longer-term careers or, even better, achieved icon status. Mostly based around action, crime or horror genres, often with a political message (in *Shaft* the eponymous private eye defeats a white crime boss with the help of militant black activists), these films were hugely popular. *Live and Let Die* borrows several features common to the genre – noticeably the flamboyant outfits and the heroin plot, a widespread concern of the time especially relevant to black communities and dramatised in many Blaxploitation pictures. While it could never be said that *Live and Let Die* is truly a Blaxploitation film (the hero is not himself black), it is clearly more than a mere shadow of the genre. It is a product of the same period, as opposed to a later pastiche, and it adopts much of the fascinations of these films unselfconsciously into both the script and production design.

The incorporation of supernatural elements causes some problems. The laughing Baron Samedi reappears on the front of Bond's locomotive at the end of the film, despite having been killed earlier, and thus he inarguably has real magical powers. Equally, Solitaire's powers of prediction are absolutely genuine. Competing with this, though Kananga places great faith in Solitaire's abilities, there is ambiguity over whether he genuinely believes in voodoo. A cynical villain using a religion as cover for his gang is a fine idea. A genuinely supernatural villain is also perfectly acceptable, but mixing the two does not feel right – its almost as if some of the production team are embarrassed to admit they are making something which is, in part, a horror movie. This is a shame, as the voodoo elements are the aspect of the film best remembered by the general public and a little more of this element would surely have helped the picture.

CRITICS: Roger Moore's debut was received positively. The critic for the *Daily Express* was quite happy with the change in Bond actor. 'The new James Bond will do very nicely thank you' (Ian Christie, 4 July 1973). Others attributed Moore's suitability for the role to the change in tone of the films. Christopher Hudson in the *Spectator* (14 July) pointed out that 'Roger Moore has none of the gravitas of Sean Connery' but that 'he does fit slickly into the director's presentation of Bond as a lethal comedian.' As Arthur Thinkell put it in the *Daily Mirror* on 6 July, 'It is as if Moore, and probably the producers too, decided that Bond's licence to kill should be extended to become a licence to frill.' Dilys Powell in the *Sunday Times* on 8 July hit the nail on the head when she pointed out, 'who wants [an] Olivier-type playing in a crocodile pool?' Roger Moore was perfectly suited to this undemanding role.

Critics welcomed this approach to Bond films, 'good lively mindless entertainment . . . Long gone are the days when we took any of it seriously' (Derek Malcolm in the *Guardian*, 5 July). They were also well on the road to being accepted as family entertainment. As Malcolm went on to put it, 'The deaths are now just a screech and a thud with scarcely a hint of Peckinpah ketchup.'

It is perhaps best to leave the last words to Kenneth Bailey of the *Sunday People* (8 July). 'Roger Moore is 45. I predict he could now be playing Bond into his fifties.' He couldn't know how true this would turn out to be.

BOX OFFICE: A worldwide gross of $126 million saw the picture's earnings just outstrip those of its immediate predecessor. Between them it seemed, Saltzman and Moore had saved the Eon series. The next film, *The Man with the Golden Gun* was rushed into production to be ready for 1974, temporarily returning the series to its 'a movie a year' roots. But there were harder times ahead.

AWARDS: The McCartneys' title song was nominated for the best original song Oscar, but lost out to the theme from *The Way We Were* (Sydney Pollack, 1973) written by Marvyn Hamlisch and Alan and Marilyn Bergman. Hamlisch would later write the score for *The Spy Who Loved Me*. Ironically, one of the presenters of the Oscars that year was Diana Ross (see **PRINCIPAL CASTING**).

MARTINIS, GIRLS AND GUNS: In the quickest seduction in film history, Bond is snuggling in with a buxom Italian lovely from the moment we see him. He follows this up by scoring with the gorgeous, tragic Rosie Carver and the prim and proper Solitaire. A good treble for the new 007. Bourbon with water appears to have replaced the vodka Martini as Bond's drink of choice. Moore is less bloodthirsty than

Connery – he kicks someone off a cliff during the raid on Solitaire's house, one gangster is immolated at the end of the boat chase, and two people are killed during the voodoo ceremony – plus Kananga and Tee Hee. We're not giving him Baron Samedi because, as demonstrated by the final frame he is, literally, 'the man who cannot die'. Incidentally, at one point Mr Big claims that Bond killed one of his men in Harlem, but all Moore does is punch the guy to the ground, so either he was particularly weak or Big is lying.

THE ONE WITH . . .: all the voodoo and the alligator farm.

THE LAST WORD: 'Sheer magnetism, darling.' *Live and Let Die* does not fit into the image of a stereotypical Bond film. Bond's opponent is not an evil genius. He doesn't have a particularly outrageous lair and his masterplan is simply criminal. And yet, somehow *Live and Let Die* works. More than that, it works *beautifully*. The script is fast, funny and well structured, with thought given to thematic concerns (it's about 'masks' and personae, in essence). Roger Moore makes an impressive debut and the supporting cast, with the possible exception of Jane Seymour, are all tremendously good. The first hour in particular is a hugely impressive contrast to the flabby, inconsequential *Diamonds are Forever*. Only the overlong boat chase fails to excite interest. The great Yaphet Kotto is a fantastic villain (actually two fantastic villains) and Sheriff JW Pepper is actually quite amusing. Great stuff.

GIRLS	22
MARTINIS	5
DEATHS	96

Racism?: 'Take this honky outside and waste him.'

Ian Fleming's novels are a hotbed of casual racism. A believer in inherent racial characteristics, Fleming demonised the Chinese and Bulgarians, and was casually hostile to most other nationalities. His attitudes to black people were somewhat more ambiguous (he found much to admire in what he saw as the innate characteristics of Jamaicans) but were patronising at best. Quarrel in the novel of *Doctor No* is the archetypal loyal, yet simple, servant familiar from much colonial and early American fiction.

Some of these attitudes are carried over into the film version of *Dr. No*. John Kitzmuller gives a great performance as Quarrel, but the part is inevitably limited by what the script gives him. The character is presented as superstitious (but, in mitigation, so is Honey Ryder) and servile, and there is a particularly painful moment when Bond orders Quarrel to 'fetch my shoes'.

The most prominent – for some most problematic – Bond film in this respect is *Live and Let Die*. Some find it inherently racist that the principal villain is black, and the hero is white. Also dubious is the presentation of Solitaire – a young white girl imprisoned by, and in the power of, these villains, who is saved by Bond. This reading, however, is slightly reductive. The part of Solitaire was written for a black woman (screenwriter Tom Mankiewicz wanted Diana Ross cast) and a white actress was only hired because United Artists made clear to Eon that it would be difficult for them to sell a picture with a white leading man and a black leading lady in several American states.

Closer inspection makes it clear that a lot of effort has been put into avoiding an even superficially 'racist' element; that the picture is deliberately going far out of its way to avoid a correlation between race and sophistication and/ or virtue.

Kananga's appropriation of the stereotype of a crime lord is, like his acquisition of the voodoo cult, role-playing to achieve his ends. Dr Kananga himself is an educated, well-spoken and hugely sophisticated man who runs rings, intellectually and socially, around all of his opponents for the bulk of the film. He knows these are simplifications and clichés and he uses them against people who don't, backed by an entourage as clued up as he. Kananga can in no way be termed a 'race warrior' – he isn't fighting on behalf of America's oppressed minorities, he's simply making a lot of money from exploiting the (largely black) people of some of America's poorest urban areas.

It is commonly asserted that the film implies all black people in America are in league with Kananga. In fact two of Bond's most helpful allies are black – the charismatic, well-dressed CIA man Strutter and the charming, skilled Quarrel Jr. The way both these characters are introduced imply they are members of Big's gang. This expectation is then deliberately confounded and undermined.

Additionally, in a reversal of expectations, it is Rosie Carver (a sophisticated American black woman) who demonstrates the most overtly patronising attitude to a black character (Quarrel Jr, a Cayman Islander) where she speaks to him overly slowly and in simple English. Bond himself never makes a single statement, suggestion or joke which could be considered remotely racist, (contrast with the overt sexism of *Moonraker*).

The key problem that many have – Bond's victory over Kananga – is easy to explain. The villain ultimately loses, like so many before him, because he is up against James Bond. Bond is the hero – it's his movie. End of story.

The Man with the Golden Gun (1974)

Albert R Broccoli and Harry Saltzman
Screenplay by Richard Maibaum and Tom Mankieweicz
Directors of Photography: Ted Moore, BSC, Oswald
Morris, BSC
Production Designer: Peter Murton
Music composed, conducted and arranged by John Barry
Title song sung by Lulu
Edited by John Shirley, Raymond Poultoun, GBFE
Directed by Guy Hamilton

PRINCIPAL CAST: Roger Moore (*James Bond*), Christopher Lee (*Scaramanga*), Britt Ekland (*Goodnight*), Maud Adams (*Andrea*), Hervé Villechaize (*Nick Nack*), Clifton James (*JW Pepper*), Richard Loo (*Hai Fat*), Soon-Tek Oh (*Lieutenant Hip*), Marc Lawrence (*Rodney*), Lois Maxwell (*Moneypenny*), Bernard Lee (*M*), Desmond Llewelyn (*Q*), Marne Maitland (*Lazar*), James Cossins (*Colthorpe*), Chan Yiu Lam (*Chula*), Carmen du Sautoy (*Saida*), Gerald James (*Frazier*), Michael Osborne (*Naval Lieutenant*), Michael Fleming (*Communications Officer*).

PRE-CREDITS AND TITLES: Another Bondless sequence, and for the first time the villain takes precedence over the hero. A game of cat and mouse takes place between Scaramanga and an American hitman (Rodney). Scaramanga wins. The setting for this is a funhouse (which appears to have been put together by Saul Bass and Rod Serling, presumably when they were both having off days). Although meant as an involving action sequence à la *From Russia with Love*, this generates no tension, despite John Barry's fantastic barrel organ version of the theme song.

The title sequence is a slight improvement. Maurice Binder provides a fairly standard set of visuals, but Lulu's fast, energetic song is great, with a deliberately comical lack of subtlety to its lyrics: 'He has a powerful weapon . . . who will he bang?'

SUMMARY: Bond is tracking down a British scientist named Gibson, inventor of the 'Solex Agitator'. This harnesses solar power and could end the energy crisis. He is taken off this assignment when a golden bullet is delivered to the Secret Service inscribed with the number '007'. It appears as though Bond is the next target of assassin Francisco Scaramanga – the man with the golden gun.

Bond decides to track Scaramanga down and kill him first. He travels to Beirut and acquires one of Scaramanga's bullets, used to kill 002. Analysis of this establishes that the bullet sent to him was genuinely from Scaramanga's stock and was not a hoax.

From there Bond tracks Scaramanga's lover, Andrea Anders, to Hong Kong where he discovers that the man himself has a meeting at the Bottoms Up club. His appointment is an assassination, but instead of Bond, Scaramanga kills a stranger who turns out to be the scientist, Gibson.

It emerges that Gibson had been working for Taiwanese industrialist Hai Fat, and that attempts by the Englishman to return home resulted in his liquidation. However, Gibson has completed a working Solex and Bond persuades Anders to steal it. For this she is killed and Bond obtains the Solex, but only for a few minutes. Scaramanga kidnaps the inept British agent, Mary Goodnight, to whom it has been entrusted. Bond tracks Scaramanga to his secret island base, kills him in a duel, rescues Goodnight and takes the Solex.

UNIVERSAL EXPORTS:

BOND, JAMES BOND: A smug, cold man in a dreadful white jacket; his reputation is sufficient that Scaramanga, his mistress Andrea and weapons dealer Lazar have all heard of him. Odd for a *secret* agent. He continues the British tourist tradition of speaking loudly and slowly in English at foreigners in order to make himself understood, despite previously stating that he took Oriental Languages at Cambridge (see **You Only Live Twice**). He's verbally and physically aggressive, basically torturing information out of Andrea Anders by repeatedly slapping her, and then threatening to break her arm. (Roger Moore looks particularly uncomfortable in this scene.) He smokes big cigars as a matter of course, and has a good understanding of solar energy. He isn't a funny or appealing lead character.

M: M is in a particularly foul mood. When Bond is reluctant to give up the search for Gibson, M rather abruptly offers him the choice of leave of absence or resignation. His temper has not improved when their paths next cross aboard the *Queen Elizabeth*. By the time Bond and Hip have incompetently lost Goodnight and the Solex, M is positively incandescent. Bernard Lee plays these later scenes with great comic timing. We see M's office for the first time since *On Her Majesty's Secret Service*, and his bust of Pepys is back.

MARY GOODNIGHT: An inept employee of the Secret Service on a 'two-year posting to Staff Intelligence'. She knows Bond, nursing an affection for him and, simultaneously, a knowledge of his throwaway attitude to women. For a while it appears as though she will be the first woman to resist his charms but she swiftly succumbs, admitting that her 'hard-to-get act didn't last for very long'. She plays little part in the film and when she *is* called on to help she fails. Miserably. Firstly she is asked to hold the Solex for a few minutes but, in the process gets kidnapped by Scaramanga. When Bond arrives she proves to be the greatest threat there, starting a destructive chain reaction by pitching a guard into some super-coolant then nearly cutting Bond in half with the solar energy beam. Along with the Solitaire of *Live and Let Die*, Goodnight goes some way towards negating the more assertive Bond women of earlier films.

MONEYPENNY: After the redrawing of their relationship in *Live and Let Die*, Bond and Moneypenny are back to the old flirtation here.

Q: More bouncy and enthusiastic than ever, Q is on hand to brief M and Bond on the significance of the Solex. His breeziness riles Bond and even gets to M, who twice tells him to shut up.

CALTHORP: The Secret Service's ballistics expert. He helps Q with the analysis of the golden bullet. In the original screenplay, Calthorp was referred to as Boothroyd. This was changed when it was pointed out that Boothroyd is Q's name.

CHIEF OF STAFF: A brief first appearance for a man known in the original novels as Bill Tanner, Bond's closest friend in the service. This is not apparent from his dour and severe portrayal here.

OHMSS: The Secret Service have a base in the wreck of the *Queen Elizabeth*, inside Hong Kong harbour – the only place in the area which isn't bugged by either the Chinese or the Americans. 002's name was Bill Fairbanks, both Bond and Moneypenny knew him well and were aware that he was killed by Scaramanga in 1969.

ALLIES:

LIEUTENANT HIP: It is unclear whether Hip is a Secret Service agent or a liaison with Hong Kong police. In any event he is one of Bond's least helpful allies. On his first appearance he fails to inform Bond who he his, apparently taking him into custody, causing Bond to regard him as a potential enemy. He rescues Bond from the karate school only to abandon him moments later. He also makes a serious misjudgement in leaving the Solex in the hands of Goodnight. This much attention gives a false view of Hip's importance – he is of no consequence to the film.

JW PEPPER: The comedy redneck of *Live and Let Die* returns here. This was judged important enough to warrant a mention in the trailer. Pepper is the embodiment of what separates this film from *Live and Let Die*. In the former film he's a negative figure – you laugh *at* him, and with his casual racism and inflated ego he's a despicable character. Here Pepper appears as a loveable comic buffoon, and one who actually gets most of the film's few funny lines.

ANDREA ANDERS: Scaramanga's abused girlfriend, whom he only seems to keep around to have sex with before undertaking a hit (he believes it improves his eye). It is she who sends the golden bullet with 007 engraved into it to the Secret Service in the hope that Bond will hunt down and kill Scaramanga in order to save his own life, and that in the process she will be rescued from him. A wannabe tragic figure, the potentially fascinating character of Anders is all but thrown away by a combination of the screenplay's indifference and a dull performance from Maud Adams.

THE OPPOSITION:

SCARAMANGA: Born in a circus of a (possibly) Cuban ringmaster father and an English snake-charmer mother, he was a trick-shot artist at ten and renowned Rio gunman at fifteen. At some point during these years the young Scaramanga experienced an epiphany when a friendly trick-performing elephant went berserk after being mistreated by his handler. The handler killed the elephant and was, in turn, killed by Scaramanga. As he put it, 'I always thought I liked animals, then I discovered I liked killing people even more. He joined the KGB in South America and was trained in Europe as an assassin. 'Overworked and underpaid', he left the Russians in the late 50s. His price is $1 million a 'hit'. His main identifying characteristic is a superfluous papilla – a third nipple.

Scaramanga is based on an island off the coast of China, held rent-free (apart from the occasional 'favour' done for the communist government). It incorporates a 'funhouse' of mirrors, dummies and confusing lights which he uses to hone his skills. This island is also the location for the prototype solar-power plant built by Hai Fat Industries.

The assassin's scheme is to sell off the plans for the solar power plant to the highest bidder. He is foiled in this ambition when Bond kills him.

Scaramanga is one of the most interesting Bond villains. He is not a grotesque mastermind like Goldfinger nor a brawny muscleman like Grant. He is not a ranting megalomaniac nor a mob boss. His closest resemblance is to the Blofeld of Charles Gray but he is as believably deadly as he is charming. A skilled professional, he is meant to represent the dark side of Bond; they share the same abilities, same expensive tastes (Scaramanga makes notes of wine suggestions made by Bond) and a Cold-War background. The one proper confrontation, held over dinner with each man espousing their views, is the most interesting the film gets. It is painful to see this fascinating idea overshadowed by the tedious Solex plot – planning to run a franchise of solar power plants is hardly the apex of villainy.

NICK NACK: Small French manservant of Scaramanga, Nick Nack's help is not limited to cooking (he is a cordon bleu chef) and polishing the silver; he is involved in his boss's attempts to secure the Solex. As part of his training programme, Scaramanga has arranged to leave his island base to Nick Nack in his will. This leads Nick Nack to bring a stream of prospective assassins to the island in order to gain his prize. Scaramanga believes these duels keep his skills well honed.

A low point in villainous henchmen, Nick Nack is the least menacing minor villain in the series, his status not helped by the 'amusing' incidental music which accompanies his arrival onscreen. On top of this the film refuses to clarify his relationship with Scaramanga. In some scenes he is a loyal servant, participating in the villain's schemes, in others he is a figure whose greed plants him on the side of Scaramanga's enemies. Another interesting ambiguity thrown away by bland scripting and inappropriate performance.

HAI FAT: An industrialist who fills a similar role to that of Osato in *You Only Live Twice*, albeit in a more interesting manner, Hai Fat has brought in Scaramanga as a junior partner and 'troubleshooter'. This turns out to be a mistake, as Scaramanga kills him and takes control of his company. In contrast to the majority of characters in this film, Osato proves that characters who are ultimately plot devices (where, otherwise, would the industrial muscle for the power plant come from?) can be interesting in their own right.

LAZAAR: A Portuguese gunsmith resident in Macau, Lazaar manufactures Scaramanga's golden bullets. Not strictly a villain, Lazaar is honoured to be in Bond's presence.

RODNEY: Hapless Mafia gunman. Hindered by his name and set of dated gangster clichés, Rodney blunders around the funhouse, apologising to a model of Al Capone for inadvertently shooting him before, mercifully, being despatched by Scaramanga.

Rodney is played by Marc Lawrence, last seen as another stereotypical mob man in *Diamonds Are Forever*.

PRINCIPAL CASTING: For the first time in seven years there was no worry over who would play James Bond. Moore's contract for *Live and Let Die* obliged him to appear in a further two Bond films should Eon require him to. After the success of *Live and Let Die* there was no doubt that Moore would return, and the actor was enthusiastic about it.

For the part of Scaramanga, Eon looked to Christopher Lee. Lee was Ian Fleming's cousin and frequent golf partner, and Fleming had suggested him for the role of Doctor No. An experienced film actor, best known as Hammer's Dracula, Lee's deep voice and charismatic screen presence made him ideal for the role of the complex villain ousted screenwriter Tom Mankiewicz had fashioned.

Swedish-born leading lady Britt Eckland had featured in *Get Carter* (Mike Hodges, 1971) and *The Wicker Man* (Robin Hardy, 1973) and had rather more English language film experience than the average Bond girl. She had also formerly been married to one time 'Bond' Peter Sellers. She lobbied for a role in a Bond picture, citing *Dr. No*'s Ursuala Andress as a major influence on her life.

French artist Hervé Villechaize is, apart from *The Man with the Golden Gun*, best known for his performance opposite Ricardo Montalban in 70s TV series, *Fantasy Island*.

DIRECTOR AND CREW: This was to be Guy Hamilton's last Bond film. Although initially slated to direct *The Spy Who Loved Me*, he jumped ship to pursue the opportunity to direct *Superman – The Movie*, a job which eventually went to Richard Donner. Hamilton's contributions to the series had a number of common characteristics. All of them hinge on a criminal endeavour rather than political intrigue or megalomania, and all of his villains seek financial reward. In addition, all of his Bonds feature a brief coda after the main plot has been wrapped up. This normally consists of the villain's henchman (or, in *Goldfinger*, the villain himself) returning to battle Bond in hand-to-hand combat. Sometimes very effective, as in *Live and Let Die*, this feature reached its nadir on *The Man with the Golden Gun*. Hamilton's films also initiated the practice of using a script solely to link together elaborate set pieces.

Production designer Peter Murton had been part of the team working under Ken Adam on *Thunderball*, as well as being part of the crew on Harry Saltzman's first two Harry Palmer pictures. *The Man with the Golden Gun* was to be his first and last Bond. He has continued to work as a production designer on films as diverse as *Superman II* (Richard Lester/Richard Donner, 1980), *Spies Like Us* (John Landis, 1985) and *Stargate* (Roland Emmerich, 1994). Murton's sets (particularly the sunken *Queen Elizabeth*) are one of the film's few points of interest.

Regular cinematographer Ken Moore fell ill and was replaced at the last minute by Oswald Morris, a distinguished director of photography with a reputation for versatility. He had been nominated for an Oscar for *Oliver!* (Carol Reed, 1968) and had been responsible for the cinematography on *Lolita* (Stanley Kubrick, 1962) and *Look Back in Anger* (Tony Richardson, 1958). Sadly, the cinematography on *The Man with the Golden Gun* is limited by the bland (and often dark) locations.

MUSICAL NOTES: As with *Diamonds are Forever*, John Barry appears to be attempting to compensate for the lack of visual thrills by providing exemplary music. Of particular note are Lulu's top-drawer, guitar-thwacking, hammered-out title song and the various renditions of it used throughout the film (especially excellent is the barrelhouse organ version played over the Western section of the pre-credits sequence).

SET PIECES: In a slack film much has been made of the river-leap stunt. Designed on computer at Cornell University, the stunt involved a car performing a full 360-degree roll after leaping off a ramp. Although technically possible, attempting the leap was regarded as near suicidal. On the day, cranes, ambulances and divers were all in place but the jump was executed perfectly on the first try. Guy Hamilton thought that the stunt might have been too well done and wanted a second take, but driver 'Bumps' Willard refused to perform the manoeuvre for a second time.

Despite the undeniable skill involved in performing this set piece, the final result is ineffective. It brings into focus the lack of excitement in the rest of the film and is spoilt by the use of 'comedy' sound effects.

POSITIVELY SHOCKING: A noticeable lack of violence here. Some rather tame bullet wounds, and a lot of unimpressive karate. It seems very much as though violence has been deliberately toned down for the crucial family market.

CUT SCENES: In one of the trailers there is a glimpse of a different version of the final duel. This included a drawn-out beach gunfight, in which both men leap for cover after walking twenty paces. Bond then calls out, 'Now I know how you do it Scaramanga.' The villain goes on to reply, 'The secret of success, Mr Bond, never take chances.' Bond hurls a thermos flask/grenade during this sequence while Scaramanga stalks around forcing Bond to use up his ammunition. Scaramanga fires off his one shot but as he runs towards the entry to his funhouse, he grins and loads a second golden bullet. The action then moves to the internal confrontation, familiar from the final version.

MEMORABLE QUOTES:

JW Pepper: 'Who you after boy? Commies? I'm with you all the way!'

JW Pepper: 'I know you. You're that English secret agent. From England.'

Bond (whilst threatening to shoot off Lazaar's genitals): 'Speak now or forever hold your piece.'

Bond (having swallowed and excreted a golden bullet that Q is now studying): 'You've no idea what it's been through to get here.'

FASHION VICTIMS: The 70s Bond films are the ones which suffer the most sartorial flak. Here Moore sports a nasty white tux and 'that' safari jacket. A large part of the blame must be laid at the door of Moore himself; he had famously taken much credit for personally designing his own wardrobe in the TV series, *The Persuaders!*.

The key problem was the need to present Bond as 'classy'. This could apply, as it had done with early Connery, to a subdued but definite style – smart but not so on the cutting edge of fashion as to become swiftly outdated.

In the book, *Dressed to Kill*, Nick Sullivan argues that Moore's Bond, like Connery's, merely reflected the tastes of his time, saying of his wardrobe that it is a simple, understated version of the prevailing and often outrageous trends in [mainstream] menswear [at that time].' In the same book, Moore's costume designer Doug Hayward spoke of the difficulty of dressing Bond in the 70s: 'During the time that we were making clothes for Roger Moore there were a lot of new styles and colours being promoted for men.' He did not believe that these should unduly influence the style of Bond. 'I took a view . . . that we should keep noticeable details . . . to a minimum.'

As seen *Diamonds are Forever*, Connery was not immune to the extravagances of the 70s, but Moore was their real fashion victim. Despite the attempt to minimise contemporary influences, his clothes have dated especially badly.

PRODUCT PLACEMENT: Top of the list comes Sony, supplier of all the CCTV monitors and of an entire window display in Hong Kong that Bond spends an inordinate amount of time gazing into. Nikon also have products positioned prominently in the window. Bond displays his Rolex watch on more than one occasion. The series' concentration on brand name drinks is expanded by the addition of Guinness. Scaramanga is shown enjoying Black Velvet (half champagne, half Guinness).

The most gratuitous product placement came from American Motors. The river-jumping stunt (see **SET PIECES**) was devised for one of their publicity tours, so it is no surprise to see their name feature prominently. However, for Bond go to a showroom in Bangkok plastered with their logo is cheeky.

GADGETS: Q-branch lets everyone down here, providing only a fake third nipple, allowing Bond to pose as Scaramanga. The villain has access to a much better arsenal of goodies than Bond – a laser gun, a luxurious junk, even a flying car – not to mention the 3-D jigsaw joy that is the golden gun itself.

SOURCE TO SCREEN: It had been suggested that the Fleming novel of *The Man with the Golden Gun* should form a basis for a film as early as 1966. The intention had been to set it in Cambodia. However, the instability caused by the Vietnam War rendered this impossible.

In 1973 Tom Mankiewicz wrote a first draft script which was essentially a duel of wills between Bond and Scaramanga, a character he envisaged as Bond's dark alter ego. Tension between and Mankiewicz and Guy Hamilton led to the screenwriter being removed from the project and replaced by Richard Maibaum, who then rewrote Mankiewicz's draft. This introduced the 'MacGuffin' of the Solex Agitator and the energy crisis subplot.

The competition between these two plot strands is immediately obvious and they sit uncomfortably together. Quite by chance Bond, who had been searching for the Solex, is brought into conflict with Scaramanga, who possesses the Solex and who decides to set up a duel. This is irritatingly obvious at the film's conclusion. Scaramanga's death is clearly supposed to be the climactic moment, but the film drags on for another ten minutes or so while Bond retrieves the ostensible object of his mission, the Solex.

It is not just a bad adaptation. As with the previous two films, the plot of the novel had been all but thrown away with only character names and the title remaining, but the weak source novel was no better. It follows on from the end of the novel, *You Only Live Twice*, when Bond returns to England, having been brainwashed and programmed to kill M. This attempt is foiled and Bond is left a broken man. M assigns him a supposedly, impossible mission which he knows will either make or break his best agent. Bond is sent to Jamaica to deal with gunman Scaramanga who is working with a cartel of gangsters, and the KGB, to sabotage various Caribbean industries for reasons of profit and revolution. Bond infiltrates the organisation and kills Scaramanga in a swamp shoot-out.

The literary Scaramanga is little more than a flamboyant thug and the development of the man into a dark reflection of Bond's bon viveur is intriguing. It is a great shame that this is so sidelined. The only other character (apart from Bond) to survive the transition to screen was Mary Goodnight. Originally Bond's secretary (with brief appearances in Fleming's *On Her Majesty's Secret Service* and *You Only Live Twice*), Bond chances upon her in Jamaica while on his mission. In the film, she is only in a couple of scenes and comes across as a rather hapless, bumbling member of Secret Service staff. She and Bond do, however, become lovers.

The one interesting point to be made about *The Man with the Golden Gun* is its origin in a growing production-line ethos. This had been an element in Bond filmmaking from the very beginning. While it is debatable how rigidly, or indeed how consciously, applied the Bond 'formula' is there are certain elements generally thought of as being common to all Bond films: girls, gadgets, chases, stunts, Martinis, flirtations with Moneypenny and suitably impressive villains.

On Her Majesty's Secret Service tried to strike out for something more complex (while admittedly retaining many of the film series' other perceived conventions). The comparative failure of that film had led to a retreat into safety, and the result was a more formulaic approach – one where the eccentricities and occasional subtleties of Fleming would be eschewed for a more obvious 'shopping list' of elements. By *The Man with the Golden Gun*, this approach had worn stale – the primary concern of the screenplay is a joyless adherence to established Bond, and it has more than one eye always on the release date. There seems to be little interest from the filmmakers in how the elements they feel they *have* to include play out. This picture is tired; the result of people creatively worn out and uninspired by their own endeavours. The film ticks all the requisite boxes; however, it either misjudges their application or fails to integrate them into a coherent story. The 'formula' plays a part in making a film recognisably Bondian, but is no guarantee of quality on its own.

IN THE REAL WORLD: The film's plot is grounded in the 'energy crisis' of the early 1970s, a solution to which is apparently to be found in the solar power to be provided by the Solex. The roots of the 'energy crisis' are in the Yom Kippur war of 1973, in which attacks by Syria and Egypt on Israel coincided with a Jewish national holiday. A direct result of this conflict was the embargo put on Middle Eastern oil exports by the Arab nations of OPEC (Organisation of Petroleum Exporting Countries). This had dramatic repercussions across the western world, especially in Britain where oil supplies from North Sea fields had not yet come on line. Petrol rationing and widespread panic caused economic and social chaos. At this time, the quest for a 'holy grail' of energy production (such as solar power) seemed a great idea for the core of a film – in much the same way North Sea oil rigs would provide a topical location for a later Roger Moore vehicle, *North Sea Hijack* (Andrew McLaglen, 1979).

In reality the repercussions of this crisis were not as critical as initially believed. Many of the ill effects had been created by the fear and panic of consumers rather than the embargo, and both Britain and America were possessed of oil reserves to help cushion the impact of future oil-price fluctuations. Subtle, long-term economic problems which were to plague successive British governments, rather than the imminent collapse of Western civilisation, were the real results of the OPEC crisis.

One of the film's more imaginative aspects is the location of the regional Secret Service station, the *Queen Elizabeth*. Sister ship of the *Queen Mary*, the *Queen Elizabeth* was one of the largest passenger liners in the world. She was launched in 1938 and served as a troop ship during World War Two. With profits falling in the late 60s she (and her sister ship) were set up as stationary hotels off the coasts of Florida and California respectively. This venture failed and the *Elizabeth* was sold to a Taiwanese buyer, CY Tung, in 1970, who intended to turn the ship into a floating university (she was tentatively renamed *Seawise University*). She was taken to Hong Kong for a refit, and, when refurbishment was almost complete, she was gutted by fire, started by an unknown arsonist. The wreck of the ship was removed from Hong Kong harbour in 1974, shortly before this film's release.

CULTURE VULTURE: As *Live and Let Die* had borrowed from Blaxploitation, *The Man with the Golden Gun* was 'inspired' by another film genre – the martial arts film.

These had recently been made popular by stars such as Bruce Lee and films such as *Fist of Fury* (Lo Wei, 1972) and *Enter the Dragon* (Robert Clouse, 1973). The Kung Fu picture has remained significantly popular in the West ever since, with the most spectacular recent example being the Oscar-winning *Crouching Tiger, Hidden Dragon* (Ang Lee, 2000).

The way in which the genre is incorporated into this Bond film is exceptionally clumsy; a brief karate battle is inserted into the middle third of the film. There have been ways in which the series has been successfully updated (see **The Spy Who Loved Me**), but this lazy attempt at bandwagon-jumping is not one of them. (For another such example, see the SF antics of **Moonraker**.)

Fleming obviously drew his book title from the film, *The Man with the Golden Arm* (Otto Preminger, 1955) which starred Frank Sinatra as a heroin-addicted card sharp. Visually influenced by expressionist filmmaking, the picture was nominated for three Oscars, including one for Sinatra himself.

CRITICS: In the *Sunday Times* of 22 December 1974, Dilys Powell described the film as 'unfailingly enjoyable' but she went on to say that 'it lacks, I think, the bite of earlier examples'. Others were more critical. David Robinson, writing in *The Times* (20 December) suggested several areas of weakness: 'Roger Moore . . . is no match for his predecessor . . . Britt Ekland . . . is the least appealing of Bond heroines.' On the production side, Robinson was unhappy with changes to the crew: 'Ken Adam, whose inventions as production designer were a good deal of the attraction of previous films, has now been replaced by decorators of competence but with little of his flair.' Jay Cocks of *Time* (13 January

1975) was more focused in his criticism of the stunts: 'Overtricky, uninspired, these exercises show the strain of stretching fantasy well past wit.'

People found positive aspects in the most unusual places. Virginia Dignam of the *Morning Star* (23 December) spoke well of John Stears's special effects but also praised 'Herve Villechaize as the sinister midget manservant'. This was supported by Alexander Walker in the *Evening Standard* (19 December) who described Nick Nack as 'the best sidekick since Oddjob'. Even less explicably, John Coleman of the *New Statesman* (20 December) wrote, 'Nice to see slack-faced Sheriff JW Pepper retrieved from *Live and Let Die*'. Dilys Powell went a step further: 'the presence of Clifton James as Sheriff Pepper is still a delight.'

BOX OFFICE: Worldwide, *The Man with the Golden Gun* took $97 million dollars, a substantial reduction on recent Bonds. Admissions in the US were a paltry 11.1 million, the lowest for any Bond before or since. It seemed that again there would have to be a rethink; but before progress could be made on another Bond picture Broccoli was to find other, less creative, endeavours occupying his time (see **TRIVIA**).

MARTINIS, GIRLS AND GUNS: Bond scores with the tragic, much-abused Andrea Anders and the dim-witted Mary Goodnight. He doesn't order a Martini, and kills only one man – the eponymous villain.

TRIVIA: Chan Yiu Lam's character is named Chew Me in the film, but credited as Chula on screen. The most important event connected with this production is the collapse of the Saltzman/Broccoli partnership. The way the partnership worked is difficult to unravel; certainly in the early days Saltzman (credited as lead producer) was the driving force behind the pictures. As the series went on, Saltzman's roving eye led him to become interested in other projects, leaving much more of the Bond stable in the hands of his partner (see **Thunderball**). By *On Her Majesty's Secret Service* the two were alternating responsibility for the films: Saltzman being effectively in charge of *On Her Majesty's Secret Service* and *Live and Let Die*, and Broccoli running *Diamonds are Forever* and *The Man with the Golden Gun*.

It was Saltzman's interest in outside projects that was to cause the final split. He became involved in the takeover of Tecnicolor and the purchase of a French camera company. In doing this, it seems, he had accrued substantial debts and had pledged either his half (or in some reports the whole) of Danjaq (see **Introduction**) to Swiss banks as collateral.

The loans were called in and a brutal legal battle was sparked between Broccoli and the Swiss banks. Broccoli's argument was that Saltzman had no right to sign over a company that was only half his. Even if, as some reports attest, Saltzman had pledged only his share, there was no way that its financial value could be realised without liquidating the company – something Broccoli wasn't going to let happen without a fight.

Pre-production of *The Spy Who Loved Me* went on as the battle continued, with Broccoli bringing in his stepson and future Eon Executive, Michael G Wilson to handle his legal affairs. This was a decision that was to have great financial and creative impact on the series in the long term. The legal feud was not resolved until 1975, when United Artists, the film company that had for so long distributed Eon's films bought out Saltzman's share of Danjaq for a reported $20 million. The production company was saved and the films would go on under a single producer. The series had overcome its second major legal hurdle.

THE ONE WITH . . .: Christopher Lee and the tiny Frenchman.

THE LAST WORD: 'There's a useful four-letter word – and you're full of it.' A tedious empty vessel of a picture, *The Man with the Golden Gun* demonstrates that you can stick rigorously to a preconceived idea of a Bond film and still produce a dull, joyless slog. Despite being stocked with action (rather cynically toned down for family viewing), chases, colourful villains, the usual recurring characters, exotic locations and a tongue-in-cheek line in dialogue, the film misfires in every possible way. Ultimately a bad script is the central problem but it is possible to rescue such a film by performing well in other areas. Sadly, such a salvaging does not take place. An exciting Barry score and wonderful Lee performance are not able to change the nature of this beast. *The Man with the Golden Gun* is a very bad film.

GIRLS	24
MARTINIS	5
DEATHS	97

The Spy Who Loved Me (1977)

Produced by Albert R Broccoli
Screenplay by Christopher Wood and Richard Maibaum
Director of Photography: Claude Renoir
Production designed by Ken Adam
Music by Marvin Hamlisch
'Nobody Does it Better' lyrics by Carole Bayer Sager
'Nobody Does it Better' performed by Carly Simon
Editor and 2nd Unit Director: John Glen
Directed by Lewis Gilbert

PRINCIPAL CAST: Roger Moore (*James Bond*), Barbara Bach (*Major Anya Amasova*), Curt Jurgens (*Stromberg*), Richard Kiel (*Jaws*), Caroline Munro (*Naomi*), Walter Gotell (*General Gogol*), Geoffrey Keen (*Minister of Defence*), Bernard Lee (*M*), George Baker (*Captain Benson*), Michael Billington (*Sergei*), Olga Bisera (*Felica*), Desmond Llewelyn (*Q*), Edward de Souza (*Sheikh Hosein*), Vernon Dobtcheff (*Max Kalba*), Valerie Leon (*Hotel Receptionist*), Lois Maxwell (*Miss Moneypenny*), Sydney Tafler (*Liparus Captain*), Nadim Sawalha (*Fekkesh*), Sue Vanner (*Log Cabin Girl*), Eva Rueber-Staier (*Rubelvitch*), Robert Brown (*Admiral Hargreaves*), Marilyn Galsworthy (*Stromberg's Assistant*), Milton Reid (*Sandor*), Cyril Shaps (*Bechmann*), Milo Sperber (*Markovitz*), Albert Moses (*Barman*), Rafiq Anwar (*Cairo Club Waiter*), Felicity York, Dawn Rodrigues, Anika Pavel, Jill Goodall (*Arab Beauties*), Shane Rimmer (*USS* Wayne *Captain*), Bryan Marshall (*HMS* Ranger *Captain*).

PRE-CREDITS AND TITLES: After a new gun-barrel sequence (required because *The Spy Who Loved Me* used a wider screen ratio than the previous two films) in which Roger Moore wears enormously flared evening wear, a British submarine is forced to the surface in mysterious circumstances. Back in London, M is told that it has disappeared. Shortly after this, Russian General Gogol is informed that a Soviet submarine has similarly vanished. He assigns his best agent, 'Triple X' to the case. Audience expectations are subverted when this agent turns out to be a beautiful girl, not the Bond-a-like agent she's seen in bed with.

Bond is recalled from a liaison with a beautiful girl in the Austrian Alps. As he skis away he is intercepted by a Soviet assassination team. A violent chase ensues, featuring the death of one of the KGB agents (see

ANYA AMASOVA), and ends when Bond leaps off a cliff, apparently to his death. But his Union Jack parachute opens and the 'James Bond Theme' kicks in.

This is possibly the most cinematic title sequence so far, with soaring vocals and a vintage set of Maurice Binder visuals perfectly complementing one another. The combination of this amazing stunt and hugely enjoyable title routine is difficult to resist.

SUMMARY: Bond's lead on the missing submarine is a tracking system that someone is trying to sell to British intelligence. He tracks the source of this offer to a man called Fekkish (and his master Max Kalba) in Egypt. However, it becomes clear that the Soviets are also trying to obtain the tracking system, through Russian agent Anya Amasova, and that a third party is killing anyone who has had contact with it. The KGB and Secret Service pool their efforts and discover that this third party is Karl Stromberg, a shipping magnate with a sub-aquatic headquarters called Atlantis off the coast of Sardinia. It was Stromberg's company who originally developed the tracking system. While following a suspicious tanker, owned by Stromberg, Bond and Amasova discover that he is using this ship, the *Liparus*, to capture nuclear submarines (thus explaining the earlier disappearances). The American sub they are aboard is in turn captured. Stromberg intends to start World War Three through the destruction of New York and Moscow. He will then construct a new civilisation under the sea. He leaves the tanker for Atlantis, with a captive Amasova in tow. Bond leads a revolt and manages to fool the stolen British and Russian subs (crewed by Stromberg's men) into firing their missiles at each other. He then sets off for Atlantis himself, kills Stromberg and rescues Amasova before the US Navy finally destroys the undersea base.

UNIVERSAL EXPORTS:

BOND, JAMES BOND: Bond's marriage is referred back to for the first time since *On Her Majesty's Secret Service*. It is confirmed that he went to Cambridge University, and is not ashamed to take advantage of the 'old boy network' to get information in Cairo. While undercover he displays a working knowledge of marine biology, probably due to a fearsome cramming session.

There is an interesting glimpse of the character's naval background. We see his full naval uniform for the second time (the first was in *You Only Live Twice*) in which he receives and returns salutes at Faslane submarine base. While aboard the USS *Wayne*, he wears a uniform that asserts his official rank. It is revealed that he did his service on the aircraft carrier HMS *Ark Royal*. This Bond is an actual Navy man, unlike both Fleming and the literary Bond (who, like his creator, had not been a serving officer but an intelligence operative with largely ceremonial rank).

M: Once again M deems it necessary to travel the world with both Q and Moneypenny in tow. We discover that his first name is Miles (perhaps indicating that, as in the novels, his full name is Miles Messervy). He uses the odd, Americanised phrase 'Mr Prime Minister' when talking to the PM on the phone (US officials tend to have 'Mr' prefixed to their form of address, UK ones don't).

M usually snipes constantly at Bond's behaviour. However, in this case, when Bond is in competition with the Russian Amasova, M is almost cloying in his congratulation of Bond's knowledge and skills.

MONEYPENNY: Doing less than ever here, her role is scarcely worth commenting on.

Q: It is once again confirmed that Q's surname is Boothroyd, and that he carries the Army rank of major. He is also involved in high-level briefings, an extension of his duties in *The Man with the Golden Gun*, filling in the Minister of Defence, senior naval staff and Bond on the submarine-tracking system. He travels out to Egypt with M and Moneypenny and personally delivers the Lotus to Bond on Sardinia. He seems to have been promoted in recent years, given this and his status in *The Man with the Golden Gun*.

OHMSS: The secret service has a base, complete with its own Q-branch, hidden inside an ancient building in Egypt. Does the Egyptian government know? (By the end of this film the Soviets certainly do.)

ALLIES:

MAJOR ANYA AMASOVA (AGENT 'TRIPLE X'): A top Russian agent chosen to solve the riddle of the missing Soviet submarine *Potemkin*. She initially competes with Bond over the microfilm of the submarine-tracking system and usurps him when it comes to gadgetry, knowing how to operate the submersible Lotus. There is an attempt to build a subplot around the death of her lover – the Austrian KGB agent –

at the hands of Bond. This strand is sidelined and dealt with most superficially. Though threatening Bond with death come the end of the mission, she becomes a captive of Stromberg. Reduced to this stereotypical 'damsel in distress', the gratitude to Bond for saving her life overwhelms any lingering desire for revenge and she ends up in his arms. It is doubtful that this vengeance plot could have been carried any further – it wouldn't be much of a Bond film if the final reel saw a vicious fight with a Bond girl. Nonetheless, the lingering threat adds a limited edginess to the film. See **The World is not Enough** for a development of this theme in the leading women.

GENERAL GOGOL: Head of the Russian KGB and a somewhat enigmatic figure, he warmly embraces the co-operation between Russian and British services but had ordered the assassination of the very British agent involved in this operation. However, Walter Gottell plays him with great charisma and it is difficult to imagine Gogol as a real enemy, on a par with Stromberg.

FREDERICK GRAY: As Minister of Defence, The Right Honourable Sir Frederick Gray MP will enjoy a long career (see **The Living Daylights**). His relationship with Bond is difficult to assess. Bond addresses him as 'Freddie' shortly after being introduced to him by Captain Benson. It must be assumed that they know each other and that Bond and Gray were being polite in not contradicting Benson. Still, odd that a minister (given their temporary nature) should be on first name terms with a senior secret agent.

ADMIRAL HARGREAVES: Commanding officer of the Royal Navy's submarine fleet, he is obviously involved when the *Ranger* goes missing. He closely resembles to the next M (see **Octopussy**). Are they one and the same?

THE OPPOSITION:

CARL STROMBERG: One of the richest men in the world (or as Anya terms him, 'one of the principal capitalist exploiters of the West'). Possessor of a webbed hand (see the scene where he attempts to woo the captive Anya) and a penchant for fish food, Stromberg is obsessed with underwater life. The first of the truly barking-mad Bond villains, Stromberg is not interested in status (Scaramanga, the eponymous **Man with the Golden Gun**, Blofeld in **On Her Majesty's Secret Service**), revenge (Klebb and Grant, **From Russia with Love**) or money as all other villains have been. His aim is a private kingdom under the sea along with the extermination of all other kingdoms, judged by him to be 'corrupt and decadent'.

It is Stromberg who utters the oft-quoted Bond phrase, 'I've been expecting you'.

JAWS: A giant of a man, with metal teeth and almost superhuman endurance. Contrary to popular myth he's played almost entirely straight, and is totally menacing as a result. The joint most famous Bond henchman (with *Goldfinger*'s Oddjob).

SHANDOR: Inept sidekick to Jaws. Fails to kill Bond when he has the chance, then gets, rather brutally, thrown off a rooftop in the resulting fight. Bit of a shame as his bulky figure gave him the potential of a new Oddjob.

PRINCIPAL CASTING: With this film Roger Moore finished his initial three-film contract with United Artists. This was his strongest performance so far with an almost perfect balance struck between the constant self-deprecating humour and large-scale spectacle of this big dumb action film. This was the film that separated his interpretation of Bond from that of Connery.

Barbara Bach was signed up at the last minute, having been recommended to Lewis Gilbert by Danny Reisner at United Artists. She had worked mostly in European films prior to this and her subsequent film career would include little of interest. She would appear in Guy Hamilton's *Force Ten from Navarone* (1978), also featuring *From Russia with Love*'s Robert Shaw and future M Edward Fox. It would also reunite her with Richard Kiel. She also featured in Paul McCartney's critically savaged *Give My Regards to Broad Street* (Peter Webb, 1984) alongside her then husband Ringo Starr.

Curt Jurgens was a respected German actor (and concentration camp survivor) who had worked almost exclusively in European cinema. His English language appearances included *The Battle of Britain* (Guy Hamilton, 1969) and *Nicholas and Alexandra* (Franklin J Schaffner, 1971). He was cast by director Gilbert who was hugely impressed by Jurgen's ability not to simply speak six languages, but to act in all of them too.

Walter Gottell had appeared in *From Russia with Love* and had previously worked with Curt Jurgens on *Lord Jim* (Richard Brooks,

1965). His other film roles included minor parts in *The African Queen* (John Huston, 1951) and Lewis Gilbert's own *Sink the Bismarck!* (1960). This was his first of several appearances as KGB chief, General Alexis Gogol.

Former nightclub bouncer Richard Kiel would reprise the character of Jaws in *Moonraker*. His subsequent career has included a minor role in *Pale Rider* (Clint Eastwood, 1985) and cameo appearances such as that in *Happy Gilmore* (Dennis Dugan, 1996).

DIRECTOR AND CREW: With Guy Hamilton gone (see **The Man with the Golden Gun**) Broccoli was keen to have an experienced director for what was very much a make-or-break film for the series. He hired Lewis Gilbert, who had previously been in charge of *You Only Live Twice* nearly ten years before.

The film also marked a return for production designer Ken Adam after an absence of six years. Adam managed to surpass his work on *You Only Live Twice*, mainly through use of the huge 007 stage at Pinewood, custom-built for the film. This is where the internal scenes in the *Liparus* were shot, for which Adam borrowed heavily from his earlier volcano set.

John Glen acted as editor for the second time in eight years, after his debut in *On Her Majesty's Secret Service*.

The director of photography was Claude Renoir, grandson of the famous painter Pierre Auguste, and nephew of the respected French-born filmmaker, Jean. He was cinematographer on hallucinatory camp sci-fi classic *Barbarella* (Roger Vadim, 1967) and the gritty and compelling *French Connection II* (John Frankenheimer, 1975). He provides some beautiful photography and really did justice to this production's more cinematic film stock.

Veteran screenwriter Richard Maibaum was joined by Bond newcomer Christopher Wood. Wood had previously worked with Lewis Gilbert on *Seven Nights in Japan* (1976), a romance starring Michael York. Wood had also previously written screenplays for *Confessions of a Pop Performer*, *Confessions of a Driving Instructor* and *Confessions of a Window Cleaner* – three of the *Confessions . . .* series of cheap, unerotic, unfunny 'sex comedies' starring Robin Askwith. It was a series he would return to when his Bond career was over.

MUSICAL NOTES: Like many of the film's aesthetic elements, Marvin Hamlisch's music is unashamedly contemporary. A mix of synthesised noise, funky guitar licks and orchestral swells, when it works it works wonderfully. The theme song, along with the parachute jump that immediately precedes it, is one of the most fondly remembered Bond moments.

SET PIECES: Where *The Man with the Golden Gun* had failed, *The Spy Who Loved Me* triumphed, most noticeably in set pieces. The usual scene-setting (but often subdued) pre-credit sequence was jettisoned for one centred around action and a spectacular stunt – the amazing ski jump performed by Rick Sylvester. There is no slackening of pace with a bruising rooftop fight in Cairo followed by the atmospheric showdown in the Valley of the Kings. Some set pieces are multi-faceted: the car chase on Sardinia seamlessly turning into an underwater confrontation; the near-epic battle inside the huge *Liparus* is a perfect finale, making the destruction of Atlantis rather anti-climatic.

POSITIVELY SHOCKING: There is intermittent nastiness. The underwater battle sees some rather graphic display of blood and the spearing of two men on one harpoon is rather unpleasant. Bond is displayed in an oddly sadistic light. He unreasonably drops Shandor off a rooftop, and the four shots used to dispatch Stromberg seem gratuitous – a throwback to the excessive brutality shown to Professor Dent in the edgier *Dr. No*.

MEMORABLE QUOTES:
Chalet Girl: 'But James, I need you.'
Bond: 'So does England.'

Bond: 'When in Egypt, one should always delve deeply into its treasures.'

Kalba: 'I think you will find the lady's figure hard to match.'

FASHION VICTIMS: The introduction to Bond is rife with mid-70s chalet style, from the couple spread out on a bearskin rug in front of a roaring log fire, to the violent colours of the ski-wear and the tacky digital watch with bracelet wristband. Bond has adopted the flared trouser leg in a particularly uncompromising suit, worn to the pyramids, and even applied to his evening wear. He earns a last-minute reprieve thanks to the natty uniform he wears for the last segment of the film and the incredibly cool naval regalia he wears at the Faslane briefing.

Sadly, the same cannot be said of the opposition. Stromberg occupies a twisted middle ground between the *de rigueur* Mao-collared tunic of the Bond mastermind and the pizzazz of heavies such as Largo, as seen in his cravat and patent leather brogues. This results in complete failure, compounded by the silly uniform worn by his lackies. The rakish berets are an especially unpleasant touch.

Once again the female lead is untouched by these disasters, with Barbara Bach looking lovely in both her evening gown and her fetching Red Army uniform, complete with furry hat.

PRODUCT PLACEMENT: Once again Sony features prominently. Bond is seen to travel BOAC, though association with the world's top secret agent didn't save the now defunct airline. Lotus provided the first Bond car since the Aston Martin, though their Esprit has failed to achieve the same level of fame as the earlier car. The most subtle bit of product placement comes when Bond orders Anya's drink of choice – 'Bacardi on the rocks'. Why she couldn't just order white rum and ice is a mystery.

GADGETS: Bond's rather cheap-looking digital watch with ticker-tape gets things off to a bad start but swift compensation follows with the missile firing ski-stick. The cigarette case/lighter microfilm viewer is upstaged by Anya's sleeping gas cigarettes. A visit to Q's workshop in the Secret Sevice's Egypt base gives a look at works in progress; a levitating/decapitating tray ('I want that ready for Akmed's tea party'), a hookah-cum-machine-gun and an anti-personnel spike built into a camel saddle.

The film features the first gadget-laden vehicle since *You Only Live Twice*'s Little Nelly, a gadget-packed Lotus that is an indisputable series highlight. The car features rear firing cement guns (to blind pursuers) and becomes a submersible, armed with torpedoes, anti-aircraft missiles, an oil slick 'smokescreen' and explosive mines.

Q provides another means of transport – a 'wet-bike' for the short journey to Atlantis that, in a similar way to Little Nelly, was assembled from parts transported in a large hold-all. Then a new invention, this sit-down jet-ski is now commonplace at many beach resorts.

SOURCE TO SCREEN: On the instruction of Ian Fleming, no part of his novel, *The Spy Who Loved Me* could be used in a film utilising its title. By 1977, this condition was largely irrelevant; no Bond film had adhered closely to its source novel's plot since *On Her Majesty's Secret Service* in 1969. Even if Eon had been allowed to use Fleming's *Spy*, it's doubtful they would have done given the nature of its narrative. Both an anomaly within Fleming's canon and an intriguing literary experiment

The Aston Martin has been a classic Bond motif from *Goldfinger*'s DB5 (1964, *right*) to the Volante of *The Living Daylights* (1987, *below*)

B549 WUU

Left Sean Connery (1962–67, 1971)

Below left David Niven (1967)

Below right George Lazenby (1969)

Left Roger Moore
(1973–85)

Below left Timothy
Dalton (1987–89)

Below right Pierce
Brosnan (1995–)

Left Bernard Lee,
Fleming's admirable
Admiral, M

Below left Judi Dench, a
new era for Bond's boss

Below right Desmond
Llewelyn as Q, Roger
Moore and a very
expensive egg in
Octopussy (1983)

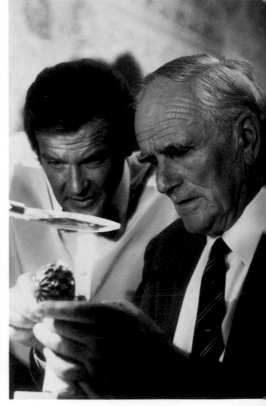

Right Bond's most
persistent adversary,
Ernst Stavro Blofeld, as
played by Telly Savalas
in *On Her Majesty's
Secret Service* (1969)

Below Mr and Mrs
Bond on their wedding
day

Above left Terence Young – 'He really was James Bond' – during the making of *Thunderball* (1965)

Above right Guy Hamilton directs Sean Connery in *Goldfinger* (1964), the first of his four Bond films as director

Right Lewis Gilbert was responsible for the most iconic screen Bonds: *You Only Live Twice, The Spy Who Loved Me* and *Moonraker*

Director John Glen *(left)* on the set of the last of his five directorial efforts, *Licence to Kill* (1989), with producers Michael G Wilson and Albert R 'Cubby' Broccoli

The man who started it all: Ian Fleming with Ursula Andress on the set of *Dr. No* (1962)

Ken Adam's cavernous set design for *You Only Live Twice* (1967)

... not dissimilar to that he provided for *The Spy Who Loved Me* (1977)

on his part; the novel (published in 1962) is told in the first person by a French–Canadian girl, Vivien Michel, who is in temporary charge of a motel. Two gangsters – Slugsy and Horror – force their way into the building and demand that she makes them food. After Vivienne refuses his unsubtle advances, Slugsy attempts to rape her. It is only now, over halfway through the novel, that Bond himself enters the story. On his way back to Britain after completing an assignment in Toronto, Bond's car has developed a flat tyre and he is looking for an opportunity to fix it. He rescues Vivienne from the two hoods (who were, it turns out, planning to frame Vivienne for setting fire to the motel as part of an insurance scam organised by the motel's owner) and a four-way gun battle takes place. Bond and Vivienne kill their opponents and later they make love, but Bond leaves before she wakes up. The book ends with Vivienne vowing never to forget 'the spy who loved me'.

Despite Fleming's instructions, two points from his story are tangentially used in the picture's screenplay. The metal-capped teeth of Stromberg's henchman, Jaws, are inherited from the novel's villain, Horror, and an incident from the novel where Vivienne finds Horror hiding in her wardrobe was adapted into a similar moment: Anya finds Jaws in her wardrobe aboard the Orient Express.

Aside from these minor details, the screenplay is entirely the creation of the screenwriters Richard Maibaum and Christopher Wood – although it owes a great deal to Roald Dahl's script for Lewis Gilbert's previous Bond picture, *You Only Live Twice*. Before Maibaum and Wood were brought on board, several other writers were asked to develop plots around Fleming's title. Most intriguingly, Anthony Burgess, a prolific novelist whose most famous work is *A Clockwork Orange*, worked on an avowedly political plot with a group of young anarchist terrorists as the villains. Like Stromberg in the finished film, they plan to destroy the world because they are disgusted with it. Unlike him they don't plan to spare themselves the death of the rest of the human race. Tinged with elements of magic realism, and the writer's commonly used nihilism, the Burgess plot was ultimately rejected by Eon.

Due to the massive differences between the film and Fleming's original novel a tie-in, paperback novelisation of the film script was published by Panther books under the title *James Bond, The Spy Who Loved Me*.

Published by the time of the film's release, and available in the UK for a princely 75 pence, it was written by primary screenwriter Christopher Wood in a chatty, readable style that does a reasonable job of impersonating Fleming's own prose. The novelisation is interesting because it represents a slightly early draft of the screenplay than the one eventually filmed. Anya Amasova's superior is SMERSH head, Colonel-General Nikitin (a character from Fleming's novel *From Russia with Love*), not the original creation, Alexis Gogol. Stromberg's Christian name is Sigmund, not Carl, and Jaws dies in the shark pool at the end (as arguably he should have done in the film) rather than escaping. In a particularly nasty bit of almost pornographic violence, Bond leaves the giant's face stuck (thanks to his metal teeth) to the magnet as he thrashes around in the water. Desperate to free himself from this hold he does some damage to his own face before finally succumbing to the great white sharks circling around him. The 'Keeping the British end up!' finale of the film is also eschewed in favour a more subtle final scene of Bond and Anya enjoying breakfast.

IN THE REAL WORLD: As with other Bond films, the plot of *The Spy Who Loved Me* was a development of contemporary fears given an improbable twist. The outbreak of a mutually destructive war between Russia and America, sparked by a third party, is very close to the story of *You Only Live Twice*, but as opposed to the rather vague threat of war – never clearly conventional or nuclear – here we have a genuinely apocalyptic vision of nuclear destruction caused by both countries' hair-trigger responses to any threat. Stromberg is certain that the result of the war would be global, total annihilation.

More positively, this film features détente in action, instead of the earlier vision of the superpowers as totally unco-operative. It is rather anachronistic to see this symbolised by Russo–British partnership, with the US largely sidelined (though the American sub captain seems quite happy to have a KGB agent aboard) though ultimately Russia and America are still the key powers – Stromberg's targets are New York and Moscow. Bond's participation is an attempt to prove that Britain could still be a major player.

CULTURE VULTURE: Anya's music-box communicator plays 'Lara's Theme' from *Doctor Zhivago* (David Lean, 1965) – strange, given that Lean's film was banned in the Soviet Union at this time. Another Lean reference is the use of the theme to *Lawrence of Arabia* (1962), played as Bond and Anya walk across the sand dunes to the oasis. The troublesome journey of a decrepit van across the desert seems to be a reference to the John Mills-starring, lager-advertising war-film, *Ice Cold in Alex* (J Lee Thompson, 1958).

Stromberg's aquarium is reminiscent of that owned by *Doctor No*.

The name *Jaws* was also the title of the 1975 shark-attack film directed by Steven Spielberg.

Though the name *Ranger* appears to be without significance, *Potemkin* was the name of a warship that played a key role in the Russian Revolution of 1905. It was made cinematically famous in the silent masterpiece, *Battleship Potemkin* (Sergei Eisenstein, 1925). USS *Wayne* shares the name of renowned Western actor John Wayne. Appropriately enough, the *Wayne* acts as the cavalry, coming to the rescue in the destruction of the *Liparus* and of Atlantis (the former named for an obscure figure in Greek mythology involved in the settling of the Aeolian Islands, now known as the Lipari, the second for a mythical city, that was either destroyed in a cataclysm or survives under the sea, depending which conspiracy theorist you believe).

CRITICS: Nell Myers of the *Morning Star* was feeling generous: 'audiences clap and cheer after each number' she observed on 8 July 1977, calling Moore's Bond 'a moderately funny acceptable joke'. She was prepared to go further, praising Claude Renoir's photography and the 'lovely' Curt Jurgens – a far cry from Nina Hibbin's polemic rage of the early 60s. In the *Sunday Telegraph* of 10 July, Tom Hutchinson called *Spy* 'the tenth and one of the best' of the series. 'The action is pushed to the limits of humorous outrage by director Lewis Gilbert'.

Others were less kind: 'Some day, around 2001 perhaps, the NFT is going to run a retrospective of Bond films,' wrote the *Sunday Times*' Alan Brien on 10 July. 'A new generation will stare aghast at these grandiose, megaloptic visions,' he continued. Of the film he thought little, disliking its 'feeble *Carry On*-style puns' and its 'useless opulence, indiscriminate slaughter, callous cynicism [and] fear and hatred of any independent female'. Interestingly, his review completely fails to consider the idea that the Bond series could still be running in 2001; the entire piece is based on the notion that by that far distant date, Bond would be a cultural curio. In its own way, Brien's review is the single most objectively wrong review of a Bond film ever written.

The NFT's Bond retrospective, by the way, was in 1999.

BOX OFFICE: *The Spy Who Loved Me*'s worldwide grosses exceeded $185 million, a massive increase on *The Man with the Golden Gun*. This more than justified the increased expenditure and Broccoli's hard-fought battle to both keep control of the series and his determination to keep it going.

AWARDS: Although nominated for three Academy Awards (for Ken Adam's set, Marvin Hamlisch's score and Hamlisch and Sayer's theme song), two BAFTAs (for production design and score) and one Golden Globe (for the score), *The Spy Who Loved Me* failed to win anything.

MARTINIS, GIRLS AND GUNS: Again, Bond is seen with a pretty girl as the film begins and he later goes on to score with the eponymous Major Amasova. In between he spends the night at Sheikh Hosein's tent with the girl Hosein 'offers' him.

Anya knows enough of 007's history to order a vodka Martini, shaken not stirred. Odd, given that he's not had one since *On Her Majesty's Secret Service*. Maybe the KGB file is out of date. Furthermore, maybe it's Anya who gets him back on them.

As far his licence to kill goes, Bond despatches fourteen. Anya's lover Sergei in the pre-credits sequence, the bald lummox Shandor (pushed off a building), three in Jaws's car, the ravishing Naomi (whose helicopter he blows out of the sky), two divers working for Stromberg (the submarine pilots are blown up by Anya), a further two Stromberg employees skewered on a single harpoon, three machine-gunnings in the battle for the *Liparus*, and Stromberg himself – shot four times just to make sure. He is additionally responsible for the dozen or so deaths caused when he blows Stromberg's control room open, but it would be impossible to arrive at an exact number.

THE LAST WORD: 'Keeping the British end up, Sir!' A slick, pacy 'greatest hits' package which reuses aspects of many previous Bond films, but has the sense to do so with pace and style, *The Spy Who Loved Me* is a joy. It's visually inventive, with atmospheric lighting and sharp cinematography providing a glossy flair that sets it far apart from any other Bond film of the 70s. The chase through the darkened pyramids is one of the best lit, directed, edited and photographed in any Bond picture. It features a good cast of typical Bond characters, a very wide selection of impressive stunt and action scenes and a script that keeps the film coherent and enjoyable.

GIRLS	27
MARTINIS	6
DEATHS	111

Sexism? 'Dink, say goodbye to Felix . . . man talk.'

Despite this – the most chauvinist line to appear in a Bond film so far – the series is by and large innocent of the charges of sexism frequently levelled against it.

The basic substance of such accusations comes in the form of the stereotypical helpless Bond girl, incompetent in the field and existing solely as an attractive trophy for Bond at the mission's end. A 'trophy' he will have jettisoned by the next mission in favour of an identical brainless beauty.

It must be said that these claims do have *some* ground. Mary Goodnight (*The Man with the Golden Gun*) and Stacey Sutton (*A View to a Kill*) are both shallow incompetents whose misadventures cause Bond no end of troubles and whose ultimate purpose is to provide an attractive face. It is no coincidence that both characters feature in two exceptionally boring Bond films of the lowest quality.

In the majority of the series there is a range of developed female characters whose relationships with Bond provide much of interest. The end result is perhaps not as noble as this makes it sound. A lot of the time the 'interest' comes from an ambiguous female character being 'charmed' by Bond to join the side of good; Tania (*From Russia With Love*), Tiffany (*Diamonds Are Forever*) and Octopussy to name but three. The 'girls' come from the same twilight world as Bond, with similarly dark backgrounds making them intriguing, if not wholly original.

There are also the 'bad girls', whose resistance to Bond's charm has become a stereotype in itself. That these sexually predatory, independent-minded women invariably meet a sticky end could be regarded as the series' most overtly sexist message – were it not for the fact that they are villains, allied with an evil scheme and therefore, in this fantasy world, deserving of punishment for their failure to repent. The only exception here is May Day (*A View to a Kill*) whose death counts as noble sacrifice.

Ultimately, Bond is the hero and so female characters do not necessarily get the prominence some would like. On several occasions the female lead is used simply to give Bond impetus to defeat the villain in the film's climax. However, more frequently, the 'helpless' Bond girl is an important asset to Bond, possessing a vital skill (*Moonraker, Licence to Kill, GoldenEye, The World Is Not Enough*), providing assistance or important resources (*Goldfinger, You Only Live Twice, For Your Eyes Only, Octopussy*) being on a par with Bond professionally (*The Spy Who Loved Me, Tomorrow Never Dies*) or even, in a reversal of traditional expectations, saving his life (*From Russia With Love, Thunderball, On Her Majesty's Secret Service, GoldenEye*). In *The World Is Not Enough* the prime candidate for the role of Bond girl is revealed to be the villain of the piece.

Bond's personal attitude, as M points out in *GoldenEye*, is that of a 'sexist, misogynist dinosaur'. The films have treated his 'Bond girls' much better than this, better than credited by popular opinion, better than Fleming did the female characters in his books and better than many female characters are presented in other 'action adventure' films of today.

Moonraker (1979)

Produced by Albert R Broccoli
Executive Producer: Michael G Wilson
Screenplay by Christopher Wood
Director of Photography: Jean Tournier
Music composed and conducted by John Barry
Title song lyrics by Don Black
Title song sung by Shirley Bassey
Directed by Lewis Gilbert

PRINCIPAL CAST: Roger Moore (*James Bond*), Lois Chiles (*Holly Goodhead*), Michel Lonsdale (*Drax*), Richard Kiel (*Jaws*), Corinne Clery (*Corinne Dufour*), Bernard Lee (*M*), Geoffrey Keen (*Frederick Gray*), Desmond Llewelyn (*Q*), Lois Maxwell (*Moneypenny*), Toshirô Suga (*Chang*), Emily Bolton (*Manuela*), Blanche Ravalec (*Dolly*), Irka Bochenko (*Blonde Beauty*), Michael Marshall (*Colonel Scott*), Leila Shenna (*Hostess Private Jet*), Anne Lonnberg (*Museum Guide*), Jean Pierre Castaldi (*Pilot Private Jet*), Walter Gotell (*General Gogol*), Douglas Lambert (*Mission Control Director*), Arthur Howard (*Cavendish*), Alfie Bass (*Consumptive Italian*), Brian Keith (*US Shuttle Captain*), George Birt (*Captain Boeing 747*), Kim Fortune (*RAF Officer*), Lizzie Warville (*Russian Girl*), Nicholas Arbez (*Drax's Boy*), Guy Di Rigo (*Ambulance Man*), Chris Dillinger (*Drax's Technician*), Claude Carliez (*Gondolier*), Georges Beller (*Drax's Technician*), Denis Seurat (*Officer Boeing 747*), Chichinou Kaeppler, Christina Hui, Françoise Gayat, Nicaise Jean Louis, Catherine Serre, Béatrice Libert (*Drax's Girls*).

PRE-CREDITS AND TITLES: A Moonraker space shuttle, being transported from the US to the UK on top of a Boeing 747, is stolen by two men in slacks. Informed of this, M immediately sends for 007, whom we see canoodling with a girl on board a small aeroplane. A small group of thugs, who include Jaws, then throw him out of the plane, and after a struggle in freefall he manages to pull the parachute from one of his assailants and float gently to the ground. An effective sequence spoiled by 'comedy' music, the presence of Jaws (already tiresome) and its resemblance to the far superior opening of *The Spy Who Loved Me*. The title sequence is distinctly unmemorable too, although Shirley Bassey's theme song, lush and lyrical, is the best of those she performed for the series.

SUMMARY: Industrialist Hugo Drax arranges for the theft of a Moonraker shuttle that his company built for the American government. He does this because one of the six Moonrakers he had built for his own purposes has developed a fault. He needs six Moonrakers because he has built a huge orbiting space station to which he is going to take a specially selected handful of the 'elite' of mankind. Once ensconced there he is going to wipe out the population of the Earth using poison developed from orchids. He and his minions will then return to the 'cleansed' planet to begin a new life. Bond, assisted by a CIA agent with NASA training, follows Drax across the globe and then into space, preventing his intended apocalypse, and ultimately killing him. Sounds a bit like *The Spy Who Loved Me*, doesn't it? It is. Almost everything in this film is like *The Spy Who Loved Me*, except not actually good.

UNIVERSAL EXPORTS:

BOND, JAMES BOND: Bond is currently drinking Bollinger 69, and has returned to that old standby, the vodka Martini. He displays expertise in skydiving and seems quite at home on a space station. His naval expertise covers both hi-tech speedboats and Venetian gondolas.

In this film Bond is at his most patronising towards women (with the possible exception of his 'man-talk' line in *Goldfinger*). He is supercilious and borderline rude.

Once again Bond is world-famous, with Drax commenting on his reputation preceding him. Maybe Stromberg (see **The Spy Who Loved Me**) missed the meeting of the world villains' club where Bond's photo was passed around.

M: Yet again, M seems willing to travel all over the world at a moment's notice. Once more, he has Q and Moneypenny in tow, this time travelling to the South American interior. Strangely he also travels with Bond (and incredibly, the Minister of Defence) to investigate an accused criminal in person. Even given Bond's story of deadly nerve gas, it is difficult to imagine these senior figures travelling to a foreign country to investigate a private lab – which doesn't even belong to a British citizen.

MONEYPENNY: Reduced again to the background role she performed in *The Spy Who Loved Me*, she has seemingly been demoted to receptionist.

Q: Another decent rack of air miles for Major Boothroyd. This time, after aiding with Bond's initial briefing, he is shipped out to South America to provide technical support to the rainforest excursion.

OHMSS: The Secret Service apparently has another base (again complete with its own Q-branch) somewhere in South America – presumably Brazil, although the film doesn't specify.

ALLIES:

HOLLY GOODHEAD: Alumna of Vasser College, NASA astronaut and CIA agent, Holly was assigned to infiltrate Drax's organisation. It must be said that she has not done a great job given that Drax has been able to construct an entire space station and formulate a potent nerve-gas with none of these activities coming to her attention. Despite this there is no need for her to be treated as badly as she is by Bond, and it is entirely forgivable that she avoids working with him for as long as possible.

Another attempt to construct a strong female character which once again falls down at the final hurdle, following the requirement that every Bond film end with the 'Bond girl' melting in the agent's arms. There is something particularly likeable about Holly, perhaps her attempt to slap Bond sardonically down at every opportunity

CORINNE DUFOUR: Pilot employed by Drax who becomes a little more involved with Bond than is healthy. He seduces her and uses her to get access to the villain's personal safe. In an exceptionally nasty sequence Drax shows his displeasure by having his Doberman dogs chase her down.

FREDERICK GRAY: Bond and Gray's relationship has changed since *The Spy Who Loved Me*, with Bond now addressing him as 'Minister' rather than 'Freddie', while at one point Gray describes Bond to M as 'your man', almost as if he doesn't know him. Maybe they've fallen out?

THE OPPOSITION:

HUGO DRAX: A sinister French industrialist played with icy relish by Michael Lonsdale, despite the inadequacies of the script. Drax isn't a subtle man: during his first meeting with Bond he may as well jump up and down shouting 'I'm the villain! Don't you see?' but he gets a lot closer to succeeding than most of Bond's foes. He likes tea and cucumber sandwiches, has enough money to import buildings and pheasants into California to allow him to live the life of a pseudo-country squire, and has elegant, if chintzy, taste in gentlemen's outdoor clothing. He has trained his dogs to hunt and kill people as well. Which is charming. He gets the script's best lines – all five of them.

Another villain in the Stromberg School (see **The Spy Who Loved Me**), he is utterly bonkers. A serious megalomaniac with a definite Hitler complex, his plans for world domination are firmly rooted in eugenics.

CHANG: Drax's martial arts expert hitman, he is bumped off by Bond in Venice, necessitating the hiring of:

JAWS: The former employee of Karl Stromberg returns, initially, it seems, out to kill Bond for reasons of his own. He's later employed by Drax for the same job. Towards the end of the film Jaws falls in love with buxom, pigtailed, comically short Dolly, forming the world's oddest couple. When he realises that neither he nor she will fit into Drax's eugenically 'perfect' world, he turns against his master.

Bizarrely Jaws's change of heart doesn't stop at Drax's defeat. Once Drax has been beaten, Jaws cheerfully tries to save Bond's life, despite having been trying to kill 007 minutes before. If his attacks on Bond are financially motivated rather than personal, why does he try to murder him in the pre-credits sequence?

A dreary second outing for the character, packed with bad comedy antics and dreadful mugging from Richard Kiel. Quite how Jaws and Dolly survive the destruction of Drax's space station is unclear.

PRINCIPAL CASTING: Anglo-French actor Michael Lonsdale works mainly in European cinema. Before *Moonraker* his English-speaking roles included parts in *The Trial* (Orson Welles, 1962) and *The Day of the Jackal* (Fred Zinnemann, 1973). He has also appeared in *Chariots of Fire* (Hugh Hudson, 1981) alongside Sean Connery in *The Name of the Rose* (Jean Jacques Annaud, 1986) and in *Ronin* (John Frankenheimer, 1998) in which he appeared with fellow Bond villains, Jonathan Pryce and Sean Bean. Lonsdale reportedly accepted the role of Drax, due to its being the kind of part rarely – if ever – available in French cinema.

Lois Chiles had been approached to play Anya in *The Spy Who Loved Me*, but was unavailable. Her agent claimed she was in temporary retirement, when in fact she was studying acting in New York. One of the first of the model-turned-actress breed now common in screen acting, she had appeared in *The Way We Were* (Sydney Pollack, 1973) and

Death on the Nile (John Guillermin, 1978) but had been stung by critics who suggested that she was little more than set decoration and a clothes-hanger. Leaving her career behind to study for a while was her way of proving them wrong. She was cast by Lewis Gilbert after a chance encounter on a plane. After *Moonraker*, she appeared in the long-running TV super-soap *Dallas* and movie *Broadcast News* (James L Brooks, 1987). She also had a cameo role in Bond spoof *Austin Powers: International Man of Mystery* (Jay Roach, 1997).

DIRECTOR AND CREW: After the success of *The Spy Who Loved Me*, as much of the crew (as well as much of the plot) as possible were retained for its successor. This included director Lewis Gilbert, screenwriter Christopher Wood, 2nd unit director/editor John Glen and production designer, Ken Adam. That more crew than this could not be retained was due to the film's production base in France, and its status as an Anglo-French co-production (galloping inflation in 1978–79 made the cost of filming in England prohibitively high). Thus the minor posts were filled with local talent rather than familiar faces from the series' Pinewood outings. This was the first Bond film not to be made at Pinewood studios, and the last until *Licence To Kill*. Since 1989 only one Bond picture (*The World Is Not Enough*) has been shot at the series' spiritual home.

This was to be director Lewis Gilbert's final Bond film; after finishing work on this, his third in the series, he would go on to further acclaimed work. He directed *Educating Rita* (1983) for which he won a BAFTA award for best film (actor Michael Caine received an Oscar nomination), and *Shirley Valentine* (1989) for which star Pauline Collins was Oscar-nominated. The now octogenarian Gilbert continues to work, directing *Before You Go*, featuring John Hannah and Julie Waters, released in June 2002.

Despite the lacklustre nature of this picture, Gilbert's contribution to the Bond series is enormous. His three instalments are all among its highest earners, and his version of the character – a superman repeatedly quipping bad puns and innuendos as he saves the world from stateless, sexless maniacs hell-bent on Armageddon – is the one most easily recognised by the public. For his first two pictures at least Gilbert showed an aptitude for staging and executing elaborate set pieces in exotic locations and pushing the envelope of what was technically possible; developing a version of the Bond picture more flippant, but with higher stakes than that presented before.

FASHION VICTIMS: Bond starts off in a pair of slacks accompanied by a double-breasted navy jacket over a white polo neck. This is a particularly vile outfit that overshadows the rest of the film's sartorial mediocrity. Drax is, like many megalomaniac Bond villains, a fan of beige tunics, and has dressed his work force in nasty primary-colour, polyester jumpsuits.

SET PIECES: The free-falling opening is impressively handled by stuntmen BJ Worth and Jake Lombard, but is ruined all the same (see **PRE-CREDITS AND TITLES**). The cable-car fight, which features some astounding stunt work from the great Richard Graydon, is rendered laughable by terrible back projection. The sequence with the Gondola and the double-taking pigeon is neither funny nor thrilling. Bond's fight with a rubber snake is more amusing, but for all the wrong reasons. The boat chase, during which we hear John Barry's '007 theme' is really good, but rather spoiled by its 'comedy' ending and yet more substandard back projection while the final space encounter is slow and marred by a reliance on ropy special effects; in fact the only bit of tension in the whole film comes when Bond shoots Drax's poisonous globes out of the sky. Shame it was done so much better in *Star Wars*. As clumsy an attempt at bandwagon-jumping as *The Man with the Golden Gun*.

MEMORABLE QUOTES:

Drax (to Bond): 'Your country's one indisputable contribution to Western civilisation – afternoon tea. Can I press you to a cucumber sandwich?'

Drax: 'Look after Mr Bond, see that some harm comes to him.'

Drax: 'James Bond. You appear with the tedious inevitability of an unloved season.'

GADGETS: The technology really goes into overdrive here, with a Gondola that transforms into a hovercraft, the first incarnation of the Q-boat (see **The World is not Enough**) armed with mines, homing torpedoes and a roof that converts into a hangglider, and a dart-firing, wrist-mounted gun thing (the first piece of 00 Branch standard issue kit since *From Russia with Love*'s attaché case), all of which are provided by Q-branch. M's office has a computer screen behind one of its paintings, and Bond has an x-ray cigarette case (for unlocking safes, or sneaking a peek through a woman's undergarments) and a natty micro-camera which, bizarrely, has his code number on it.

Q's South American lab is seen to be testing a machine gun disguised as a sleeping Mexican peasant and a laser that looks suspiciously similar to that employed by Drax's space patrol. Is Q doing a bit of moonlighting?

We also get a glimpse of CIA-issue gadgets as well, courtesy of Holly Goodhead. A dart-firing diary, a highly flammable perfume spray, a radio transmitter built into a handbag and a pen with extendable stiletto point which Bond swipes and which is greatly useful in his epic snake battle.

All this is overwhelmed by the technology possessed by Drax. He has no less than six 'Moonraker' shuttles, one with a built-in laser; he is also the proud owner of a space station with a radar-jamming system and, as pointed out by a contemporary *New Scientist* article, correctly generated artificial gravity (through its rotation). Fortunately the United States has several platoons of space marines on constant standby at Vandenburg airbase.

CULTURE VULTURE: It is worth emphasising the impact of *Star Wars* (George Lucas, 1977) on not only genre pictures but on the movie-making industry as a whole. Though *Star Wars'* forebears were not so much Bond as Westerns, war films and the Japanese cinema of Akira Kurosawa, almost in spite of itself it began the trend towards big budget action films designed to take hundred of millions at the box office. Many of these would owe a great debt to Bond, the pioneer of the action-dominated adventure genre. A victim of its own success, the Bond series would have a hard time competing against these spiritual heirs.

There are a couple of musical references. The keypad on Drax's lab has, as its access code, the distinct motif of John Williams's score for *Close Encounters of the Third Kind* (Steven Spielberg, 1977). Bond gallops across the South American plains to Elmer Bernstein's rousing score for *The Magnificent Seven* (John Sturges, 1960).

IN THE REAL WORLD: The intention with *Moonraker* was for its release to coincide with the launch of the USA's first reusable space vehicle, the Space Shuttle, in 1979. Technical problems were to set the programme back and the first operational Space Shuttle flight, made by *Columbia*, did not actually take place until 1982. While the film correctly depicted the way in which shuttles were transported over long distances – piggyback on a 747 – they were not in reality transported this way while fully fuelled. Additionally it is difficult to say why a shuttle was being transported to the British Isles in the first place, given the lack of a British space programme, or even a pad from where it could be launched.

SOURCE TO SCREEN: Christopher Wood's screenplay, while nominally based on Fleming, retains only the names of its villain, and of the eponymous space vehicle. In the book, Sir Hugo Drax, Liverpudlian industrialist, has used his own funds to build a long-range missile to be used for Britain's defence. James Bond is assigned to investigate the murder of a Ministry of Supply security expert at the missile site. He discovers that Drax is, in fact, a Nazi terrorist named Graf Hugo von der Drache and has been posing as an Englishman since the end of World War Two (the novel had been published in 1955). He intends to destroy London with a Soviet-supplied atomic device mounted on Moonraker. Bond redirects the missile to destroy the Russian submarine on which Drax had been attempting to escape.

The true source of the film can be found in Lewis Gilbert's previous two Bond films, *You Only Live Twice* and, especially, *The Spy Who Loved Me* on which Christopher Wood had also worked.

The pre-credit sequence is a carbon copy of that to *The Spy Who Loved Me*; the villain's plot is initiated, M is informed, Bond's presence is requested, Bond is seen with a beautiful girl (who turns out to be treacherous), Bond is attacked and escapes by the medium of an impressive stunt sequence. The main plot is little better. A fabulously wealthy madman sets out to destroy the human race with the aim of replacing it with a worthier civilisation, bred in an outlandish location. The main difference is in the simplification of the story. Stromberg's plan hinges on the irony of the superpowers destroying themselves through misdirection (itself very similar to *You Only Live Twice*). Drax simply intends to gas everyone.

Moonraker also draws heavily on 1965's *Thunderball*. The intervention of massed American forces takes place at the end of both films (and also features heavily in *The Spy Who Loved Me*, though this is an international force). The centrifuge scene is very similar to the 'rack' at Shrublands health farm and the carnival in Rio is (less surprisingly) very much like that which takes place in Nassau. There is also a homage to the bridge over the deadly piranha pool in *You Only Live Twice* (Bond carefully steps around Drax's snake pool only to be flipped in by a trick stone). However, while this last scene is a deliberate reference by the production designer and director of the earlier film, when it comes to *Thunderball* and *The Spy Who Loved Me*, one cannot help but get the feeling that this film cannibalises its predecessors.

Christopher Wood turned his own script into a mass market paperback novella (*James Bond and Moonraker*) sold to publicise and accompany the film. Although he largely follows both the spirit and the letter of his own screenplay, Jaws is absent from the adaptation of the events in the pre-credits sequence and many later scenes, and is not so much of a buffoon as presented onscreen.

MUSICAL NOTES: Once again Broccoli engaged the services of the series' most frequent composer, John Barry, who provides another top-notch score. There is also a strangely enjoyable disco remix of the title song runs over the credits.

BOX OFFICE: *Moonraker* took a little over $200 million, with US admissions being a startlingly impressive 25.5 million people. The picture's receipts were bolstered by the success of *The Spy Who Loved Me*, and *Star Wars*' whetting of the movie-going public's appetite for space opera.

AWARDS: A nomination for the 1980 Academy Award for Best Effects, Visual Effects (for John Evans, Derek Meddings and Paul Wilson).

CRITICS: Writing in the *Evening Standard* of 28 June 1979, Alexander Walker called *Moonraker* 'the biggest and most expensive box of tricks' of the series and 'as before, only more so'. He was generally indulgent to the film, praising Jean Tournier's photography, Maurice Binder's titles and the way Roger Moore 'got exactly the right measure of the part'. In the *Finanical Times* of the same day, Nigel Andrews found that 'the present movie bears hardly the skeleton of a resemblance' to Fleming's novel of the same name. Andrews felt he detected 'a gallic influence' which lifted '*Moonraker* one notch of refinement higher than its predecessors'. The unnamed reviewer of the *Daily Telegraph* was less swayed by the film's Anglo-French status, finding it 'a fascinating success of pitiful ambition, no sensitivity and altogether too much wet humour ...' Susan Lardner of the *New Yorker*, writing on 9 July, was also unimpressed. '*Moonraker* is a traditional, not to say, repetitious entry in the ranks', she complained, and compared the Broccoli series to the way Roman dictators kept order by organising lavish amphiteatrical slaughters. On 27 June *Variety*'s Har said of the picture, 'more than ever producer ... and director ... seem to be strapped for fresh thrills, falling back on formula'. There was approval for Moore and the series' longevity, but *Moonraker* was compared unfavourably with *The Spy Who Loved Me* and *Goldfinger* all the same.

PRODUCT PLACEMENT: In the most blatant examples of product placement in the entire series, the ambulance carrying Bond and Holly up a hill passes a series of billboards containing hugely visible adverts for various products such as 7up, Seiko and Marlboro which, coincidentally, also appear at other points in the film. Dr Goodhead has a packet of Marlboro cigarettes in her desk drawer, Bond sports a thoroughly tacky Seiko watch and the cable-car station demolished by Jaws is plastered by adverts for 7up. A sight gag involving one of the fake ambulancemen being wedged through one of these billboards leads to a lingering shot of a British Airways advertisement. Bond, however, flies Air France.

MARTINIS, GIRLS AND GUNS: Despite Bond's thoroughly unpleasant attitude he attracts an awful lot of female attention, managing to bed Colleen, his Secret Service contact in Rio and the lovely Dr Goodhead herself. In the second instance he even gets himself served a Martini.

Another fourteen deaths are added to his total so far: the silly-hatted pilot in the pre-credit sequence, Drax's tree-based sniper, the knife-thrower in the coffin, Chang, one of the fake ambulancemen, eight of the pursuers on the Amazon and finally Drax himself. For reasons of fairness the following have been discounted: the female passenger on the pre-credit plane (no idea what happens to her), the scientists in Drax's lab (it's not Bond's fault they're clumsy) and the occupants of Jaws's boat (if he survives, so might they).

THE LAST WORD: 'On behalf of the British Government, I apologise.' There is a school of *Moonraker* apologists. These people believe that *Moonraker* is fun. They believe that people who don't like *Moonraker* are taking the whole Bond thing too seriously. These people are quite simply wrong. It's not fun – it's *dull*. It's a lazy travelogue through boringly shot locations culminating in some slightly-below-par space work. Given his previous experience of writing formula comedies, it is perhaps unsurprising that screenwriter Christopher Wood's second Bond film is also unrelentingly formulaic – a soulless, wretched, sparkle-free retread of his first – but it is disappointing nonetheless. *Moonraker*'s set pieces lack excitement and verve and there's not one laugh-out-loud joke. Its heroine is anonymous, its villain is wasted and its hero is visibly bored. *Moonraker* is ghastly, painful viewing.

GIRLS	30
MARTINIS	7
DEATHS	125

For Your Eyes Only (1981)

Produced by Albert R Broccoli
Executive Producer: Michael G Wilson
Screenplay by Richard Maibaum & Michael G Wilson
Director of Photography: Alan Hume
Music by Bill Conti
Title song performed by Sheena Easton
Lyrics by Michael Leeson
Production designed by Peter Lamont
Directed by John Glen

PRINCIPAL CAST: Roger Moore (*James Bond*), Carole Bouquet (*Melina*), Topol (*Columbo*), Lynn-Holly Johnson (*Bibi*), Julian Glover (*Kristatos*), Cassandra Harris (*Lisl*), Jill Bennett (*Brink*), Michael Gothard (*Locque*), John Wyman (*Kriegler*), Jack Hedley (*Havelock*), Lois Maxwell (*Moneypenny*), Desmond Llewelyn (*Q*), Geoffrey Keen (*Minister of Defence*), Walter Gotell (*General Gogol*), James Villiers (*Tanner*), John Moreno (*Ferrara*), Charles Dance (*Claus*), Paul Angelis (*Karageorge*), Toby Robins (*Iona Havelock*), Jack Klaff (*Apostis*), Alkis Kritikos (*Santos*), Stag Theodore (*Nikos*), Stefan Kalipha (*Gonzales*), Graham Crowden (*First Sea Lord*), Noel Johnson (*Vice Admiral*), William Hoyland (*McGregor*), Paul Brooke (*Bunky*), Eva Reuber-Staier (*Rublevich*), Fred Bryant (*Vicar*), Robbin Young (*Girl in Flower Shop*), Graham Hawkes (*Mantis Man*), John Wells (*Denis*), Janet Brown (*The Prime Minister*).

SIGNIFICANT UNCREDITED CAST: John Hollis (*Blofeld – Body*), Peter Marrinker (*Blofeld – Voice*), Jeremy Bulloch (*Smithers*).

PRE-CREDITS AND TITLES: Visiting his wife's grave, Bond is interrupted by a call to arms, and boards a helicopter bearing the Universal Exports Logo. Shortly after take-off, his pilot is electrocuted, and a sinister voice fills the helicopter. Blofeld. We see the bald, cat-stroking maniac taunting Bond from a wheelchair as he operates the aircraft by remote control. The plan is to humiliate 007 before killing him. Fighting his way onto the outside of the speeding chopper, Bond climbs inside the front and disconnects the remote control. He seeks out Blofeld, and picks up the former SPECTRE chief's wheelchair with the helicopter's landing skids. Despite Blofeld's protests Bond drops him down a chimney stack to his death, and Tracy is revenged at last. Tightly edited, backed with terrific wah-wah guitar noises and rich in character impact (listen to the way Bond says 'It always is' after the priest has told him that the situation that requires his presence is an emergency). This is great stuff, setting up the picture's themes (revenge, and the idea of Bond as an ageing figure, with a painful past) while being roaringly enjoyable. Full marks.

SUMMARY: A British spy ship is sunk off the coast of communist Albania. On board is an ATAC (Automatic Targeting Attack Communicator), a device used to direct the Polaris missiles on British nuclear submarines. After the initial British salvage team (led by Sir Timothy Havelock and his wife) is murdered, Bond is sent to interrogate the Cuban assassin responsible, Hector Gonzales, at his villa near Madrid and find out who ordered the execution.

Gonzales is killed by Melina, Sir Timothy's daughter, and she escapes with Bond's help. Bond identifies a man sent to pay Gonzales as Emile Locque, and then tracks him to Italy. Here Bond meets a decorated ex-Greek resistance fighter, Kristatos, and requests his help in finding Locque and his alleged employer – the smuggler Columbo, who it is supected will be the man employed by the Russians to retrieve the ATAC from the sunken wreck of the *St Georges*.

Columbo kidnaps Bond and then informs him that it is Kristatos, not he, who is Bond's enemy and the employer of the murderous Locque. Moreover, it is Kristatos whom the Russians have employed to retrieve the ATAC. Bond and Columbo decide to work together. Bond kills Locque, and he and Melina use her parents' equipment to salvage the ATAC themselves. In the course of this mission they are captured by Kristatos, who takes the device from them and leaves.

Bond, Columbo and Melina follow Kristatos to St Cyril's Monastery, where he intends to hand the ATAC to the Russians. They infiltrate the monastery and Columbo kills Kristatos. Bond is confronted by the Russian General Gogol, who has come to collect the ATAC on the KGB's behalf. Rather than surrender the ATAC, Bond destroys it. With nothing left to fight over, the Russians leave.

UNIVERSAL EXPORTS:

BOND, JAMES BOND: This is a more contemplative, less flippant Bond than usual. First seen standing by his wife's grave, it is clearly stated that Bond has been active for at least the past twelve years. He also kills the man responsible for Tracy's death, dropping him down an industrial chimney.

It is hard to believe this is the same man who was so unpleasant in *Moonraker*. His rejection of revenge to Melina could be seen as hypocritical, as he twice takes revenge on his enemies, killing Blofeld and Locque.

This new maturity comes to a head with Bond's destruction of the ATAC. Although supposed to be a nod to détente, it is a false gesture. Surely it doesn't matter to the British if just one ATAC is destroyed?

MONEYPENNY: Moneypenny's brief appearance and banter with 007 seems to be included almost solely out of audience expectation. Though she imparts the news that M is on holiday, her presence here is of little other interest.

TANNER: With M absent, the Chief of Staff, Bill Tanner, is running the Service. Briefly seen in *The Man with the Golden Gun*, though played there by Michael Goodliffe, the Chief of Staff is a gruff, authoritarian figure who addresses Bond with formality. An adequate temporary replacement, it is nevertheless good to have the familiar face present in the character of Freddie Gray.

Q: Probably the cosiest Q/Bond moment of the series sees them working together on the Identograph, bickering over cups of coffee. There's also the wonderful 'confessional' scene (see **MEMORABLE QUOTES**).

OHMSS: Maintains connections with people such as Havelock who, while not necessarily fully fledged agents, have skills that are, on occasion, useful to the Service.

ALLIES:

MELINA: The half-Greek daughter of Sir Timothy Havelock, Melina is strong willed and possessed of a fiery temperament. She is skilled in diving and underwater work, which is useful when it comes to investigating the wreck of the *St Georges*. She is also an expert shot with a crossbow; with it she kills Gonzales, and it later proves useful during the attack on St Cyril's.

What is remarkable about Melina is her own, separate character arc. Coincidentally she becomes involved with Bond's hunt for the ATAC, but her primary concern is to avenge her parents. In the end she realises that killing Kristatos – the man responsible for their deaths – will not bring them back to her.

MILOS COLUMBO: A smuggler in harmless luxury items, Columbo operates in the central Mediterranean. He is rarely seen without a bag of pistachios. A genial character, very much in the mould of loveable rogues such as Kerim Bey or Marc-Ange Draco, Columbo readily throws his lot in with Bond. His rivalry with Kristatos goes back to World War Two when both fought in the resistance together. This ties in with the film's concern with growing old and the ending of vendettas. Columbo ends his by killing Kristatos as the treacherous smuggler is about to knife Bond in the back.

Columbo is a great supporting character, and steals every scene he is in. It is unfortunate that there are so few.

COUNTESS LISL VON SCHLAF: Mistress of Columbo and regular habitué of night clubs, where she acts like a classier Plenty O'Toole (see **Diamonds Are Forever**), taking high rollers for a ride, then ditching them when the money runs out. When Columbo hears the recorded conversation in which Kristatos accuses him of being a Russian agent, he orders the Countess to seduce Bond. In the course of this he discovers her secret . . . she is just a girl from Liverpool pretending to be an Austrian countess.

She is killed by Locque, her death being especially poignant given her short time onscreen. She is one of the 'sacrificial lambs' who make an impact as interesting characters in their own right.

SIR TIMOTHY HAVELOCK: Marine archaeologist with a Greek wife, employed by the Secret Service to investigate the sinking of the *St Georges*, for which activity he is killed by Gonzales. He keeps a parrot named Max, who has a conveniently selective memory.

FREDERICK GRAY: Still Minister of Defence, despite the election in late 1979 of a new government from a different party to the one in power when he first appeared in 1977. Gray, it seems, has pulled off the biggest party political defection in British history, and managed to keep his old job into the bargain. It is not a surprise to see Gray take such an interest in the ongoing investigation as ATAC is something that involves the entire defence community.

BIBI DAHL: Precocious teen skating star, sponsored by Kristatos, who develops the hots for Bond. After the (un)pleasantries of the monastery encounter she is taken under Columbo's wing.

THE OPPOSITION:

ARIS KRISTATOS: He won the King's medal for work in the Greek resistance during World War Two, while (according to Colombo) secretly fighting for the Communists all that time. He certainly does the Russians' dirty work for them in the present (he is Gogol's 'usual man in Albania') but is also a heroin smuggler. He is the 'guardian' of, and has inappropriately lascivious eyes for, teen skating prodigy Bibi Dahl. How he came to be in the former position is never revealed.

EMILE LEOPOLD LOCQUE: Initially an enforcer for the Brussels underworld, Locque was imprisoned at Namur Prison, Belgium on 31 January 1975. He escaped by strangling his psychiatrist and went on to work for various drug-smuggling rings in Hong Kong and Marseilles. This led to his involvement with Kristatos who employed him to arrange the assassination of Havelock and then to try and kill Bond and Melina on the slopes of Cortina. It also seems that he had some involvement with Kristatos's heroin-smuggling operation in Albania. Bond pursues Locque after the assault on this warehouse and, in a tense scene, kicks Locque's car – in which the killer is still sitting – off the cliff edge.

ERIC KRIEGLER: East German skiing champion and biathelete, Kriegler is a KGB agent and acts as the liaison between Kristatos and Gogol. He also works with Locque in an attempt to kill Bond on the slopes of Cortina, but fails. He fails again during the fight in the monastery when Bond flings him off the mountain.

HECTOR GONZALES: A Cuban hitman employed by Locque to kill Havelock, he is himself killed by Melina. He recognises the gun used by Bond.

GENERAL GOGOL: Alexis Gogol returns, this time as an opponent of the Secret Service. However, the character remains ambiguous. He does not order the death of the Havelocks, nor directly orders the salvage of the *St Georges* but merely asks for Kristatos to be contacted. When Kristatos obtains the device, Gogol is contacted and arrives with the intention to buy it. The destruction of this device does not lead to reprisal from Gogol, merely a weary smile. He holds no grudge against Bond (quite the reverse one imagines) and acknowledges this is just a round in the greater game, a round that he happens to lose.

BLOFELD: Blofeld is never explicitly called so on screen (see **TRIVIA**). We never see his face, but physically he's reminiscent of Donald Pleasence, and vocally Peter Marrinker's performance hints at Telly Savalas. He's bald too, and his injuries suggest those that he sustained at the end of *On Her Majesty's Secret Service*. It's almost as if this film is ignoring *Diamonds Are Forever* altogether. (Which, given that *Diamonds* ignores *OHMSS*, is arguably fair enough.) Just before Bond kills him he begs for his life, offering 007 a deal. He says he'll buy him 'A delicatessen, in stainless steel!' Quite why the bald maniac seems to think that his purchasing for Bond a small, albeit shiny, establishment from which he would sell cheese and meat products would make up for the brutal murder of Bond's beloved wife on their wedding day is anybody's guess.

PRINCIPAL CASTING: By now Roger Moore was selling his services to Eon on a film by film basis; each new production saw a game of brinkmanship between producer Broccoli and Moore himself, with the latter not confirming his involvement until the last minute in order to push up his earnings from the film. This led to many auditions of actors to take over the role of Bond, part of Broccoli's bluff to force Moore into accepting whatever salary offer was on the table at that time. Among these was Julian Glover, who asked to be considered for the role after being cast as Kristatos. However, Moore eventually struck a deal with Broccoli and was back on board.

Chaim Topol was cast as Kristatos's opponent, Columbo. Topol is most famous for his Oscar-nominated performance in *Fiddler on the Roof* (Norman Jewison, 1971) but he also comprised the 'Bond ally' part of a Bond triumvirate in *Flash Gordon* (Mike Hodges, 1980) along with Max von Sydow (Blofeld in *Never Say Never Again*) and latterday Bond, Timothy Dalton. His casting was largely due to serendipity. Cubby and Dana Broccoli met him at a cocktail party and the producer's wife suggested he be cast.

RADA graduate Julian Glover had appeared in a number of horror films and historical epics before working on *For Your Eyes Only*. Almost always cast as a villain, his other major roles include the brutal General Veers in *The Empire Strikes Back* (Irvin Kershner, 1980) and the treacherous Walter Donovan in *Indiana Jones and the Last Crusade* (Steven Spielberg, 1989). In 1993 he won the Laurence Olivier award for best actor for his performance in the title role of *Henry IV* Parts One and Two.

French actress Carole Bouquet had her first (and only) major role as Melina Havelock. All her work since has been in low-key European cinema. Her Bond role did, however, help her secure a lucrative contract as the face of Chanel.

Playing a comparatively minor character in the film, Countess Lisl was actress Cassandra Harris. During production she married actor Pierce Brosnan, who later came to visit the set and met producers Cubby Broccoli and Michael Wilson. Sadly, Ms Harris died of cancer in 1991 after a long illness. The lull in her husband's career between the late 80s and his resurgence as Bond is attributable to the years he took out from his career to care for her and their children.

Q's assistant Smithers (who would reappear in *Octopussy*) is played by Jeremy Bulloch, the actor who played Boba Fett in *The Empire Strikes Back* (Irvin Kershner, 1980) and *Return of the Jedi* (Richard Marquand, 1983).

DIRECTOR AND CREW: Cubby Broccoli asked John Glen to take over the director's chair, a position he would occupy for eight years and five films – longer than any other Bond director. Previously an editor by profession, Glen had worked on several classic 1960s TV shows (*Danger Man*, *Man in a Suitcase*, *The Avengers*). His first Bond film was *On Her Majesty's Secret Service*, where he worked on the editing alongside the director Peter Hunt, as well as carrying out some second unit work on the spectacular skiing and bobsleigh scenes. He went on to work alongside Hunt on *Gold* (1974) and *Shout at the Devil* (1976), both films starring Roger Moore. He also worked with Moore on *The Wild Geese* (Andrew McLaglen, 1978). As a director, Glen seems happiest with action set pieces, though a reliance on suddenly intrusive humour can sometimes undermine the effect. He has adopted as his motif a pigeon fluttering out of a nest to add shock to tense moments. Additionally, an abnormally large number of deaths in his films are caused by falling from a great height (a theme that also emerges in the pre-credit sequences of *The Spy Who Loved Me* and *Moonraker* – both sequences shot by Glen).

Peter Lamont, production designer for the first time on this film, was a Bond veteran with associations going back to *Thunderball* (where he worked as a uncredited set-dresser). Lamont provided understated sets that complemented the return to less fantastic stories and settings. He would go on to win an Oscar for his work on *Titanic* (James Cameron, 1997).

Alan Hume made his Bond debut as cinematographer. A man with a long pedigree of work on the *Carry On* films, Hume would go on to work on many films in the 1980s, including *Return of the Jedi* (Richard Marquand, 1983), *A Fish Called Wanda* (Charles Crichton, 1988) and *Shirley Valentine* (Lewis Gilbert, 1989).

MUSICAL NOTES: Bill Conti provides the competent score. Note: playing flamenco guitars over shots of obviously Greek olive groves does not make a location Spanish.

Conti also wrote the title song, the singer of which, Sheena Easton, became the first and to date only Bond song artiste to appear in the title sequence. A good number, quite well suited to the low-key nature of the film, it became disproportionately popular and was nominated for an Oscar, losing out to Burt Bacharach's 'Between the Moon and New York City (Theme From Arthur)'.

SET PIECES: *For Your Eyes Only* is guilty of some of the crimes committed by *Live and Let Die*'s boat chase. The ski scene in particular is overlong and uninspired. However, redemption comes in the great, unconventional car chase scene with Bond ditching his flashy Lotus for a battered Citroen 2 CV. It was put together by the Remy Julienne driving team. They had been responsible for the awesome stunts in *The Italian Job* (Peter Collinson, 1969) and would return for many subsequent Bond films.

The mountain-climbing sequence at the end is especially well staged. The actual climbing was done by Rick Sylvester, the extreme skier who performed the opening stunt for *The Spy Who Loved Me* and, for once, the long shots of the stunt and close-ups of Moore are put together skilfully enough to make each viewing a tense one. It is during this climb that Glen's pigeons make their first appearance (see **DIRECTOR AND CREW**).

POSITIVELY SHOCKING: Not so much a visceral as an emotional shock is the brutal murder of Melina's parents. As they wave to the returning sea-plane, their looks turn from happiness to horror; the welling music and the look on Melina's face as the camera pans in is enough to make this scene comparable with the killing of Tracy in *On Her Majesty's Secret Service*.

When Bond pushes the helpless Locque off the side of the cliff, this is cold-blooded murder, an action almost out of character for Moore's Bond.

MEMORABLE QUOTES:
Bond (entering a confessional booth for a meeting with Q): 'Forgive me Father, for I have sinned.'
Q: 'That's putting it mildly, 007.'

PRODUCT PLACEMENT: Limited to a plug for Olin skis, the requisite appearance of Bond's Seiko watch and a brief appearance by the Lotus, which this time stays firmly on dry land. There is also a clear shot of a box of Kellogg's All-Bran during the 10 Downing Street scene.

GADGETS: One of the least gadget-reliant films. In one case, they work against Bond – the rather extreme security device on the Lotus deprives him of an obvious escape route. Bond's digital watch has a two-way radio (very Dick Tracy) and Q-branch are working on an umbrella which spikes the user's head on contact with water ('stinging in the rain, Q?') and a spring-loaded plaster cast – surely a predecessor of Q's wheelchair rocket in *GoldenEye*. The lab also houses the Identograph. This is basically a machine for creating a photo-fit picture that is plugged into the databases of the FBI, Interpol and various other law enforcement agencies allowing for instant identification of felons.

SOURCE TO SCREEN: *Moonraker* had marked the nadir of the Bond film as an empty attempt at spectacle. Even Broccoli seemed somewhat ashamed of it and a decision was made to bring Bond, both literally and figuratively, back to Earth. With this in mind, Richard Maibaum was once again brought in to write the screenplay, this time assisted by Broccoli's stepson, Michael G Wilson. Wilson was already being groomed to take over the franchise from Broccoli, and had been credited as an executive producer on *Moonraker*. Wilson's involvement led to the series dropping its apolitical outlook. The Cold War would, for the next four films at least, became far more prominent in the plots. Many critics have understandably assumed that the Bond pictures became less Cold War-centred as time went on. Yet any comparison between the 70s creed of stateless psychopaths such as Blofeld, **The Spy Who Loved Me**'s Stromberg or **Moonraker**'s Drax and the 80s run of Soviet-backed (Kristatos) Soviet-trained (**A View To A Kill**'s Zorin, **The Living Daylights**' Koskov) or even hard-line Soviet Communist villains (**Octopussy**'s Orlov) can only lead to the opposite conclusion.

Linked to this new politicisation was an attempt at a less fantastical tone to Bond's adventures, which would become more concerned with the minutiae of spying and would not involve a plot to destroy the whole world again. Some have seen this as a return to 'realism', although it could equally be argued as the trading of a previous self-consciously large-scale fantasy for a new unselfconsciously grubbier and more mundane one. Regardless of what this approach would bring in future, however, it must have been as manifest to everyone at the time as it is to any viewer of the film now, that after *Moonraker* drastic change was needed to stop the series collapsing under the weight of its own repetitions.

There was, in tandem with this, also a return to the work of Ian Fleming. Though *Moonraker* had seen the use of the last James Bond novel (albeit in title only – see **GoldenEye**) there were still two volumes of accomplished short stories: *For Your Eyes Only* (published in 1960) and *Octopussy* (published posthumously in 1966). The former comprised five short stories, several of which had been adapted from ideas Fleming had suggested for a possible television series (see **Introduction**); the latter essentially a miscellany containing practically all of Fleming's uncollected Bond pieces.

Wilson and Maibaum's screenplay was to utilise elements of two stories from *For Your Eyes Only*. The first was the title story itself, a small-scale revenge tragedy set in Vermont on the Canadian border. In it, a former Nazi named Hammerstein is attempting to buy property in Jamaica, to allow his 'retirement' from the Cuban secret police. An agent of the dictator Batista, he is trying to secure a new base in light of the ongoing revolution (the story was written before Fidel Castro came to power on the island). An expatriate British family, the Havelocks, are killed by Hammerstein's agent, Hector Gonzales, in an attempt to frighten their daughter – Judy Havelock – into selling up. M, who had been at the couple's wedding, sends Bond, with the agent's willing agreement, on a revenge mission. He is, quite simply, to kill Hammerstein. When Bond arrives in Vermont he encounters Judy, who is herself out for revenge, having tracked Hammerstein down through Havana's casinos. Bond unwillingly agrees to let her kill the ex-Nazi and together they wipe out Hammerstein and his gang.

From this story the film takes its leading lady, the ongoing revenge subplot and the character of Cuban hitman Gonzales. Incidentally, the Havelocks of the story share a distinctive characteristic with the Ryders from Fleming's novel *Doctor No*. Members of both families were, according to Fleming, granted land on Jamaica by Oliver Cromwell in return for being signatories of the death warrant of Charles I.

In addition to *For Your Eyes Only* the screenplay borrows heavily
from 'Risico'. This is a tale of smuggling set in Venice and Albania,
where Bond is sent to track down a major supplier of heroin. Though M
expresses distaste at sending his agents on what is essentially either a
customs or criminal matter, he is swayed by the Prime Minister's belief
that the smuggling of hard drugs into the West is in fact a psychological
warfare tactic employed by communist powers (this assumption turns
out, in the context of the story, to be entirely correct). Bond meets the
supposedly reliable Ari Kristatos, who accuses the smuggler Columbo of
being responsible for the supply of heroin. This Columbo kidnaps Bond
(who has been rumbled due to a tape recorder hidden in a chair) and
reveals that Kristatos is the real enemy, taking Bond to the Albanian
warehouse where Kristatos receives his Soviet heroin. Together they
mount a raid on the warehouse and kill Kristatos.

The story is faithfully transcribed, almost in its entirety, to make up
the film's middle section. The major changes are threefold: the relocation
of the initial meeting between Bond and Kristatos to Cortina, the
incorporation of the dune buggy set piece and a slight change to the
ending. Kristatos's henchman, Locque, is killed in the film's warehouse
raid, with Kristatos surviving until the final reel.

The novel *Live and Let Die* provided the sequence where Bond and
Melina are keel-hauled. There proved to be no appropriate moment to
insert this set piece in the film of *Live and Let Die*, despite producer
Harry Saltzman's enthusiasm for it. Its use here provides one of this
picture's most satisfying sequences.

These elements of original Fleming are a real boost to a film series that
had spent more than a decade deliberately ignoring its heritage. The first
short story provides real backbone to the Melina character. 'Risico'
lends itself to a great mid-film action sequence as well as providing the
interesting Columbo/Kristatos by-play. Coupled with the Cold-War
story, these elements make this the first Bond film to try to work in a Le
Carré/Deighton mould since *From Russia with Love*. That film is itself
plundered for plot inspiration – the ATAC maguffin owes more than a
little to the Lektor decoder.

IN THE REAL WORLD: Although Kristatos is Greek he is employed by
Russians. This is the first time that Soviet powers had been the guiding
hand directly behind a cinematic Bond villain, reflecting a rise in
Cold-War tensions. In 1981 détente had faltered 1979–80 had seen
renewed Soviet expansionism (most clearly expressed through the
invasion of Afghanistan) and the election of a Republican US President –

Ronald Reagan – whose arms-stockpiling policies were openly designed to discourage American–Russian co-operation. This brought the American government broadly into line, politically speaking, with Britain, where a Conservative party which had moved noticeably to the right while in opposition, had won a general election in September 1979. The then Prime Minister actually 'appears' in the film, in the form of an impersonator; the first time a real political figure is featured. Previous politicians had been either anonymous or not obviously based on any one person, or both. Although the sequence with Mrs Thatcher is played strictly for laughs, it still underlines the production team's desire to provide as many links as possible between their film and what their audience would recognise as 'reality'.

If the Bond films were keen to drop their apolitical stance, then making Russia Bond's opponent was understandable. What is interesting is the way in which the film presents Russian villainy. Very much in the background for most of the film – the war is being fought by proxy – the country is represented by General Gogol, who had been Bond's ally in less tense times. Despite his orders, and the frustration of his objectives, Gogol remains well disposed towards Bond as an individual, taking the loss of the ATAC very well indeed. There is a marked reluctance to let the Russians become the undisputed 'bad guys'.

It is also worth commenting on Kristatos's war record. When Columbo speaks of him fighting for the communists at the end of the war, this refers to a bitter factional struggle that occurred in Greece, to decide who would run the country. As indicated, one of these factions was communist and civil war raged through to 1949, when a democratic government was finally installed.

CRITICS: 'For Your Eyes Only grabs you from the start', opined Alan Frank of the Daily Star (27 July 1981) proclaiming 'it's a winner all the way'. 'One of the better Bonds,' was the more muted praise of the Daily Express of the 24 July, 'with a nice balance between humour and excitement.' Their critic Ian Christie was also positive about the 'return to earth' after Moonraker and the 'touch of credibility' afforded the plot. Nigel Andrews in the Financial Times (26 June) was less enthused, feeling that Bond had 'come back to Earth with a baleful and bathetic thud'. He felt the plot was 'reheated' and missed the presence of a clear villain, the 'guess-the-baddie play-off between two colourlessly shady Greek tycoons' failing to pique his interest. The Times' David Robinson, writing on the same day, felt that the new picture was 'not very much different from its immediate predecessors', and 'no better or worse' than the bulk of Bond pictures. Alexander Walker in the *Evening Standard* (25 June) was a happier man, 'Bond is back in flesh and blood . . . *For Your Eyes Only* puts humanity before the hardware.' Comparing the film favourably with *From Russia with Love*, he praised Moore's 'elegance' and called the ending 'the best in the series'. The *Morning Star* (26 June) once again had political truck with the picture. 'Each Bond adventure,' said correspondent Virginia Durham, 'however adroit and escapist, perpetuates the myth of the Red threat, the lurking menace, the unseen but ever present aggressor.' In fact this was the first time Bond had honestly fought against communists in the whole of the film series, and that the menace in this case is clearly visible in the final scenes.

BOX OFFICE: The worldwide gross for *For Your Eyes Only* was $195 million, a little down on *Moonraker* but this was more than compensated for by the reduced production costs.

MARTINIS, GIRLS AND GUNS: Bond is not only surprised, but also embarrassed, when the teenage Bibi offers herself on a plate. 'Put your clothes on and I'll buy you an ice cream,' he deadpans, turning away. Of far more interest is the Countess Lisl – a woman nearer his own age, who knows exactly what she's getting herself into, and whom he spectacularly fails to save from Kristasos's thugs. Although he forms a partnership with Melina Havelock he doesn't seem to be concerned about seducing her. That said, he certainly doesn't object when she throws herself at him in the final reel. A gentlemanly two.

Once again a fairly dry adventure, save a couple of glasses of fine wine and an unforgivable beaker of Ouzo. A respectable body count though. With Blofeld at the beginning, two men killed by the exploding Lotus, three of Locque's men killed at the docks (plus Locque himself) two men at the *St Georges* wreck, one man pulled off a mountain and the defenestration of the fearsome Kriegler a decent eleven. Good work 007.

TRIVIA: Blofeld is never named so onscreen because Kevin McClory has often claimed sole film rights to the character. A claim refuted by Eon. The reappearance and killing of Bond's 60s nemesis here is a deliberate statement by Broccoli of his lack of need to use the character. (See **Never Say Never Again**.)

THE ONE . . .: that no one remembers.

THE LAST WORD: 'When setting out for revenge, first dig two graves.' *For Your Eyes Only* tries hard to be *On Her Majesty's Secret Service* and succeeds about as often as it doesn't. Given the sheer quality of *OHMSS* that's still very good going. In its favour are Moore's most complex performance as Bond – he turns in an impressive, reflective study of Bond as an ageing hero – and a deceitful, twisting plot structure which depends on people at least as much as on machines. It even tries to be *about* something – the pain of growing old and the pitfalls of becoming obsessed by revenge. Against it, almost every set piece goes on that little bit too long, and the picture lacks a single, identifiable iconic 'moment'. Except in the pre-credits, even its best scenes fail to stand alongside the series' signature sequences.

An enjoyable, well-crafted thriller whose unfortunate reward for its attempt to give the world a low-key, high-quality Bond film is anonymity among the overblown spectacle of *Moonraker* and the colourful nonsense of *Octopussy*.

GIRLS	32
MARTINIS	7
DEATHS	136

Octopussy (1983)

Produced by Albert R Broccoli
Executive Producer: Michael G Wilson
Screenplay by George MacDonald Fraser, Richard Maibaum
and Michael G Wilson
Director of Photography: Alan Hume
Music composed and conducted by John Barry
Song 'All Time High' performed by Rita Coolidge
Music by John Barry
Lyrics by Tim Rice
Production designed by Peter Lamont
Supervising Editor: John Grover
Directed by John Glen

PRINCIPAL CAST: Roger Moore (*James Bond*), Maud Adams (*Octopussy*), Louis Jourdan (*Kamal*), Kristina Wayborn (*Magda*), Kabir Bedi (*Gobinda*), Steven Berkoff (*Orlov*), David Meyer (*Twin One – Mischka*), Anthony Meyer (*Twin Two – Grischka*), Desmond Llewelyn (*Q*), Robert Brown (*M*), Lois Maxwell (*Miss Moneypenny*), Michaela Clavell (*Penelope Smallbone*), Walter Gotell (*Gogol*), Vijay Amritraj

(*Vijay*), Albert Moses (*Sadruddin*), Geoffrey Keen (*Minister of Defence*), Andy Bradford (*009*), Philip Voss (*Auctioneer*), Bruce Boa (*US General*), Richard LeParmentier (*US Aide*), Paul Hardwick (*Soviet Chairman*), Suzanne Jerome (*Gwendoline*), Cherry Gillespie (*Midge*), Dermot Crowley (*Kamp*), Peter Porteous (*Lenkin*), Eva Rueber-Staier (*Rublevitch*), Jeremy Bulloch (*Smithers*), Tina Hudson (*Bianca*), William Derrick (*Thug with Yo-yo*), Stuart Saunders (*Major Clive*), Patrick Barr (*British Ambassador*), Gabor Vernon (*Borchoi*), Hugo Bower (*Karl*), Ken Norris (*Colonel Toro*), Tony Arjuna (*Mufti*), Gertan Klauber (*Bubi*), Brenda Cowling (*Schatzi*), David Grahame (*Petrol Pump Attendant*), Brian Coburn (*South American VIP*), Michael Halphie (*South American Officer*), Roberto Germaines (*Ringmaster*), Richard Graydon (*Francisco The Fearless*).

PRE-CREDITS AND TITLES: Bond infiltrates a South American airbase disguised as one Colonel El Toro. His objective is to sabotage an experimental plane. He is captured, but escapes by using an Acrostar mini-jet which he has concealed within a horsebox. A missile is fired after him, but thanks to Bond's piloting skills it destroys the experimental plane instead, completing his mission for him. Bond lands at a nearby petrol station and asks the attendant to 'fill her up please'. An entertaining teaser, but for the first time in the series there is no link, not even tangential or thematic, to the rest of the film. The titles are low-rent Maurice Binder. The song is excellent but the cheap laser-light visuals leave a lot to be desired.

SUMMARY: Soviet General Orlov wants to start an 'easily winnable' conventional war with the West. To do so he has to neutralise the US nuclear deterrent. He cultivates a smuggling route using a travelling circus run by the all-women Octopus cult. He uses this route to sell pre-revolution Russian jewellery (which he has stolen, and of which he has had copies made to take their place in the archives) in order to (a) gain the trust of the smugglers and (b) make himself some money on the side.

Bond is investigating this jewellery smuggling and suspects Afghan Prince Kamal Khan of being involved. He tracks Khan to India and discovers the Octopus cult's involvement. He befriends their leader Octopussy and learns that she owns a circus troupe.

Bond goes to their next performance in East Germany, where he realises that Orlov is using the smuggling route to get a low-yield nuclear bomb into an American airbase. Once there it will be detonated. With no possibility of this being a Soviet attack (the early warning sensors would have indicated it) the Americans would inevitably assume that this was an accident involving one of their own weapons. Left-wing pressure within Europe would force total nuclear withdrawal, leaving mainland Europe ripe for conquest by Orlov's conventional troops. Octopussy herself is unaware of Orlov's plans, she thinks that they're merely smuggling jewellery.

The Soviet authorities learn of Orlov's plan, and he is killed by his own troops. Bond infiltrates the circus and defuses the bomb, then returns to India with Octopussy where they destroy Khan's organisation.

UNIVERSAL EXPORTS:

BOND, JAMES BOND: Bond knows something about Fabergé eggs, has a working knowledge of nuclear bombs and some skill at backgammon. He can fly a plane and looks like South American General Toro. He was implicitly in the Secret Service a few years after the end of the Korean war. He has some ability with throwing knives, and is revolted by the idea of eating baked sheep's eyes. Bond takes the alias Charles Moreton when travelling.

M: This film sees the debut of the 'new' M. It is unclear whether Robert Brown's M should be seen as the same man played by the late Bernard Lee, or whether the idea was that this was a new leader for the Secret Service. While Robert Brown did play Admiral Hargreaves in *The Spy Who Loved Me*, there are no indications of a change in leadership such as those in *GoldenEye* or even *Never Say Never Again*. If only to preserve the memory of Bernard Lee as separate from this rather huffy individual, it would be nice to believe that Hargreaves has been promoted since *For Your Eyes Only* and Admiral Miles (Messervy?) is enjoying his retirement.

MONEYPENNY: She is seen here training her alleged replacement, Penelope Smallbone, whom Bond takes an instant fancy to. (We never see Smallbone again – Moneypenny must have a vicious streak.) The time was long overdue for Maxwell to leave the role.

Q: Back in the field and as unhappy as ever, Q sees real action here. He takes part in the surveillance of Octopussy's floating palace, and it is he who finds Vijay's body. He is also employed in giving Bond transport during the final attack on Khan's Monsoon Palace in a hot air balloon (cunningly camouflaged by a monstrous Union flag on the side). His seeming PA Karen, from *For Your Eyes Only*, has been replaced by one called Sharon. His assistant Smithers turns up for the second and last time.

OHMSS: Another unfortunate 00 agent is killed – 009 – though we never learn either his name or what the original mission was that led to the infiltration of Octopussy's circus. The Secret Service has a team in India comparable to that run by Kerim Bey – a group of streetwise, intelligent individuals easily able to outfox the opposition. The London station also has access to an art expert, Jim Fanning. This is presumably a similar relationship to that they have with Sir Timothy Havelock (**For Your Eyes Only**) and Sir Godfrey Tibbett (**A View to a Kill**).

ALLIES:

OCTOPUSSY: The mysterious smuggler of the title, Octopussy is the daughter of one Major Smythe, a looter of Chinese gold who had been hunted down by James Bond shortly after the Korean war. Bond gave Smythe the opportunity to commit suicide rather than be arrested and court-martialled, and Smythe thus preserved his honour. Octopussy has long wanted to meet Bond to thank him for giving her father this chance.

Octopussy was once employed in small-scale smuggling on behalf of the Hong Kong-based smugglers that dealt with the gold stolen by her father. Discovering her calling in life from this service, she revived the all-woman octopus cult and turned it into an efficient smuggling operation, employing female drifters from all over the world. This group has diversified into shipping, hotels and the circus. The circus is actually a front for the transport of stolen Soviet jewellery to auction in the West. This jewellery is sold to a fence in Zurich who disposes of the goods in the auction houses of London. Octopussy is unaware of the plan to use this pipeline to transport a nuclear device into an American air base.

Tough and independent, Octopussy is a spiritual heir of Pussy Galore (see **Goldfinger**) but there is no similar 'ideological realignment'. She is like **For Your Eyes Only**'s Columbo – a rogue who does not live within the boundaries of the law but who does have her own strong personal code of ethics. She is horrified by the plans of the real villains of the piece. Despite her protests of being different to Bond (very like his own to Scaramanga – see **The Man With The Golden Gun**) they are ultimately both on the same side.

MAGDA: Octopussy's right-hand woman. She conveys to Khan the need to buy back the original Fabergé egg and seduces Bond in order to retrieve it. She moonlights as a conjurer at the circus and she initially warns Octopussy against trusting Bond but, once Khan and Orlov's apocalyptic agenda is revealed, she joins the side of right.

VIJAY: The first decent sidekick since Quarrel Jnr (**Live and Let Die**), and the first really effective 'sacrificial lamb' since Aki (**You Only Live Twice**). Vijay is a cheerful, gregarious Secret Service agent with a part-time job as a tennis pro. It is heartening to see a Bond character who really engages with the audience (it is difficult not to smile, even at the silliest scenes in the car chase). This makes it all the more affecting for the audience when Vijay is killed by Khan's mercenaries.

FREDERICK GRAY: There is no real reason for the Minister of Defence (still going strong after six years) to be present during the early part of this film. Indeed, it must undermine M's authority somewhat to have the internal affairs of the Secret Service continually scrutinised like this.

GENERAL GOGOL: Gogol has always existed in the moral greys of Bond's world. Here he returns to being an ally, though not quite as emphatic an ally as in *The Spy Who Loved Me*. He is part of a politburo meeting debating a response to calls by NATO to attend disarmament talks and is very much the 'dove' to Orlov's 'hawk' (see **IN THE REAL WORLD**). He chases down the rogue general towards the end of the picture, and he is the only one to hear Orlov's last words (see **MEMORABLE QUOTES**). However, he remains very much a Soviet Russian official, without the overtly friendly face he sports in the earlier film or the later *The Living Daylights*. He appears briefly at the conclusion to request (politely) the return of the Romanov Star, used by Bond to persuade Octopussy of Khan and Orlov's treachery.

THE OPPOSITION:

KAMAL KHAN: An exiled Afghan prince, Khan is easily a match for Bond in terms of snobbery, living in the luxurious Monsoon Palace and being driven around in a Rolls-Royce. Khan has keen interests in polo, cricket and tennis. He also plays backgammon well, although this is probably due to the loaded dice he uses.

Khan's criminal life is a mystery. He has become involved with Octopussy but has a well-funded organisation of his own. His relationship with General Orlov is badly defined (it is odd that he works so closely with a fanatical Russian considering Soviet support for the communist puppet government then in control of his homeland). It seems likely that he brought Orlov and Octopussy together with the aim of supporting the general's scheme. What Khan has to gain from this is unclear. It is difficult to see how a communist Western Europe would aid his empire, and financial gain seems an unlikely motive – not only is he fabulously rich but, as we see at the end, he has printing plates for all major currencies. It seems that he's just 'evil'.

Khan plays a major role in the convoluted opening story of the Fabergé egg smuggling. Here is a brief summary of this complicated sequence: X represents the real Fabergé egg, Y the forgery. Orlov takes X from the repository, creates copy Y of it, and then sends X down the smuggling pipeline. Somehow 009 gets hold of Y and ends up dead in East Germany, leaving the egg in the hands of the British ambassador. Y is sent to M, who sends Bond to the auction of X to investigate the matter.

Meanwhile, Orlov has received notice of the loss of Y and orders Khan to buy back X, so that it can be placed back in the archives in time for an inspection. At the auction Bond switches X for Y, leaving Khan paying £500,000 for Y.

Bond travels to India where Q fits a homing device to X. Khan knows his stuff and is fully aware that Bond is in possession of X when the secret agent reveals his egg at the backgammon game. Magda steals this back so Khan is in possession of both X and Y. When Orlov's men take the container back to his helicopter we initially assume that he has taken possession of X. However, when he smashes what we assume to be Y, Khan spots the homing device. The only explanation is that Khan tried to fob Orlov off with the fake egg, keeping the real one for his own benefit.

GENERAL ORLOV: Fanatical Soviet general. His ultimate aim is to invade and conquer Western Europe. To this end he first cultivates a pipeline for pre-revolution Russian jewellery which he steals from the archives and replaces with forgeries. This pipeline will carry the nuclear bomb, destined for an American airbase.

A full-on Cold Warrior, Orlov embodies the worst fears of Western strategists in the 1980s, and even today: a rogue military commander with access to nuclear weapons. He is a lone voice among a horde of politburo figures calling for arms talks with the West. The filmmakers clearly did not want Bond to become *too* political.

GOBINDA: Large brutish henchman to Khan – he is in the Jaws mould (see **Moonraker**). His weapon of choice is an archaic blunderbuss. He is given one indisputably great moment – when Khan instructs him to battle Bond on the outside of a plane there is real disbelief on Gobinda's face before he reluctantly agrees. He falls to his death as a consequence. At one point Gobinda crushes Khan's loaded dice in an explicit reference to Oddjob crushing his master's golf ball in **Goldfinger**.

MISHKA AND GRISHKA: Though they are referred to as 'Twin 1' and 'Twin 2' in the credits, it is not hard to fathom the characters' actual names from the film. They are expert knife throwers who are in Khan's inner-circle of confidants (they are to be evacuated from the nuclear blast site). Their first appearance hints at the potential they have to be great henchman but the film throws this away. They are separated and killed individually by Bond with no ceremony at all.

INDIAN MERCENARIES: Cash-hungry, loincloth-wearing criminals from the slums. Employed by Khan to kill Bond at Octopussy's palace (leaving Octopussy untouched). One of their number has a nasty razor-edged yo-yo that was inexplicably marketed as a child's toy.

PRINCIPAL CASTING: After another round of bluff and counter-bluff between Moore and Broccoli – and the selection by Broccoli of a clear favourite, American actor James Brolin, to succeed Moore – the ageing actor agreed to what he again insisted was to be his final film as James Bond.

Maud Adams was cast as female lead Octopussy. She had also played the ill-fated Andrea Anders, mistress of *The Man with the Golden Gun*. With the exception of a small role in violent future-sport classic *Rollerball* (Norman Jewison, 1975) this would be the extent of Maud Adams's mainstream film career.

Louis Jourdan's casting as Khan occurred for similar reasons to the casting of Topol in *For Your Eyes Only* – Broccoli suggested him to Glen after attending one of the actor's parties. A former maquis, Jourdan had appeared in a number of nondescript films as the stereotypical European lover, before going on to be typecast as the suave villain in *Octopussy* and films such as the atrocious comic-book adaptation, *Swamp Thing* (Wes Craven, 1982).

A playwright and theatre director, most of Steven Berkoff's film work takes the form of scenery-chewing villains, roles chosen (as the actor openly admits) more for the pay packet than for any potential he sees in the character. Aside from General Orlov, examples of these incarnations can be seen in *Beverley Hills Cop* (Martin Brest, 1984), *Rambo: First Blood Part II* (George Pan Cosmatos, 1985) and Cindy Crawford's film debut *Fair Game* (Andrew Sipes, 1995).

One of the film's actors also had relevance in the world outside the cinema. Vijay is played by Vijay Amritraj, a professional tennis player. Cue much hilarity as he fends off assailants with his tennis racquet. He also holds the honour of being the first ever non-Caucasian captain in *Star Trek*, thanks to his appearance in *Star Trek IV: The Voyage Home* (Leonard Nimoy, 1986).

DIRECTOR AND CREW: John Glen was asked by Broccoli to direct *Octopussy* before *For Your Eyes Only* was even released, so pleased was the producer with how that film had turned out. Like *For Your Eyes Only*, this film contains Glen's directorial 'signature' moment, a pigeon appearing out of nowhere at moment of intended tension; here it takes place as Bond negotiates his way around Khan's Monsoon Palace.

Bond newcomer George MacDonald Fraser provided the first draft of the screenplay. Fraser is best known not as a screenwriter, but as the novelist responsible for the bestselling 'Flashman' series of adventure novels, the eponymous hero of which is, of course, the school bully from Thomas Hughes' *Tom Brown's Schooldays. Octopussy* was the first of only two screenplays in Fraser's career, the other being that of *Red Sonja* (Richard Fleischer, 1985). It is hardly surprising that, after these two efforts, Fraser instead chose to concentrate on his prose career, which has seen him win great acclaim and high sales. Most of Fraser's initial ideas were, by all accounts, heavily rewritten by Maibaum and Wilson, who would go on to write the next three Bond films with no outside contribution. Fraser's key contribution was the Indian setting.

With this one major exception, the rest of the crew of *Octopussy* consisted of the usual roster of Bond regulars, some with pedigrees stretching back to the Connery years, others who had come on board only in the last few years. In many ways it seems, working on a Bond film was more a career than a job.

MUSICAL NOTES: John Barry returned to the Bond fold to provide one of his less distinguished efforts. Pleasant rather than earth-shattering, the score cannot save the picture. Having said this, the title song is one of the best. Rita Coolidge belts out the tune with gusto, the lyrics provided by West End musical regular Tim Rice. The soundtrack was the first in the series to be issued on CD.

SET PIECES: The aerial battle that marks the climax of the film is well up to usual Bond standards. However, it is let down by the preceding hundred or so minutes. The pre-credit sequence is great fun, but hardly spectacular, with some appalling back projection and some deeply unsatisfying model work. The fights are rather limp, the chase involving the ubiquitous three-wheeled Indian form of transport – the 'tuk-tuk' taxi – is predictable and littered with annoying 'jokes'. The train-top sequence, which should be impressive, just feels clichéd (this is the fourth time Bond has run into trouble on this particular form of transport). The only other times it comes to life are the Berlin Wall pursuit at the beginning and the bomb defusal at the end; both are well-executed sequences with genuinely tense moments. What is really admirable is the way they avoid self-parody, despite the Secret Service protagonists (009 and Bond respectively) both being dressed as clowns.

POSTIVELY SHOCKING: Vijay's death is rather gruesome and not in keeping with the farcical nature of Bond's crocodile-submarine infiltration. Aside from this *Octopussy* is one of the most 'family friendly' of the series.

MEMORABLE QUOTES:
Bond (on his Latin American alter-ego): 'El Toro . . . sounds like a load of bull.'

Khan: 'Mr Bond is a rare breed. Soon to become extinct.'

Khan (to Bond): 'You have a nasty habit of surviving.'

Gogol calls the dying Orlov a disgrace to his uniform, and **Orlov** replies: 'Yes, but tomorrow I shall be a hero of the Soviet Union.'

FASHION VICTIMS: Bond has to be forgiven his clown suit and nifty red-and-black knife-thrower garb. He is, after all, undercover. Overall he is well turned out in very smart suits or suave all-black spy gear (very much like that in *Live and Let Die*. Khan's clothing marks a brief return to neutral-coloured jerkins for the villain. The real fashion victims here are the members of the Octopus cult, in flowing silk sarongs and sparkly, bright (and very tacky) jumpsuits. These were dated before the film had even finished production.

PRODUCT PLACEMENT: Bond's pen provided a hefty plug for Mont Blanc, and he once again sports his digital Seiko watch. Both BMW and

Mercedes cars were used for the race across Germany, while his South-American contact uses a Land Rover.

GADGETS: Q's Indian base has the usual regionally accented items – this time a mechanical variant on the Indian rope trick, not quite perfected. Q has also developed a wrist-mounted LCD television, used in the final attack on the Monsoon Palace. Bond's eccentric transport takes the form of an Acrostar mini-jet (powered by the solid fuel motor used in cruise missiles – which, incidentally, makes it impossible for the plane to be refuelled at local petrol stations) hidden in a horsebox. Additionally, he makes use of a water craft disguised as a crocodile to cross the river to Octopussy's base, and the Indian branch of the Secret Service has access to a customised 'tuk-tuk'. The version built for the stunt scenes at Pinwood was capable of reaching 70 mph. The only other notable gadget is his adapted fountain pen, fitted with a receiver for the tiny microphone in the bugged Fabergé egg, and a small reservoir of acid to aid escape from prison cells.

SOURCE TO SCREEN: The thirteenth James Bond film took the title of the one remaining James Bond book, *Octopussy*, a collection of short stories published in 1966, two years after Ian Fleming's death. An odd collection of writings, this work consisted of a short story – 'Octopussy' – in which Bond played an incidental, but important, role; and two pieces Fleming wrote for other publications. 'Property of a Lady' – a short sketch of espionage at an auction was written for a Sotheby's catalogue, and 'The Living Daylights' was written for the first issue of the *Sunday Times* colour magazine. The last of these would ultimately merit a film all of its own, but *this* film made liberal use of the other two.

Like *For Your Eyes Only*, only elements of the two source stories were taken – one to provide background to the 'Bond girl', the other to provide plot points and the basis for one of the film's set pieces. An entirely new plot was constructed around them, once again taking the heightened Cold War for inspiration.

'Octopussy' the story marked one of the few occasions on which Fleming departed from accepted Bond style. An ex-military man (Major Dexter Smythe), retired and living in Jamaica is revealed to be a criminal whose luxurious lifestyle is based on stolen Nazi gold. Bond tracks the man down in a personal vendetta – the major had killed a German guide who had taught Bond to ski – and prepares to take him into custody, but Smythe takes one last swim and is accidentally drowned by a beloved octopus that lives by the reef near his house (the 'Octopussy' of the title).

Bond leaves, convinced that the major committed suicide to avoid dishonour. A rather melancholy piece, written towards the end of Fleming's life and reflecting his preoccupation with his own mortality, this story is strip-mined to provide Maud Adams's Octopussy's back-story. In the film, Major Smythe stole *Chinese* gold from *Korea* and unquestionably *did* kill himself to preserve his honour.

'The Property of a Lady' is used for the rough basis of the jewellery-smuggling subplot. A Russian mole within the Secret Service is being paid off for her years of service. This pay-off will come in the form of a piece of Russian jewellery sold, on her behalf, by the KGB. The Service know of this mole and decide that the KGB director himself would be present at the auction to bump up the price (so important is the mole that he would be the only man at the Russian embassy to know about her). The very simple story of Bond identifying this man is swathed in glossy description by Fleming of lush jewellery and the thrill of the auction house. In the film, the jewellery forms part of Orlov/Khan and Octopussy's complex smuggling/counterfeiting operation. The auction-room scene is one of the high points of this film, despite Roger Moore's deliberate mugging.

Where *For Your Eyes Only* deploys the source material it uses with skill, those elements of Fleming's fiction that appear in *Octopussy* seem almost randomly chosen, and haphazardly slotted in. Putting Smythe's story in as Maud Adams's character motivation is done clumsily and serves little purpose other than as a way for her and Bond to become acquainted quickly.

IN THE REAL WORLD: One of the most interesting aspects of *Octopussy* is its attitude to the Cold War. The film's characters, including Bond and General Orlov, believe that in a conventional war between the USSR and Western European democracies, the USSR would win with ease. This is the stance adopted by the picture itself, which is earnestly convinced that it is the nuclear deterrent, indeed the very presence of US airbases in Europe, which prevents an inevitably successful Soviet ground invasion. However, the reality is that by 1983 the military forces of the USSR were in no position even to contemplate such action – although no one in the West knew this at the time. This, more than anything, marks *Octopussy* as a product of its time – its political position is now little better than laughable.

The pre-credit sequence refers to events outside Europe. While it is generally assumed that the mysterious Latin American country that Bond is attempting to infiltrate is supposed to represent Cuba, at the time of production British forces had just fought a limited war against Argentina in the Falkland Islands. The anonymous country is probably supposed to represent all such 'troublesome' nations.

CULTURE VULTURE: The nuclear disarmament plot of *Octopussy* bears the closest resemblance, not to any work of Fleming, but rather to the writings of another spy writer, Frederick Forsyth. Like Fleming, a journalist turned novelist, Forsyth developed a style of writing that dealt with minor matters (such as obtaining a false passport) in great detail, keeping them as real as possible, so as to distract the audience from the absurd plot at the heart of every book. In *The Fourth Protocol*, he describes how a Soviet agent is sent to Britain on order to detonate a nuclear bomb at an American airbase in East Anglia. The intention behind this is that the public will be shocked into supporting unilateral disarmament and will therefore vote in the Labour party. Forsyth contended that hard left-wing elements within the party would then conspire to overthrow the leadership, installing a 'Marxist Leninist' prime minister – with apocalyptic results.

Incidentally, this potential Stalin is implied to be future London Mayor and popular media pundit Ken Livingstone. Although this is of circumstantial interest there is no way this plotline could have influenced the filmmakers, as the book was not published until 1984 – a year after the movie's release.

CRITICS: 'Part parody and part travesty', said the legendary Pauline Kael of *The New York Times* (27 June 1983). She considered herself 'resigned' to Roger Moore: 'He may not be heroic, but he's game,' she said. She thought even less of the women: 'Maud Adams is disappointingly warm and maternal . . . the role is a washout.' In the *Observer* Philip French (12 June) wasn't interested in yet another Bond picture. 'Writing about the Bond cycle is like reporting on the Ziegfeld Follies [which appeared annually on Broadway every year from 1907 to 1931] the shows get more opulent, new fashions are incorporated and the only real change is the date.' The *Sunday Express*'s Richard Barkley (12 June) thought *Octopussy* 'soothing escapist . . . Tomfoolery [which] dazzles the eye with action and locations . . . then suddenly condenses a vital plot twist into a burst of dialogue lasting microseconds. Fun though.' The *Morning Star* (10 June) ran its usual ideological piece: 'blatantly jingoistic and anti-Soviet', claimed Virginia Dignam, with some justice, admittedly, while conceding that 'the stunts are sometimes astonishing'. 'Bond without Bite', was the judgement of the *Scotsman*'s Michael Wigan (11 June), 'too little is incisive and clear cut, Bond's laconic and macabre wit is absent'. Unimpressed, he contemplated the idea that his lack of enthusiasm was his own fault: 'Maybe it's the palate that's jaded.'

BOX OFFICE: An opening weekend gross of $8 million in the US led to a substantial gross of $34 million in that market. Worldwide however, the picture took $188 million. This was down on *For Your Eyes Only*, which had itself seen a fall in receipts since *Moonraker*.

MARTINIS, GIRLS AND GUNS: One of Khan's thugs is spiked to death by a bed of nails, another dies with an octopus on his face. Three Russian soldiers are machine-gunned by Bond as he attempts to board the train. Twin 1 (Mishka) is smacked in the head with a heavy prop cannon while twin 2 (Grishka) is stabbed with his brother's knife. Six guards in Khan's palace cop it, and finally Khan's henchman Gobinda who – like a lot of characters in Glen-directed Bond films – falls to his death. A grand total of fourteen. A mere two notches on the 007 bed post and a solitary Martini.

THE ONE WITH . . .: the circus.

THE LAST WORD: 'Having trouble keeping it up?' *Octopussy* is a blackly comic Cold-War thriller – except for when it's a sub-Merchant Ivory Indian adventure. Part anti-Soviet melodrama (featuring classic espionage flashpoints such as the Berlin Wall and Checkpoint Charlie) and part ludicrous travelogue, it is satisfying as neither. It wants to have both joke-laden set pieces (the interminable jungle hunt) and moments of real tension (the bomb-defusing scene). It aims for emotional impact by trying to create well-drawn characters (hence the backstory of Octopussy herself) and still bursts with cheap innuendo ('I need filling up'). It wants both villains with terrifying goals (Orlov) and villains with no motives at all (Kamal Khan). In the process it fails to achieve any of these extremes as, just when one is becoming interesting, its polar opposite intrudes. Compounding this is the lack of any real flow to the confused narrative creating tedium where there should be tension. A plotless, witless, irredeemable mess.

GIRLS	34
MARTINIS	8
DEATHS	150

Bond's Colleagues: 'This was recovered from 004's body.'

Fleming's original Bond had two colleagues, 006 and 008, whose involvement was peripheral, although occasionally their missions or status would be mentioned. The cinematic Bond is part of a larger department, comprising nine agents (*Thunderball*), though this appears to have shrunk to six by *The World Is Not Enough*. Though Bond is the best agent the Service has, 008 seems to be next in line – twice M considers assigning him Bond's mission (in *Goldfinger* and *The Living Daylights* when he is to be recalled from Hong Kong).

The survival rate in the 00 branch is not good. Captain Nash (no number but possessing a piece of 00 equipment) dies at the hands of SPECTRE-assassin, Donald Grant (*From Russia With Love*). Bill Fairbanks (002) was killed by Scaramanga in Beirut in 1969. 009 is killed while on a mission in East Germany (*Octopussy*) while 003 dies shortly after retrieving a Russian microchip from Siberia. (*A View to a Kill*). The agent who inherited the number 002 survived the assassination policy of rogue Russian General Koskov (*The Living Daylights*) though 004 was not so lucky. 009 failed in his mission to kill Victor Zokas (*The World Is Not Enough*).

The most notorious 00 agent is 006 who faked his own death and formed a criminal group with the intent of launching an attack on London (*GoldenEye*).

Never Say Never Again (1983)

Produced by Jack Schwartzman
Executive Producer Kevin McClory
Written by Lorenzo Semple Jr
Based on an original story by Kevin McClory,
Jack Whittingham & Ian Fleming
Director of Photography: Douglas Slocombe, BSC
Production designed by Philip Harrision, Stephen Grimes
Music by Michael LeGrand
Title song lyrics by Alan and Marilyn Bergman
Title song sung by Lani Hall
Supervising Editor: Robert Lawrence
Directed by Irvin Kershner

PRINCIPAL CAST: Sean Connery (*James Bond*), Klaus Maria Brandauer (*Largo*), Max von Sydow (*Blofeld*), Barbara Carrera (*Fatima*), Kim Basinger (*Domino*), Bernie Casey (*Leiter*), Alec McCowen (*Q Algy*), Edward Fox (*M*), Pamela Salem (*Miss Moneypenny*), Rowan Atkinson (*Small-Fawcett*), Valerie Leon (*Lady in Bahamas*), Milos Kirek

(*Kovacs*), Pat Roach (*Lippe*), Anthony Sharp (*Lord Ambrose*), Prunella Gee (*Patricia*), Gavin O'Herlihy (*Jack Petachi*), Ronald Pickup (*Elliott*), Robert Rietty, Guido Adorni (*Italian Ministers*), Vincent Marzello (*Culpepper*), Christopher Reich (*Number 5*), Billy J Mitchell (*Captain Pederson*), Manning Redwood (*General Miller*), Anthony Van Laast (*Kurt*), Saskia Cohen Tanugi (*Nicole*), Sylvia Marriott (*French Minister*), Dan Meaden (*Bouncer at Casino*), Michael Medwin (*Doctor at Shrublands*), Lucy Hornak (*Nurse at Shrublands*), Derek Deadman (*Porter at Shrublands*), Joanna Dickens (*Cook at Shrublands*), Tony Alleff (*Auctioneer*), Paul Tucker (*Ship's Steward*), Brenda Kempner (*Masseuse*), Jill Meager (*Receptionist at Health Spa*), John Stephen Hill (*Communications Officer*), Wendy Leech (*Girl Hostage*), Roy Bowe (*Ship's Captain*).

PRE CREDITS AND TILES SEQUENCE: There's no pre-credits adventure (see **CUT SCENES**). The credits run over a sequence of Bond gaining entry to a villa in South America, where he attempts to rescue a kidnapped woman. Once he's freed her, however, she knifes him. We are then told that this is a Secret Service exercise to test Bond's fitness, and in this scenario the kidnapped girl had been brainwashed by her terrorist captors. It's all rather involving and well shot. Shame about the horrendous theme song and dodgy caption cards.

SUMMARY: SPECTRE, on the orders of Blofeld, have gained the services of USAF officer Jack Petachi, by addicting him to heroin and threatening his sister, Domino. Petachi is recovering from an operation to replace his right eye with a corneal replica of that of the President of the United States at Shrublands, a health farm where M has, coincidentally, also sent a semi-retired Bond. His suspicions raised by late-night violence, Bond investigates Petachi's room and discovers little more than a matchbook featuring a curious design. In the process of this, Bond is recognised by SPECTRE Number Twelve, Fatima Blush, who is 'caring' for Petachi.

Petachi uses his false eye to arm cruise missiles, intended for a test flight, with real nuclear warheads. He is then killed by Blush, and the warheads are intercepted by SPECTRE. The ransom for the return of these warheads is set at 25 per cent of the Gross Domestic Product of the NATO powers.

Bond's 007 status is reactivated and he is ordered to search for the warheads. The matchbook he found in Petachi's room is emblazoned with the same logo as several other items and properties, including a

yacht, belonging to millionaire Maximillian Largo who is currently in
the Bahamas. Bond follows him there, later re-acquainting himself with
Fatima Blush, who tries to kill him with a remote-controlled shark. He
follows Largo's boat to the South of the France, where he contacts
Largo's mistress Domino and meets Largo himself – later gaining access
to his yacht, *The Flying Saucer*. Bond informs Domino of the death of
her brother, and seduces her, enraging Largo. Fatima makes another
attempt to murder Bond, but he kills her instead.

Bond follows Largo again to North Africa, where Largo tells him that
the first bomb is in Washington DC. Bond deduces that a pendant given
to Domino by Largo shows the location of the other bomb; planted to
cause maximum destruction to the Middle Eastern oilfields. Bond finds
the bomb and defuses it, and Domino kills Largo. Bond and Domino
seemingly retire together to the Bahamas, with Bond swearing that his
secret service days are over.

UNIVERSAL EXPORTS:

BOND, JAMES BOND: An ageing figure who spends most of his time
teaching or participating in training exercises and war games. An
effective fighter, with an eye for the ladies and keen deductive skills, he
has retired by the end of the film. Bond smokes cigars (though he prefers
thin cheroots to Moore's hand-rolled Cubans). Bond is also skilled in
the playing of video games – Secret Service training obviously keeps all
bases covered.

M: Clearly a different character to Bernard Lee's M. This is a head of the
Secret Service, played very effectively by Edward Fox. He has little time
for the 00 section, and is hostile towards Bond. His attitude changes
completely in the aftermath of the mission. He realises that which we all
knew beforehand – without Bond the safety of the civilised world is
at risk.

MONEYPENNY: A simple, but enthusiastically friendly figure. Utterly
forgettable and in truth not much different to Lois Maxwell's
interpretation – she is clearly meant to be the same person.

Q: Again clearly meant to be the same character (his name is Algernon)
but played by a different actor. Alec McCowen, a fantastic stage actor
with many of the great roles of the English-speaking theatre under his

belt, delivers a stuttering and faintly unsavoury performance – one rather reminiscent of Michael Palin's 'Ken Shabby' character from *Monty Python's Flying Circus*.

ALLIES:

DOMINO: Largo's girlfriend, sister of the much-abused Jack Petachi. Vacant and unassuming, she switches sides to Bond the first chance she gets, and demonstrates little strength or steel. Her killing of Largo at the end (cathartic in *Thunderball*) seems out of character here.

FELIX LEITER: The most compelling Felix Leiter since Jack Lord. Sadly he gets little to do except swap a couple of quips and get Bond access to a US Navy submarine.

NICOLE: A field assistant assigned to Bond, she has what is presumably a French accent. She's killed by Fatima Blush after less than half a dozen lines of dialogue, and never demonstrates a personality.

THE OPPOSITION:

ERNST STAVRO BLOFELD: Now the SPECTRE 'Supreme Commander' rather than Number One (that designation belongs to Largo) he seems to be an inoffensive old man with a white cat who sounds a lot like he did in *From Russia with Love* and *Thunderball*.

MAXIMILLIAN LARGO: About as threatening as the middle-ranking bank official he so strongly resembles, this Largo has none of the piratical swagger of his previous incarnation. Klaus Maria Brandeur is a fine actor, with roles in many great films. His mistake with Largo is to try and deliver a convincing portrayal of a psychotic monster. When up against a smirking Sean Connery and the wooden Kim Basinger, it's somehow Brandeur's detailed, skilled performance that comes across as silly.

FATIMA BLUSH: A cackling femme fatale, all ostrich feathers and leather trousers who manages the unique feat of being both utterly over the top and exceptionally bland. The filmmakers clearly think there's something excitingly dangerous-kinky-sexy about her dealing out of both pain and pleasure and her (ridiculously dangerous) habits of keeping a syringe full of heroin in her garter and a large snake in her car. There isn't. She is killed by Bond's exploding fountain pen.

PRINCIPAL CASTING: Sean Connery had expressed an interest in returning to the role of James Bond as early as 1976, and had been involved in the writing of McClory's earlier aborted *Thunderball* remake, *Warhead*. He had walked away from that project when legal difficulties arose, and was only prepared to star in *Never Say Never Again* once he had been given assurances that the picture was 'legally bona fide'. In the early 80s Connery's career was, if not in decline, temporarily stalled – he was no longer a young leading man, but he hadn't yet achieved his future position as elder statesman and versatile character actor. This was the dry middle period of his Hollywood life, and the thought of returning to his star-making role must have appealed to him – he was also paid an undisclosed but reportedly impressive fee.

Distinguished German stage actor Klaus Maria Brandauer had won acclaim for his performance in *Mephisto* (Istvan Szabo, 1981). After *Never Say Never Again* he would receive an Oscar nomination for his work on *Out of Africa* (Sydney Pollack, 1985).

Max von Sydow provided suave support in the role of Blofeld. Best known for his chess game against Death in *The Seventh Seal* (Ingmar Bergman, 1957), and his performance as an elderly priest in *The Exorcist* (William Friedkin, 1973), his sepulchral tones and elegant manner are largely wasted here.

In 1983 model Kim Basinger was just beginning her film career. After her big break in *9½ Weeks* (Adrian Lyne, 1986), she would go on to appear in *Batman* (Tim Burton, 1989) before winning an Oscar for *LA Confidential* (Curtis Hanson, 1997).

Bernie Casey, who played Felix Leiter, was a veteran of Blaxploitation cinema including a great performance in the title role of *Hit Man* (George Armitage, 1972), a remake of the seminal *Get Carter* (Mike Hodges, 1971).

DIRECTOR AND CREW: Irvin Kershner had directed *The Empire Strikes Back* (1980), the follow up to *Star Wars* and one of the few sequels universally held to be as good as its predecessor. He was later responsible for the gory and inferior *Robocop 2* (1990). Credited screenwriter Lorenzo Semple Jr has also turned out work of varying quality, having worked on fantastic post-Watergate paranoia film *The Parallax View* (Alan Pakula, 1974) as well as on the 60s kitsch-a-thon *Batman* TV series and spin-off film (Leslie Martinson, 1966).

British scriptwriters Dick Clement and Ian La Frenais, known for sitcoms such as *Porridge* and *Whatever Happened To The Likely Lads?* performed uncredited rewrites on the screenplay at Sean Connery's personal request. They would later go on to write the hit comedy, *Vice Versa* (Brian Gilbert, 1988). Clement's films as director include *The Commitments* (1991).

It is also generally accepted that multi-Oscar winning director/ screenwriter Francis Ford Coppola (*The Godfather*, *Apocalypse Now* etc.) – the brother of Talia Shire, part owner of the production company responsible for this film – had an uncredited hand in rewrites.

Second unit director David Tomblin had been a successful television writer/director/producer in Britain in the 60s (he had produced *The Prisoner*) before moving to Hollywood to perform second unit duties on films such as *Raiders of the Lost Ark* (Steven Spielberg, 1980) and its sequels.

MUSICAL NOTES: The score is bizarrely intermittent; often ridiculously intrusive and as frequently noticeably absent. It's part sub-John Williams parping (the shark attack) and part-pseudo Nino Rota French comedy stylings. Neither work.

SET PIECES: *Never Say Never Again* has the feel of forced economy. The 'grand' car chase features three cars and a motorbike; the underwater sequences lack flair and there isn't so much a finale as a sort of gradual halt. *Thunderball* had a specially staged carnival in Nassau; *Never Say Never Again* has eight men in fright masks with party hooters.

POSITIVELY SHOCKING: The tone of the picture is all wrong; there's something strangely adolescent about the film's lame attempts to use heroin and nurse's outfits to titillate and seem 'grown up'. It also has any Bond film's closest thing to a 'traditional' sex scene (Fatima and Bond on the boat) which it cuts to and from in a way which is meant to be 'arty'.

CUT SCENES: One draft of the script contained a pre-credit sequence, in which two knights at a pseudo-medieval pageant are seen jousting. One kills the other with an armour-piercing lance, and a third knight (revealed as he removes his helmet to be Bond) gives chase.

MEMORABLE QUOTES:
M (talking about free radicals): 'Toxins which destroy the body and the brain. Caused by eating too much red meat and white bread – and too many dry Martinis.'

Bond: 'Well I shall endeavour to cut out the white bread, sir.'

Q: 'Good to see you Mr Bond, things have been awfully dull round here . . . now you're on this I hope we're going to have some gratuitous sex and violence.'

FASHION VICTIMS: Another let down. A nice little linen suit shows early promise but soon Bond is shamelessly strutting around in a grotesque pair of dungarees. Largo swaggers around his yacht with a sweater 'nonchalantly' draped over his shoulders. Domino does better, but even she's not infallible with her penchant for legwarmers. The final indignity comes in the form of Blush's disgraceful outfits of fur and leather, 'specially designed for Barbara Ferrera by Fendi'.

PRODUCT PLACEMENT: When smuggling luxury food and drink into health farms, Bond prefers Absolut vodka. An odd example of product placement comes with the positioning of numerous mid-80s arcade classics (such as *Centipede* and *Robotron*) at Largo's charity ball.

GADGETS: Q talks of budget cuts, so it is small wonder that Bond has little impressive gadgetry. An unimpressive, but very useful, watch-mounted laser and fountain pen that fires a small (but very explosive) rocket make up Bond's arsenal, along with a special motorbike that seems rather a rushed job by Q-branch. Its only special features are front and rear bumpers and a rocket motor. Blush has no excuse for her total ineptitude at assassination. She has access to remotely detonated explosives and a remote-controlled shark. SPECTRE is also equipped with a TV camera hidden in a metal casting of a skull and technology that allows them to duplicate presidential release authority for American nuclear warheads.

SOURCE TO SCREEN: This film is best classified as a curio thrown up by the legal wrangling over *Thunderball*. Though Kevin McClory had made a deal with Harry Saltzman and Cubby Broccoli to make this 1965 Bond film, he had retained the right to the film elements he had won as a result of his legal battle with Ian Fleming (see **Thunderball**). There were periodic threats from McClory that he would make a rival Bond picture but it was not until 1983 that his plans came to fruition. With backing from Warner Bros, in a deal engineered by attorney Jack Schwartzman, Lorenzo Semple Jr was commissioned to write a screenplay that had, by legal necessity, to occupy certain well-defined boundaries. McClory's victory was far from absolute. He had won the film rights to the novel, *Thunderball*, and the unused script material upon which it was based. Any Bond film he might try to make had to be developed from this one storyline; any attempt to deviate significantly from this plot would incur legal action from Eon. McClory was imprisoned by a highly restrictive set of plot criteria. This explains the fundamental resemblance to *Thunderball* – all changes are basically cosmetic. For instance, nuclear bombs become cruise missiles. There was a threat of a further McClory Bond film in 1997, but this never materialised. This would have had to be yet another remake of *Thunderball*.

Production on *Never Say Never Again* was troubled. Producer Jack Schwartzman later admitted that he had seriously underestimated the cost of making an action film on this scale. After the production budget ran out, he funded the picture out of his own personal wealth. Connery would later criticise those involved in the picture, and argue that he and second unit director David Tomblin had effectively produced the film between them. After completing this film Connery would not make an appearance on the cinema screen for nearly two years (in Russell Malcahy's cult classic *Highlander*), suggesting more than ample truth to his claims that *Never Say Never Again* had all but exhausted him.

IN THE REAL WORLD: *Never Say Never Again* makes a few gestures to updating the *Thunderball* story. Cruise missiles were the latest (and most controversial) addition to the NATO arsenal while the optical recognition system needed to arm the warheads was way ahead of its time. As an aside it is not necessarily true that the president would have to travel to England to arm the warheads – SPECTRE hack into the arming system. It could be assumed that the retinal authorisation would be transmitted from overseas. A final update comes from the change of targets, the Middle Eastern oilfields were strategically vital.

A non-vital plot element worth mentioning is the story's use of video games that, at the time of filming, were becoming a worldwide craze.

CRITICS: Respected American commentator Roger Ebert captured the mood of many reviewers when he wrote 'there was never a Beatles reunion . . . but here, by God is Sean Connery as Sir James Bond. Good work 007'. David Castel in the *Sunday Telegraph* (18 December 1983) and Derek Malcolm in the *Guardian* (15 December) both heaped qualified praise on Connery's return to Bondage. Castel arguec that *Never Say Never Again* was the first time 'in a decade that the Bonds have had a new look' and Malcolm simply enjoyed Connery's 'effortless traversing' of the part that had once been solely his.

BOX OFFICE: The second Bond film of the year, *Never Say Never Again* benefited from the publicity surrounding the 'Battle of the Bonds' (a journalistic invention that never affected Sean Connery and Roger Moore's very good personal relationship) and took around $9 million in its opening weekend. This was a million more than *Octopussy*, and must have given McClory much cause for celebration. Ultimately *Never Say Never Again* took less than *Octopussy* across the whole of its cinema run, chalking up a (still impressive) $28 million – substantially less than *Octopussy*'s $34 million.

MARTINIS, GIRLS AND GUNS: Bond drinks two Martinis, one in the Bahamas and one on Largo's yacht. He kills four people – the brawny assassin sent to despatch him at Shrublands, Fatima Blush with a rocked pen, and two in his escape from the fort where Largo plans to sell Domino as a slave. There are three more notches on the 007 bedpost: a nurse at Shrublands, Domino and Fatima, who at this point stops being merely tedious and turns into a caricature of a psycho ex-girlfriend from hell.

THE LAST WORD: 'Do I look like the sort of man who'd make trouble?' *Never Say Never Again* scores in a number of areas early on before comprehensively falling to pieces around fifteen minutes in. There's some witty dialogue, and the idea of Bond as a middle-aged man coming out of retirement for one last job is intriguing, but the notion is not exploited to its fullest. The production chaos is visible on screen, with frequently mediocre editing, direction, stunt work and photography all emerging from the restricted budget. For most of the film there is little reference to the stolen nuclear devices (the lynchpin of the 'plot') and little sense of global threat. At the time, *Never Say Never Again* got away with it, thanks to public and critical pleasure at seeing Connery again. Now it is dated, slow and (worst of all) looks cheap, faring badly when compared to even the poorest of the Eon films. Pointless.

GIRLS	3
MARTINIS	2
DEATHS	4

A View to a Kill (1985)

Produced by Albert R Broccoli and Michael G Wilson
Screenplay by Richard Maibaum and Michael G Wilson
Music composed and conducted by John Barry
Title song performed by Duran Duran
Title song composed by Duran Duran and John Barry
Production designed by Peter Lamont
Editor: Peter Davies
Directed by John Glen

PRINCIPAL CAST: Roger Moore (*James Bond*), Christopher Walken (*Max Zorin*), Tanya Roberts (*Stacey Sutton*), Grace Jones (*May Day*), Patrick Macnee (*Tibbett*), Patrick Bauchau (*Scarpine*), David Yip (*Chuck Lee*), Fiona Fullerton (*Pola Ivanova*), Manning Redwood (*Bob Conley*), Alison Doody (*Jenny Flex*), Willoughby Gray (*Dr Carl Mortner*), Desmond Llewelyn (*Q*), Robert Brown (*M*), Lois Maxwell (*Miss Moneypenny*), Walter Gotell (*General Gogol*), Geoffrey Keen (*Minister of Defence*), Jean Rougerie (*Aubergine*), Daniel Benzali (*Howe*), Bogdan Kominowski (*Klotkoff*), Papillon Soo Soo (*Pan Ho*), Mary Stavin (*Kimberley Jones*), Dominique Risbourg (*Butterfly Act Compere*), Carole Ashby (*Whistling Girl*), Anthony Chinn (*Taiwanese Tycoon*), Lucien Jérôme (*Paris Taxi Driver*), Joe Flood (*Police Captain*), Gerard Buhr (*Auctioneer*), Dolph Lundgren (*Venz*), Tony Sibbald (*Mine Foreman*), Bill Ackridge (*O'Rourke*), Ron Tarr, Taylor McAuley (*Guards*), Peter Ensor (*Tycoon*), Seva Novgorodtsev (*Helicopter Pilot*).

PRE-CREDITS AND TITLES: It's Bond versus communists on ice again. A less spectacular reprise of the opening of *The Spy Who Loved Me* as Bond retrieves a microchip from the deceased 003. It's fun all the same, with an impressive helicopter crash and some neat skiing stunts, although the dubbing on of The Beach Boys' 'California Girls' is ludicrous. The mini-submarine (with Union Jack interior hatch, comfortable sofa and scantily clad, eyebrow fluttering captain) is staggeringly ridiculous. The title sequence is, hands down, the worst for any Bond film, with nasty laser-light visuals and neon body paint. It does not deserve Duran Duran's superb title song.

SUMMARY: Millionaire industrialist Max Zorin wants to corner the global market in microchips. To this end he initiates Project Mainstrike.

By pumping water into California's geological faults and then blowing up key 'locks' (formations of rock which prevent the faults from moving simultaneously) Zorin hopes to flood Silicon Valley. Then he, with the support of the cartel of microchip companies put together for this purpose, will dominate production.

The Secret Service become suspicious when a secret British microchip design is found in Soviet hands. Bond infiltrates Zorin's French mansion and discovers that the industrialist is hoarding computer chips. In tandem with geologist, Stacey Sutton, Bond then investigates Zorin's mining and drilling operations in California, discovers his scheme and kills him.

UNIVERSAL EXPORTS:

BOND, JAMES BOND: Once again Bond demonstrates an enthusiasm for being as rude as possible to his host (see **Thunderball**). He believes that 'a successful cover becomes second nature'. He doesn't know a great deal about horses, but is successful at betting on the winners at the track. He uses the alias 'James St John Smythe' while at the horse sale and 'James Stock of the London Financial Times' while in San Francisco. In one of the most disturbing moments of the series he treats Stacey Sutton to a tasty home-made quiche. James Bond – gentleman spy, lover, killer, scourge of the Soviets and saviour of the free world – bakes a quiche.

SIR GODFREY TIBBETT: Secret Service agent and expert in horses, Sir Godfrey accompanies Bond to Zorin's horse sale to provide expert assistance. The banter between the obnoxious 'James St John Smythe' and his faux-valet Tibbett is the highlight of the film. This makes Tibbett's death at the hands of May Day genuinely upsetting.

M: Flustered and generally put out by Bond's irreverent approach, a far cry from the calm, collected Bernard Lee. M assigns Bond to investigate Zorin and, reluctantly, bails him out of trouble with the French police. This M seems rather blasé about British intelligence secrets – for the second time, the head of the KGB is invited into his office.

MONEYPENNY: As well as performing the usual witless innuendo scene, Moneypenny is invited on what appears to be an MI6 company outing to the races. There is also a brief glimpse of her at the close of the film, as M imparts the news that Bond is missing and she infers the worst. This was to be the last sight of the original screen Moneypenny, crying into her handkerchief.

Q: Helps out in M's initial briefing, explaining the functions of the Electro Magnetic Pulse resistant microchip.

OHMSS: Agent 003 was lost in the first attempt to recover the microchip from Siberia. The Service seems to run company outings to the races. In attendance are Q, Moneypenny and M. This cosiness is a far cry from the professional – albeit good-natured – agency from around the time of **From Russia With Love.**

ALLIES:

STACEY SUTTON: Heir to a Californian mining family, whose company Zorin has tried to buy up. Fighting him in the courts has reduced her to relative penury (though she still has her family mansion) and she has taken the job of state geologist.

Bond first sees Sutton at Zorin's stud auction. He learns that she has been given a cheque by Zorin so assumes she is on his payroll. On discovering they are fighting the same enemy they work together to stop Zorin.

Having said this, Sutton is second only to Goodnight (**The Man with the Golden Gun**) for the title of least useful and least interesting Bond girl. She spends a large part of the film screaming while dangling from great heights. The nadir comes when she gallops across a field into Bond's arms, completely oblivious of the huge airship looming behind her. She is utterly inconsequential and very annoying.

POLA IVANOVA: Russian agent who sleeps with Bond and with whom he has had prior involvement. In this mission he meets her by accident. She had been sent to destroy Zorin's offshore oil platform at the same time that Bond is investigating it to learn more about Zorin's plan.

CHUCK LEE: Agent for the CIA and Bond's contact in San Francisco. Though Tibbett serves as the film's 'sacrificial lamb', Lee is also killed off in a similar manner. However, we hardly know the character and there is little pathos as a result of his death, which takes place primarily to prevent any official help reaching Bond.

FREDERICK GRAY: The ageing politico is present for Bond's briefing. It is tricky to justify the head of the ministry being present for such a matter, although, as with *Octopussy*, the visit of the head of the KGB would count as a ceremonial matter in which he should be involved.

GENERAL GOGOL: While the British are investigating Zorin, the KGB are trying to kill him. A former employee, he is guilty of trying to leave the Service. The Russians must either be running low on resources, or regard the mission as very important as General Gogol personally visits Zorin, and participates in Ivanova's attempt to destroy the drilling platform. This leads to an absurd moment where Gogol – who is both a Soviet general and the head of the KGB – acts as the getaway driver to one of his agents in an operation on American soil.

Though not formal allies, the aims of the Russians are commensurate with those of the British. Indeed, Gogol seems so pleased that he offers Bond Russia's highest decoration – the Order of Lenin – at the close of the mission. Presumably this is for disposing of a rogue KGB agent rather than for protecting Soviet technological growth which, a beaming Gogol states, relies on stolen Western technology.

It si likely that the fact that Bond has twice prevented World War Three in recent years (*The Spy Who Loved Me* and *Octopussy*) is also taken into account.

THE OPPOSITION:

MAX ZORIN: The product of Nazi experimentation on women held in concentration camps, Zorin is a genuinely psychotic, blond-haired blue-eyed Aryan superman. He was born in Dresden in 1945, and fled East Germany to the West in the 1960s. He has a French passport, is regarded as 'a staunch anti-communist' and owns racehorses. M claims Zorin can speak five languages without a trace of any accent. Given his bizarre combined middle-European/Anglo-American drawl it can perhaps be assumed that English is his sixth language. He is an important industrialist with involvement in oil and gas, electronics and hi-tech companies.

Zorin is in many ways an updating of Auric Goldfinger. His key objective is global dominance in his particular field of interest – microchips. What is especially interesting is how close his character comes to genuine social critique. All Zorin does is take the tenets of capitalism to their logical conclusion: in co-operation with his business partners he sets out to bury the opposition (literally). Of course, this symbolism is fudged by the character being, simultaneously, a Communist and a Nazi, but it is still amusing to see this particular motivation for a Bond villain in the mid-80s, a time of Yuppies, 'greed is good' and all-round enthusiasm for ruthless business practices.

MAY DAY: Companion and martial arts trainer to Zorin, their exact relationship is ambiguous. Her reaction to Zorin's advances in the training room is hostile, and he seems very ready to let her sleep with Bond, but they are very close initially. She acts as his right-hand woman and carries out assassinations on his behalf. She seems deeply committed to his cause and, even having slept with Bond, her allegiance remains the same, trying to kill Bond at City Hall. However, Zorin all but turns against her in the final third of the film, killing her female assistants and being surprisingly flippant about her fate. In one of the most surprising change of sides, she joins with Bond because she 'thought that creep loved me'. Indeed, Zorin seems not to realise how much he did love her – there is real shock on his face when he sees her fiery death.

May Day is an interesting variation on the Fiona Volpe (**Thunderball**) character. She is in thrall neither to Zorin nor Bond and makes her own choice of final allegiance on her own terms, not dictated by who she last slept with but on the grounds of her betrayal at the hands of Zorin.

DR CARL MORTNER/HANS GLAUS: He carried out Nazi experiments under the name of Glaus then worked for the Soviets under the name of Mortner, developing steroids for their athletes. He has adapted this into a technique for providing horses with a brief boost of natural steroids, giving them the impetus to win a race, without the risk of anything showing up in a drugs test.

Mortner has a paternal attitude to Zorin and is heartbroken to see his 'son' fall to his death off the Golden Gate bridge. He himself is killed with Scarpine as they fumble around for a dynamite stick, lit with the intention of blowing up Bond.

SCARPINE: Zorin's reptilian head of security. Scarpine, it turns out, is his closest associate – even closer than May Day – as it is only he and Mortner who survive the massacre in the mine. He helps Zorin in this massacre and pilots the airship at the end, an airship on which he and Mortner perish.

BOB CONLEY: Zorin's mining expert. He was the chief engineer at an African mine which collapsed, killing twenty miners. He now runs oil rigs and mines essential to Project Mainstrike, the rigs pumping water into geological seams, the mine acting as the focal point for the blast that will set the faults moving. Conley is killed, along with all his workers, in Zorin's gun rampage at the end of the film.

PRINCIPAL CASTING: Despite his advanced age, Roger Moore was once again signed up for what was to be his final appearance in the role of Bond. In this picture he is playing opposite a leading actress almost exactly half his age (Tanya Roberts was 30. Moore was 58). Moore had played Bond in seven films, a total so far unmatched by any other actor. Since retiring from Bond, Moore has continued to work in films, such as *Spiceworld: The Movie* (Bob Spiers, 1997) and the abysmal Michael Winner comedy *Bullseye!* (1990) alongside his friend Michael Caine. He has also hosted numerous documentaries and appeared in tribute programmes to other British stars. In 2002 he was cast as an enigmatic, aged British agent in deliberately ludicrous US action series, *Alias*.

Tanya Roberts attracted attention for her appearance as one of the Angels in final season of *Charlie's Angels* (1980–1). She appeared, though most of her clothes did not, in a number of low-budget/low-quality films such as *Beastmaster* (Don Coscarelli, 1982). She is unfortunate enough to have *A View to a Kill* as the peak of her movie career. She is now a regular in the popular US sitcom *That '70s Show*.

Conversely, Christopher Walken is one of the most talented and well-known actors to appear in a Bond film. A former child actor, Walken won an Academy Award for *The Deer Hunter* (Michael Cimino, 1978). His long and distinguished CV includes *The King of New York* (Abel Ferrara, 1990), *Batman Returns* (Tim Burton, 1992), *True Romance* (Tony Scott, 1993) and *Pulp Fiction* (Quentin Tarantino, 1995).

Flamboyant 80s singing star Grace Jones took the role of May Day. She had previously appeared in terrible fantasy sequel *Conan, The Destroyer* (Richard Fleischer, 1984). Her only other film performance of note is a distinctive cameo in the underrated Eddie Murphy film *Boomerang* (Reginald Hudlin, 1992).

Casting Patrick Macnee alongside Roger Moore put the two elder statesmen of 60s British spy series on screen together. Macnee had become a star through his performance as John Steed in *The Avengers*, just as Roger Moore came to prominence for his role in *The Saint*. With the exception of this picture Macnee's cinema career has been restricted to enjoyable cameo roles.

This would be the last appearance by Lois Maxwell. As with Roger Moore, it was simply a matter of age. She had appeared in *Lolita* (Stanley Kubrick, 1962) but became typecast in the role of Moneypenny. Unlike Roger Moore, Maxwell was singularly reluctant to leave the series and suggested that she be kept on as Moneypenny's mother or, a less realistic suggestion, as M.

DIRECTOR AND CREW: Another demonstration of the tight-knit 'Bond family': director John Glen (pigeons replaced by a caged bird in Sutton's San Francisco mansion), composer John Barry, cinematographer Alan Hume, editor Peter Davies and production designer Peter Lamont were all Bond veterans.

MUSICAL NOTES: A terrific theme song from Duran Duran, an act then at the top of their game (the band would perform it at Live Aid that summer), forms the melodic basis for yet another terrific John Barry score. Particular highlights are the fantastic deep string and stings of the pre-credits action and the beautifully lush orchestral rendition of the title song.

SET PIECES: The structure of *A View to a Kill* is stranger than that of any other Bond film. Though all of them are guilty, to an extent, of providing ludicrous excuses so that certain action sequences can be shot, around 45 minutes of *A View to a Kill*, from the moment Bond arrives at the stud farm to his arrival in San Francisco, serve no narrative purpose. Bond discovers Zorin's hoard of microchips and meets Stacey Sutton. Why not just stage this in a five-minute warehouse sequence? Because setting it on an estate devoted to horses allows for a horse-race set piece – Zorin's steeplechase of death.

Though there are some good stunts in the film, May Day's Parisian parachute jump especially, it is ultimately underwhelming. For some reason, none of the set pieces spark any real interest in this badly put together story.

POSITIVELY SHOCKING: Zorin's killing spree is a gruesome way of tying up the loose end of the fate of all those mine workers. Tibbett's death is unpleasant, more because of the regard built up for the character.

CUT SCENES: One slight, amusing scene cut from the finished picture was of Bond having his possessions returned after having spent the night in a French police cell. These include a watch with a garrotte wire ('From Russia, with love', Bond quips to M with a raised eyebrow) and a lighter that fires a burst of flame. Bond signs the paper allowing him to take his possessions with a pen which then burns up the document he has signed.

MEMORABLE QUOTES:
Zorin: 'Intuitive improvisation. The mark of genius.'

Zorin: 'This is going to hurt him more than it hurts me.'

Bond (after sleeping with May Day): 'I was a little restless but I got off eventually.'

FASHION VICTIMS: An undistinguished outing all round. The men are uniformly attired in business suits, though the lightweight suit worn by Bond in San Francisco is worth a mention. The only clothing that really stands out is that worn by May Day, designed by the Azzedine Alaia label and the vile, fur-hooded ski-suit worn by Bond.

PRODUCT PLACEMENT: Bond and Jones drink Stolichnaya vodka on the motorised iceberg. Apart from that the film features an esoteric selection of brands. Tibbett chooses a BP (British Petroleum) petrol station – in France! – to wash his car, Zorin possesses a Diners Club card and Philips computer. Bond questions the content of Sutton's larder, suggesting they might have to dine on 'Whiskas'.

GADGETS: Q isn't exactly overemployed here, providing a number of rather mundane gadgets, all of which have rather unfortunate drawbacks. Bond's signet ring-camera has a flash making it all too obtrusive, his sunglasses, while eliminating all reflections and thus allowing him to peer into a room from outside, require him to stare fixedly into the window in question and, most ridiculously, the bug detector, designed to help him find listening devices emits a piercing beep when it finds one.

There is also a small robot which resembles a mechanical dog on wheels. The purpose of this metal beast is allegedly surveillance, though it is itself easy to detect. Its only use comes when the Service are searching for 007, Q using it to spy on Bond and Sutton in the shower.

The jury is still out on the motorised iceberg. On the one hand it is a handy way of infiltrating Siberia, but on the other it seems most unprofessional to have decorated the inside like a 60s bachelor pad.

SOURCE TO SCREEN: *A View to a Kill* follows in the footsteps of *The Spy Who Loved Me*, borrowing the title of a literary Bond, but none of its names or plot elements. In this case, the filmmakers return to the *For Your Eyes Only* collection of short stories. 'From a View to a Kill' sends Bond to France to solve the mystery of disappearing NATO dispatch riders from SHAPE (Supreme Headquarters, Allied Powers Europe) near Paris. Despite the American base commander's dislike of Bond, the agent discovers a small group of Russians living in an underground base. Like

BOND FILMS A View to a Kill

several of its companion stories, this began life as one of Fleming's screen treatments for a proposed Bond TV series and, as it stood, would have made a nice, short drama. For the film the makers jettison any reference to the plot, and the first word of the title. It is easy to see why. There is no way the plot could have been stretched over two hours and it does not rank as one of Fleming's most inventive pieces.

Instead, the plot of *Goldfinger* was recycled, with the more relevant resource of the microchip replacing gold, Auric becoming Max, a business meeting between Goldfinger and gangsters becoming the formation of a business cartel and Fort Knox becoming Silicon Valley. There is even a stud farm in both films. The addition of a horse-racing scene, the usual Maibaum/Wilson hint of Cold War topicality and a link to earlier history – Zorin's Nazi heritage – completes the mix.

IN THE REAL WORLD: The microchip is a logical substitute for gold – Zorin states as much when he draws attention to the new value attached to the abundant mineral silicon at his business meeting. The most important technological development since the transistor, this small component became vital in nearly all everyday electrical appliances, making global control of this market a desirable objective indeed.

The ubiquity of this component also meant that any threat to it had to be taken very seriously indeed. In dealing with the danger posed by Electro Magnetic Pulse, the Secret Service is on the cutting edge. See **GoldenEye**.

CULTURE VULTURE: Following the famous sequence in *Indiana Jones and the Temple of Doom* (Steven Spielberg, 1984) a mine setting of some description was a must for action films. It is impressive that the Bond team resisted the temptation to put 007 in a mine-cart.

CRITICS: Reviewers were not slow to pick up on Roger Moore's advanced age. In *The New York Times* (24 June 1985), Janet Maslin comments that 'the effort involved in keeping Roger Moore's 007 impervious to age . . . seems overwhelming.' This aside, critics generally appeared unimpressed by the film or the actor. Maslin refers to the globetrotting nature of the film in a negative way: 'As the scenery improves, the Bond films lose personality.' She goes on to comment on the 'less than dynamic plot twists' and to refer to the less than able Miss Roberts as 'a barbie doll brought to life.'

Alexander Walker of the *Evening Standard* (13 June) was more positive, referring to *A View to a Kill*'s many predecessors: 'It would be odd after thirteen successes if they got the recipe wrong', though, even with all his enthusiasm, he is forced to admit that 'Those of us who wistfully recall the days when the chips Bond handled were the ones in *Casino Royale*, won't warm to silicon chips in quite the same way.'

BOX OFFICE: A worldwide gross of $153 million was impressive, but represented a general decline in the series' takings since the mid-70s. Worse, in America the 16.6 million admissions demonstrated a loss of nearly ten million viewers since *Octopussy*.

AWARDS: John Barry and Duran Duran received a much-deserved Golden Globe nomination in 1986 for their title song. Tanya Roberts also received a 1986 nomination – for the Golden Raspberry worst actress award. Not an award as such, but Duran Duran's title song became the Bond series' only UK number one hit single. It was backed by a superb promotional video featuring clips from the film and the band's leader introducing himself as 'Bon, Simon Le Bon.'

MARTINIS, GIRLS AND GUNS: Though Bond consumes no Martinis, he does sleep with four women – a joint record with *From Russia With Love*: Agent Kimberley Jones on the fake iceberg in the pre-credits sequence, May Day, Pola Ivanova and Stacey Sutton. His only definite kills are the two Russian pilots in the pre-credit sequence and Zorin himself. As for the deaths of Mortner and Scarpine in the airship explosion, it is Bond's action causes them to lose the dynamite leading to the explosion so he deserves the credit there, too. Five kills for Bond.

THE ONE WITH . . .: Grace Jones and the fight on the Golden Gate Bridge.

THE LAST WORD: 'If you're the best they have, they'll more likely try and cover up your embarrassing incompetence.' Uninspired and uninvolving, *A View to a Kill* is a barely efficient retread of *Goldfinger*, minus the swagger. In its favour is the fact that it *is* quite funny and that the acting is generally of a high standard. Of special note is the wonderful chemistry between Roger Moore and Patrick MacNee. Moore shines, actually, and you have to give credit to the only 58-year-old man in history able to convincingly play a secret agent little more than half his own age. A potentially crackerjack finale above the Golden Gate Bridge is ruined by poor front (and back) projection. *A View to a Kill* is desperately ordinary. While not actively offensive, it is scarcely interesting enough to merit contemplating viewing it.

GIRLS	38
MARTINIS	8
DEATHS	155

The Living Daylights (1987)

Produced by Albert R Broccoli and Michael G Wilson
Screenplay by Richard Maibaum and Michael G Wilson
Director of Photography Alec Mills
Music composed and conducted by John Barry
Title song performed by a-ha
Title song composed by Pal Waaktaar and John Barry
Production Designed by Peter Lamont
Editors John Grover and Peter Davies
Directed by John Glen

PRINCIPAL CAST: Timothy Dalton (*James Bond*), Maryam d'Abo (*Kara Milovy*), Jeroen Krabbé (*General Georgi Koskov*), Joe Don Baker (*Brad Whitaker*), John Rhys-Davies (*General Leonid Pushkin*), Art Malik (*Kamran Shah*), Andreas Wisniewski (*Necros*), Thomas Wheatley (*Saunders*), Desmond Llewelyn (*Q*), Robert Brown (*M*), Geoffrey Keen (*Minister of Defence*), Walter Gotell (*General Anatol Gogol*), Caroline Bliss (*Miss Moneypenny*), John Terry (*Felix Leiter*), Virginia Hey (*Rubavitch*), John Bowe (*Colonel Feyador*), Julie T Wallace (*Rosika Miklos*), Kell Tyler (*Linda*), Catherine Rabett (*Liz*), Dulice Liecier (*Ava*), Nadim Sawalha (*Chief of Security, Tangiers*), Alan Talbot (*Koskov's KGB Minder*), Carl Rigg (*Imposter*), Tony Cyrus (*Chief of Snow Leopard Brotherhood*), Atik Mohamed (*Achmed*), Michael Moor (*Kamran's Man*), Sumar Khan (*Kamran's Man*), Ken Sharrock (*Jailer*), Peter Porteous (*Gasworks Supervisor*), Antony Carrick (*Male Secretary, Blayden*), Frederick Warder (*004*), Glyn Baker (*002*), Derek Hoxby (*Sergeant Stagg*), Bill Weston (*Butler, Blayden*), Richard Cubison (*Trade Centre Toastmaster*), Heinz Winter (*Concierge, Vienna Hotel*), Leslie French (*Lavatory Attendant*).

PRE-CREDITS AND TITLES: A very traditional version of Monty Norman's 'James Bond Theme' plays as Timothy Dalton's Bond walks the pinhole camera walk in evening dress. This cuts to three 00 agents parachuting out of a C130 Hercules transport plane over Gibraltar to take part in a training exercise. They're observed from the ground by a figure who then murders one of them, after showing him a note reading 'Smiert Spionem'. Bond gives chase, leaping on top of a Land Rover and holding on as it winds down the mountain roads. The Land Rover launches off the rock at high speed, and thanks to Bond's efforts, explodes. Bond parachutes to safety, nay luxury, landing on a yacht. Here he encounters a short-haired, bikini-clad brunette, who is complaining into her telephone that she can't find herself 'a real man'. After introducing himself Bond resolves to stay for an hour or two. Combining excellent stunt-work, macabre touches, some wit and a little sex appeal this is one of the best pre-credits sequences in the series. The title sequence is not really much fun, but the theme song is 24-carat pop gold.

SUMMARY: KGB General Georgi Koskov and American arms dealer Brad Whitaker have cooked up a 'get rich' scheme. Koskov will authorise the advancement to Whitaker of a down payment of $50 million for some weapons. Whitaker will then use this money to purchase diamonds from the Netherlands; these will be smuggled into Afghanistan where (as non-traceable currency) they can be used to buy opium. This opium can then be sold on the streets of America for approximately half a billion dollars.

They will use some of this money to purchase the weapons, delivering them to the Russians as per agreement, then covering up their tracks and resulting a clear profit of around $450 million.

As a further protective measure, Koskov tries to arrange to have his KGB superior general Pushkin (who does not trust him or Whitaker) murdered by British intelligence. Koskov fakes his own defection and convinces MI6 that Pushkin is responsible for a programme named *Smiert Spionem* – a systematic murdering of British Intelligence operatives that he has been organising with Whitaker. Once Pushkin is dead, Koskov will return to Russia several million dollars richer and 'prove' that his defection was faked and that he was on a special assignment which only the late Pushkin knew about.

Acting on a hunch, Bond (who has been instrumental in Koskov's defection) investigates the holes in Koskov's cover story, follows the trail to Afghanistan via Bratislava and Tangiers and destroys the raw opium which is, in effect, Koskov and Whitaker's collateral and profit. Collaborating with Pushkin, Bond has Koskov arrested by the KGB. Whitaker, he kills.

UNIVERSAL EXPORTS:

BOND, JAMES BOND: An acerbic, deep-voiced man in his forties. He's worked with Czech-based British Agent Rosika Miklos before, and knows KGB general Leonid Pushkin both professionally and personally. His relationship with M is warmly professional rather than friendly. Bond's reputation as a ladykiller precedes him as far as Bratislava, and the idea that he's Britain's best agent has permeated the higher echelons of the KGB. He's honestly capable of violent, even homicidal rages and, while he's good at his job, he doesn't relish it. He winces when downing a sub-standard Martini, but lies about its quality so as not to upset Kara. He obviously seduces Kara to make her open up to him about Koskov, but then develops real affection for her (watch the way he smiles as she embraces him). A brooding man whose humour is sardonic rather than flippant; he also smokes like a chimney. An effective leading man for this Cold War crime caper.

M: It is a source of pride to M that the 007 section has been chosen for the training exercise at the film's outset. He is enthused by Koskov's defection but visibly balks at the price MI6 has to pay for the hamper selected for the Russian from Harrods. He has no hesitation in ordering Bond to go and kill a man he knows well when political circumstances demand it. Equally, he isn't particularly keen to favour 007's instincts over what appears to be substantive evidence (the *Smiert Spionem* cards and Koskov's testimony).

MONEYPENNY: A pretty woman, a little younger than Bond, and clearly infatuated with him. Less confident than Lois Maxwell's version, she gives as good as she gets for a while, but once he actually deigns to touch her she melts.

Q: The ever-helpful, ever-constant Q regards this Bond with avuncular amusement and seems to believe that this enthusiasm for his craft is infectious. He accompanies Bond on his initial jaunt to Bratislava where he uses an adapted gas-pipe cleaning tool to smuggle Koskov to Austria. He also has a Harrier jump jet on hand to ferry the general back to England.

SAUNDERS: The not-exactly practical head of Station V Vienna, Saunders is officious and snide. He doesn't know Bond, although he knows of him, and on first meeting he doesn't take to him at all. He regards Koskov's defection as his baby, and is rather antagonistic about Bond's methods. He comes to appreciate Bond's skills though, and Saunders's brutal death has real pathos.

004: 004 is murdered on Gibraltar by an unnamed employee of Whitaker and Koskov.

002: Also taking part in the Gibralter training exercise, 003 is 'killed' by one of the paintball gun-armed SAS men, but escapes actual death at the unnamed assassin's hand.

OHMSS: The Secret Service is based in a corner of Trafalgar Square, and has vast labs and tunnels within its headquarters. It also has numerous external safehouses, which are themselves equipped with all sorts of technology (weapons detectors hidden in rakes, for example). What the one we see (Blayden) lacks, however, is the ability to stand up to a really determined assault by a grenade-throwing fake milkman.

ALLIES:

KARA MILOVY Koskov's girlfriend. An accomplished cellist, Koskov asks her to pretend to be a KGB sniper out to kill him on the night he stages his 'defection', setting her up to be killed by Bond. Bond, acting on the hunch that she isn't a professional assassin ('the girl didn't know one end of a rifle from the other'), shoots the gun out of her hands rather than kill her. It is she who provides the link in Bond's investigation into Koskov's disappearance; he returns to Bratislava to meet her and try to work out what is going on by interviewing her. He pretends to be a friend of Georgi's sent to fetch her to him, but she slowly falls for Bond during their acquaintance. He clearly comes to feel something for her too, despite his initial seduction showing all the hallmarks of the classic 007 'sex to bring someone over to your side'. She shows no hesitation in leading an attack on a convoy. She can ride a horse and (despite what Bond says) fire a gun. She can't, however, fly a plane.

KAMRAN SHAH: An Oxford-educated Afghan Mujaheddin leader fighting a guerrilla war against the Soviet occupation. He has a tendency towards theatricality and, while ostensibly a Muslim, is clearly Westernised in his ways. He thinks nothing of providing escorts for opium shipments in exchange for cash, reasoning that the drugs are headed for the Soviet Union and that it doesn't matter if Russians die from drugs or bullets.

GENERAL LEONID PUSHKIN: The recently installed head of the KGB, known to both M and Bond. Thought of as a moderate, the idea that he is behind *Smiert Spionem* disturbs both M and Bond. After Koskov's 'defection' he moves against Koskov and Whitaker (whom he has suspected for a long time), asking for the Soviet Union's money back, but is too late to stop their plan swinging into action. Pushkin willingly co-operates with Bond in his own staged assassination in order to draw the culprits out, and saves Bond's life at the very end of the film.

FELIX LEITER: Sighted briefly (for the first time since **Live and Let Die**) and portrayed by mullet-sporting American actor John Terry, Felix is using an espionage-equipped yacht to keep and eye on Brad Whitaker. After having Bond abducted from a marketplace, he furnishes him with some information about the 'major' and we see no more of him. He and Bond at least have some warmth in their relationship, but their scene is too fleeting to have any real impact.

THE OPPOSITION:

'MAJOR' BRAD WHITAKER: A rotund middle-aged American, he considers himself 'an old soldier', but was actually expelled from West Point for cheating and subsequently spent some time as a mercenary in the Belgian Congo before setting himself up as an independent arms dealer. He has an obsession with military figures throughout history and has a waxwork gallery of 'great' generals, including Genghis Khan and Hitler. He is rich enough to buy a $150,000 Stradavarius cello on Koskov's behalf and is described by Kara as a 'patron of the arts'. A tedious military fetishist, but nonetheless a formidable opponent for all his bluster. His plan for making a fortune out of the Soviets comes very close to succeeding.

GENERAL GEORGI KOSKOV: A plausible schmuck of a KGB man; a lying, double-dealing, charming, flamboyant con man and the co-architect of the above scheme. Calls caviar 'peasant food' which is 'all right with champagne'. He's prone to bursts of enthusiasm and sudden loud laughter. At one point he dances a little jig when excited. He is absolutely convinced of his own infallibility and even tries to lie his way out of arrest right at the very end.

In a similar way to *From Russia with Love*, these two individuals share villain duties. The overall scheme is rather mundane when viewed in isolation, but is actually carefully constructed. Taking in corruption in political circles, the arms trade, drug smuggling and the Russian invasion of Afghanistan, the film rejects outlandish megalomania and is a topical thriller.

NECROS: Yet another Donald Grant wannabe (see **From Russia with Love**). Blond-haired muscleman Necros is a Communist, working for world revolution on behalf of his 'revolutionary brothers and sisters'. It seems that by doing Koskov and Whitaker's dirty work he's going to receive a handsome pay-off. His stake in the scheme is financial gain to be put to political use.

PRINCIPAL CASTING: Roger Moore was not coming back. Both producer and actor knew that Moore, at nearly 60, was too old for the part. Several actors were screen-tested by Glen – who got them to perform favourite scenes from early Bond pictures. For a while Sam Neill, then known as television's *Reilly, Ace of Spies*, was the front runner, but Broccoli, final arbiter on all things, was unconvinced. Also seen was Welsh actor Timothy Dalton, who since turning the part down in 1969 had carved out an impressive career on the stage. Although interested, Dalton had stage commitments that would prevent him making the filming dates. Among the other candidates was Irish-born Pierce Brosnan, the star of the recently cancelled television series, *Remington Steele*. Brosnan had first met Broccoli in 1980 during filming of *For Your Eyes Only*, in which his wife Cassandra Harris had appeared. According to Broccoli's widow Dana, Cubby came away from this initial meeting convinced that Brosnan would make a great James Bond. Eventually the producer and his team were all agreed, and Brosnan signed up to become Eon's fourth 007.

Then fate, in the form of Brosnan's contract for *Remington Steele*, intervened. The production company that made the series, and which had prior claim on Brosnan's services, retained him to produce more episodes; activating their option to recall him on the last day that they were able to do so. Frustrated, Brosnan had to bow out and another round of interviews began. There was no time to spare, pre-production on the film being in an advanced stage. Of those seen Timothy Dalton was judged to be by far and away the most suitable. After extricating himself from his stage commitments, Dalton signed an initial three-film contract, as Roger Moore had done, and began filming *The Living Daylights* within 96 hours of being informed that he'd got the job.

Maryam d'Abo had originally been hired to provide a female foil for screen-testing Bond hopefuls (she played the role of Tatiana Romanova in scenes from **From Russia with Love**). She sufficiently impressed John Glen to be given the film's principal female role herself as reward.

Welsh actor John Rhys-Davies, cast as General Pushkin, was becoming known internationally thanks to roles in film such as *Raiders of the Lost Ark* (Steven Spielberg, 1980) and *Victor/Victoria* (Blake Edwards, 1981). The initial screenplay featured General Gogol – a veteran of every Bond picture since 1977 – in the plot role occupied in the finished film by Pushkin. However, Walter Gotell's age and ill-health caused the film's insurers to refuse to cover him for a sizeable role in the picture. Despite producer Broccoli's offer to cover Gotell's insurance out of his own pocket, there was no wavering, and thus the character of Pushkin was created and Gogol relegated to a cameo in the film's final scene. This is ultimately to the film's benefit, as Rhys-Davies's boisterous yet subtle performance is one of the picture's highlights. Since 1987 Rhys-Davies has starred in several seasons of sci-fi series *Sliders* and appeared in films such *Indiana Jones and the Last Crusade* (Steven Spielberg, 1989) and *The Lord of the Rings: The Fellowship of the Ring* (Peter Jackson, 2001) and its two sequels.

Dutch actor Jereon Krabbé, like so many Bond actors, was best known for his work in European language cinema. As he had hoped, the role brought him more exposure in America. Since *The Living Daylights*, Krabbé's English-language films have included *Kafka* (Steven Soderbergh, 1991), *The Fugitive* (Andrew Davies, 1993) with Harrison Ford, Profumo-era exposé, *Scandal* (Michael Caton-Jones, 1989) and Beethoven biopic *Immortal Beloved* (Bernard Rose, 1994).

DIRECTOR AND CREW: For John Glen's fourth Bond film the crew would remain largely static. John Barry, Maurice Binder, Peter Lamont were all retained from the previous film, as were screenwriters Wilson and Maibaum. Alec Mills, a camera operator since *The Spy Who Loved Me* was promoted to director of photography when Alan Hume decided to shoot *A Fish Called Wanda* (Charles Crichton, 1988) instead. Glen's 'signature' pigeons feature in the attack on Whitaker's compound.

MUSICAL NOTES: John Barry's final score for the series on which he had such a profound influence draws heavily on the melody lines for two of the film's songs. Of particular note is the terrific music which accompanies the fight outside the plane.

SET PIECES: The terrific airborne fight scene (which looks so dangerous precisely because it is), the impressive explosion of a bridge, the 'seizing' of Koskov from Blayden, the staged defection all exist to serve the story rather than dominate. The car chase seems like an afterthought but, silly though it occasionally is, it's thrilling all the same.

POSITIVELY SHOCKING: The fight in the kitchen in the MI6 safehouse is really nasty stuff, especially when Necros holds a man's head against a hot plate. The way the piece of cardboard with '*Smiert Spionem*' scrawled on it slides down to the terrified 004 on a rope is disturbing rather than gruesome.

CUT SCENES: One scene snipped from the Tangiers segment saw Bond slapping a rug over some descending telegraph wires and riding down them as if on a magic carpet. Included on the DVD release as an extra, it's not a very funny idea quite poorly executed and cut with good reason. Earlier drafts of the screenplay featured a 'terrorist bazaar' on the Afghanistan border, where every conceivable kind of weaponry was available to buy. This was dropped, although something similar appeared in *Tomorrow Never Dies* ten years later. Other versions of the screenplay eschewed Bond and Kara's escape from the damaged plane in favour of a sequence where Bond has to pilot the gargantuan craft, low on fuel, into landing on an American aircraft carrier.

MEMORABLE QUOTES:
Gray: 'Smiert Spionem?'
Bond: 'Death to spies, Minister.'

Kara: 'We're free!'
Bond: 'Kara, we're inside a Russian airbase in the middle of Afghanistan.'

Q (on his bazooka mounted in a stereo): 'Something we're making for the Americans. It's called a ghetto blaster.'

Rosika (slapping her superior after having practically sexually assaulted him): 'What kind of girl do you think I am?'

FASHION VICTIMS: Whitaker's beige non-denominational uniforms deserve scorn. Georgi almost always looks like he's about to go boating. Bond is at times far more casual than ever before, with a rumpled leather jacket and his hands shoved into his pockets. He can still dress to kill though, as his tuxedo proves, and the one which (thanks to velcro) allows him to cover up his white shirt collar recalls the glories of *Goldfinger*. Most of the clothes though, are functional rather than ornate.

PRODUCT PLACEMENT: The logo of Carlsberg is very prominent when Bond is in Vienna and both Harrods and Bollinger are ostentatiously mentioned. The Aston Martin Volante is a return to the glory days of Bond product placement as well (see **Goldfinger**). Not exactly product placement, but the emblem of the International Red Cross was used in the film without the organisation's permission, resulting in a brief fracas of correspondence between it and Eon.

GADGETS: Bond's Aston Martin complete with jet-propelled engine, front-loaded missiles and skiing function. Q also gives Bond a key ring which bleeps when you whistle at it (very 80s) but with modifications. If you whistle the first few bars of 'Rule Britannia' it expels enough gas to disorientate someone for several minutes; if you wolf-whistle it explodes – this is Bond's personal code that works only on his key ring. Q has also designed a sofa that swallows people.

SOURCE TO SCREEN: *The Living Daylights*, the last Fleming title to be used for a Bond picture, was a short story written by the author for the first issue of the *Sunday Times* magazine in February 1962. The story, like the first fifteen minutes or so of the film after the titles, concerns a defection from East to West, with Bond sent to kill a KGB sniper who is going to bring down the defector. In both story and film the sniper is a blonde cellist whom Bond has earlier been admiring, although the story takes place in Berlin (right by Checkpoint Charlie) rather than in Bratislava (Czechoslovakia). As in the film Bond shoots to wound instead of kill. Fleming's officious, antagonistic Captain Sender becomes Saunders, head of Station V Vienna. After having deliberately failed in his mission Bond says, 'With any luck it'll cost me my double 0 number' – the origin of the film Bond's comment, 'If he [M] fires me I'll thank him for it.' The screenplay, the rest of which is the invention of the screenwriters, then picks up by following the consequences of the defection (revealed to have been staged) and answering the literary Bond's question as to what the unlikely-looking sniper was doing there.

IN THE REAL WORLD: The use of Afghanistan for the setting of much of film's final third is interesting, especially with regards to the portrayal of the native 'resistance' who are led by a cultured, smooth-talking Westernised man, Kamran Shah. The Soviet invasion of Afghanistan in

December 1979 had already provided some background colour to Bond pictures (see **For Your Eyes Only** and **Octopussy**) but this is the first time Bond actually goes there on screen. Those native Afghans who fought the Communists were widely celebrated in the Western media in the mid-80s (*Rambo III* contains the credit 'This film is dedicated to the gallant people of Afghanistan'), although even at the time some of *The Living Daylights* press coverage found people willing to quibble with their portrayal in the Bond film. 'There is some atrocious guff about the gallant Afghan resistance which those puritanical Moslem fundamentalists would no doubt find profoundly offensive', stated the *Scotsman*, with some justification. The Afghan resistance did eventually expel the Soviets from their native land, and set up a Moslem fundamentalist government, which became the bête noire of the Western world after the events of 11 September 2001.

Koskov terms his operations against British agents *Smiert Spionem*, the Russian for 'Death to Spies'. When questioned General Pushkin claims that *Smiert Spionem* is an abandoned operation dating 'from Stalin's time'.

He is correct, as in 1943 this phrase, contracted to SMERSH, became the name given to a new Soviet military counter-intelligence service. The organisation was disbanded in 1946, although there are countless examples – including the use of the name on official paperwork – of Soviet personnel referring to themselves as working for SMERSH into the mid-1950s.

SMERSH's responsibilities included the internal security of the Russian state, and its official duties were roughly equivalent to those of MI5 in Britain, although its unsavoury working methods invite comparisons with the Gestapo. SMERSH became infamous in the West for its actions in the satellite communist countries of Eastern Europe, especially Germany, immediately after World War Two. Ian Fleming used a fictionalised version of the organisation as the main adversary of the literary Bond. SMERSH agents appear in the novels *Casino Royale*, *Live and Let Die*, *Moonraker*, *From Russia with Love*, *Doctor No* and *Goldfinger* (see also **Casino Royale**).

CULTURE VULTURE: General Pushkin is, like his predecessor Gogol, named after a celebrated Russian author. When in Austria Bond and Kara ride on the same big wheel on which Orson Welles's Harry Lime and Joseph Cotton's Holly Martins famously discussed morality in *The Third Man* (Carol Reed, 1949), a film on which director John Glen had worked as a sound editor.

CRITICS: Reception for *The Living Daylights* was divided between people who thoroughly approved of the changes made to the series since *A View to a Kill* and those who disliked the fact that such changes had been made at all. 'Bond is now more upper cut than below the belt', complained Tom Hutchinson in the *Mail On Sunday*'s 5 July 1987 edition. 'The result is a licence to dull those notorious, bad taste wisecracks', he continued, denouncing the film as 'dedicated to dismantling the legend' of James Bond. Whatever that means. The *Scotsman* of 11 July was muted in its praise: the increase in character involvement was seen as a good thing with ' a plot . . . more dependent on suspense and . . . less on gimmicks' giving 'a chink for character to be portrayed, and Jeroen Krabbé. Joe Don Baker and Maryam d'Abo seize their chance.' Dalton's script-led approach to the role came in for some friendly mocking. 'He does not bump into the furniture unless the script requires it, and when it does he bumps into it very hard indeed.'

'More compelling than any recent Bond film', was Iain Johnstone's judgement. Writing in the *Sunday Times* on 5 July, he was equally sure of the reason for this: 'We care.' Johnstone also had praise for Jereon Krabbé's portrayal of Koskov, saying that like Shakespeare's Richard III he could 'smile and murder while he smiles'. Judging Dalton to be 'reinventing a role which seemed to hang on Moore like an unwanted suit' he enthusiastically looked forward to a future series of Bond pictures that would 'run. And run' due to Dalton's 'throwing down a potent challenge to writers who must now accommodate a man'. The *Sunday Telegraph*'s review of that same weekend saw Richard Mayne use the medium of fiction, and the character of a (presumably non-fictional) James Bond himself to judge the new picture and new screen Bond. He found neither wanting, but wasn't happy about the portrayal of Felix Leiter. Nigel Andrews of the *Financial Times* felt the film signalled Bond 'not so much in control of the hardware as engulfed by it', presumably unaware that such claims had been made as early as *Thunderball*. The *Observer*'s Philip French, though, was impressed with the overhaul, claiming Dalton as 'a darkly handsome public-school type . . . like the figure on the covers of the 50s Pan paperbacks'. He found the picture '. . . the most likeable Bond since the Connery days [which] should ensure the future of the series'.

BOX OFFICE: *The Living Daylights* took $191 million dollars worldwide at the box office, an increase on *A View to a Kill* and the series' best grosses since *For Your Eyes Only* in 1981. The series' decline in box-office fortunes had been stalled, although it had not yet returned to its *Moonraker* heights.

MARTINIS, GIRLS AND GUNS: Three twos for our new 007: two girls (Kara and the bikini-clad playgirl in the pre-credits) two Martinis (Kara makes him one, another is sent to his hotel room, although he asks for neither) and two kills. Whitaker is killed right at the end (finally facing his Waterloo, he is crushed by a bust of the Duke of Wellington) and the thug Necros, who gets tossed out of a plane to his doom. It's a John Glen film – *someone* has to fall to their death.

TRIVIA: On the end credits to this film General Gogol's forename is given as Anatol, despite him being addressed as 'Alexis' in *The Spy Who Loved Me.*

THE ONE WITH: The rock of Gibraltar, the milkman and the cello.

THE LAST WORD: 'You didn't think I'd miss this performance?' Although it uses many of the props of the later Moore films (Gogol, criminals taking advantage of the Cold War, Anglo-Soviet relations etc.) and occasionally lapses into farcical humour at odds with the rest of the film's tone, *The Living Daylights* is a breath of fresh air. Dynamic, strong on character, and well paced, it's a largely straight-faced action adventure/detective story helped enormously by the fact that when the jokes do come they're genuinely funny. The entire supporting cast are superb and Koskov's staged defection is the tensest sequence in a Bond picture since George Lazenby hung from a cable car. The best Bond picture since the 60s.

GIRLS	40
MARTINIS	10
DEATHS	157

Continuity 2: 'He was married, once.'

When, in *The Spy Who Loved Me,* Anya Amasova refers briefly to Bond having been married, and he cuts off her description with a pained expression, it is the first time the events of *On Her Majesty's Secret Service* have been even obliquely referred to in dialogue since the end of that film. *For Your Eyes Only* (two films later) opens with Bond visiting his wife's grave (her death is even dated to the year *OHMSS* came out). The film sees Bond in an unusually philosophical mood, reflecting on his advancing age (Moore was 53 at the time).

The recurring supporting cast and occasional references to past Bond pictures seem designed to remind you of the longevity of the character, and to firmly push home the idea that the Bond of *A View to a Kill* is the same man we first met in *Dr. No*. Given that Roger Moore is in fact slightly older than Sean Connery (and was a TV star when *Dr. No* was released) it is at least plausible that the first fourteen Eon Bond pictures take place in one single (reasonably) internally consistent world.

Where this begins falling to pieces is in *The Living Daylights*. Timothy Dalton's Bond is clearly too young to have been an agent in 1962 (let alone have bought a Bentley in 1933, as the novel *Casino Royale* says the literary Bond did), and his relationships with Q and Moneypenny (who is not only a different actress, but a markedly different character) are fundamentally not the same. Yet the film contains continuity references back to *The Spy Who Loved Me*, which itself referred back to *On Her Majesty's Secret Service*. *Licence to Kill* also makes specific reference to Bond's marriage (indeed the entire plot is arguably predicated on it) despite Dalton's Bond being too young to have experienced it (let alone be the ageing figure of *For Your Eyes Only*).

GoldenEye is another matter. While it is becoming increasingly clear as the Brosnan films progress that nothing before them is considered particularly relevant, *GoldenEye* itself depends on the audience knowing Bond and what he's like – understanding his past and his relationship with the previous M.

It is conceivable that this 'past' is meant to be the previous two films, but that merely opens up the same old problems. Bond producer Michael G Wilson has publicly questioned whether Brosnan's version of Bond loved and lost Tracy Di Vincenzo, or whether that event is now too far in the past to be considered 'current'. In any event the family motto of the modern Bond remains the same (see *The World Is Not Enough*).

Licence to Kill (1989)

Produced by Albert R Broccoli and Michael G Wilson
Screenplay by Richard Maibaum and Michael G Wilson
Director of Photography: Alec Mills
Production designed by Peter Lamont
Original score composed and conducted by Michael Kamen
Editor: John Grover
Directed by John Glen

PRINCIPAL CAST: Timothy Dalton (*James Bond*), Carey Lowell (*Pam Bouvier*), Robert Davi (*Franz Sanchez*), Talisa Soto (*Lupe Lamora*), Anthony Zerbe (*Milton Krest*), Frank McRae (*Sharkey*), Everett McGill (*Killifer*), Wayne Newton (*Professor Joe Butcher*), Benicio Del Toro (*Dario*), Anthony Starke (*Truman-Lodge*), Pedro Armendariz (*President Hector Lopez*), Desmond Llewelyn (*Q*), David Hedison (*Felix Leiter*), Priscilla Barnes (*Della Churchill*), Robert Brown (*M*), Caroline Bliss

(*Miss Moneypenny*), Don Stroud (*Heller*), Grand L Bush (*Hawkins*),
Cary-Hiroyuki Tagawa (*Kwang*), Alejandro Bracho (*Perez*), Guy De Saint
Cyr (*Braun*), Rafer Johnson (*Mullens*), Diana Lee (*Hsu Loti*), Christopher
Neame (*Fallon*), Jeannine Bisignano (*Stripper*), Claudio Brook
(*Montelongo*), Cynthia Fallon (*Consuela*), Enrique Novi (*Rasmussen*),
Osami Kawawo (*Oriental*), George Belanger (*Doctor*), Roger Cudney
(*Wavecrest Captain*), Honorato Magaloni (*Chief Chemist*), Jorge Russek
(*Pit Boss*), Sergio Corona (*Bellboy*), Stuart Kwan (*Ninja*), José Abdala
(*Tanker Driver*), Teresa Blake (*Ticket Agent*), Samuel Benjamin Lancaster
(*Della's Uncle*), Juan Pelàez (*Casino Manager*), Mark Kelty (*Coast Guard
Radio Operator*), Umberto Elizondo (*Hotel Assistant Manager*), Fidel
Garriga (*Sanchez's Driver*), Edna Bolkan (*Barrelhead Waitress*), Eddie
Enderfield (*Clive*), Jeff Moldovan, Carl Ciarfalio (*Warehouse Guards*).

PRE-CREDITS AND TITLES: The opening gun-barrel sequence from
The Living Daylights is reused, this time underscored with a version of
Monty Norman's theme from which the melody appears to have been
stripped. This leads into an uninspiring pre-credits sequence in which
Bond – who is getting ready to be best man at Felix Leiter's wedding –
becomes involved in an attempt to arrest drug Baron Franz Sanchez, who
has unexpectedly arrived in the United States. Sanchez has entered the
US in order to recapture and 'discipline' his mistress, Lupe, who has been
sleeping with another man. Despite being officially 'an observer' on this
mission, Bond is instrumental in Sanchez's capture (although Sanchez
doesn't actually see him) thanks to his willingness to climb out of an
aeroplane in mid-flight and winch himself across to another. After this
victory, Bond and Felix parachute into Leiter's wedding. There are
several reasons for this sequence's failure. One is the flat lighting and the
resolutely unexciting location (the Florida Keys), another is the slack
editing. There's also a really nasty sub-*Platoon* slo-mo close up of Felix
and his DEA buddies running towards camera, which is unintentionally
hilarious.

After this we're treated to a Maurice Binder title sequence which,
while an improvement on those to the last four or five films, features
whacking great close-ups of a visually very boring domestic camera. The
song is dire.

SUMMARY: Sanchez escapes from the DEA, and returns to his
drug-smuggling operation. In revenge for Leiter arresting him, he has
Leiter's wife Della murdered, and feeds Leiter to a shark. Somehow
(presumably because Sanchez always wanted him to) Leiter survives this

attack, and Sanchez leaves him unconscious near the body of his murdered wife, with a sign reading 'He disagreed with something that ate him' around his neck.

Enraged by this, Bond wages a personal war against Sanchez, one that does not let up even after M comes to Florida to order him to stop. Bond resigns from the Secret Service, and M revokes his licence to kill. After assaulting one of M's guards, Bond runs off to continue his vendetta. He causes problems for Sanchez's cocaine-smuggling operations, before flying into Isthmus City where Sanchez is based, infiltrating the drug lord's inner circle, turning his own men against him and destroying his base. He finally kills Sanchez after letting him know why it is he's gone through hell to do this.

UNIVERSAL EXPORTS:

BOND, JAMES BOND: This version is prone to violent rages (witness his shoving a gun in Pam Bouvier's face at the slightest sign of treachery or the way he knocks Q about) and has no compunction about holding a knife to Lupe's throat to extract information out of her. He still smokes like a chimney, and is a skilled housebreaker. He orders a Bud-with-a-lime in the Barrelhead bar but doesn't drink it. He's slightly balding and has large side-burns. He takes his coffee black and unashamedly enjoys the view when Pam has to strip down to her underwear in front of him. He's visibly disgusted by Sanchez during their initial meeting in the casino. He is prepared to go to almost any lengths to revenge Della Leiter, though perhaps not the cost of his own life. (He could easily have killed Sanchez on several occasions when he's at his house, but Sanchez's guards would have cut him down afterwards.) He doesn't say a lot, either.

The script doesn't make enough of the fact that the reason Bond becomes so psychotically obsessed with revenging Della on Felix's behalf is because the murder of his friend's wife on their wedding day reminds him of his own brutally cut-short marriage. Della and Felix clearly mean more to him than his career. Once Sanchez is dead, Bond clearly doesn't care one iota that the unstable Lupe retains all his drug money and is going to shack up with a corrupt and incompetent president; outside concerns are of no interest to him. He's frankly self-absorbed. Reckless, brutal, prone to nervous laughter and sentimental outbursts – a rather interesting figure to watch, and Dalton is brilliant. Again. The screenplay to *Licence to Kill* tacitly acknowledges, as do those for *GoldenEye* and *The World is not Enough*, that Bond is probably insane, or at least seriously disturbed.

M: M only turns up twice. The second time is the brief sequence with Moneypenny (see **MONEYPENNY**) but the first is more memorable. Bond is captured on the streets of Miami by armed men, and taken to an ominous building. Here Bond is walked along a balcony until he comes across a figure, facing away from him, who is surrounded, Blofeld-style, by cats. The figure whirls around to reveal himself to be M. M orders Bond to cease his vendetta, and when he refuses, accepts his resignation. Bond hands over his gun, but attacks one of M's bodyguards and flees. Some commentators have suggested that Bond assaults M here, but a close viewing of the scene makes it clear that it is the security man nearest to him that Bond kicks in the chest. It is disturbing though that the stated reason for M stopping his men from shooting Bond is that there are 'too many people' around.

MONEYPENNY: After only one film Caroline Bliss's Moneypenny finds herself reduced to one scene. In this, she's ticked off by M for her sloppy typing and then reveals herself to be authorising Secret Service resources to be used in looking for Bond. It's a dull exchange, but in a strange way its also pivotal, as at the end of it Moneypenny calls Q branch to tell its head about 007's latest escapade.

Q: Given a decent slice of the action, even more so than in *Octopussy* or *Diamonds are Forever*. Learning of Bond's actions from Moneypenny, Q takes some leave, and makes his way to Isthmus City. Here he supplies Bond with a variety of gadgets which he hopes will enable 007 to complete his vendetta and then get back to work. 'If it wasn't for Q-branch you'd have been dead long ago' he points out to Bond when 007 expresses surprise that he's made the trip. Desmond Llewelyn shines in his expanded role, indulging in excellent comic business (such as eye-rolling, knocking back drinks when no one is looking and checking the softness of both beds before choosing the best one for himself) while always coming across as genuinely concerned about Bond's fate. He seems aware of Bond's tendency to sleep with women in order to gain information from them/bring them over to his side; 'field operatives must often use every means at their disposal to achieve their objectives', he claims, defending Bond against Pam.

OHMSS: The Secret Service's base now appears to be on Whitehall. They seem to control, or have access to, Hemingway House in Miami. A representative of the service (played by former *Colditz* star Christopher Neame) is helping the Hong Kong narcotics bureau. He, possibly along with all other Secret Service personnel, seems to have been informed of 007's actions and ordered to bring him in if possible.

ALLIES:

FELIX LEITER: Bond's long-time ally, on the cusp of a happy marriage with Della Churchill, appears to have been reassigned to the DEA (Drug Enforcement Agency). Deeply involved in the prosecution of Sanchez, and responsible for his capture, it is no surprise that he is targeted by Sanchez on his escape. Though Della dies, Felix survives (albeit minus a leg) and seems cheerful when one considers what he's been through.

The real weak link in the film's story is the building of the vengeance plot around the character of Leiter. Despite a brief appearance in *The Living Daylights* (and there played by an actor of a completely different age and appearance) Leiter had not been seen in a Bond film since 1973's *Live and Let Die*. One can understand how Maibaum, involved in many films which featured the character, considered him familiar, but he had neither played a big enough, nor a consistent enough part in the series for this idea to work. With so many changes of actor, and so many gaps between appearances, even a relatively well-informed audience is not going to link the portly character from a TV viewing of *Diamonds are Forever* with this smooth cop-style Leiter. They aren't really the same character at all. After all this, the producers don't even have the guts to kill Leiter off (which would have added something to Bond's pursuit of revenge). That the revenge plot works at all is down to Dalton, Hedison and Barnes's playing in the early scenes, and nothing to do with the audience's pre-supposed affection for the character. From the audience's point of view it would have been much more effective to base a similar story around M, Q, or even Moneypenny. He is played, as in **Live and Let Die**, by David Hedison.

PAM BOUVIER: An enigmatic character – former army pilot, well-acquainted with South America, DEA informer and messenger on behalf of the US state department – it must be assumed that Bouvier is an American agent, working on the fringe of Sanchez's organisation and used to convey the pardon to Heller.

Pam is very much in the tradition of strong Bond female characters. The recurring line, 'Why don't you wait until you are asked?' with the response, 'Why don't you ask me?' bounces back and forth between her and Bond and is a sign of their equality. She can handle a gun, a plane and explosives with great skill too. However, she also takes great offence at Bond's relations with Lupe, which could be seen to imply that, despite her tough exterior, she is as vulnerable to Bond's charms as most other women in the series.

LUPE: Sanchez's mistress endures great cruelty at his hands; she seems to be under the impression that all men are like him. She's not dissimilar to *The Man with the Golden Gun*'s Andrea Anders; both use Bond to rid themselves of cruel, villainous lovers. Like Anders, Lupe sleeps with Bond but, unlike her predecessor, she survives the film, ending up in the arms of President Lopez.

SHARKEY: A straight copy of both Quarrels (see **Live and Let Die, Dr. No**) but based in the Florida Keys rather than Jamaica. An instantly likeable character, not possessed of all Bond's foolhardy bravado, but prepared to back him in his revenge mission. Saves Bond's life when he follows the agent into Krest's warehouse, momentarily disorientating Killifer. He is murdered by Sanchez's men for acting as Bond's support for the infiltration of the Wavekrest, but is instantly avenged by Bond who puts a harpoon through the man responsible for Sharkey's death

THE OPPOSITION:

FRANZ SANCHEZ: A drug dealer with a self proclaimed 'invisible empire' stretching from Chile to Alaska, and with aims to expand his operations into the Pacific Rim. Prime target of the American DEA, Sanchez's main weakness is his fixation on loyalty; he claims to value it highly (though he demonstrates no such trait himself) and risks his freedom to punish an errant mistress. Any hint of treachery among his own men turns him into a complete paranoiac. Bond uses this against Sanchez to bring down the drug baron's organisation.

Sanchez has no clever gimmicks or hideous deformities, he is a simple, though vicious, hoodlum. Though played well by Robert Davi, he remains just a variant on the many other Latin American drug lords seen in countless action films of the time (see **CULTURE VULTURE**). Even **Live and Let Die**'s Kananga had his voodoo, his hook-handed henchman and a twist to the drug-smuggling plan – a distribution of free heroin. All Sanchez wants is to expand his markets. If he hadn't crossed Felix Leiter it's doubtful his world and Bond's would ever have come into contact.

DARIO: Formerly of the Nicaraguan contras before being kicked out, Dario is a nasty little thug with a flick-knife always at his side. Carries out Sanchez's most despicable orders: the removal of Lupe's boyfriend's heart, the rape and murder of Della and the attempted killing of Bond.

KILLIFER: An American agent probably for the DEA (it is he who takes responsibility for Sanchez) but he is transporting the drug dealer to Quantico, Virginia, where the FBI is based. In any case, he is swiftly tempted by Sanchez's doubling of his usual $1 million bribe. 'Two million is a hell of a chunk of dough', he comments, after switching sides. He's visibly disturbed by what Sanchez does to Leiter, but realises that he can do nothing to dissuade him from his actions. Bond feeds Killifer to the sharks in an act of cold-blooded murder.

COLONEL HELLER: Military man of unclear origins. Sanchez's head of security also has some authority in the army of Isthmus, leading the tank assault on the (un)safehouse of the Hong Kong Narcotics Bureau. He is involved in a side deal of his own. The US state department has offered him immunity from prosecution in return for the return of Stinger missiles in Sanchez's possession. Bond hints of this to Sanchez and Heller is killed with a forklift truck.

HONG KONG NARCOTICS BUREAU: Bond disrupts a planned infiltration of Sanchez's operation by this small group of agents. It's a rather clever attempt to beef up the plot by showing the wider repercussions of Bond's maverick actions.

PRINCIPAL CASTING: *Licence to Kill*'s consistently impressive supporting cast was drawn from a variety of sources: Robert Davi had previously appeared in *The Goonies* (Richard Donner, 1985) and *Die Hard* (John McTiernan, 1988) before being cast as this film's main villain. Since 1989 he has continued to work on unremarkable thrillers, including *Showgirls* (Paul Verhoeven, 1995) and *Predator 2* (Stephen Hopkins, 1990). He was reunited with *Licence to Kill* director John Glen on *Christopher Columbus – The Discovery* (1992).

Carey Lowell *Licence to Kill*'s effective leading lady, had previously been a model and had had parts in films such as 1986's *Club Paradise* (directed by *Ghostbusters*' Harold Ramis and starring Robin Williams and Peter O'Toole). Since *Licence to Kill* she has appeared in Tom Hanks's comedy *Sleepless in Seattle* (Nora Ephron, 1993) and John Cleese's *Fierce Creatures* (Fred Schepisi, 1996), and played Jamie Ross in NBC's crime drama *Law & Order* between 1996 and 1998.

Talisa Soto had previously featured in David Lynch's brilliant comic short *The Cowboy and the Frenchman* (1988) but her films since have been rather less impressive. She was the eponymous *Vampirella* (Jim Wynorski, 1996) and has appeared as the Princess Kitana in no less than three *Mortal Kombat* straight-to-video features.

Experienced stage actor Anthony Zerbe had appeared in *Cool Hand Luke* (Stuart Rosenberg, 1966) with Sidney Poitier in *They Call Me Mister Tibbs* (Gordon Douglas, 1970) and in *Rooster Cogburn* (Stuart Millar, 1975) with John Wayne. Interestingly, he had also appeared in the TV movie *The Man from UNCLE, The Fifteen Years Later Affair* (Ray Austin, 1983) in which George Lazenby unofficially reprised his role as James Bond. Since *Licence to Kill*, Zerbe has memorably played an amoral admiral in *Star Trek: Insurrection* (Jonathan Frakes, 1998).

RADA-trained Everett McGill, who added real substance to the role of corrupt government man Killifer is one of David Lynch's regular collaborators, appearing in his films *Dune* (1985) *The Straight Story* (1999) and his TV series *Twin Peaks* (1990 to 1991). Other films include Wes Craven's *The People Under the Stairs* (1991).

The part of 'Professor' Joe Butcher was taken by Las Vegas entertainer, Wayne Newton, who has a high profile in the United States thanks to his charity work. This is a piece of 'stunt' casting reminiscent of **Diamonds Are Forever**.

One relatively minor role in the film, that of Sanchez's henchmen Dario, was taken by a then very young Benicio Del Toro. Before *Licence to Kill*, Toro had only made one feature, Paul Reubens's vehicle *Big Top Pee-wee* (Randall Kleinman, 1988), but his career has since sky-rocketed. He made a memorable appearance in *The Usual Suspects* (Brian Singer, 1995) and was truly outstanding in Terry Gilliam's pin-sharp adaptation of Hunter S Thompson's classic of Gonzo journalism, *Fear and Loathing in Las Vegas* (1998). After an amusing cameo in *Snatch* (Guy Ritchie, 1998), Del Toro won just about every supporting acting award conceivable, up to and including an Oscar, for his portrayal of a quietly spoken, much-put-upon narcotics agent in Steven Soderbergh's masterful *Traffic* (2000).

Aside from Timothy Dalton, this was also to be the last Bond outing for two short-lived regulars. This was Robert Brown's final appearance as M. Although effective in the role, Brown had never been given the chance to distinguish himself from Bernard Lee's formidable admiral and thus had never escaped his shadow. *GoldenEye* would see the introduction of a noticeably different Secret Service head. Caroline Bliss would not reprise the role of Moneypenny when the series returned after an unprecedented gap of six years, choosing primarily to concentrate on stage work.

Despite frequent public assurances from both Broccoli and Dalton during the early 90s that this wouldn't be the case, when *GoldenEye* eventually began shooting, there was a new 007. Since leaving the secret service behind Dalton has continued to work as an actor on stage, screen and television. He became one of the first of the 90s Hollywood tradition of British-accented bad guys in *The Rocketeer* (Joe Johnston, 1993) and played Rhett Butler in *Scarlett* (John Erman, 1994), the sequel to *Gone With The Wind* (Victor Fleming, 1939). In 1999 he was reunited with *The Living Daylights*' Art Mailk in *Cleopatra* for *Quadrophenia* director and *MasterChef* creator, Franc Roddam.

Dalton's departure from the role, despite having only fulfilled two-thirds of his three-film contract, was something agreed by both parties. The actor has remained close to the Broccoli family, and was one of the pall-bearers at the producer's funeral in July 1996.

DIRECTOR AND CREW: Director John Glen was retained for his fifth consecutive Bond picture, breaking Guy Hamilton's record for directing the most Bonds and becoming the series' most frequent director. It would also be his last Bond picture, and an end to a twenty-year association with the series. Since 1989 he has directed *Christopher Columbus the Discovery* (1991) *Aces: Iron Eagle III* (1992) with Lou Gosset Jr and *The Point Men* (2001) with Christopher Lambert and *The Living Daylights*' Maryam D'Abo. He was also responsible for several episodes of Gerry Anderson's TV series *Space Precinct*, in most of which he utilised cast members from his Bond pictures, including d'Abo, *For Your Eyes Only*'s Jack Hedley and *Octopussy*'s Steven Berkoff.

Glen's departure also heralded the break-up of much of the team he had established for the 80s Bond pictures. Alec Mills, director of photography since *The Living Daylights* and a cameraman on many previous Bond films, also departed. He continued his relationship with Glen, providing the same role on all of Glen's post-Bond pictures, as well as working on multi-award winning children's TV series *Press Gang*. Editor John Grover, who had cut both *For Your Eyes Only* and *The Living Daylights* for Glen, also left the series at this point.

MUSICAL NOTES: Michael Kamen was an experienced film composer whose credits included *Die Hard* (John McTiernan, 1988) and *Lethal Weapon* (Richard Donner, 1987), both cinematic antecedents of *Licence to Kill*'s new style for the Bond films, as well as the brilliant BBC television series *Edge of Darkness*. Here he contributes his only Bond score. To be honest, there's not a lot to it. It heavily utilises the 'James Bond Theme' but, because it has no relation to the film's title song, has no other main melody with which to play. There are unimaginative splatterings of Spanish guitar here and there, and a few brass-based orchestral parps which could have come straight from John Williams's *Return of the Jedi* (Richard Marquand, 1983) score. It's a real disappointment considering Kamen's form. Since *Licence to Kill* Kamen has worked on all of the *Die Hard* and *Lethal Weapon* sequels, Terry Gilliam's *Fear and Loathing in Las Vegas* (1998), the chronically underrated *Last Action Hero* (John McTiernan, 1993) and the terrific *X-Men* (Bryan Singer, 2001).

SET PIECES: *Licence to Kill* is noticeably short of large-scale set pieces. The pre-credits sequences, despite impressive stunt work, is rather dull, but the waterskiing sequence is exemplary and the truck chase finale is a truly exhilarating bit of action filmmaking. To compensate there are more than a few fist-fights and gun battles, all of which have real impact. Bond's attack on Sanchez's cocaine boat is effective. The drugs foaming away into the water is one of the picture's most striking images.

POSITIVELY SHOCKING: *Licence to Kill* is substantially nastier, perhaps not in incident, but certainly in presentation and spirit, than any Bond film before or since. There are two shark-maulings, one of which is fatal (and that's orchestrated by Bond himself). Then there's Colonel Heller's vampire-like staking with a forklift truck; Dario being pulverised as he slowly slips into a cocaine grinder; the (thankfully offscreen) rape and murder of Della Leiter; Sanchez cutting Lupe's lover's heart out; the killing and meat-hanging of Sharkey; Bond setting fire to a petroleum-soaked Sanchez who then staggers around for a bit before dying; Bond knocking a man into a water-filled tank containing an electric eel and locking another in the drawer full of writhing maggots (which then eat him) and finally Krest being put into a decompression chamber and then exploded across its four walls. Plus the usual assortment of shootings.

CUT SCENES: There are several different versions of *Licence to Kill* in circulation thanks to the sequence where Krest is exploded. The US version is slightly more graphic than the UK cut, and the Japanese edition is reportedly longer still. These cuts make no real difference to the sense and flow of either the scene nor the film as a whole.

MEMORABLE QUOTES:

M (when Bond attempts to resign from the Secret Service): 'We're not a country club, 007!'

Sanchez (explaining his vision): 'East meets West, drug dealers of the world unite!'

Sanchez (subtly threatening the puppet ruler of Isthmus): 'Remember, you're only president for life.'

Sanchez (killing his annoying accountant): 'I guess it's time to start cutting overheads.'

FASHION VICTIMS: A good show on Bond's part. He appears once in a particularly smart tuxedo and sports a succession of very nice suits with open-neck shirts for the majority of the film. He definitely has the jump on most of Sanchez's men, who appear to be dressing for an episode of *Miami Vice* (perhaps influenced by the flat, TV-style lighting). Sanchez himself is the worst offender. Pink pastel shirts, dazzling white suit jackets and, a sartorial low-point for the Bond villains, slip-on moccasins with no socks. Quite frankly, burning alive is too good for him. Also, the Barrelhead Bar is not merely the most 80s thing in a Bond picture, it's the most 80s thing ever.

PRODUCT PLACEMENT: Bond flies Pan American airlines, and despite ordering an entire case of Bollinger RV, he seems to be enjoying a different kind of alcoholic drink; Carlsberg and Michelob both get a lot of coverage in the Barrelhead Bar, and Budweiser gets a mention. It is clear Sanchez would not dream of transporting his cocaine on anything other than a Kenworth truck.

GADGETS: Once Q turns up he presents Bond with a suitcase which contains 'everything for a man on holiday'. This includes an X-ray camera with a laser gun in the flash, a cummerbund containing a wire which supports 007's weight, a 'signature gun' disguised as a movie camera (which is keyed so that only Bond can use it) and a tube of plastic explosive disguised as 'Detonite' toothpaste. Bond uses the explosives, the wire and the signature gun as part of his first attempt to kill Sanchez, but fails. None of the items proves to be pivotal in his final victory over the drug lord, but all are good fun.

SOURCE TO SCREEN: Although credited jointly to both Michael G Wilson and Richard Maibaum, the *Licence to Kill* screenplay was primarily Wilson's responsibility. Maibaum had collaborated with the young producer on an outline (and according to some commentators a first draft script) but Maibaum's fidelity to the rules of his union, the Screenwriters Guild, meant that he was unable to work during the long Writers Strike of 1988–89. This left Wilson to write much of the script on his own. By 1988, the year that Wilson and Maibaum began their outline, the only pieces of Fleming's writings unused in any way by the film series were two short stories, both from the *For Your Eyes Only* collection.

The first, 'Quantum of Solace', was a tale of domestic love and hate in the Caribbean with Bond reduced to a passive observer, and was thus utterly useless to them. The other, 'The Hildebrand Rarity', had some potential. It features Bond investigating the possibility of the Royal Navy using the Seychelles as a fall-back base in the event of their losing control of the Maldives. Bond finds himself aboard a marine research vessel belonging to the odious Milton Krest. The Krest Foundation carries out marine research solely for tax reasons and in the least ethical ways possible (Bond is witness to a vivid description of the slaughter of a marine community for the purpose of obtaining one rare fish, the titular rarity). Krest is abusive to his wife and intolerably rude to his guests, and is suffocated one night with the precious fish he was sent to capture. A story not of espionage but of the limits of torment one can endure, it is strongly implied that Krest's put-upon wife was responsible for his death. Here we find the basis for the film's Milton Krest, a boorish drunken chauvinist whose marine research foundation is cover for a drug-smuggling operation. The film also borrows one of Krest's most unpleasant marital habits for Sanchez: both characters 'discipline' their abused partners with the dried tail of a stingray.

Aside from this, *Licence to Kill* borrows from a further range of Bond sources, including the novels *Live and Let Die* and *The Man with the Golden Gun* (the latter had been all but ignored by the film which took its title), as well as Guy Hamilton's 1973 film of *Live and Let Die*.

Fleming's *The Man with the Golden Gun* arguably provides the main structure of *Licence to Kill*'s second hour. In that novel Bond infiltrates Scaramanga's operation as a freelance operative, trying to earn his trust before carrying out his mission of assassination. Of course, in *Licence to Kill*, Bond is not actually working for the Secret Service but his methods remain. In both, Bond obtains the trust of the villain with impressive speed, and the villain develops an irrational attachment to Bond despite the concerns of his employees. Bond then exposes the villain's operation and defeats his organisation from within. Of course, Fleming did not have a monopoly on the destruction-from-within storyline, and writer/producer Michael G Wilson has openly admitted that much of the inspiration for this aspect of his screenplay came from Japanese *Ronin* tales and their cinematic appropriation by directors such Akira Kurosawa and Sergio Leone.

Nineteen fifty-four's *Live and Let Die* had been systematically strip-mined by the film series. As well as the film which appropriated its title, it had also given one of its set pieces to *For Your Eyes Only* and some incidental details to the film of *Dr. No*. It provides *Licence to Kill* with one of its most memorable sequences. In the Fleming, Felix Leiter visits the Ouroubouros bait warehouse and is kidnapped. He is later returned to his colleagues, having been mauled by a shark (losing his right arm and half his left leg in the process). He has with him a covering note which reads 'He disagreed with something that ate him (PS we have plenty more jokes as good as this)'. Bond returns to the warehouse and, after a firefight, pitches the villain responsible into his own shark pit. With a couple of small changes, such as leaving out of the second part of the message attached to Leiter, this sequence makes up Bond's first action against Sanchez's people and concludes with the death of corrupt government man, Killifer.

Another big influence on *Licence to Kill* is the film of *Live and Let Die*, one of the few Bond pictures Maibaum had not worked on. Once the revenge element is removed, there is a striking similarity between Sanchez and Kananga. Both, in different ways, are rulers of 'rogue' Atlantic states; both are ruthless heads of drug cartels and both have large-scale drug production at the heart of their respective plans. The main difference is in the detail of their operations, and that is rooted in the changes in illegal narcotics in the real world. Finally, the character of Sharkey – a friend of both Bond and the Leiters – is named after a boatman Fleming knew in the Seychelles in the late 1950s.

Licence to Kill was the first Bond film not to take its title from a Fleming book or short story. Since 1989 none of the remaining Fleming titles – 'Risico', 'Quantum of Solace', 'Property of a Lady', 'The Hildebrand Rarity' – have been used, although the films have continued to take ideas, characters and sequences from his work.

The script for *Licence to Kill* has exactly the opposite problems to those of most the previous Maibaum/Wilson/Glen films. Whereas all the others had been somewhat confused in terms of both plot and plotting, *Licence to Kill*'s (admittedly straightforward) storyline is well worked through. What it lacks is the throwaway humour that had sometimes been the saving grace of the weaker Moore films. Equally, it could be suggested that all the previous 80s pictures begin well (certainly their pre-credits sequences are well up to par) before dropping off around the one-hour mark. *Licence to Kill* has a distinctly lacklustre pre-credits sequence, and an unremarkable first half-hour before really kicking into gear when we reach Isthmus City.

IN THE REAL WORLD: Recreational use of cocaine had received continually increasing attention from the Western media throughout the 1980s. Its popularity among yuppies, and the spectacle provided by crack-cocaine gang wars, made it a bigger story than reports on heroin junkies.

Many films took this opportunity to dramatise South American drug cartels (see **CULTURE VULTURE**). *Licence to Kill* did have some roots in reality. The pock-marked drug baron, Franz Sanchez, with control over his kingdom of Isthmus, bears a resemblance to pock-marked General Manuel Noriega. After seizing control of Panama (clear inspiration for the fictional Isthmus) in a coup in 1983, former CIA agent Noriega attracted the wrath of America through his practice of drug smuggling. Captured after the US invaded Panama in 1989, Noriega was tried and, in 1992, sentenced to 40 years in prison. Not quite as bad as Sanchez's 936 years, though.

Another contemporary area of Latin American affairs is covered by mention of the Contras. The name is a diminutive of 'counter-revolutionary forces' – these were groups of guerrillas who fought against the Sandinista government of Nicaragua in the 1980s. Originally funded by the United States, who were far from happy to see a left-wing revolutionary government in their back yard, Congress later enacted laws to prevent the support of these groups. In 1986 it emerged that funding had continued covertly, with proceeds of arms sales to Iran going to the contras. These groups became increasingly involved in kidnapping and drug smuggling to fund their cause, and it is quite believable that they would sell Stinger missiles to a someone like Sanchez.

CULTURE VULTURE: Cocaine was to action films of the 80s what heroin had been to thrillers of the 70s. The largely black, poor pushers of Harlem dealing drugs in crumbling tenement buildings evolved, cinematically, into ludicrously wealthy Latinos decked out in designer clothes, operating above the law, and often based in Miami or Los Angeles, rather than New York.

The examples of violent action films whose villains are involved with

South American (usually Colombian) drug cartels are too numerous to list here. *Lethal Weapon* (Richard Donner, 1987) pitted maverick cops against the drug smugglers. *Beverley Hills Cop II* (Martin Brest, 1987) saw a wisecracking loose cannon policeman out of his jurisdiction and battling with a drug smuggler hiding behind wealth and class. The remake of *Scarface* (Brian de Palma, 1983) saw violent cocaine dealers fighting it out in Miami. Only a year after *Licence to Kill*, *Delta Force II: The Colombian Connection* (Aaron Norris, 1990) put a US special forces trooper up against a Colombian cartel.

These were all descendants of the action-oriented heritage of Bond, adapting his violent but witty style to an American environment (usually putting the high level of violence above a high level of wit). In *Licence to Kill*, Bond made the mistake of poaching on their turf. Audiences were either used to greater violence and bigger thrills, or were unprepared to stomach the new look of Bond. From the filmmakers' perspective, an updating of the drug-smuggling politician Kananga must have been appealing and logical. However, they failed to appreciate the cinematic atmosphere of the time. Taking Bond so far out of his environment, making him a maverick loose cannon and pitting him against the stereotypical South American drug dealer was simply too similar to many other, more effective films. This was a flawed attempt at reinvention, to try and get a foothold in saturated market.

CRITICS: If *Licence to Kill* had been intended to impress American *critics*, then at least according to the *Variety* of 14 June 1989 it had succeeded. 'A cocktail of high octane action, spectacle and drama', wrote Coop who went on to praise Dalton's 'physicality and vigour' in the lead role and the way the 'exotic set pieces . . . serve the narrative rather than provide a glossy travelogue'. The film, the magazine felt would 'rate among the best in the United Artists 007 series'.

In Britain it was a very different story; whereas *Variety* had felt *Licence to Kill* gave Bond its 'second wind', UK reviewers seemed to be suffering ennui with the series as a whole and with this film in particular. '*Licence to Kill* doesn't work in any shape or form', complained *The Face*, calling the film 'a mind-numbing caper movie' and the script 'the most tedious ever to grace the screen'.

Derek Malcolm, writing in *Midweek* (15 July), complained about everything, from the presence of 'more daft stunts than good lines' to the length of the end credits. 'A vintage effort it is not', he concluded at the end of a review which actually spends most of its time talking about other things entirely.

One of the more positive UK reviews was in music paper, *NME* (10 July) whose reviewer called it 'the best Bond film for simply ages', saying 'the puns are probably the worst of any Bond film, the violence the vilest and the stunts are the silliest'. He meant those as compliments.

BOX OFFICE: US takings for *Licence to Kill* were just over $34 million, a share of worldwide gross of around $157 million. Although substantial, it was less than the producers had been expecting and over 30 million less than *The Living Daylights* two years before. This can, in part, be explained by the film's 15 certificate in the UK, which cut down on admissions.

Another important factor is the competition. The following year *The Economist* would call 1989 'the most financially successful year in Hollywood history'. Certainly the sheer number of popcorn movies vying for the audience's money was impressive and would not be surpassed until 1999's even more excessive crop of Hollywood product. Other features on release across Summer 1989 included *Batman* (Tim Burton), *Lethal Weapon 2* (Richard Donner), *Star Trek V: The Final Frontier* (William Shatner), *Indiana Jones and the Last Crusade* (Steven Spielberg).

MARTINIS, GIRLS AND GUNS: Bond feeds the treacherous Killifer to the sharks, and one of Sanchez's goons to some maggots; he electrocutes another with a tank full of water and an eel. He throws two of Sanchez's men out of a plane, harpoons Sharkey's murderer on the deck of the *Wavekrest*. Four people die in the car crash Bond causes in the final chase, Dario is ripped to pieces by the cocaine grinder and Sanchez is set aflame in a final moment of fiery catharsis. A total of twelve. He scores with Pam (initially on the boat, although she turns him down for a second liaison a day or so later, forcing him to bunk up with Q) and then later sleeps with Lupe right under Sanchez's nose. This is despite the fact that it's an extremely dangerous thing to do, not to mention an action that jeopardizes his self-appointed mission. It is implied, yet again, that he's doing this to bring the girl over to his side. It works, too. He orders one vodka Martini; well, actually he gets Pam to order it for him, and she makes a rather unflattering gesture towards him as she does so.

TRIVIA: During the fight on the drug-pulverising machine, Benicio Del Toro cut Timothy Dalton's hand, leaving the actor with a permanent scar.

Pedro Amendáriz, who appears as President Lopez, is the son of the Pedro Amendáriz who played the great Kerim Bey in **From Russia with Love**.

Due to financial considerations, no part of *Licence to Kill* was shot in Britain. All studio seqeunces were undertaken at Churubusco Studios, Mexico where films such as David Lynch's *Dune* (1985) had previously been based.

As has been often reported, the picture was originally entitled *Licence Revoked*, and indeed publicity material bearing this title still exists. This was changed after research in the American market confirmed that 'Licence Revoked' was a common phrase suggesting the withdrawal of a driving licence. The idea that most American consumers did not know the meaning of the word 'revoked' appears to be an urban myth originating in British newspapers.

Sanchez, Lupe and Dario are all prone to mood-swings and make snap irrational decisions. The implication seems to be that all three of them use their own products a bit too much, but the point is not made clear – perhaps because the sight of a character snorting cocaine on camera was considered at the time automatically to guarantee an 18 certificate.

THE ONE WITH . . .: the fifteen certificate.

THE LAST WORD: 'God help you, Commander.' Easier to appreciate now that it is no longer an indication of the series' ongoing direction, *Licence to Kill* is neither the chronic misinterpretation of Bond some fans seem to think it is, nor the misunderstood masterpiece that many of its production team would have you believe. It is a brave attempt to push Bond in a new direction, and one genuinely born out of a real desire to give the series new life. A noticeably more violent film, it is well paced, contains many excellent performances, and gets increasingly exciting as the plot unfolds (a trick that many of its predecessors seem to find difficult). The film's biggest flaw is, in all honesty, how quickly the Secret Service welcome Bond back to the fold after his solo actions, and even this could have been smoothed over if a new Bond picture had emerged two years later. Yes, there are better films in the series than this, but there are many far worse as well.

GIRLS	42
MARTINIS	11
DEATHS	169

Smoking: 'It could save your life, this cigarette.'

The Bond of Fleming's novels, a consumer of up to 60 Morland specials a day, was never seen onscreen. Connery's Bond might be seen occasionally puffing on a filterless cigarette, most notably during the famous introduction at Les Ambassadeurs in *Dr. No*, but he was not the chainsmoker of the novels. Though he would later be seen sharing a smoke with Leiter, this was an increasingly rare sight, and by *You Only Live Twice*, the cigarette had become a useful weapon rather than a lifestyle choice. Lazenby smoked at the opening of *On Her Majesty's Secret Service* but this was more to provide a visual signifier – to assert his identity as Bond.

Moore's arrival in the role involved a major change. For the next few years Bond would be a smoker of fat Havana cigars, a reflection of Moore's personal habits. Connery's Bond had turned one down at dinner in *Goldfinger* and Moore looked ridiculous. When Connery briefly returned to play Bond in *Never Say Never Again*, he did carry a cigar case which contained several thin cheroots.

Dalton's desire to play Bond as Fleming intended saw him constantly puffing away on cigarettes throughout his two films. This made the producers so nervous, given the increasing awareness of the danger of smoking and the status of the Bond films as family movies, that they placed a health warning in the credits of *Licence to Kill*. In recent years Bond has become a definite non-smoker. For Pierce Brosnan, an active supporter of cancer charities, to be any other way would be unthinkable.

GoldenEye (1995)

Produced by Michael G Wilson and Barbara Broccoli
Written by Jeffrey Caine and Bruce Fierstein
Story by Michael France
Music by Eric Serra
'GoldenEye' performed by Tina Turner
Director of Photography: Phil Meheux, BSC
Production designed by Peter Lamont
Edited by Terry Rawlings
Directed by Martin Campbell

PRINCIPAL CAST: Pierce Brosnan (*James Bond*), Sean Bean (*Alec Trevelyan*), Izabella Scorupco (*Natalya Simonova*), Famke Janssen (*Xenia Onatopp*), Joe Don Baker (*Jack Wade*), Judi Dench (*M*), Robbie Coltrane (*Valentin Zukovsky*), Tcheky Karyo (*Dimitri Mishkin*), Gottfried John (*General Ourumov*), Alan Cumming (*Boris Grishenko*),

Desmond Llewelyn (*Q*), Samantha Bond (*Moneypenny*), Michael
Kitchen (*Bill Tanner*), Serena Gordon (*Caroline*), Simon Kunz
(*Severnaya Duty Officer*), Pavel Douglas (*French Warship Captain*),
Cmdt. Olivier Lajous (*French Warship Officer*), Billy J Mitchell
(*Admiral Chuck Farrell*), Constantine Gregory (*Computer Store
Manager*), Minnie Driver (*Irina*), Michelle Arthur (*Anna*), Ravil Isyanov
(*MiG Pilot*), Vladimir Milanovich (*Croupier*), Trevor Byfield (*Train
Driver*), Peter Majer (*Valentin's Bodyguard*).

PRE-CREDITS AND TITLES: Nineteen eighty-six – the Soviet Union. A
black-clad figure infiltrates the Arkangel Chemical Weapons Facility.
After bungee-jumping into the base, he knocks out a guard before being
revealed to the audience as James Bond, 007. Shortly afterwards he is
intercepted by another figure in black, Alec Trevelyan, 006. Together
they break into the main storage facility before being surrounded by
Russian troops. 006 is captured and apparently shot dead by base
commander Ouromov. 007 escapes, and the explosives he has planted
blow up the base.

This cuts into the most impressive title sequence since *The Spy Who
Loved Me*. Like this predecessor, *GoldenEye*'s titles visually refer to the
plot of the film: symbols of the crumbling Soviet system, such as statues
of Lenin and Stalin, a two-faced woman (to represent Janus – the villain
of the piece) and numerous motifs representing the 'GoldenEye' itself. To
an extent the wonderful credits are damaged by a terrible song rolling
over them – an ugly pastiche of Shirley Bassey via Tom Jones's
'Thunderball', courtesy of U2's Bono and The Edge, and sung by
Tina Turner.

SUMMARY: Nine years later, a top-secret helicopter, radar-invisible
and proofed against the electromagnetic effects of a nuclear blast, is
stolen from the South of France by Ouromov and a woman, Xenia
Onatopp, both of whom are in the employ of the Janus crime syndicate.
Ouromov and Onatopp then use the helicopter to go to Severnaya, a
Russian Space Centre, which is the home of a first strike nuclear weapon,
GoldenEye, developed by the Soviet Union during the Cold War. It
works by exploding a nuclear device in orbit, and then targeting the
resultant Electro Magnetic Pulse on an area on Earth. The effect of the
pulse is to destroy the functionality of any electronic device in the area.
They take the control of the software necessary to fire GoldenEye
satellites, and then use one of them to destroy Severneya, covering up all
traces of their crime.

Bond travels to St Petersberg and arranges a meeting with the head of Janus, who turns out to be Alec Trevelyan, not so dead after all. The erstwhile 006 intends to detonate a second GoldenEye to wipe all computer records in London – after having transferred vast amounts of money into his own foreign accounts. This is not simply theft however: Trevelyan has other motives too (see **ALEC TREVELYAN**).

Bond kills Ouromov and tracks Trevelyan to his base of operations in Cuba. There 007 destroys the weapon's control system, and the second satellite GoldenEye harmlessly burns up in the Earth's atmosphere. Bond kills Onatopp and the treacherous Trevelyan.

UNIVERSAL EXPORTS:

BOND, JAMES BOND: An experienced Secret Service man of around forty, he was orphaned when his parents died in a climbing accident. He has pre-existing warm relationships with both Q and Moneypenny – M's secretary – but is unsure of where he stands with the new M. He clearly had some regard for her predecessor. Off duty he drives an Aston Martin DB5, registration BMT 214A. He prizes his loyalty to the service, and his country, very highly. Like the hero of *The Living Daylights*, he explains his job with the phrase 'I work for the British Government'. He is personally affected by Alec Trevelyan's betrayal. He's secretly aware that suggestions that he drinks to block out the screams of the men he has killed, and that he sleeps around in a quest for forgiveness for all the women he has failed to save have a ring of truth to them, claiming that being 'cold' is what keeps him alive. Very good at his job, he can drive a tank and a motorbike, fly a plane, bungee-jump, skydive and bring down a helicopter with a machine gun. He's given to making quips in the form of puns, albeit with an apologetic glance as he does so, and is flippant, but not crass. He lives by the words 'enjoy it while it lasts' but claims never to have acquired the skill to quit while he's ahead. He casually adjusts his tie after surviving a ludicrous tank chase.

M: The recently installed head of MI6, regarded by some as 'an accountant' and dismissed by MI6's Chief of Staff, Bill Tanner as 'the evil queen of numbers'. She certainly has put too much faith in analysts whose predictions (such as the idea that GoldenEye cannot possibly exist) occasionally turn out to be very inaccurate. She professes a personal dislike of Bond, and in perhaps the film's most celebrated line calls him 'a sexist misogynist dinosaur, a relic of the Cold War'. She knows of his reputation as a ladykiller – she refers to his 'boyish charms'

– yet still sends a seemingly insecure young woman to evaluate his fitness for service. She drinks bourbon with ice, and has no compunction about sending men out to die, though she claims she'd never do it on a whim. Having said all this, her briefing of 007 ends with her saying, 'Bond – come back alive.'

MONEYPENNY: An attractive, together woman a few years younger than Bond. She and Bond have never had sex, and while she's clearly not averse to the idea (she flirts with him mercilessly) she's clearly absolutely aware that their relationship is flirtation and nothing more. She's been called in from a date at the theatre due to an emergency, and is thus dressed rather more formally than one might expect for an average day at the office. The most successful version of this character yet presented.

Q: Since his adventures in *Licence to Kill*, Q has returned to his usual duties in the workshop. This is no bad thing. In a scene of only a few minutes he strikes up an affectionate and enjoyable rapport with the new Bond, on a par with the Q/Bond relationship of the 60s.

OHMSS: The Secret Service is based in Millennium House on the South Bank of the Thames (as indeed it is in reality). This has an Operations room which is run by Bill Tanner – with whom Bond has a friendly relationship, addressing him by his surname in a distinctly old school tie manner – and is linked to a network of spy satellites independent of those used by any other country.

ALLIES:

NATALYA SIMONOVA: Systems programmer at the Severnaya facility who gets caught up in the theft of the GoldenEye. Her escape from the ruined base is seen by Janus as a loose end to be tied up. Bond rescues her and she becomes an invaluable ally. Not only is she able to hack into Boris's computer systems, allowing the location of the second control dish, but it is her computer skills that result in the destruction of the second satellite. Though not as skilled as Boris, her experience with satellite re-entry systems allows her to put the weapon on a self-destructive orbit. Bond sabotages the control system, preventing Boris from correcting this course, and the weapon is destroyed.

Simonova has skills vital to the completion of Bond's mission. Though she falls for Bond she has no illusions about his profession – far from considering it romantic she lectures him on how it renders him an emotional cripple. Additionally, in an echo of the actions of Pam Bouvier (**Licence to Kill**), it is she who saves Bond, commandeering the helicopter that rescues him from the crippled communications dish.

VALENTIN DIMITROVITCH ZUKOVSKY: Former KGB agent turned gangster, Zukovsky has had an earlier (unseen) run-in with Bond, over the course of which Bond 'shot him in the leg, stole his car and took his girl'. It emerges that Bond, in fact, spared Zukovsky's life out of 'professional courtesy' (a courtesy he has yet to show anyone else in the series). Zukovsky's operation is based in a night club in St Petersburg. He helps Bond by putting him in contact with Janus.

JACK WADE: The CIA liaison with Bond, he appears to have replaced Felix Leiter. There is perhaps an oblique reference to Bond's old friend when Wade mentions that he obtained the Cessna plane, used by Bond to land in Cuba, from a friend at the DEA – the DEA being the agency for whom Leiter worked in *Licence to Kill*. Wade provides assistance in St Petersburg and helps with Bond's incursion into Cuba, though he seems doubtful about the expedition. This doubt does not prevent him arriving on the island with a detachment of marines to provide support.

THE OPPOSITION:

ALEC TREVELYAN (JANUS): The former 006 who faked his own death to become involved in Russian organised crime. He eventually became head of a large criminal empire, under the alias Janus. At some point in the 90s he formulated the GoldenEye sting – a combination of mass-extortion and straightforward revenge. His parents were Lienz Cossacks (see **IN THE REAL WORLD**). Trevelyan's parents survived Stalin's purges but years later his father killed his mother and then himself – an action for which Trevelyan blames the British government. At one point Trevelyan claims that half of everything is luck, and the other half is fate. We don't get to find out which he thinks it is that brings him and Bond back into contact after nine years. Although they were once fast friends and friendly rivals – indeed Alec claims that he considered asking James to join in 'defecting' – Trevelyan now holds a personal grudge against Bond. This is because, during the Arkangel incident (see **PRE-CREDITS AND TITLES**), Bond re-set charges that had been primed to go off in six minutes so they would explode in only three. The resultant explosion injured Trevelyan and permanently scarred his face. The fact that Alec was defecting at the time, and that Bond believed his friend dead and mourned him for nine years, didn't seem to enter into Trevelyan's self-pitying pysche.

As a former 00 agent, Trevelyan is a formidable opponent. Like Zorin (*A View to a Kill*) Sanchez (*Licence to Kill*), and Scaramanga (*The Man with the Golden Gun*), he is a principal villain who is physically threatening on his own terms. His abilities are enhanced by a lack of scruples. He uses both Bond and Natalya as hostages at different stages and doesn't think twice about sacrificing Ouromov. Having said this there is no 'luck' to Bond's eventual victory: whatever Trevelyan's beliefs 007 is simply better than 006.

GENERAL ARKADY OUROMOV: Former Colonel in command of a chemical weapons plant in Arkangel. Despite this plant's destruction, by 1995 Ouromov has been promoted to General in charge of Russia's Space Division while the Secret Service analysts see him as 'the new iron man of Russia'.

As well as helping to fake Trevelyan's death, he is key to the theft of the Tiger helicopter. His motives are never fully explained. It is possible he hoped to secure political power with the backing of the Janus group, or perhaps he was just in it for the money. It is unlikely that he is part of, or even aware of, Trevelyan's desire for vengeance. He is visibly shocked when Bond reveals Trevelyan's origins – clearly he has no time for Cossacks. It is during this confrontation that Bond shoots him dead.

XENIA ONATOPP: A former Soviet fighter pilot, it is she who flies the stolen Tiger helicopter. She also acts as Trevelyan's assassin – sent to murder the admiral, whose identity is used in the helicopter theft, and also to make attempts on Bond's life, both before the meeting in Statue Park and in the Cuban jungle. It is on this second occasion that she meets an ugly end, crushed after a helicopter drags her into a tree.

Her assassination method is different to say the least, consisting of crushing the ribcage of her victims, mid-coitus.

BORIS GRISHENKO: Computer genius and high-level programmer at Severnaya, Grishenko helps Trevelyan target the second GoldenEye on London while his hacking skills allow for the theft of money from the Bank of England. He's vital for these two reasons but this doesn't prevent Trevelyan treating him like dirt. He is an annoying character, so this attitude is understandable. He meets his end in a suitably humiliating way when he is frozen by an exploding vat of liquid nitrogen.

PRINCIPAL CASTING: Despite press suggestions of other actors up for the role, and the drawing up of an internal shortlist, it seems that the Broccoli family only ever really wanted one man to be their fifth 007 – Pierce Brosnan. Like his two immediate predecessors, he signed a contract to appear as James Bond in three films. With this key piece of casting in place, the producers began to replace other figures at MI6. Caroline Bliss – Moneypenny a mere twice – was not asked to return, and instead stage actress Samantha Bond was contracted.

Perhaps due to an awareness that Robert Brown's M had never had room to breathe, the decision was made to cast a woman. Judi Dench, a stage, screen and television figure of enormous experience and colossal range, took the role at a time when she was on the verge of large-scale Hollywood exposure. She would win an Oscar for a comic cameo as Queen Elizabeth I in *Shakespeare in Love* (John Madden, 1999) and be nominated for two others – one for movingly portraying Queen Victoria in *Her Majesty, Mrs Brown* (John Madden, 1998) and another for *Iris* (Richard Eyre, 2001) in which she played novelist, Iris Murdoch.

Desmond Llewelyn, clearly beloved of the films' audience, was inevitably asked back to continue portraying Q. Another actor engaged with an eye to return appearances was Michael Kitchen, cast as Bill Tanner. Tanner is MI6's Chief of Staff, and a character who had appeared in Fleming novels, beginning with *Casino Royale*. Despite being previously seen onscreen in *The Man with the Golden Gun* (played by Michael Goodliff), and *For Your Eyes Only* (portrayed by James Villiers), Tanner was a character the film series had not chosen to make much of. A busy actor, whose most memorable roles include playing the future King Charles III (that is to say, the present Prince of Wales) in satirical political drama, *To Play the King*, Kitchen's other commitments would prevent him from appearing in *Tomorrow Never Dies* (1997) and *Die Another Day* (2002), though he would reappear in *The World Is Not Enough* (1999).

Although Bond required a CIA contact, this would no longer be the much-abused Felix Leiter, whose erratic screen appearances had rendered the character damaged goods in cinematic terms. Instead, a new recurring character, bumbling Jack Wade – played as comic relief by *The Living Daylights*' villain, Joe Don Baker – was introduced with the intention that he should reappear when required by any future films. Baker had previously worked with director Martin Campbell on *Edge of Darkness* (1986). Although Wade would appear in *Tomorrow Never Dies*, he would not be reused in *The World Is Not Enough*, and by *Die Another Day* a potential replacement character was being drafted.

Former *Comic Strip Presents* funnyman, Robbie Coltrane, cast as Bond's former enemy and unlikely ally, Valentine Dmitrivitch Zukovsky, had altered his career trajectory by taking on the difficult role of psychologist Fitz in socially aware screenwriter Jimmy McGovern's series *Cracker*. He would win three consecutive BAFTA awards for the role. During the filming of *GoldenEye* he publicly expressed a hope that he would be able to reprise the role of Zukovsky some day. He would get this chance in *The World Is Not Enough* four years later.

Sean Bean, a TV star thanks to his role as the eponymous *Sharpe* in the series based on Bernard Cornwell's adventure novels, was cast as 006 partially because he had been on the shortlist to play 007. Bean's other film work has included *Patriot Games* (Philip Noyce, 1992) in which he was also a revenge-obsessed villain and *Ronin* (John Frankenheimer, 1998). In 2001 he won acclaim for his portrayal of Boromir in *The Lord of the Rings: The Fellowship of the Ring* for director Peter Jackson.

Like many Bond actresses, 'bad girl' Famke Janssen was a former model with little screen experience. She had, however, appeared in *Clive Barker's Lord of Illusions* alongside future captain of the starship Enterprise, Scott Bakula. Since then Janssen's career has been the very antithesis of that of the typical ex-Bond girl. Her films have included Woody Allen's *Celebrity* (1999) with Kenneth Branagh, monster-movie hit *Deep Rising* (Stephen Sommers, 1998) highly regarded indie flick *Love & Sex* (Valerie Breyman, 2000) and Bryan Singer's stunning *X-Men* (2000).

Polish-born Izabella Scorupco had been both a model and pop singer in Sweden before being cast as Natalya. Since then she has continued to work in Europe (she is fluent in four European languages) but her only mainstream US film since *GoldenEye* has been *Vertical Limit*.

Alan Cumming, cast as Boris, has won many plaudits for projects as diverse as playing Hamlet at the National Theatre and writing and starring in exceptionally camp 90s aeronautical sitcom, *The High Life*. Since *GoldenEye* he has carved out a niche as a certain kind of Hollywood villain, appearing in *Spy Kids* (Robert Roderiguez, 2001) and *Josie and the Pussycats* (Harry Elfont, Deborah Kaplas, 2001). He has also made memorable guest appearances on television, including in HBO's *Sex and the City* and ABC's *Third Rock from the Sun*.

GoldenEye contains a blink-and-you'll miss it appearance by future Hollywood favourite Minnie Driver as Zukovsky's girlfriend. Driver's hit movies include *Grosse Pointe Blank* (George Armitage, 1997), *Good Will Hunting* (Gus Van Sant, 1997) and *The Governess* (Sandra Goldblacher, 1998).

DIRECTOR AND CREW: Director Martin Campbell had an extensive résumé, encompassing both film and television. His work included sex satire *Eskimo Nell* (1975), episodes of action-packed television series *The Professionals*, police drama *Bergerac* and cockney hi-jinks show *Minder*, as well as instalments of American TV's *Homicide Life on the Street*. Since *GoldenEye* he has directed action films ranging from the outstanding – *The Mask of Zorro* (1998) – to the utterly mundane – *Vertical Limit* (1999).

Screenwriting duties were handed to Bond newcomers Jeffrey Caine, who had previously worked on low-quality British series *Dempsey and Makepeace* and *CATS Eyes*, and Bruce Feirstein, a writer with no big-screen credits. They developed a story by Michael France, the writer responsible for Sylvester Stallone vehicle *Cliffhanger* (Renny Harlin, 1993).

Ian Sharp, second unit director responsible for much of the action, was himself an action feature director, with *Who Dares Wins* (1982) to his credit. He had also shot episodes of *The Professionals* and the first season of the highly regarded *Robin of Sherwood*. Cinematographer Philip Mayheux had worked with Sharp on *Who Dares Wins*. Other work included the powerful *Scum* (Alan Clarke, 1979) and the influential *The Long Good Friday* (John Mackenzie, 1980).

Another Bond newcomer was Terry Rawlings who took over as editor. A man with much experience, Rawlings had edited *Alien* (Ridley Scott, 1979), *Chariots of Fire* (Hugh Hudson, 1981) and *Legend* (Ridley Scott, 1985) – during the shooting of which the original 007 sound stage in Pinewood was burnt down.

MUSICAL NOTES: Frenchman Eric Serra provided the post-industrial score for *GoldenEye*. Distinctive, but alien to the musical heritage of the series, its atonal noises and funky synthesiser breaks make it an effective oddity among Bond scores.

SET PIECES: Where to start? The knock 'em dead pre-credits sequence? The escape from KGB headquarters? The destructive tank chase? The final guns-blazing run-around in Cuba? First rate, the whole lot of them. Shot with gusto and edited with precision.

POSITIVELY SHOCKING: A violent film but without the protracted nastiness of *Licence to Kill*. Having said this, the scenes showing Onatopp's killing technique seem drawn out.

CUT SCENES: The UK DVD of the film has one of its fights between Bond and Onatopp trimmed to remove a headbutting.

MEMORABLE QUOTES:

Bond (on being told to come out of his hiding place with his hands up): 'How original.'

Bond (complaining at those who have captured him): 'No one takes the time to do a really sinister interrogation any more. It's a lost art.'

M: 'If I want sarcasm . . . I'll talk to my children.'

006: 'What's the matter James? No glib remark? No pithy comeback?'

006 (envisaging Bond's funeral): 'With only Moneypenny and a few tearful restaurateurs in attendance.'

FASHION VICTIMS: For the first time, Bond looks outside England for his tailoring: all of his suits and tuxedos were made by Brioni of Italy. There is no drop off in quality – Bond looks as good as ever, even in a potentially dangerous navy blazer and slacks combination. He spends much of the film in military assault gear.

Boris favours an unpleasant selection of Hawaiian shirts and Onatopp an outfit perilously close to that worn by **Never Say Never Again**'s Fatima Blush. Only Trevelyan really looks the part – and that's probably due to his 00 training.

PRODUCT PLACEMENT: Many companies were eager to have their names mentioned in the new Bond film. Q has a gadget built into a British Telecom phone box and a grenade built into a Parker pen. Bond flies British Airways, drives a BMW, and wears an Omega watch. Zukovsky drinks Smirnoff and St Petersburg computer dealers stock IBM machines. The most blatant placement comes when Bond drives his stolen tank through a lorry carrying Perrier mineral water.

GADGETS: Q's laboratory contains a missile built into a plaster leg cast, a phone box that traps its victim with an expanding air bag and an X-ray document scanner in a tea tray. Bond is equipped with a class four grenade in a pen (three clicks to arm, another three to disarm) used to great effect in Trevelyan's Cuban base, a belt with 75 feet of steel cord attached to a piton launcher used to escape KGB headquarters and a BMW equipped with Stinger missiles that, sadly, are never used. His watch has a handy laser and doubles as a detonator for the bombs he

plants in the Cuban control centre. In a badly explained sequence it is
revealed that Trevelyan knows of this function – he has an earlier model
of the same watch – enabling him to defuse the bomb. Bond's old DB5
(**Thunderball** et al) has a few new tricks. It can receive fax and voice
transmissions from Secret Service headquarters, responding to requests
for information sent by a digital camera carried by Bond. Most
importantly, the arm-rest that housed the control system for the gadgets
in the previous car is now used to chill champagne.

SOURCE TO SCREEN: The six-year absence of Bond, the longest
since the series began, was due to the franchise's third big 'behind the
scenes' dispute.

In the early 80s, United Artists (UA) faced financial ruin after the
costly flop, *Heaven's Gate* (Michael Cimino, 1980). Transamerica, the
holding company which owned UA, sold the studio to MGM for
$380 million. This did not have serious effects on the Bond series for
some years – the films were a profitable part of the studio's portfolio.
However, throughout the 80s MGM/UA, as the studio was known, was
almost constantly subject to rumours of takeover bids and the Bond
name and back catalogue became a chip in these high-stake financial
poker games. In 1990 Pathe Communications, in fiscal partnership with
Time-Warner, launched a takeover bid. As part of the deal, Pathe's
Giancalo Paretti hoped to sell off the rights to all sixteen Bond films at
very low prices. This could have great repercussions on the Bond series,
and would certainly have diminished the massive power that Danjaq –
the company which owned the cinematic Bond copyright – would have
over future Bond production. Danjaq filed numerous lawsuits and the
resulting court action prevented a new addition to the series from being
made for several years. In 1993, this was finally resolved and the video
and TV rights that had been so contested remained in MGM/UA hands.
Once the Bond production line had started running again, work began
on *GoldenEye*.

By *GoldenEye*, much had changed. The old political order had
collapsed, a key crew member, screenwriter Richard Maibaum, had died
(in January 1991) and other long-term screenwriter, Michael Wilson,
had taken up residence in the producer's office. What is more, the
Fleming legacy had apparently been stripped bare. It is not surprising
that many people have seen *GoldenEye* as a completely new direction
for Bond.

In fact, a lot of the perceived alterations were cosmetic. The use of
Russia as an enemy was itself a comparatively recent development, the

collapse of the Soviet Union was not a disaster for the films so much as a potential plot. Early films provided inspiration: the underwater satellite dish was taken straight from *You Only Twice*, Xenia Onatopp borrowed from *Thunderball*'s Fiona Volpe and *Never Say Never Again*'s Fatima Blush; the idea of a third party stealing a piece of hi-tech equipment from one country and blaming it on another is familiar from *From Russia with Love* and the famous Aston Martin DB5 made its first appearance since *Thunderball*. There was some inspiration from the books. The opening chase between Bond's Aston and Onatopp's Ferrari could have been taken straight from the opening pages of the novel *On Her Majesty's Secret Service*, right down to Bond recognising the car of his racing partner outside a casino. Trevelyan's revenge plot also seems familiar; a disfigured man seeks vengeance on the British for a defeat inflicted during World War Two by wiping out London could also refer to Hugo Drax in the novel of *Moonraker*. Even the title had a Fleming pedigree. GoldenEye had been the name of Fleming's house in Jamaica, itself named after a contingency plan on which Fleming worked for intelligence operations were Germany to invade Spain during World War Two.

As always, the watchwords for this Bond film were change and continuity. Indeed, recognition of political change allowed for continuity. In answer to the challenge of being a 'relic of the Cold War' Bond would go back to fighting the non-nation-specific megalomaniacs he had faced before his politicisation in the 80s. In the tradition of previous Bond films, topical events, in this case the collapse of the Soviet Union, would be incorporated into the plot.

IN THE REAL WORLD: The break-up of the Soviet empire, which effectively began in 1989, dominates the plot of *GoldenEye*. As recently as 1987's *The Living Daylights*, the Soviet Union was a powerful, conquering force, in active opposition to countries in the West. Growing economic problems, military setbacks in Afghanistan and a more liberal leader at the head of the politburo (Mikhail Gorbachev) led to a gradual fracture of the Eastern European communist bloc. By 1991, the Soviet Union itself had split into fifteen different countries, and free elections had made Boris Yeltsin president of a Russian Federation. Ouromov highlights this trend when he blames the theft of the GoldenEye on 'Siberian separatists.' Political freedom has not inevitably led to economic success and, in the new Russia, it is mostly the criminal gangs and black-marketeers who have prospered. Janus is an extreme example; Zukovsky is the more realistic face of the ex-official-turned-gangster.

The massacre of the Cossacks of Lienz was a real event. In the closing days of the European war, around 30,000 Cossacks (including women and children) who had sided with the Nazis against Communist Russia for nationalist reasons surrendered to British forces and were billeted in the Austrian town of Lienz. Whether they believed that the British would join with them to fight Stalin is unclear, but it is certain that they faced death or imprisonment on return to Russia. The Yalta conference of February 1945 laid the basis for just such repatriation with the allied leaders agreeing all prisoners of war be returned to their countries of origin. Between March and June 1945 these families were returned to Russia against their will, where many were killed or sent to the gulags.

Electromagnetic pulse joins the pantheon of scientific theories appropriated for the Bond film. The idea itself is sound and is pretty much as explained in the film. The concept is mentioned in *A View to a Kill*.

In 1992 Stella Rimington became the first woman to head Britain's internal security service (often referred to as MI5). The casting of Judi Dench in the role of M not only reflected this contemporary development but also allowed for the interesting scenes that would result between Bond and a woman in authority over him. Then Prime Minister John Major publicly commented on the resemblance between Dench and Rimington.

CULTURE VULTURE: The Russian mobsters who appear in *GoldenEye* have become a much-used resource in action films. *The Jackal* (Michael Caton-Jones, 1997) was an abysmal attempt to update Fred Zinnemann's 1973 classic with Russian gangsters based in Helsinki. The reinvention of classic Roger Moore series, *The Saint* (Philip Noyce, 1997) was an equally terrible Bond rip-off with Val Kilmer as a master of disguise against the Russian mob. *Fair Game* (Andrew Sipes, 1995) was an inferior contemporary of *GoldenEye* with Russian criminals operating in America. In a world deprived of Cold War opponents, it has become all too easy to take the standard Russian stereotypes and label them as 'mobsters'.

CRITICS: Christopher Tookey in the *Daily Mail* (8 November 1995) offered opinions in line with most film reviewers: 'Bond is back with a bang . . . this is among the finest action adventures of recent years and one of the very best Bond movies.'

Across the Atlantic, the *Village Voice*'s Georgia Brown (28 November) thought the film, 'Smoother than an unbruised vodka Martini'; although initially perplexed by the need for Bond to return at all, she seemed to be (largely) won over to his side by the film. 'The cinematography is sumptuous', she enthused, and made loud noises of approval about both Brosnan and Dench: 'You could do worse than see the new Bond', she concluded. Describing the pre-credits sequence, Quentin Curtis of the *Independent on Sunday* (26 November) noted a phenomenon observed by many paying cinema-goers: 'a cheer went round the auditorium in which I saw the film'. Finding Brosnan's Bond 'closer to Fleming than Connery' he felt 'much of the credit for this revised Bond must go to the director Martin Campbell [who] never allows the special effects or . . . humour to crowd out the core of human drama'. Derek Malcolm of the *Guardian* was of the opinion that '*GoldenEye* cleverly, and with thorough professionalism, delivers the familiar goods whilst changing the packaging a little.' He also felt that 'No one could say that the fantasy has a tinge of realism to give an edge to its absurdity . . . the movie gives its audience all they wanted while obliquely suggesting that Fleming's hero was a bit of a cad by modern standards.' He concluded with a note of hope for the British film industry, 'If *Four Weddings and a Funeral* suggested Britain could still make highly commercial films, *GoldenEye* proves the point.'

In the *Evening Standard* (9 November) Alexander Walker was ecstatic: '*GoldenEye* is everything we hope for and nothing we feared . . . the best adventure for many a year.' He felt that Brosnan's Bond was the 'best since Connery' (a feeling echoed elsewhere in the press) and thrilled that the first instalment of the revived series was both 'confident enough in its own legend to throw a few choice bits of self criticism [and] in step with the times'. It was, in summary, '. . . the Bond film with everything.'

Geoff Brown of *The Times* was ready to take on those who labelled Bond a museum piece, 'a miracle happens in GoldenEye . . . the museum exhibit smashes out of his case'. 'Brosnan [is] an ideal Bond', he continued, '[and] Martin Campbell bombards us with action'. He finished by paraphrasing the Q of **Never Say Never Again**. ' "Good to have you back Mr Bond. Let's get back to some gratuitous sex and violence." '

BOX OFFICE: *GoldenEye*'s worldwide gross was $350 million of which $106 million was earned in the USA. American viewers totalled some 29 million people, the largest audience for a Bond film in the biggest, most vital of markets since *You Only Live Twice* thirty years before. The Broccolis' gamble had paid off – *GoldenEye* was a brilliant success.

AWARDS: Bond's belated return earned two BAFTA nominations in 1996: Best Sound and Best Achievement in Special Effects. *GoldenEye* demonstrated Bond's continuing appeal to a younger generation at the MTV movie awards, picking up the Best Fight award for the sauna tussle between Bond and Onatopp. Q's lunch also won an award for 'Best Sandwich in a Movie'.

MARTINIS, GIRLS AND GUNS: Bond seduces (much to M's disapproval) Caroline, the girl sent to psychologically evaluate him. He also scores with the comely Natalya. Again, there's a single Martini ordered, but at least here he drinks it. Bond despatches quite a few Red Army troops during the course of his adventures this time round – eight to be precise. He shoots Ouromov, smashes Onatopp into a tree, guns down a helicopter which crashes, killing its pilot, and then drops Alec Trevelyan from a great height, before subsequently dumping an entire radio telescope on him. A total of twelve.

THE ONE WITH . . .: the bungee jump and the tank chase.

THE LAST WORD: 'Ready to save the world again?' The first Bond film in six years, this was do or die for Eon – a last chance to relaunch the series. Fortunately for all concerned, *GoldenEye* is a triumph. It is neither an epic adventure, nor a consciously 'deep' character piece – it is a seemingly effortless blend of both, which is a *hugely* difficult trick to pull off (see **The World Is Not Enough**). Jokey enough to appease hardcore Moore fanatics, well thought through enough to engage fans of *On Her Majesty's Secret Service* and self-aware enough to work in an era when the very series of which it is a part has become the stuff of common currency. Part reinvention, part restatement, *GoldenEye* brings Bond firmly into the milieu of the modern action film, while retaining his own distinctive appeal *and* adding more than a few ideas uniquely its own. By the end of these 124 minutes Pierce Brosnan *was* James Bond. No question. A brilliant success.

GIRLS	44
MARTINIS	12
DEATHS	181

Tomorrow Never Dies (1997)

Produced by Michael G Wilson and Barbara Broccoli
Written by Bruce Feirstein
Music by David Arnold
'Tomorrow Never Dies' performed by Sheryl Crow
Director of Photography Robert Elswit
Production designed by Allan Cameron
Edited by Dominique Fortin and Michael Arcand
Directed by Roger Spottiswoode

PRINCIPAL CAST: Pierce Brosnan (*James Bond*), Jonathan Pryce (*Elliot Carver*), Michelle Yeoh (*Wai Lin*), Teri Hatcher (*Paris Carver*), Ricky Jay (*Henry Gupta*), Götz Otto (*Stamper*), Joe Don Baker (*Wade*), Vincent Schiavelli (*Dr Kaufman*), Judi Dench (*M*), Desmond Llewelyn (*Q*), Samantha Bond (*Moneypenny*), Colin Salmon (*Robinson*), Geoffrey Palmer (*Admiral Roebuck*), Julian Fellowes (*Minister of Defence*), Terence Rigby (*General Bukharin*), Cecilie Thomsen (*Professor Inga Bergstrom*), Nina Young (*Tamara Steel*), Daphne Deckers (*PR Lady*), Colin Stinton (*Dr Dave Greenwalt*), Al Matthews (*Master Sergeant*), Mark Spalding (*Stealthboat Captain*) Bruce Alexander (*Captain, HMS Chester*), Anthony Green (*Firing Officer, HMS Chester*), Christopher Bowen (*Commander Richard Day, HMS Devonshire*), Andrew Hawkins (*Lieutenant Commander Peter Hume, HMS Devonshire*), Dominic Shaun (*Lieutenant Commander, HMS Devonshire*), Julian Rhind-Tutt (*Yeoman, HMS Devonshire*), Gerard Butler (*Leading Seaman, HMS Devonshire*), Adam Barker (*Sonar, HMS Devonshire*), Michael Byrne (*Admiral Kelly*), Pip Torrens (*Captain, HMS Bedford*), Hugh Bonneville (*Air Warfare Officer, HMS Bedford*), Jason Watkins (*Principal Warfare Officer, HMS Bedford*), Eoin McCarthy (*Yeoman, HMS Bedford*), Brendan Coyle (*Seaman, HMS Bedford*), David Ashton (*First Sea Lord*), William Scott-Masson (*Staff Officer 1*), Laura Brattan (*Staff Officer 2*), Nadia Cameron (*Beth Davidson*), Liza Ross (*Mary Golson*) Hugo Napier (*Jeff Hobbs*), Rolf Saxon (*Philip Jones*), Vincent Wang (*MiG Pilot*), Philip Kwok (*General Chang*).

PRE-CREDITS AND TITLES: In the most viscerally satisfying pre-credit sequence of the series, Bond acts as a scout for a military strike on a terrorists' arms market near the Russian border. Watched by M and several other observers thanks to remote cameras, he is forced into action by a poorly thought-out cruise-missile strike ordered by Royal

Navy Admiral Roebuck. The market contains a plane equipped with nuclear torpedoes which will, if hit by the missile, detonate, causing a nuclear catastrophe. Bond seizes control of the plane, and flies it away before the explosion spreads the radioactive plutonium in the bombs over the Northern Hemisphere.

The pounding Sheryl Crow title song is accompanied by an impressive visual sequence based on the film's theme of media domination. There are the requisite scantily clad ladies and one particularly fine sequence where a diamond necklace turns into an orbiting ring of diamonds representing satellites.

SUMMARY: Media Mogul Elliot Carver intends to engineer war between Britain and China in order to gain broadcast dominance over Chinese territory. He finances the construction of a boat which is invisible to radar and uses it to sink a British frigate – HMS *Devonshire* – and destroy a Chinese MiG fighter plane while the respective crews are quarrelling about whether the boat is in international or Chinese territorial waters.

It later turns out that Carver has used a GPS (Global Positioning Satellite) encoder – stolen from the Americans – to lead the *Devonshire* off course and into Chinese waters. With the British Government convinced that the Chinese Airforce sunk the frigate and murdered the survivors, and the Chinese Government certain that the British frigate invaded their waters and destroyed the MiG, tension between the countries increases and the British Navy is sent to the South China Sea.

Carver has struck a deal with a Chinese general, Chang. Once war starts, the stealth boat will destroy a meeting of the Chinese Government, allowing Chang to take control, broker a ceasefire and emerge as his country's leader. Carver will be given broadcasting rights in China for the next hundred years as payment for his part in this particularly bloody coup. Following the trail of the stolen decoder, and later in concert with Chinese Agent Wai Lin, Bond hunts Carver down, kills him, arranges for his boat to be destroyed by the British Navy and prevents war.

UNIVERSAL EXPORTS:

BOND, JAMES BOND: Bond uses the operation code signal 'white knight'. He once had a relationship with Eliot's wife, Paris, and has confided with Moneypenny about this, (she, rather unfairly, appears to have briefed M on it). He carries naval rank (and looks good in uniform) and has a working knowledge of Global Positioning Satellites. He is still driving an Aston Martin DB5 in his own time and a BMW on the firm's and is having an affair with Professor Inga Bergstrom of Oxford University. He has no qualms about killing Dr Kaufman in cold blood for personal revenge.

M: M is pitted against the chest-beating macho men of the British armed forces. She comes out on top in this contest, humiliating Admiral Roebuck, thanks to Bond's work in the field. She has mellowed towards 007 since their first encounter, not only backing him to the hilt in official matters but putting up with his sexual antics. She has a personal car and driver, in which she rockets around London with full police escort.

MONEYPENNY: Reprises the sharp sarcastic style from *GoldenEye*. She has a detailed knowledge of Bond's history – probably from all his pre-mission bragging.

Q: Assigned to the field as he was in *Thunderball* and *The Spy Who Loved Me*, Q delivers Bond his customised BMW. Undercover as a rental agency official Q bickers with Bond in the usual entertaining manner.

CHARLES ROBINSON: Suavely played by the excellent Colin Salmon, Robinson is a late replacement for a scripted appearance by Bill Tanner which had been dropped when Michael Kitchen proved unavailable. Rather than recast the character, a substitute was created. Robinson knows Bond well enough to call him 'James' and to exhibit personal concern for his well-being. It isn't made clear if he's Tanner's deputy or of equal rank.

OHMSS: The Secret Service has contacts in Saigon though Bond never meets them. They are also involved in operations with the military (and with Russian forces) conducted from a control room in the Ministry of Defence.

ALLIES:

WAI LIN: Colonel with the Chinese People's External Security Force, Wai Lin is Bond's opposite number. She is a truly effective agent in her own right, who only comes to rely on Bond at the very end of the mission and is quite capable of functioning without him. Wai Lin is an expert martial artist skilled at operating undercover at dinner parties – a perfect match for Bond. It is a shame in a way that the time needed to develop Paris Carver's character couldn't have been spent on Wai Lin.

PARIS CARVER: Elliot's high-class wife was once involved romantically with Bond (who was probably a secret agent at the time – he slept 'with a gun under his pillow'). This was at a time in her life when her drink of choice was a straight tequila shot – hardly the drink of high society. Further details of her past are elusive, though she once lived in Zurich. As a character Paris works as a 'sacrificial lamb'. It is clear that she means something to Bond and is quite convincing as a character from his past. Her death is genuinely affecting and we can see that Trevelyan's question in *GoldenEye* – whether Bond's affairs distract him from the women he failed to protect – has deep roots. However, it is Paris's prior conversation revealing intimate knowledge of Bond that has already sealed her fate.

JACK WADE: The CIA's top buffoon returns for a cameo. A latterday JW Pepper, Wade provides comic relief, as well as acting as a link to the brief scene at the American airbase. This is his last appearance.

ADMIRAL ROEBUCK: The belligerent Roebuck is a shoot first, consider the consequences later man. This creates problems both when he nearly causes nuclear disaster by ordering a cruise missile strike on an arms market and later when he backs sending the British Navy to China.

THE MINISTER OF DEFENCE: A rather limp, stuffy figure – it seems that Freddie Gray couldn't make the political manoeuvres necessary to get into Tony Blair's cabinet (see **For Your Eyes Only**). He gamely goes along with the jingoistic response to events in the South China Sea.

THE OPPOSITION:

ELLIOT CARVER: Head of the Carver Media Group Network, a nebulous organisation with links to newspapers, magazines and television news channels. Carver had worked in Hong Kong on a small, low-quality newspaper at the age of sixteen and has, presumably, crawled his way to the top of his profession. He wants to take what he sees as the next step – creating the news through manipulation of countries, and the staged war between China and Britain is the first step. A combination of **The Spy Who Loved Me**'s Stromberg and **A View To A Kill**'s Zorin, Carver is a maniac with global power his ultimate goal.

STAMPER: A blond-haired, blue-eyed Aryan sociopath in a tight black T-shirt. Regards Dr Kaufman as his mentor, and claims to think of him as 'a father'. In an early draft of the script (and in Raymond Benson's novelisation), Stamper had a brain abnormality that caused pleasure to register as pain and vice versa. This brilliant idea was reserved for partial use in the next Bond film (where it was badly employed) and leaves Stamper as yet another Donald Grant (**From Russia with Love**) clone, albeit an efficient one.

HENRY GUPTA: A 60s student radical, Gupta has become a 'techno-terrorist', selling his skills with electronics and computers to the highest bidder. It is he who purchases and reprogrammes the GPS encoder and arranges for the *Devonshire* to be sent off course. He also intercepts a conversation between Bond and Paris, leading to the death of Carver's wife. If the heroin and pornography in his safe are anything to go by, Gupta has some unpleasant personal habits.

DR KAUFMAN: A skilled assassin with a PhD in forensic medicine, Kaufman carries out murders made to look like suicides. He specialises in the 'celebrity overdose' but is a skilled pistol marksman able to make a gunshot wound from any distance appear self-inflicted. He is skilled in torture, but regards this as a hobby. One of the most interesting henchmen in the entire series, his brief screen appearance and abrupt death prevent his character from receiving the recognition it deserves.

GENERAL CHANG: A vital part of Carver's plan, albeit one only seen onscreen for a few seconds, it is Chang who is the true beneficiary of the manufactured war – securing the leadership of China.

PRINCIPAL CASTING: The filmmakers opted for a less overtly physical villain, choosing versatile British actor, Jonathan Pryce. An accomplished stage performer, Pryce is best known cinematically for his lead role in Terry Gilliam's dystopic *Brazil* (1985). He had also played Argentinian president Perón in the musical Madonna vehicle *Evita* (Alan Parker, 1996). It is a measure of his ability as an actor that, in the same year he played the insane Elliot Carver, he gave a beautifully understated performance in *Resurrection* (Alan Parker, 1997). Fans of his performance as Carver will enjoy his equally eye-rolling turn as The Master in *Doctor Who and the Curse of Fatal Death* (John Henderson, 1998).

Teri Hatcher was best known as Lois Lane in the Superman series *Lois & Clark*. Film roles before Bond include the token love interest in *Tango and Cash* (Andrei Konchalovsky, 1989) and the dreary *Heaven's Prisoners* (Phil Joanou, 1996).

Michelle Yeoh came to Bond on the back of many impressive Chinese martial arts films. She performed all her own stunts in *Tomorrow Never Dies*.

A fine supporting cast of memorable character actors included British sitcom star Geoffrey Palmer, famous stage magician Ricky Jay, and hounddog-faced American actor, Vincent Schiavelli.

DIRECTOR AND CREW: As opposed to the continuity seen in the 'Bond family' of crew members in the 60s, 70s and 80s, the 90s would see much more change in the key backstage roles.

By now the series was effectively on a 'guest director' footing. Martin Campbell was replaced by Roger Spottiswoode who had begun his career editing films – including *Straw Dogs* (1971) – for director Sam Peckinpah. He went on to helm a series of unremarkable action films such as Mel Gibson vehicle *Air America* (1990) and ill-advised Sylvester Stallone comedy *Stop! Or My Mom will Shoot* (1992). His best work is rightly felt to be *And The Band Played On* (1993), a complex critique of mainstream America's reactions to the Aids epidemic. The production designer Allan Cameron had worked with Spottiswoode on *Air America*.

Shortly before shooting *Tomorrow Never Dies*, cinematographer Robert Elswit had fulfilled DOP duties on *Boogie Nights* (PT Anderson, 1997). He returned to work with Anderson on the critically acclaimed *Magnolia* the following year.

The one main crew member (with the exception of the producers) to remain on board was Bruce Feirstein, who would contribute to the script for all of Brosnan's first three films.

This was the first Eon Bond film produced without Cubby Broccoli, who had died in June 1996 shortly after the international success of *GoldenEye*. His daughter Barbara and his stepson Michael G Wilson were now fully in control of Eon after long apprenticeships. It was agreed that Cubby's name would be included on the opening credits of all future Bond productions. A caption card at the end of *Tomorrow Never Dies* dedicates this film to his memory.

MUSICAL NOTES: Composer David Arnold was a great fan of John Barry and of Bond songs in general, overseeing an album of cover versions by artists such as Chrissie Hynde and Pulp released in 1997. Responsible for the excellent score to *Independence Day* (Roland Emmerich, 1996), Arnold brought a rich, funky jazzy feel to the soundtrack, echoing the classic score of *Goldfinger* but with effective modern twists. Arnold collaborated with British dance act Propellerheads for 'Backseat Driver', the music for the car-park chase. Arnold also wrote 'Surrender (Tomorrow Never Dies)' for use as the film's title song. Sung by kd Lang this was ultimately relegated to the closing credits. As with *Thunderball*, a new (in this case theoretically more commercial) song was recorded late in the day. Written by Sheryl Crow and her usual writing partner, Mitchell Froom, and sung by Crow, it's an effective theme song, but bears no resemblance to Arnold's score, which frequently reprises lines from 'Surrender' in the same way that John Barry's scores had utilised aspects of his title songs.

SET PIECES: A joy from start to finish. The pre-credit sequence, a top-notch shootout in Germany, an inventive car chase (filmed at Brent Cross shopping centre) a motorbike escape and final stealthboat battle which are both spectacular.

This is Bond as unashamed action film, fast paced and well directed. The suggestion that Bond films' stories exist only to put the action sequences in some order is hard to refute in the case of *Tomorrow Never Dies*.

POSITIVELY SHOCKING: There is plenty of implied unpleasantness in Paris Carver's death, the presentation of the Chakra torture instruments and Elliot Carver's ultimate fate courtesy of the sea drill. However, none of this is actually shown in any detail. As with all the other films, the high body count is largely sanitised. The violence is that of any film aimed at a young teenage audience.

MEMORABLE QUOTES:
Moneypenny: 'You always were a cunning linguist, James.'

Admiral Roebuck: 'Sometimes M, I don't think you've got the balls for this job.'
M: 'Perhaps, but the advantage is I don't have to think with them.'

Carver: 'Mr Stamper, will you please kill those bastards!'

Admiral Roebuck on Bond: 'What the hell's the man doing?'
M: 'His job.'

FASHION VICTIMS: Bond once again looks the business in his tailored Brioni suits and a gorgeous light-brown overcoat. Carver reprises the infamous tunic of *Dr. No* fame while his stealthboat crew are uniformly attired in tight black T-shirts and his media centre guards wear humiliating blazers. Wai Lin has great taste in oriental style dresses and special mention must go to Paris Carver for coping with an ostrich feather-heavy evening number.

PRODUCT PLACEMENT: As with *GoldenEye*, most of Bond's gadgets are built into brand name items; his grenade/lighter is Dunhill, his versatile phone is an Ericsson, his watch (or rather the one he borrows from the Chinese Secret Service) is Omega and his car is a BMW (as is the motorcycle he steals). The Secret Service supply their vehicles by masquerading as Avis car hire. When Bond waits for Paris Carver in his hotel room he consumes half a bottle of Smirnoff Red vodka.

GADGETS: Q supplies Bond with two very useful items. His BMW saloon car is bullet-proof and has CS gas dispensers and electrically charged door handles to deter thieves. For more extreme situations there is a roof-mounted rack of missiles, a rear-spike dispenser, re-inflating tyres, and a chain cutter concealed under the front BMW badge. It also has a concealed weapon tray, perhaps in homage to a similar idea built into the Aston Martin in *Goldfinger* but never shown onscreen. Bond's fully functional mobile phone is also an electric stun gun, a lock-pick, a fingerprint scanner (which duplicates the scanned print on the display screen allowing the opening of fingerprint-coded doors) and a remote control for the BMW.

The Chinese People's External Security Force has its own Q-branch, including a fire-breathing dragon statue, a paper fan that fires darts and a whole arsenal of guns and explosives. Among these are an updated Walther pistol – the rather bulky P99 – that Bond adopts as his preferred side arm, and a variant on his Omega watch with a detachable, remote-controlled detonator that he uses to cause havoc on the stealth boat.

SOURCE TO SCREEN: *Tomorrow Never Dies* marks a total separation from Fleming. No elements are taken from the novels and the title, for the first time, is a complete invention. The books had been of little consequence for some time now, but the occasional incorporation of a set piece or name from Fleming's work acted as a reminder of 007's origins.

However, the film does keep up links with Bond's cinematic past. The plot is basically a reworking of *The Spy Who Loved Me*: a lone madman manipulates two countries into war for his own benefit. Indeed, the film makes direct reference to this earlier work, putting Bond back into the naval uniform he had not worn since 1977. Wai Lin of the Chinese People's External Security service is a rough analogue of that film's Anya Amasova too, although one more inclined to fisticuffs, and working with Bond of her own volition rather than on the orders of her government. On top of this, Bruce Feirstein built a fairly simple story, which ultimately suffered from the many rewrites it went through. Trouble with location shooting (the Vietnamese government rescinded permission and substitute locations in Thailand had to be found) and tension between Feirstein and the director, led to a great many last-minute changes and rewrites. While the picture holds together pretty well there are moments when it feels as though dialogue has been rushed to justify a particular action sequence (for instance when Bond and Wai Lin steal a bike outside the CMGN building in Saigon). Still, such things can be said about any Bond movie, though most do hide this feature of their scripts better. Ultimately the script does all it needs to do – it keeps the film rolling along fast enough to prevent the audience spotting the problems.

It was at the time that this film was made that the threat of a rival film, based on the legacy of Kevin McClory, manifested itself for the last time. Sony Pictures had acquired the rights that Kevin McClory had won from Ian Fleming some thirty years previously (see **Thunderball**) as well as the rights to the book *Casino Royale*. It has been suggested that Sony's actions were directly related to the move by former UA executive John Calley (who oversaw production of *GoldenEye*) to Sony's filmmaking subsidiary. Though in reality the deal between Sony and McClory had begun long before Calley arrived at Sony, he did step up efforts to finalise arrangements and plans were announced to produce a rival picture named *Warhead 2000*. At one point there was even news of attempts to hire Sean Connery to play the villain. The constrictive requirements of the rights to Bond owned by McClory (see **Never Say Never Again**), combined with Eon/MGM's litigious stance to any attempts to produce a rival Bond, led to Sony admitting defeat in early 1999. Over the course of the next few years Danjaq acquired the rights to *Casino Royale* from Sony. McClory launched a last-ditch lawsuit in 1998 in which he claimed joint ownership of the actual character of Bond, and demanded royalties from every film so far made! Unsurprisingly this was unsuccessful and by 2001 he had lost the case and failed in his appeals. With the majority of Bond material in the hands of Danjaq, and McClory having lost so many court cases against the Bond producers, it seems unlikely that a rival series, or even another rival picture, will emerge.

IN THE REAL WORLD: The script makes several indirect comparisons between Carver and numerous real media moguls. His basic desire to obtain broadcast rights in China parallels the attempts of Rupert Murdoch to broadcast his Sky satellite channels in that country. The reference to CMGN's software division is a cheeky joke at the expense of Microsoft owner, Bill Gates. The use of inflammatory editorials and newspaper articles to trigger a war is comparable to the actions of William Randolph Hearst. When Carver himself quotes Hearst as saying 'you provide the pictures and I'll provide the war' he is referring to Hearst's incitement of war between America and Spain in 1898 over Cuba. Hearst's newspapers published stories exaggerating and inventing acts of cruelty and tyranny on the part of the Spaniards in their former colony, leading to action by America. M's press release, covering up Carver's death, draws on the details surrounding the death of newspaper baron Robert Maxwell who drowned, under suspicious circumstances, while cruising the Mediterranean on his private yacht. The character of Carver is not based on any one individual, but an exaggerated amalgam of them all.

The series' apparent vendetta with China came to an end with this film, which presented the country in a light comparable to the Russia of *The Spy Who Loved Me* – a country normally friendly to Britain but misled. This was commensurate with China's evolving real-world status – a participant in a form of détente with the West since the early 70s and a respected trading partner. The fall of the Soviet Union left China the only realistic opposition to America, and so the film runs with the implication that China could present a threat were the current, friendly government replaced by more unpredictable elements.

Where the plot departs from any concept of reality is in the power and influence it attributes to the British Navy. The proclamation of Admiral Roebuck, 'we're sending the fleet to China', borders on laughably unrealistic. But this is far from new in a Bond film – previous portrayals of the global prominence of Britain (in *You Only Live Twice*, *The Spy Who Loved Me* and with the extensive satellite network of *GoldenEye* for instance) have been similarly fantastic.

Carver's stealth boat capitalises on the growing interest in stealth technology. The US military first admitted to using stealth aircraft to attack key targets in Operation Desert Storm, 1990–91. Since then they have seen regular use in operations in the former Yugoslavia and

Afganistan. The actual design of the boat is based on a real stealth ship that has undergone tests with the American Navy.

The use of cruise missiles to eliminate terrorist targets also has basis in military fact. After the US Army took disastrous losses in Mogadishu at the start of the 90s, President Bill Clinton adopted a policy of attacking suspected terrorist sites with cruise missiles, a policy which (as Russian General Bukharin points out in the film) avoids any risk of unpopular casualties being inflicted. As in the film, the viability of this tactic is debatable in real life; several such strikes hit civilian buildings and factories in Somalia rather than actual terrorist bases.

CULTURE VULTURE: As *The Man with the Golden Gun* had incorporated a sequence inspired by the popular martial arts films of the time, so *Tomorrow Never Dies* owes a debt for its stealth boat shoot-out to the action films of Hong Kong director John Woo. Titles such as *The Killer* (1989) and *Hard Boiled* (1992) introduced his distinctive directing style, replete with balletic violence and slow-motion footage, that he later brought to Hollywood with the disappointing *Broken Arrow* (1996) and the amazing *Face/Off* (1997). Spottiswoode borrows heavily from this oeuvre for the prolonged climactic shoot-out with several gratuitous (and misjudged) uses of slow motion and the two-handed gunplay that began as a signature of Woo but has become *de rigueur* in every Hollywood blockbuster. Spottiswoode keeps up the Bond tradition of making reference to the dominant action genre, a tradition seen in other films such as *Live and Let Die* and *Licence to Kill*. However, his rather lazy incorporation of the clichés of this style count as one of the less effective examples of this.

CRITICS: The reception of *Tomorrow Never Dies* was generally negative. Alexander Walker in the *Evening Standard* (11 December 1997) was initially positive, 'The film opens promisingly enough . . . but then things go wrong.' The *Daily Telegraph*'s Quentin Curtis was more exact in his criticism. Writing on 12 December he claimed that 'After its promising and amusing start, the movie is little more than a series of sequences – exciting and sometimes breathtaking ones . . . but largely unconnected.' Philip French, of the *Observer* (14 December) made similar criticism, accusing the films of recently 'sacrificing everything to a relentless, unvaried pace'. That same day Matthew Sweet's review for the *Independent on Sunday* covered similar ground when it suggested that the character of Bond had become 'marginal to his own adventures'. Sweet attributed this to the progress of time leaving Bond an anachronism.

There were a few dissenting voices. In the *Sun*, Nick Fisher described *Tomorrow Never Dies* as 'quite possibly the best film ever'. Nigel Andrews, of the *Financial Times*, dwelled on the film's production problems, saying that its release was due to Eon's determination 'not to let a cash cow expire'. He went on to torture this metaphor, praising the film in the process: 'The cow here is a brindled thing, part bad part good. But it moves like merry thunder. This cow could win the Grand National.'

Even the positive reviews, with the exception of the *Sun*, were ambivalent. Anne Billson, writing in the *Sunday Telegraph* (14 December), adopted a pastiche of Ian Fleming's style, a device reviewers had first adopted in the 1980s, to make a disturbing suggestion that, 'James Bond was . . . perplexed. It seemed like only yesterday that colleagues had been patting him on the back . . . on a spiffing return to form in *GoldenEye*.' Now, however, 'He could hear them muttering the dreaded words "past his sell-by date" and "*Moonraker*." ' Whatever they may say, the critics had to face one fact. As Jason Cowley put it in an article for *The Times*, 'You can say many things about James Bond . . . but what you cannot do . . . is ignore him.'

BOX OFFICE: *Tomorrow Never Dies* compounded *GoldenEye*'s box-office performance by taking over $300 million worldwide in its initial run.

AWARDS: Though not a winner, Sheryl Crow's title song picked up two major nominations at the Golden Globes and Grammy Awards for the title song.

MARTINIS, GIRLS AND GUNS: Bond beds three: Professor Ingrid Bergstrom at Oxford, Paris Carver and Wai Lin, just after the credits begin to roll. He also has one Martini, ordered for him by Paris at Elliot Carver's reception.

Bond's body count for this mission is 25. Amazingly he makes no clean kills on the ground at the arms market, but does kill the co-pilot of his plane and the pilot of the one that's following him at the end of this sequence. Two of Carver's guards are killed during his raid on the Carver building in Hamburg before Dr Kaufman is shot dead at the hotel (he kills no one in the car park). Three guards are dead when Bond and Wai Lin escape from the Saigon building and four are killed when the Carver helicopter goes down. Bond claims thirteen lives in the gunfight on the stealth boat – eleven guards, Stamper and Carver.

THE ONE WITH . . .: Lois Lane and the remote-controlled BMW.

THE LAST WORD: 'There's no news like bad news.' Despite its torturous production and troubled shoot, *Tomorrow Never Dies* works very well. The plot is deceptively simple, the set pieces are uniformly excellent and there's an abundance of good dialogue. With a terrific heroine, a hugely amusing villain and a confidently brash tone, *Tomorrow Never Dies* is the best straightforward action movie in the series.

GIRLS	47
MARTINIS	13
DEATHS	206

The World Is Not Enough (1999)

Produced by Michael G Wilson and Barbara Broccoli
Screenplay by Neal Purvis, Robert Wade and
Bruce Fierstein
Director of Photography: Adrian Biddle, BSC
Music by David Arnold
Lyrics by Don Black
'The World Is Not Enough' performed by Garbage
Editor: Jim Clark
Directed by Michael Apted

PRINCIPAL CAST: Pierce Brosnan (*James Bond*), Sophie Marceau (*Elektra*), Robert Carlyle (*Renard*), Denise Richards (*Christmas Jones*), Robbie Coltrane (*Valentin Zukovsky*), Judi Dench (*M*), Desmond Llewelyn (*Q*), John Cleese (*R*), Maria Grazia Cucinotta (*Cigar Girl*), Samantha Bond (*Moneypenny*), Michael Kitchen (*Tanner*), Colin Salmon (*Robinson*), Goldie (*Bull*), David Calder (*Sir Robert King*), Serena Scott Thomas (*Dr Molly Warmflash*), Ulrich Thomsen (*Davidov*), John Seru (*Gabor*), Claude-Oliver Rudolph (*Colonel Akakievich*), Patrick Malahide (*Lachaise*), Omid Djalili (*Foreman*), Jeff Nuttall (*Dr Arkov*), Diran Meghreblian (*Coptic Priest*), John Albasiny (*Helicopter Pilot*), Patrick Romer (*Pilot*), Jimmy Roussounis (*Pipeline Technician*), Justus von Dohnanyi (*Captain Nikoli*), Hassani Shapi (*Doctor*), Carl McCrystal (*Trukhin*), Martyn Lewis (*Newscaster*), Kourosh Asad

(*Russian Radio Operator*), Daisy Beaumont (*Nina*), Nina Muschallik (*Verushka*), Daz Crawford (*Casino Thug*), Peter Mehtab (*Casino Dealer*).

PRE-CREDITS AND TITLES: Bond retrieves a vast sum of money from a Swiss banker in Bilbao, Spain. This had been the sum paid by British industrialist Sir Robert King for the return of a report stolen from a murdered MI6 agent. Bond demands the name of the man responsible for the murder but the banker is killed by one of his assistants. In the confusion Bond escapes.

Back in London he oversees the return of the money to Robert King, an old personal friend of M's. However, it turns out that the cash has been sabotaged and is, in fact, a powerful bomb that explodes, killing King. Bond chases after an assassin who was stationed on the river to kill anyone who survived the blast. The chase runs the length of the Thames, ending at the Millennium Dome where the girl commits suicide rather than be captured.

An incredibly long sequence – in fact, by the time it ends it is easy to forget that the credits have not yet been shown. This length reduces the impact of the boat chase which is a shame because it is really such an impressive sequence, surpassing that seen in *Live and Let Die*.

Another quality title sequence follows this, Daniel Kleinman really going to town on the film's primary motif of oil. The song isn't bad either, belted out by Shirley Manson of Garbage, backed by a lot of strings.

SUMMARY: British mogul Sir Robert King's daughter Elektra plans to monopolise oil production in the Caspian Sea, and win great prosperity for Azerbaijan and international renown for herself. In order to do this she has had her terrorist henchman Renard steal some weapons grade plutonium, which she will then use to stage an elaborate nuclear 'accident' on board a Russian Navy submarine. This 'accident' will destroy Istanbul and effectively wipe out all her competitors (who need to use the Bosphorus to transport their oil). Initially assigned to protect Elektra following her father's murder, Bond discovers that she is in fact his enemy, and that the various actions against her (such as a murder attempt and an attack on her own pipeline) have been orchestrated by her to draw attention away from her own culpability. Despite having begun a relationship with Elektra (she is manipulating his weaknesses) Bond kills her and foils her plan.

UNIVERSAL EXPORTS:

BOND, JAMES BOND: Bond has a passing knowledge of nuclear fission, but unlike in *Octopussy* doesn't know how to defuse a nuclear bomb. He speaks some Russian. He is regarded by M as the best agent she has available to her, although she states that she'd never actually tell him. She allows him considerable leeway, including overlooking two instances (one in Scotland, the other in Azerbaijan) where he explicitly criticises her decisions and questions her judgement. Bond believes that life is full of small challenges and claims that he gets through life by 'taking pleasure in great beauty', an echo of sentiments in *GoldenEye*. His family motto is still 'The World is Not Enough' (see **On Her Majesty's Secret Service**). He has previously had sex with Secret Service medic Dr Molly Warmflash, and is reticent about answering questions about whether he's ever lost a loved one. Dr Warmflash judges him to have 'exceptional stamina'. On the verge of death – due to a screw bolt putting pressure on his neck – and with nuclear catastrophe imminent, he can't resist one last sub-pun to the victorious Elektra, telling her she meant nothing to him and was merely 'one last screw'. He shows similar lack of restraint after Elektra challenges him to kill her, saying, 'You can't kill me. You'd miss me' – he guns her down in cold blood and then quips, 'I never miss.' It isn't meant to be funny, and the coldness in Brosnan's eyes makes you worry for 007's psyche like never before.

M: M read Law at Oxford (although we don't get to find out at which college) with Robert King. It is repeated that she has children, and by implication a partner still living (King says 'Best to the family' not 'Best to the children'). As Bond and Dr Jones dismantle a nuclear bomb, she confidently pronounces, 'If there's even the slightest chance then Bond will succeed.'

MONEYPENNY: After Bond returns from Bilbao he and Moneypenny indulge in their most explicit repartee in the series; she asks him if he has brought her a present back from Spain and he responds by handing her an (inevitably suggestively shaped) metal tube containing a cigar. He tells her that he's sure she knows what to do with it, and replies that she knows exactly 'where to put' such an object. She then smiles suggestively and throws it in the bin. She later indulges in some comic mock jealousy over Bond's tryst with Dr Warmflash, reminding the medic Bond essentially slept with her to guarantee that he'd be taken off the inactive roster.

Q: The last appearance of Desmond Llewelyn's Q is an alternately jolly and sombre affair. After all the puns and the usual repartee there's an earnest discussion about Q's imminent retirement. 'You're not retiring any time soon, are you Q?' asks Bond. The admirable major replies that he's always tried to teach Bond two things, firstly 'never let them see you bleed' and secondly 'always have an escape plan'. Then Q descends slowly through the floor on a hidden platform until he's out of sight; a touching onscreen finale to a career that had been dominated by the Bond series (actor Desmond Llewelyn died in a car accident shortly after filming was completed).

BILL TANNER: A more authoritative chief of staff than in *GoldenEye*. The return of Charles Robinson gives a real pecking order to the staff of MI6, and Tanner is at the top. Having said this, he shares briefing duties with Robinson. Reluctant (with good reason) to see M travel to Azerbaijan, Tanner is visibly glad to see her return.

CHARLES ROBINSON: Although ranking slightly below Tanner, his duties include field operations – he escorts M to Azerbaijan. Despite the difference in rank he is friends with Tanner and they both get on well with Bond.

OHMSS: The Service is still based in Millennium House in Vauxhall, which is seen to have a river-based boat-launching platform and extensive labs for Q to work in. There's also a secondary headquarters in Scotland, where the Service decamps after the explosion in London. This combines suits of armour and yet more Q labs with wall- and floor-mounted display screens, medical facilities, video phones and a holographic projector capable of creating an image more than three feet in diameter (in this case, Renard's head). A portrait of the late Bernard Lee (Eon's first M) is on the wall in M's briefing room. Five more 00 agents beside Bond attend M's briefing – one of them is a woman.

ALLIES:

VALENTIN DMITRIVICH ZUKOVSKY: Since *GoldenEye*, Zukovsky has made a few attempts to 'go straight'. He owns a caviar factory and a casino, but is not above taking a million-dollar bribe to secure a passage for some smuggled items on the Russian Navy nuclear submarine of which his nephew is the commander. He clearly has more affection for Bond than before, actually looking pleased to see him when Bond enters his casino unannounced. He advises Christmas against developing an attachment to Bond with the words: 'A relationship with a man like that? I wouldn't bet on it.' When he realises that Elektra is not smuggling, but has in fact planned a nuclear catastrophe and killed his nephew in the process, he resolutely allies himself with Bond, leading an armed attack on Elektra's base at Maiden's Tower. Here he takes two bullets in the chest from Elektra and, after collapsing to the ground, seemingly mortally wounded, he uses his last bullet to damage the torture chair that Bond is tied to, giving our hero the chance to escape.

DR CHRISTMAS JONES: Perhaps the most unlikely nuclear physicist in the whole of fiction (and visibly much younger than thirty), Christmas is attached to a team clearing up Russian nuclear weapons left over from the Soviet Union days. It seems that at first meeting she warns everyone from making jokes about her name ('I don't know any Doctor jokes' Bond deadpans). She speaks (at least some) Russian and has defused hundreds of small nuclear charges.

THE OPPOSITION:

VICTOR ZOKAS aka RENARD: A former KGB man 'cut loose' by his employers (the implication is it was because he was too dangerous, à la Dario and the Contras; see **Licence To Kill**), Renard is regarded by MI6 as the world's most dangerous terrorist. In the wake of Renard's mid-90s kidnap of Elektra King, M sent 009 to kill Renard. He put a bullet in Renard's head, but due to a freak incident, Renard didn't die. The bullet remains lodged in his brain, moving slowly along his medula oblongata, killing off his physical senses, including his ability to feel pain. Since then he has been seen in Pyongyang (North Korea), Moscow (in 1996), Afghanistan, Iraq, Iran, Beirut and Cambodia. It is apparently he who stole the atomic energy report from the MI6 agent and who arranges for its sale to Sir Robert King in order to get the money bomb into close proximity to its target. It is he who keeps Bond alive in the Bilbao shoot-out (so that Bond can deliver the rigged money to MI6). Initially presented as the main villain of the piece, out to gain revenge on the King family, Renard later turns out to be little more than the psychotic lapdog of:

ELEKTRA KING: Sir Robert King's daughter, and also his murderer. Several years before the events of the film Elektra had been the victim of a very public ransom extortion during which MI6 advised Robert King not to pay the ransom and let them handle matters. Renard was her kidnapper. Elektra eventually 'escaped' her captors without MI6's help, having (she claims) seduced her guards. This is truer than Bond knows; she did not just distract them to allow her escape, but actually turned them to her side. Renard feels he 'ruined her' himself and takes some of the 'credit' for transforming her from 'promise itself' to the bitter young woman she is now. (The rest of the blame, he feels, belongs to M, who left Elektra 'at the mercy of a man like [him]'.) It is Elektra who used her self-described 'power over men' to turn Renard to *her* side, and enlist him in her private war against her father. Elektra regarded Sir Robert as an exploiter of the wealth of her people, usurping the inheritance she sees as coming from her mother's side.

There had been 'henchwomen' and villainous female protagonists in Bond films before – examples include Fiona Volpe (**Thunderball**), Helga Brandt (**You Only Live Twice**), Irma Bunt (**On Her Majesty's Secret Service**), Bambi and Thumper (**Diamonds are Forever**), May Day (**A View to a Kill**) and Xenia Onatopp (**GoldenEye**). However, this is the first time in the series that the main villain has been female. The closest the series had previously got was Rosa Klebb (**From Russia with Love**) and she worked for Blofeld. What Elektra represents is an out-and-out Bond villain with her own motives and fiendish scheme. This is typical of the film. It takes a Bond theme and twists it slightly: here the main 'Bond girl' turns out to be his opposition, the one he has been sent to protect he must kill.

ARKOV: Works for the Russian Atomic Energy Commission. Has been hired by Renard to help him obtain a nuclear warhead. When he questions the sense behind continuing the operation, after Bond disposes of the parahawks Arkov had provided, Renard shoots him for showing weakness.

DAVIDOV: Elektra King's head of security and very much a part of her plans. Renard orders him to travel to the missile silo, in place of Arkov, to obtain the nuclear warhead. Bond intercepts and kills Davidov before this happens, and takes his place.

MR BULLION: Zukovsky's treacherous gold-toothed sidekick Mr Bullion is nowhere near as tough as he thinks he is. He's machine-gunned to death by the employer he betrayed and tried to murder, during the assault on Maiden's Tower.

PRINCIPAL CASTING: This was the last film in Pierce Brosnan's initial three-film contract. Although Brosnan was eventually to agree to reprise the role, it was a measure of the renewed vigour of the 90s Bond series that the question asked by the media after the release of this film was not *if* there would be a new Bond should Brosnan depart, but who it would be.

For the first time, the villain of the piece was to be a woman, and the filmmakers turned to massively experienced French actress, Sophie Marceau, who had come to prominence in English language films via Mel Gibson's execrable *Braveheart* (1995).

Glaswegian Robert Carlyle was cast as Renard. Carlyle's most famous roles include the stripping and steel comedy *The Full Monty* (Peter Cattaneo, 1997) and his portrayal of the psychotic Begbie in *Trainspotting* (Danny Boyle, 1995). On British television he had appeared in the controversial yet brilliant *Priest* (Antonia Bird, 1994) and given a frightening, yet moving portrayal of a man driven to murder and madness by the pressures of life and the deaths of 96 Liverpool FC fans at Sheffield Wednesday's Hillsborough Ground in *Cracker*, both for writer Jimmy McGovern. *The World Is Not Enough* would see him reunited with *Cracker*'s star and fellow Scot, Robbie Coltrane.

Denise Richards's big debut movie had been in the sci-fi social satire, *Starship Troopers* (Paul Verhoeven, 1997) and she had also appeared in the swamp noir thriller, *Wild Things* (John McNaughton, 1998) and spoof documentary, *Drop Dead Gorgeous* (Michael Patrick Jann, 1999) among other things.

Actors in slightly smaller roles included British drum and bass star Goldie as Mr Bullion (cast solely, it would seem, for his impressive array of gold teeth), and distinguished stage actor David Calder as Sir Robert King. An associate artist of the Royal Shakespeare Company, Calder's brief appearance here gives little indication of his range, or his complex essaying of many of the great roles of the stage.

John Cleese, the co-writer/star of the Oscar-winning *A Fish Called Wanda* (Charles Crichton, 1987) and the much-loved *Fawlty Towers*, and one sixth of *Monty Python's Flying Circus*, was selected to play Q's assistant and chosen successor, jokingly referred to (and credited) as R.

Many actors reprised their roles from earlier films. Along with Judi Dench as M, Samantha Bond's Moneypenny and Desmond Llewelyn's Q, Michael Kitchen and Colin Salmon appear together as characters that had hitherto been seen filling equivalent roles in the two earlier Brosnan films. Robbie Coltrane also returned as *GoldenEye*'s Valentin Zukovsky – Coltrane gets a lot more to do here than in his last appearance, and comes close to stealing the film thanks to a script which gives him many of the best lines.

DIRECTOR AND CREW: Michael Apted, chosen as the man to helm Eon's nineteenth Bond instalment, had had an eclectic career as both a feature-film director and a documentary filmmaker for television. A pivotal figure in the development of the *7up/14up* (et al) television series (which charted the development of a group of demographically selected British children across their whole lives), Apted's feature films included such diverse titles as *Gorillas in the Mist* (1988) with Sigourney Weaver and *Stardust* (1974) with Adam Faith, David Essex and Larry Hagman. More in the Bond mould had been Cold-War detective drama *Gorky Park* (1983) which starred William Hurt, Lee Marvin and Ian McDiarmid. Perceived as a director who could handle complex character pieces, Apted's appointment meshed with the desire of returning star Pierce Brosnan to appear in a film which would deal more with Bond as a character than *Tomorrow Never Dies*.

Aside from Apted, the majority of the crew were established members of Eon's rep. Second unit director Arthur Wooster had been part of the team, on and off, since *For Your Eyes Only* and had also worked on *Shakespeare in Love* (John Madden, 1999). Peter Lamont, production designer, had worked on most Bond pictures since *Goldfinger* in a design capacity. Lamont had been absent from *Tomorrow Never Dies* in order to work on James Cameron's *Titanic* (1997) for which he had won an Academy Award.

The other second unit director, Vic Armstrong, a stunt co-ordinator as well as an accomplished action director, had a Bond pedigree going back to *You Only Live Twice*.

Director of photography, Adrian Biddle, had been Oscar nominated for *Thelma and Louise* (Ridley Scott, 1991). A former focus-puller, he had graduated to full-blown DOP status on *Aliens* (1986) after director James Cameron fired his designated photographer and searched through the crew for a replacement.

MUSICAL NOTES: Also returning for another Bond assignment was musician David Arnold, fresh from the success of *Tomorrow Never Dies*. Since completing his first Bond assignment, Arnold had provided music for the box-office disaster *Godzilla* (Roland Emmerich, 1998). Sadly, one of Arnold's songs, a superb lounge-core anthem performed by living legend Scott Walker (the melody of which supplies the tune for much of the score) would be cut from the final print (it was to have run over the end credits) and replaced with a lengthy version of Monty Norman's 'James Bond Theme'.

SET PIECES: The pre-credits sequence is a staggering 13 minutes and 42 seconds long; the ski sequences are slick and the fight in the submarine is brutal. Most impressive is the white-knuckle ride Christmas and Bond take through the oil pipeline, while strapped to a nuclear bomb. What is key about all of these is the twist they put on the usual Bond fare. When skiing, Bond faces not other skiers on the slopes but masked men in flying ski-mobiles. The boat chase is not on some exotic tributary or in the Louisiana bayou, but on the grey water of the Thames. The 'car chase' takes place in a pipeline, and combines speedway thrills with the tension of a traditional 'bomb countdown'. A battle on a submarine doesn't take place in the horizontal but in the vertical. All in all, this contributes to a film with some very close links to reality but which comes across as rather – well, *weird*.

POSITIVELY SHOCKING: Elektra gets a sort of psycho-sexual kick out of straddling Bond as she tortures him, pointing out the inevitable outcome of a man being strangled (an erection). Renard punches a hole in a wooden box in order to illustrate that he feels no pain, visibly bloodying his hands as he does so. Earlier he has handled boiling hot rocks, and crushed one into the unfortunate Arkov's hands – with all the attendant scorching misery for Arkov.

MEMORABLE QUOTES:
Zukovsky: 'I'm looking for a submarine. It's big and black and the driver is a very good friend of mine!'

Zukovsky (on finding Christmas Jones sitting wearing a skimpy purple dress): 'How did you get in here? I'll call security . . . and congratulate them!'

Zukovsky (unimpressed by his henchman's absence): 'Where have you been you gold-plated buffoon?'

Christmas (explaining why she has to get the stolen plutonium back): 'Somebody will have my ass.'
Bond (looking her up and down): 'First things first'.

Christmas: 'Do you want to put that in English for those of us that don't speak spy?'

FASHION VICTIMS: Bond's suits are still by Brioni. Christmas Jones wears exceptionally little even by Bond-girl standards – but at least it's a practical very little as opposed to purely decorative very little (see **The Man with the Golden Gun**).

PRODUCT PLACEMENT: This film boasts a staggering degree of corporate co-operation. The by-now standard BMW is present as is Bollinger champagne. Elektra and her guards communicate by Motorola walkie-talkie and Renard's assassin flees from the attack on Millennium House in a Sunseeker motor boat. Some of the more esoteric examples of product placement are Caterpillar (the earth-moving equipment company with a sideline in boots and jackets) who have their logo emblazoned over the construction site of Elektra's pipeline, and Microsoft whose Windows CE operating system is apparently used by nuclear scientists to defuse atomic bombs. It is difficult to tell whether the Millennium Dome's appearance at the end of the opening boat chase was an attempt at a plug for the controversial landmark or just chosen as a logical end point for a Thames river pursuit. Even if intentional it failed to help disastrous attendances.

GADGETS: There's Q's self-described 'fishing boat' which comes complete with rocket propulsion, front-mounted missiles and machine guns. What's he intending to fish for? Giant sea monsters? Bond's new BMW is, according to Q, 'fully loaded' (or 'rather stocked' according to R) with side-mounted rockets and six beverage cup holders. At the Highlands MI6 base someone has a combined set of bagpipes with a machine gun and a flame-thrower. When wandering around Zukovsky's casino, Bond wears a pair of X-ray glasses which allow him to see if anyone in the room is carrying concealed weapons (as it happens, everybody is). He also uses a grappling hook watch and an inflatable ski jacket as protection against avalanches.

SOURCE TO SCREEN: *The World Is Not Enough*, like *Tomorrow Never Dies*, is made up entirely of original material. However, the title is very much drawn from Fleming. In both the novel and film of *On Her Majesty's Secret Service*, Bond visits the Royal College of Arms. Here he is told by the Sable Basilisk of the college that one of his ancestors took as the family motto the Latin phrase *Orbis non sufficit* – the world is not enough (or more literally, 'the world is insufficient').

The idea for the plot originated with co-producer, Barbara Broccoli who, while on her way back to America shortly after the premiere of *Tomorrow Never Dies*, saw an edition of US TV news programme, *Nightline*, which discussed problems with oil pipelines in Eastern Europe. This programme had details on the huge reserves of oil under the Caspian Sea, and commented that this was the last great oil discovery of the twentieth century; and had led to small local towns becoming areas of huge wealth and lavish spending habits. The programme also mentioned a dramatic rise in the number of casinos in the area, and the practical difficulties in transporting this local oil to the West. All of these would provide elements around which the script would be built.

Screenwriters Neil Purvis and Robert Wade had written the acclaimed *Let Him Have It* (Peter Medak, 1991), the story of a miscarriage of justice in the 1950s. Their initial draft of the script was rewritten by director Apted and his wife, screenwriter Dana Stevens (who expanded M's role in the story and added the idea of her being kidnapped), and then later by Bruce Feirstein, a veteran of the two previous Bond pictures who refined the characterisation of Bond.

There are numerous elements in the picture that are derived from, or heavily influenced by, earlier Bond pictures. *The Spy Who Loved Me* lends its image of a nuclear submarine and its 'Bond discovered in flagrante' finale. *On Her Majesty's Secret Service* (both book and film) inspires the skiing sequences, whereas the epic boat chase cannot help but remind a viewer of *Live and Let Die*. However, given the interesting and innovative ways in which these scenes were staged, it is perhaps more demonstrative of the way in which the series, after nearly twenty films, was running out of even remotely plausible ways in which to put its protagonist in danger.

CUT SCENES: A shot of Bond checking the fallen Zukovsky's pulse (and thus confirming his death) was cut. Given Robbie Coltrane's enthusiasm for the character it wouldn't be surprising if Zukovsky reappears in a later Bond picture, grumbling all the while that Bond left him for dead.

IN THE REAL WORLD: Aside from the main plot device of Caspian oil, the film is based very much on real world events (see **SOURCE TO SCREEN**). Some of Elektra's background and motives seem inspired by the Pattie Hearst kidnapping case. In 1974 Pattie Hearst, heiress to the Hearst publishing company millions, was kidnapped from her California apartment by a revolutionary group calling itself 'The Symbionese Liberation Army'. During the course of the captivity she was brainwashed by her kidnappers and joined their group. She assisted in bank robbery and shoplifting, before being captured. This complicity with her captors earned her a harsh custodial sentence, though she was freed by President Jimmy Carter in 1979. Though King was a rich heiress captured by a radical political group, there is an interesting twist to this source material as it appears in the film; it is King who manipulates her kidnappers, bringing Renard to her side in her private battle with her father.

A brief topical reference, on a par with *Dr. No*'s stolen Goya painting, is made at the expense of Swiss bankers. In the late 90s certain Swiss banks came under pressure for being unwilling to release the funds of Nazi holocaust victims to survivors or to families of the deceased. Claiming that lack of proper identification prevented them from returning the money held in various accounts, international pressure eventually forced the banks to concede and, gradually, control of the accounts returned to their rightful owners. When Bond speaks of Swiss bankers generally being reluctant to return money and sarcastically comments about how difficult it is to get money out of a Swiss banker, he is referring to these distasteful episodes.

On a lighter note, Bond and Moneypenny's wordplay about where to put a cigar is clearly a reference to activities practised by 42nd US President Bill Clinton (1993–2001) and White House intern Monica Lewinsky.

CULTURE VULTURE: The name of the villain of the piece, Elektra, is taken from classical mythology, as well as having resonance with psychoanalytical theory. The daughter of King Agammenon and his wife Cyltemnestra, she is the subject of Sopohocles's play *Electra* and Euripedes's later *Electra* and *Orestes*. In all these she is an instrument of vengeance on the murderers of her father (who are in league with her mother). Elektra King's name is a conceptual red herring; she is not the revenger of her father's murder, but rather its cause.

Sigmund Freud came up with the term 'Elektra complex' to describe the female equivalent of the Oedipus complex. Although not necessarily sexual in nature, the concept is based in the idea of a woman's search for a replacement father figure due to the inadequacies or absence of her natural father. This figures prominently in the writings of poets such as Sylvia Plath and her lesser emulators.

CRITICS: There was little consistency to critical opinion on this film. Antonia Quirke of the *Independent on Sunday* (28 November 1999) was lukewarm about it, '. . . less definitively feeble than other recent offerings . . . my reaction is much the same as to a new Rolling Stones album: I'm just grateful that it's not embarrassing'. She also speaks of the producers appealing to the 90s love of camp 'to legitimise their incredible slovenliness and timidity' in not varying the formula of the films. Adam Mars-Jones in the *The Times* (25 November) takes completely the opposite view, speaking approvingly of the film's approach to formula and considering the film as 'not coming close to the destructive knowingness of camp'. Andrew O'Hagan of the *Daily Telegraph* (26 November) seems ready to accept the formula too, 'the James Bond formula, like an episode of *Casualty* or a Mills and Boon book, is clear-cut and dependable'. By this point in the series there seems to be acceptance of formula. *Time Out*'s Derek Adams in the 24 November–1 December issue gives conditions for this tolerance: 'At least with a Bond flick you know what to expect . . . That said some Bonds are more watchable than others and this . . . is certainly one of the better ones.' Anthony Quinn of the *Independent* (26 November) praised the pre-credits sequence yet felt that 'once the sequence is over, there's a strange feeling that the movie itself is over too'. Yet he too accepted the principle of there being rules the film had to obey and concluded, 'Bond is now an institution.'

Pleasantly surprising was the seemingly unilateral decision by critics to not give away Elektra's status as ultimate villain.

MARTINIS, GIRLS AND GUNS: Bond sleeps with the amusedly detached Dr Warmflash, the decidedly sociopathic Elektra King and the buxom-yet-vacant nuclear scientist, Dr Christmas Jones. He orders a Martini in Zukovsky's casino.

Bond racks up nineteen kills. He shoots one man in the banker's office in the pre-credit sequence, the four parahawk pilots and Davidov. He then kills three of Renard's men in the missile silo, three of the crew of one helicopter sent to kill him at the caviar factory, two men who get off the second helicopter to kill him, before he destroys this helicopter and its two remaining crew. His final three kills are Gabor, Elektra and Renard, in that order.

THE ONE WITH . . .: the boat chase down the Thames and Q's farewell scene.

THE LAST WORD: 'There's no point in living if you can't feel alive.' The most pessimistic of the Bond films (even the title seems to suggest that life itself is somehow pointless and purposeless), *The World Is Not Enough* is fundamentally about a lot of very damaged people doing dreadful things to one another for fundamentally disturbed reasons. What's more the whole thing is arguably M's fault. Although buoyed up by much wit and consistently good performances (Brosnan is oustanding here) there's nevertheless something about the film that is raw, painful and somehow hollow. If this is a fantasy, then why are there consequences? If this is a character drama then why the never-ending boat chase? Part Bond epic, part deconstruction of the man, *The World Is Not Enough* is not wholly satisfactory as either, but it's an accomplished and arresting try.

GIRLS	50
MARTINIS	14
DEATHS	225

Saving the World: 'World domination . . . the same old dream'.

How many times has James Bond saved the world? For these purposes, any adventure where failure in his job would lead to any outcome other than the destruction of all (or the vast majority) of human life on Earth will be discounted.

With this in mind, all of his first four outings can be put to one side. They involve, at worst, limited mass destruction. Similarly, *On Her Majesty's Secret Service* is out – the UN were on the cusp of agreeing to Blofeld's demands when Bond intervened. *Diamonds are Forever* had no direct implications of imminent war or destruction, though such an event could have occurred in the aftermath. The first two Moore films revolved around strictly criminal villainy. All films in the 80s dealt with missions on a smaller scale. In the worst of these, *Octopussy*, Bond's failure would have led to localised devastation with the strong possibility of a European war, but one largely free of the risks of escalation into nuclear war. In the worst case scenario of any of the Brosnan films, there would be limited war between Britain and China were Bond not to succeed, but in this case the villains intend to stop such a war before it gets out of control.

This leaves three films where Bond's failure would have undeniably critical implications: *You Only Live Twice* – Russia and America are poised on the brink of all-out war if he fails; *The Spy Who Loved Me* – his intervention prevents global nuclear devastation; *Moonraker* – by his actions on the space station, Bond prevents the launch of Drax's gas globes.

Die Another Day (2002)

Albert R Broccoli's Eon Productions Limited present
Produced by Michael G Wilson and Barbara Broccoli
Screenplay by Neal Purvis and Robert Wade
Director of Photography: David Tattersall, BSC

Music by David Arnold
'Die Another Day' performed by Madonna
Editor: Christian Wagner
Director: Lee Tamahori

PRINCIPAL CAST: Pierce Brosnan (*James Bond*), Halle Berry (*Jinx*), Toby Stephens (*Gustav Graves*), Rosamund Pike (*Miranda Frost*), Rick Yune (*Zao*), Will Yun Lee (*Colonel Moon*), Michael Madsen (*Damian Falco*), Judi Dench (*M*), John Cleese (*Q*) Samantha Bond (*Miss Moneypenny*), Colin Salmon (*Charles Robinson*).

PRINCIPAL CASTING: Halle Berry, cast as Jinx, has described her character as 'the feminine James Bond', and 'the next step in the evolution of women in the Bond movies'. The actress herself has had a somewhat eclectic career. She made her big-screen debut in Spike Lee's critically acclaimed *Jungle Fever* after a year on US glamour soap *Knot's Landing*. Her other work is as varied, and includes Bryan Singer's *X-Men* (2000), Eddie Murphy vehicle *Boomerang* (Reginald Hudlin, 1992), political satire *Bulworth* (Warren Beatty, 1998) and the brainless *Swordfish* (Dominic Sena, 2001). In March 2002 she became the first African–American woman to win a Best Actress Academy Award, for her portrayal in *Monster's Ball* (Marc Foster, 2001) of a young woman whose husband is on death row.

Toby Stephens is the son of the late Sir Robert Stephens and the actress Dame Maggie Smith. Like his parents he has principally concentrated on stage work, and is a long term member of the Royal Shakespeare Company, for whom he memorably portrayed Coriolanus. His television work includes RSC director Peter Hall's wonderful Channel 4 adaptation of Mary Wesley's *The Camomile Lawn* and Stephen Poliakoff's *Perfect Strangers* (2001).

Rick Yune previously appeared as a motorcyclist in the intense road-race remake *The Fast and the Furious* (Rob Cohen, 2001). He also starred in a high-quality literary adaptation of *Snow Falling on Cedars* (Scott Hicks, 1999).

Michael Madsen, cast as Bond's NSA contact Damien Falco, is best known for his performance as the sadistic, jive-dancing Mr Blonde in *Reservoir Dogs* (Quentin Tarantino, 1992). He has previously worked with Bond director Lee Tamahori on *Mulholland Falls* (1996).

DIRECTOR AND CREW: To helm this 40th-anniversary Bond instalment Eon made the unorthodox choice of New Zealand-born

Lee Tamahori. The versatile Tamahori – a former commercial artist and photographer – had moved into motion pictures by working as a boom mike operator on numerous films, before becoming a second unit director on the outstanding David Bowie/'Beat' Takeshi Kitano vehicle *Merry Christmas Mr. Lawrence* (Nagisa Oshima, 1983). Several more 2nd unit assignments followed before his first major feature as director – 1994's *Once Were Warriors*, a remarkable study of alcoholism and marital violence amongst the Maori population of New Zealand. Since then he has directed brutal LA noir thriller *Mulholland Falls* with Nick Nolte and Melanie Griffith, David Mamet's *The Edge* (1997) and the formulaic serial killer film *Along Came A Spider* (2001) with Morgan Freeman. He has also directed episodes of HBO's hip gangster soap *The Sopranos*.

British cinematographer David Tattersall has a long history of working with *Star Wars* mogul George Lucas. Tattersall shot numerous episodes of Lucas's *Young Indiana Jones* TV series (1992–96) and the two *Star Wars* prequels *The Phantom Menace* (1999) and *Attack of the Clones* (2002), the latter of which was the first mainstream big-budget film to be shot on digital video as opposed to celluloid. His other work includes *Con Air* (Simon West, 1999) and *Whatever Happened to Harold Smith* (Peter Hewitt, 1999).

Editor Christian Wagner has an excellent pedigree in action films, having cut *Face/Off* (1997) and *MI-2* (2000) for John Woo, as well as the thrilling *Bad Boys* (Michael Bay, 1995) and the somewhat more complex *True Romance* (1993) and *Spy Game* (2001) for director Tony Scott.

PRODUCT PLACEMENT: Bond returns to the Aston Martin fold after fifteen years: in this film he drives a V12 Vanquish. The film also makes use of the Jaguar XKR – both former British companies are owned by the Ford motor corporation. Other companies to feature include Norelco grooming products, Philips electronics and Revlon cosmetics.

SOURCE TO SCREEN: Shooting for the twentieth Bond film began on 14 January 2002. With filming in Iceland, Cadiz (standing in for Havana) and the bio-domes of the Eden project in Cornwall – which also provided a stretch of beach to stand in for the Korean de-militarized zone – the locations are a checklist of destinations hitherto neglected by Bond.

The set pieces, too, seem designed to avoid replicating any particular Bond sequence. A lengthy surfing sequence is an obviously left-field attempt to create something memorably different, yet similar in appeal to, a skiing scene, and a hovercraft chase seems, as with the pipeline ride of *The World Is Not Enough*, to be an attempt to cosmetically spice up the requisite 'car chase'. In designing the hovercraft sequence stunt co-ordinator Vic Armstrong set out to consciously imitate part of *Stagecoach* (John Ford, 1939) in which John Wayne's coach is beset on all sides by Native Americans climbing up it as he attempts to escape. The film also features an actual car chase sequence which, somewhat less originally, is set on ice (see **The Living Daylights**).

Early publicity indicated that Rosamund Pike's Miranda Frost character was originally called Gala Brand. This, plus hints that Blades health club will appear, implies that the picture's screenplay will borrow from the under-utilised *Moonraker* novel (which was all but ignored by the film carrying its title). Gala Brand was the hero's Special Branch contact in Fleming's third Bond novel, Blades is the name of the fictional gentlemen's club of which the literary M was a member.

The sequence in which Gustav Graves parachutes to Earth outside Buckingham Palace has him employing a Union Flag parachute not entirely unlike the one used by Roger Moore's Bond in *The Spy Who Loved Me*. Equally self-referential is the sequence where Jinx emerges from the sea clad only in a skimpy bikini and carrying a diving knife – an obvious nod to Ursula Andress's iconic entrance in *Dr. No*.

IN THE REAL WORLD: One sequence was shot on location at the Eden Project in Cornwall. Funded by money from the National Lottery, the Eden Project was one of Britain's most successful millennium 'monuments' (especially when compared with the utter failure of the much-vaunted Millennium Dome – see **The World Is Not Enough**). Several diverse, tropical habitats (rainforest, desert etc) are sealed under huge conservatories, or biomes, providing examples of more exotic environments in the temperate climate of Cornwall. In the film they provide an unusual backdrop to Graves's sinister plans.

CULTURE VULTURE: The title is derived from the work of the poet AE Housman (1859–1936). Housman's signature collection *A Shropshire Lad* (1896) includes the verse 'LVI Far I Hear The Bugle Blow, The Day of Battle'. This contains a discussion of whether dying in battle/in the service of one's country really is a worthwhile thing to do. At the suggestion that it might be better to run away, and therefore live longer, the poem indicates that running away will not perpetuate the life of the soldier, merely extend it – someone who runs away just lives 'to die another day'. It goes on to suggest that cowards' funerals are less sad than those of people who have done their duty, an observation that may be meant ironically. Housman's attitude to military service varied considerably over the course of his life. His brother was killed during the Boer War and one of his most famous poems is 'Elegy on a Troop of Professional Murderers', a 'tribute' to the British Expeditionary Force that invaded France in 1914. The appropriation of Housman's ambivalent sentiments suggests that, as with *The World is not Enough*, the producers are keen to explore areas of ambiguity and untapped maturity within the Bond character, to question his creed (summed up as 'For England' in *GoldenEye*) and his motivations. The hope is that this can be done without sacrificing the character's reputation as the screen's foremost action-adventure hero.

THE LAST WORD: Despite the enormous success of *Spider-Man* and the media juggernaut that was *Star Wars: Episode II – Attack of the Clones*, excitement built across the summer of 2002 in anticipation of Eon's twentieth official Bond picture. The release of the first teaser trailer over the Internet and in cinemas on 16 May 2002 saw an almost unprecedented number of downloads from movie websites, and led to rounds of applause from some audiences.

James Bond Will Return

Appendix

The Ian Fleming James Bond Novels/ Short Story Collections:

Casino Royale, 1953
Live and Let Die, 1954
Moonraker, 1955
Diamonds are Forever, 1956
From Russia, with Love, 1957
Doctor No, 1958
Goldfinger, 1959
For Your Eyes Only, 1960 (short story collection)
Thunderball, 1961
The Spy Who Loved Me, 1962
On Her Majesty's Secret Service, 1963
You Only Live Twice, 1964
The Man with the Golden Gun, 1965
Octopussy, 1966 (short story collection)

Select Bibliography:

Amis, Kingsley, *The James Bond Dossier*. New York, New American Library, 1965.
Amis, Kingsley (as Robert Markham), *Colonel Sun*. London, Jonathan Cape, 1968.
Barnes, Alan and Hearn, Marcus, *Kiss Kiss Bang! Bang!* London, Batsford, 1997.
Bennett, Tony and Woolacott, Janet, *Bond and Beyond: The Political Career of a Popular Hero*. London, Macmilllan, 1987.
Benson, Raymond, *Tomorrow Never Dies*. London, Hodder & Stoughton, 1997.
Black, Jeremy, *The Politics of James Bond: From Fleming's Novels to the Big Screen*. Westport, CT, Praeger, 2001.
Broccoli, Cubby and Zec, Donald, *When the Snow Melts: The Autobiography of Cubby Broccoli*. London, Boxtree, 1998.
Chapman, James, *Licence to Thrill: A Cultural History of the James Bond Films*. London, IB Tauris, 1999.

Del Buono, Oreste and Eco, Umberto eds, *The Bond Affair* (trans. RA Downie). London, MacDonald, 1966.

Dougall, Alastair, *James Bond: The Secret World of 007*. London, Dorling Kindersley, 2000.

Dobbs, Michael, *Down With Big Brother: The Fall of the Soviet Empire*. New York, Alfred A Knopf, 1997.

Gardner, John, *GoldenEye*. London, Hodder & Stoughton, 1995.

Glen, John with Hearn, Marcus, *For My Eyes Only*. London, Batsford, 2001.

Hernu, Sandy, *Q: The Biography of Desmond Llewelyn*. Seaford, East Sussex, SB Publications, 1999.

Johnstone, Iain, *The World Is Not Enough: a Companion*. London, Boxtree, 1999.

Lycett, Andrew, *Ian Fleming*. London, Phoenix, 1995.

Markham, Robert, *Colonel Sun* – see Amis, Kingsley.

Marwick, Arthur, *The Sixties: Cultural Revolution in Britain, France, Italy and the United States c. 1958–c. 1974*. Oxford, Oxford University Press, 1998.

McInnerney, Jay, Foulkes, Nick, Norman, Neil, Sullivan, Nick, with Woodhead, Colin, *Dressed to Kill: James Bond, the Suited Hero*. Paris, Flammarion, 1996.

Nourmand, Tony, *The Official 007 Collection: James Bond Movie Posters*. London, Boxtree, 2001.

Pfeiffer, Lee, and Philip, Lisa, *The Incredible World of 007*. London, Boxtree, 1992.

Pfeiffer, Lee, and Worrall, Dave, *The Essential Bond: The Authorized Guide to the World of 007*. London, Boxtree, 1998.

Richards, Jeffrey, *Films and the British National Identity: From Dickens to Dad's Army*. Manchester, Manchester University Press, 1997.

Turner, Adrian, *Goldfinger: Pocket Movie Guide*. London, Bloomsbury, 1998.

Wood, Christopher, *James Bond, The Spy Who Loved Me* (novelisation). London, Panther Books, 1977.

Wood, Christopher, *James Bond and Moonraker* (novelisation). London, Panther Books, 1979.

Periodicals

In addition to the magazines/newspapers whose reviews are quoted within the text (see individual chapters for references), of specific help with background information were:

Cinefantastique, vol 4, no. 3, May 1984.
Hollywood Reporter, 13 May 1987.
Neon, no. 24, December 1998.
Starburst, no. 42, March 1981.
Variety, 25 May 1977.
Variety, 2 November 1995.
Variety, 26 October 1997.

Picture Credits

All pictures are from The Ronald Grant Archive: Page 2 (bottom left) courtesy of Columbia/MGM; all other pictures courtesy of Eon Productions/Danjaq.

Index